WELFARE ASPECTS OF INDUSTRIAL MARKETS

NIJENRODE STUDIES IN ECONOMICS

Volume 2

Welfare aspects
of industrial markets

editors

A. P. Jacquemin and H. W. de Jong

Martinus Nijhoff Social Sciences Division
Leiden 1977

ISBN 90. 207. 0625. x

Printed in the Netherlands.

CONTENTS

XVI. The abolition of cartels and structural change in the United Kingdom / 345
D. C. Elliott and J. D. Gribbin

XVII. The regulation and control of public utility prices: British experience 1960–1975 / 367
R. W. Daniels

XVIII. French antitrust legislation: an exercise in futility / 401
Frédéric Jenny and André-Paul Weber

Contributors to the volume

W. ADAMS, Professor of Economics, Michigan State University, East Lansing, United States.

W. J. ADAMS, Assistant Professor of Economics, University of Michigan, Ann Arbor, United States.

B. CARLSSON, Economist, Industriens Utrednings Institut, Stockholm, Sweden.

R. E. CAVES, Professor of Economics, Harvard University, Cambridge (Mass.), United States.

T. A. J. COCKERILL, Professor of Economics, University of Salford, Salford, United Kingdom.

R. W. DANIELS, Professor of Economics, University of Lancaster, United Kingdom.

J. R. DAVIES, Senior Lecturer in Finance, University of Strathclyde, England.

J. B. DIRLAM, Professor of Economics, University of Rhode Island, Kingston, United States.

D. C. ELIOT, Economic Advisor, Office of Fair Trading, London, United Kingdom.

J. D. GRIBBIN, Under Secretary (Economics), The Price Commission, London, United Kingdom.

L. HJALMARSSON, Associate Professor of Economics, University of Gothenburg, Sweden.

E. HEUSZ, Professor of Economics, Friedrich Alexander University Erlangen-Nürnberg, W. Germany.

F. JENNY, Professor of Economics, ESSEC, Paris, France.

J. KHALILZADEH-SHIRAZI, Economist, The World Bank, Washington D.C., United States.

D. A. KUEHN, Lecturer in Economics, University of Stirling, Scotland.

S. NYMAN, Research Officer, Nuffield College, Oxford, United Kingdom.

W. G. SHEPHERD, Professor of Economics, University of Michigan, Ann Arbor, United States.

R. SHERMAN, Professor of Economics, University of Virginia, Charlottesville, Virginia.

Z. A. SILBERSTON, Fellow of Nuffield College, Oxford, United Kingdom.

A. SINGH, Fellow of Queen's College, Cambridge, United Kingdom.

B. SOSKIC, Professor of Economics, Belgrade University, Yugoslavia.

A. P. WEBER, Professor of Economics, ESSEC and French Planning Commission, Paris, France.

C. C. VON WEISZÄCKER, Professor of Economics, University of Bonn, West Germany.

O. E. WILLIAMSON, Professor of Economics, Law and Public Policy, University of Pennsylvania, Philadelphia, United States.

INTRODUCTION

The present volume of essays on industrial organization, which are based on conferences held at Nijenrode and Brussels, differs considerably from its predecessor. Even more than in the first volume the essays demonstrate the broad scope of industrial organization analysis. Besides the traditional topics such as economies of scale, monopoly and competition policy, there are essays on methodology, on stagflation, and on the relationship between industrial structure and international trade and trade policies. The latter topics are of growing importance. The issue of restructuring industries and the question of whether free trade or some measure of protection is more appropriate are topics of increasing relevance today (and will no doubt continue to be in future years as well). The problem of persistent inflation which other essays address is also of major concern.

Apart from being broad in scope and venturing into new fields, this volume is also controversial. Its central feature is a debate about welfare aspects. Here, more than in pure analysis, economists tend to entertain different points of view. One of the participants in the Nijenrode conference, Professor John Blair, who died in December 1976 and whom we honour as having been an active promoter of this kind of meeting, wrote to the editors shortly before his death to say that the first volume had succeeded very well in acquainting the reader with the results of empirical investigations, notably on trends and levels of concentration. In contrast, many of the papers given in the 1976 conferences are policy-oriented and controversial. Presumably, one of the goals implicit in their controversial nature is to get nearer to the 'truth' by subjecting each argument to the searching criticisms of those who know their subject and who can detect weakly-based empirical and deductive statements. By so doing, one can discover other aspects of the problem and verify whether the policy conclusions correspond to the evidence and analysis presented. In this perspective, two aspects of the papers warrant particular attention. First, the usual skepticism of specialists in industrial organization towards the validity of general welfare statements is reinforced by the various contributions which highlight the complexities introduced by information costs, uncertainty, external effects and the dynamics of the structure-conduct-performance relationship. These aspects are shown to be more important than the traditional considerations, such as scale economies. Often the trade-off between competition and efficiency is a multidimensional problem; certainly it is a more complex issue than is implied in the way it is presented in static models. Second, there are great dangers in making simplistic comparisons between the performance of firms or industries in different countries, such as in the U.S. and E.E.C. countries. Distinguishable objectives and constraints, including items such as different managerial attitudes toward risk or the degree of industrial dependance upon international trade, can make behaviour or policies considered inefficient in some countries acceptable in others.

The following comprises some of the welfare controversies which arise in this volume.

In the first section, Roger Sherman, after briefly tracing the roots of industrial organization theory, focuses attention on a very old theme developed, among others, by Plato and (more recently) by Luigi Pirandello, that appearances may not be representative of reality: 'things are not always what they seem.' In industrial organization this has recently come to mean that risk, randomness and imperfect information play an important role in modifying the conclusions of neo-classical theory. He shows the broad scope of such considerations, particularly in a world dominated by large firms; and he draws attention to their implications for our theories. Sherman ends on a relatively optimistic note, suggesting 'a new wave of research', anticipated as being 'based on a theory that is more powerful because it omits less.' However, in his paper, Shepherd maintains that current theory leaves the dominant firm an unsolved puzzle. He emphasizes the analysis of the rate of change of market share (or its absence) of those firms. Exploring the causes and effects of the 'hardening of market structures' (at least in the U.S. economy), Shepherd also puts emphasis on how the firm is owned and controlled and what incentives can be used to alter manager behaviour. This fits in well with the third article in this section, in which Silberston and Nyman raise the question of ownership control versus managerial control of large firms. Consistent with other recent studies, they are relatively sceptical of the proclaimed level and trend of managerial control that prevails in large firms. A persisting question is the degree to which the differences reflect different transatlantic situations. As Silberston and Nyman also note, there is room for further research into the implications of ownership types on the welfare of firms.

In the section on stagflation, von Weizsäcker pleads for an appreciation of the importance of short-term price rigidity. Far from contributing to the destabilizing tendencies that occur in perfectly competitive markets which adapt to

upward and downward fluctuations, rigid prices promote specialisation, investment and other beneficial outcomes. Thus, competition policy should not aim at
artificially bringing about price flexibility but should have a long-term structural
perspective. The reader might wish to compare this argument with Lenel's in
favour of price intervention in the first volume (p. 316–23). Heusz uses a different
approach to explain the stagflation dilemma: the combination of external
technical progress and oligopolistic (or monopolistic) market structure induce
inflationary tendencies without securing full employment. Technical change
is differentiated into internal and external varieties, the latter gaining in
importance as market limitations become increasingly visible in many branches
of industry in the industrialized world.

Šoškić underlines the fact that stagflation problems are not absent from a
workers' self-managed economy, but are, if anything, more pronounced. He
attributes this to the shift in favour of consumption at the cost of accumulation.
Therefore, an incomes policy is necessary but it should be differentiated
according to the cyclical situation prevailing. This applies to other policies too.
Such policies should also aim at measures to push monopolistic organizations
into investing in productive output and at the removal of structural disequilibrium.

In the section on international trade and industrial organization a number of
interesting current debates are discussed. Caves and Khalilzadeh-Shirazi note
some impacts of international trade on the character of product differentiation in
industries exposed to and sheltered from trade, and on the scale of plants and the
interdependency of oligopolistic sellers. These findings support the time-
honoured position that international trade is an important variable sustaining
the competitive structure of an economy. William Adams broadens this
contention by comparing large European and North American firms. He finds
much less support for the allegation that national differences in corporate
performance are more important than is commonly assumed. Though company
structures are affected by nationality differences, this is less true for performance
variables such as cash flow, profitability or company growth. In view of the
current European debate on firm profitability, investment and employment, his
findings that firm growth 'depends on neither the availability of internal funds
nor the proportion of assets actually financed via debts' is especially interesting
(the correlation between growth in capital stock and availability of internal funds
is extremely small).

The policy question is approached with different views – and with different
conclusions – by Adams and Dirlam, on the one hand, and Singh, on the other.
The first two authors stress that import controls – or considerations to institute
them – raise far more questions than can be answered, and that a necessary

consequence of quotas is the obstruction of competition. They point out that the latter would have to be stimulated in order to restrict the welfare loss. Both alternatives – dictatorial regulation and government ownership of the industry in question – introduce rigidities and inefficiencies, and present-day governments would do well to ponder the alternatives before adopting import restrictions, measures which are now *en vogue*. Ajit Singh approaches the question from the point of view of Britain's deplorable economic performance, especially during the past ten years. In the U.K. there is less and less employment in manufacturing, though output continues to increase. Such de-industrialization exhibits the increasing failure of the manufacturing sector to pay for the growing imports by means of exports. Thus, the structure of U.K. manufacturing production needs adaptation. Though he leaves open the ways in which this can be achieved (he even suggests that the participation of the U.K. in the international economy might have to be reconsidered), Singh rejects the likelihood of a spontaneous correction by means of market forces. Also, the discussion in this paper on the relative welfare aspects of the manufacturing industry and services merits attention in view of the increase in the latter sector in nearly all western European countries.

The next section continues the debate about the virtues of competition, but from a different angle. The advantages flowing from economies of scale and monopoly come under review. Williamson continues the discussion of economies of scale as a defense in merger cases which he initiated in his article in the *American Economic Review* in 1968. His argument is that from an economic point of view, such economies should be taken into consideration, although he is not inclined to overrate their importance. Revisiting the field, he finds some signs of hope in the context of U.S. policy. For European readers, the subject is also of importance, not so much because the economies' defense has to be advocated, but because of the various considerations which have come to play a role in the trade-off between efficiency and competition (which are not always explicitly taken into account).

Hjalmarsson introduces dynamic efficiency aspects. He restricts these to the reductions in production costs due to an optimal path of capacity expansion by firms producing homogeneous goods in multiplant structures. He rightly says that this makes economies of scale an endogeneous concept imparting a dynamic impulse to industry development. This is a worthwhile first attempt, but one which has to be rounded out by other considerations. The dynamics of demand and price remain of obvious importance in a market economy.

Two papers follow on economies of scale from a comparative international perspective in industries (iron and steel and brewing) where economies of scale are said to be important. These empirical studies, by Carlsson and Cockerill, emphasize that economies of scale do play a role, but that they are only one factor (and sometimes not the most important one) in an overall assesment of the industry's performance.

The book concludes with a section on the various anti-trust and industrial policies. Apart from evaluations of U.K. and French competition policies which stand as eminent long-period surveys, these essays deal with the roles of the capital market in steering efficient industrial development and of public utility pricing. Like the empirical studies, the policy surveys have limited application: that is, to the countries and time periods to which they are relevant. Nevertheless, it remains instructive to compare experiences among countries and to benefit from their strengths and weaknesses by taking them into account when pursuing policies in other nations.

To sum up, the collection of papers presented here shows a number of dichotomies: some papers show a neo-classical approach; others diverge rather strongly therefrom. Some papers are theoretical in nature; others are mainly empirical. Some papers aim at policy conclusions or have an implicit policy message; others abstain from such recommendations. The reader can explore for himself the various combinations. By doing so, he will see how these papers broaden the traditional analytical framework used by industrial organization economists and how they provide alternative explanations for the differences among countries in their policies with respect to market structure and firm conduct and performance.

A. P. Jacquemin   H. W. de Jong

PART ONE

THEORETICAL AND STATISTICAL QUESTIONS IN INDUSTRIAL ORGANIZATION

I. THEORY COMES TO INDUSTRIAL ORGANIZATION

Roger Sherman

1. Introduction

Industrial organization knowledge is largely empirical. Some of the empirical findings tend to confirm implications from neoclassical economic theory, but the theory rarely has offered exact hypotheses. Predicted effects of explanatory industry variables could be specified in only a crude way from the theory, perhaps that A, B, and C are apt to affect D, and they were usually estimated by ordinary least squares whether that method was appropriate or not. Some of the operational measures for important explanatory variables, such as 'industrial concentration,' also were rationalized in only an informal way, and dependent variables such as industry performance were represented even less adequately. Despite these methodological weaknesses, the hunt for relationships can be defended because available economic theory was unable to predict events any more precisely, and a great many results of interest nevertheless have been found. But empirical evidence without theory cannot yield a compelling understanding of what really is going on. For clear and convincing explanations we need sound and tested theory.

Maybe no unified theory can serve the vast empirical and policy orientation of industrial organization knowledge.[1] Our institution-free, deterministic neoclassical theory repeatedly has been found inadequate to deal with specific industrial organization questions.[2] Yet the advantages of theory, for keeping track of past discoveries and for generating fruitful expectations about new ones, seems as undeniable here as it is in other areas of research. So this paper discusses the now visible prospect of elaborating our severely deterministic neoclassical model to accomodate risk, dynamic effects and imperfect information from the

---

1. Joel Dirlam kindly called my attention to the similarity between the title of my paper and the title of Robert Hichen's short story, 'How Love Came to Professor Guildea' (in Dorothy Sayers, ed., *The Omnibus of Crime*, New York: Prayson and Clarke, 1929). After he had lived most of his life without it, love ruined Professor Guildea. To a field that has developed without depending heavily on theory its arrival conceivably might bring similarly drastic consequences.

2. See, e.g., criticisms by Shubik (1970).

real world, rather like adjusting for effects of friction in physics so that pure theories could be tested. Through such elaboration we may understand more of what we see while the unity of neoclassical analysis might also be preserved, even across a broad subject like industrial organization which is concerned generally with how markets work and particularly with how the way they are organized will affect how they work.

The aim will be to express first in admittedly over-simple terms the nature of theory that has been applied in industrial organization, claiming it to be mainly deterministic neoclassical micro-theory with minor bows to oligopolistic interdependence. Then I shall illustrate, in the important case of the size distribution of firms, how crucially important our presumptions about randomness and uncertainty can be to our conclusions. Having brought out the importance of uncertainty I then make a brisk review of recent developments in risk and imperfect information that bear on industrial organization questions, in an effort to show that these efforts offer some promise of accumulating to yield a unified theoretical basis for industrial organization work. Because risk and imperfect information, and other new topics, serve so well to fill in the inadequacies of deterministic microtheory we can anticipate a great deal of theoretical work which promises to give industrial organization economists a genuine basis for testing and accumulating reliable knowledge.

2. The role theory has played in industrial organization

One might say industrial organization is well founded in theory. After all, as a special field of interest in economics it could claim theorist Augustin Cournot (1838) as its founder. He was the first to bring out how price is affected by the structure of a market, with structure varying all the way from monopoly at one extreme to competition at the other. Or we could date the field from Adam Smith (1776), who articulated so well the role of market competition in turning private, profit-seeking motives of individuals to the service of society. Alfred Marshall (1920) later codified the neoclassical theory, and provided many suggestions about the role of risk and other market imperfections. And the many oligopoly theories, plus monopolistic and imperfect competition theories of this century, provided a basis – good or bad – for industrial organization work.

It is really in this century, particularly in the last forty years or so, that industrial organization has become a focus of attention and a special field of economic and legal research. Indeed, the development of industrial organization as a field may be owed partly to the advent of modern times, with its seeming compulsion for specialization and categorization, rather than to any growing coherence in the subject.[3] I think many would agree that development of the field largely followed Edward Mason's call (1939) for empirical work describing crucial characteristics of an industry, to capture them and their effects in a quantitative way. Although prompted by work in oligopoly and the theory of the firm, early empirical efforts, starting for instance with Gardiner Means (1932), Adolph Berle and Gardiner Means (1932, 1968), and Joe Bain (1956), were attempting to describe the world and only partly to test crude hypotheses derived from theory. Yet their results and others like them would be claimed today by many to constitute much of the substance of industrial organization knowledge.

So although to a degree industrial organization can claim respectable theoretical origins, the subject matter does not rest firmly on a broad theory. All empirical efforts have not used theory; empirical work frequently was undertaken to pursue in measurable terms relationships thought to be important because of previous observations, or due to some perceived social problem or great public policy concern. In the USA, where I think it is fair to say this empirical work in industrial organization started, two forces can be seen posing problems and issues. One is a traditional academic one, where implications from the body of economic theory, largely deterministic neoclassical theory, were to be tested. The other is the world of affairs where public disputes simply had to be settled, disputes such as whether the Alcoa aluminum company was a monopoly in violation of an antitrust law, whether the marketing of milk was to be regulated, or more recently whether government certification of safety is to be required and if so whether to stop with food and drugs, rotary lawnmowers, glass shower doors, toilet seats, or whatever.

Rather than review the empirical findings, which have been summarized recently by several different authors,[4] I shall note briefly the theory underlying the early empirical work. Where theory was used it often relied on the assumption of static certainty, although imperfect information was acknowledged. The implications emphasized and, in turn, the variables chosen for observation, were drawn from neoclassical theory. Going back to Alfred Marshall (1920) there has been a faith that broad averages, typified in the analysis of 'representative' firms and consumers, would be captured sufficiently well by a deterministic theory that such a theory could serve practical ends. Based on this theory a crucial role could be seen for the condition of entry, and that role was emphasized when Bain (1956) saw imperfect information working to handicap new entrants and sought to measure effects by considering the sum of money a new entrant would have to

3. The words, 'industrial organization,' may have come into use in the late 1940's partly because John Blair created that official job title for economists employed by the US Government.
4. See Blair (1972), Phlips (1971), Scherer (1970), Sherman (1974), Vernon (1972), or Weiss (1971).

gather together in order to enter. Industrial markets could often be categorized as oligopolistic also, to be represented later by measures of economic concentration. When new entry was difficult the implication from a simple Cournot model would be relevant, that fewer firms in a market would set smaller outputs or higher prices than many competing firms would, and that the few would enjoy higher profits as a result. A number of variables that play no role in any neoclassical model (e.g., firm size) also have been included in these industrial organization studies, in part because various *ad hoc* hypotheses had been advanced which called for including them. Indeed, Mason's original urging was aimed not so much at testing hypotheses as discovering stable relationships or regularities; exploration was to be encouraged because it might possibly yield new discoveries itself.

Before Mason's plea for empirical work on industries another strand of work had begun to focus on the actions of the business firm, and today it forms an important part of industrial organization. It also came essentially from two directions. First, theoretical developments such as imperfect competition and monopolistic competition broadened the question of firm behaviour to whether competition would occur in price, advertising, product design, or other areas, and they stimulated academic interest in the theory of the firm. Second, it was shown empirically that most large corporations in the US no longer possessed a dominant ownership interest, and the question thus was raised whether the hired managers of such firms would operate them entirely in the interests of their owners. This was an old question, of course, having been treated in some detail by Adam Smith. For in his lifetime the forerunner of the modern shareholder organization, the joint-stock company, was a controversial and somewhat discredited institution largely for the very reason that owners lacked control over managers.

The development of the modern large business organization in most advanced western countries has raised a host of controversial public policy questions that have seemed beyond the reach of economic theory (and, in the case of multinational firms, perhaps outside any one country's control). With a variety of modifications, resulting work on the theory of the firm has still been based largely on the same neoclassical theory with its assumption of static-certainty conditions and occasionally with growth dynamics. The role for psychology and organization theory has grown recently, of course. Indeed, the economic theory of the firm is one of few topics that have brought economics in touch with other social sciences. But the theory relied on in early industrial organization work still was slightly modified deterministic neoclassical theory, with results from other disciplines grafted on as needed. Even the more recent sales maximization, growth maximization, and other managerial discretion theories retain essentially the deterministic form.[5]

The fruitfulness of this deterministic theory in the hands, for example, of what are called Chicago-School economists (whether or not they are or have ever been at Chicago) has been very great, and I certainly do not wish to demean it. On the contrary I would urge all who can to carry out such good work. It rests on a sophisticated and powerful view of where unlimited competitive behaviour leads, and thus it enables researchers to look in the right places for results. But for interpreting results the assumptions of static certainty which underlie such analyses can sometimes yield misleading conclusions. And some of the persisting differences that separate researchers on industrial organization issues concern the ways such results might be interpreted.

I am not dealing here with the question whether a failure to meet ideal criteria should be played down merely because no institution that can satisfy them can be invented. In such a case it is easy to be persuaded that one should simply do the best one can. The question is whether an ideal (or even a second-best) result can be defined in deterministic terms when risk or imperfect information are present in an important way. And the answer is gradually becoming clear; in many areas, it is *no*. Indeed, for conditions of risk and imperfect information the criteria that would define an ideal become elusive, and a unique expression for them may not even exist.[6]

Recent developments in probability or risk analysis and theories related to information will be especially valuable to industrial organization work by making clear such limitations, and will be emphasized here for that reason. One could make similar arguments about the role of dynamic rather than static analysis, but I want mainly to show the uses of elaborations on neoclassical theory; theories of risk and information will afford sufficient opportunity for that. In the next section I shall stress the great effect *a priori* presumptions about uncertainty can have on the conclusions we draw from observations available to us. Surely we cannot *assume* a deterministic theory if the extent to which we see the world as deterministic can be crucial to our conclusions. I shall then go on to note the prospect for elaborating neoclassical static certainty theory so it can include new knowledge about imperfect information and knowledge of probabilities and how to represent them. How such an elaboration could strengthen our ability to tackle industrial organization issues will then be sketched in a conclusion.

5. See, e.g., Baumol (1967) or Williamson (1964). Risk has been given some attention; see Cyert and March (1963) or Caves (1970).
6. Properties of equilibrium with risk and imperfect information have received considerable attention. See Arrow (1971), Grossman and Stiglitz (1975), and Spence (1974) as examples.

3. Uncertainty and interpretation of evidence in industrial organization

We can have situations today where all will agree to the observable facts and yet there is strong disagreement about causes, for there are too many possible explanations for the facts. To illustrate that problem and, at the same time, to show the importance of viewing the world as certain or as uncertain I shall focus on one of the most important issues in industrial organization, the size distribution of firms in manufacturing industries.

Early investigators took the level of concentration in an industry as given, perhaps by technological influences, and attempted to assess its effect on industry performance. The size distribution of firms was accepted by them as datum (as 'structure') and the task was to trace its consequences (as 'performance'). Many found support for the implication of simple oligopoly models that fewer firms would compete less rigorously and thus, although they would be more profitable, they would serve society less well. Others have disputed that conclusion, as the Goldschmid, Mann and Weston (1974) volume shows. In particular, Harold Demsetz (1973) regards better products and better management, or possibly the existence of genuine and desirable economies of scale, as the reasons a few firms may grow relatively large in any one industry. Thus he sees the relatively large size of a firm as an earned reward for significant accomplishment. He has been careful to derive different implications of this view and has confirmed them empirically. All have not accepted his interpretation but he argues that his intellectual opponents have a mindless adherence to a mere 'system of belief,' not a position based on careful and open interpretation of evidence.

No active party in this dispute allows much scope for randomness. But earlier, Hart and Prais (1956), Simon and Bonini (1958), and others had approached the same task of interpreting an observable size distribution of firms by presuming there is much randomness in the world. If firms in an industry have constant average costs and all face the same probability distribution for growth opportunity Simon and Bonini showed convincingly that over time the concentration in an industry would depend on the rate of new entry; with little new entry the industry would become highly concentrated. There would be absolutely no need of scale economies, skilled management, or superior products to produce high concentration. Edwin Mansfield (1962) also stressed the possibility of random effects on firm growth in examining the consequences of entry barriers, and he supported the Simon-Bonini view. Of course one cannot claim that firm growth depends only on chance.[7] But it should be realized that the size distribution of

7. For other effects on the size distribution of firms see Caves (1976) and Flaherty (1976).

firms itself is the result of a process, and to understand it we may have to give a proper role to randomness.

In rational man there probably is a tendency to deny any sizeable role for randomness in accounting for what we observe. Most parties who argue against Demsetz, for instance, do not really have a randomness rationale in mind, even though stochastic elements rather than skill and efficiency can provide an alternative explanation for the observed size distribution of firms. To illustrate our readiness to accept cause as explanation for events I like particularly this account by Fred Schwed (1955) of a great coin-flipping contest (Schwed, pp. 160–61):

The referee gives a signal for the first game and 400,000 coins flash in the sun as they are tossed. The scorers make their tabulations, and discover that 200,000 people are winners and 200,000 are losers. Then the second game is played. Of the original 200,000 winners, about half of them win again.

The third game is played, and of the 100,000 who have won both games half of them are again successful. These 50,000, in the fourth game, are reduced to 25,000, and in the fifth to 12,500. These 12,500 have now won five straight without a loss and are no doubt beginning to fancy themselves as coin flippers. They feel they have an 'instinct' for it. However, in the sixth game, 6250 of them are disappointed and amazed to find that they have finally lost, and perhaps some of them start a Congressional investigation. But the victorious 6250 play on and are successively reduced in number until less than a thousand are left. This little band has won some nine straight without a loss, and by this time most of them have at least a local reputation for their ability. People come from some distance to consult them about their method of calling heads and tails, and they modestly give explanations of how they have achieved their success. Eventually there are about a dozen men who have won every single time for about fifteen games. These are regarded as the experts, the greatest coin flippers in history, the men who never lose, and they have their biographies written.

Although corporations cannot reasonably be viewed as coin flippers, the view of firm growth as due partly to stochastic elements should not be ignored. To regard all large firms as successful and efficient, as if growth is caused by a deterministic process, may be partly like treating successful coin flippers as skilled rather than lucky. Thus, whether the theory we use in our work allows for randomness can determine the kinds of explanations we accept as consistent with given data.

Effects on interpretation similar to those of randomness will follow also when we allow for the existence of imperfect information. For some years a rational choice has been presumed on the part of individuals who add to their human capital[8] by becoming educated, for instance, and their choices are seen as efficient ones benefiting society as well as themselves. Suppose information is imperfect, though, so employers have to guess about the actual productivity of potential

8. The valuable work on investment in human capital began with Schultz (1961). See also Becker (1975).

employees from a few scraps of available data such as their education.[9] An individual's choice of education can then be influenced by his wish to 'signal' a high productivity; he may invest in more education partly to lead potential employers to *regard* him as more productive. One consequence is that private returns to education may overstate social returns. The more general result is that things are not always as they seem; observed actions need to be considered for their information-giving consequences as well as for other reasons.

More general consequences of imperfect information follow when individuals must search to obtain information and undertaking transactions then naturally becomes costly.[10] Implications of imperfect information for the modern large corporation are manifold. Affected are the sizes and the 'images' of firms, their manner of organization, who gets promoted in them, what products are offered, what consumers think of the products, how advertising is carried out, and what research is privately undertaken, among other things.[11] There also are implications for how such organizations compete, whether they grow or decline, what role vertical integration can play or how employees will fare, and for the extent to which the capital market can discipline managers to make them serve owners effectively. Not only may a corporation's success and large size be due to luck rather than better performance alone, with randomness in the world, but with imperfect information the corporation's leaders also may have been chosen partly for the positive signals they were able to generate and not solely for their raw managerial talents.

Theory that lets us deal carefully and explicitly with risk and imperfect information should enable us to express industrial organization hypotheses with more precision. For instance, we can predict effects on measures of risk, or we can control for them, when looking at average values of other variables. As a result the set of possible explanations for a given event can be circumscribed, so those who differ can examine in more detail the nature of their differences. For although the degree of randomness or of determinateness in a given situation may be what separates parties in a dispute over interpretation of evidence, we cannot even know that until the probability elements of our theories are made explicit. In addition, it will sometimes be possible to distinguish different theories by their implied effects on risk or other such measures, even though the average levels of variables may not be much affected. Thus by including risk and information conditions in our models we may perform more subtle tests. And we may also reduce the freedom we now have to embrace one or another view of the

9. Such effects of imperfect information are developed by Spence (1974).
10. The search theories were stimulated by Stigler (1961). See also McCall (1970) and Riley (1976).
11. We can only touch on these possibilities here. See Arrow (1971), Hirshleifer (1971), Johnsen (1976), and Williamson (1970 and 1976) for examples of recent work.

world we see, because the more complete theory should leave less scope for differences in individual interpretation.

4. Certainty through uncertainty

In *The Pursuit of Certainty* (1965), philospher Shirley Letwin cast 18th and 19th century efforts to explain the world through the economic efficiency idea as a hopeful search for certainty in belief. On a much smaller scale we might also describe any search for a unified understanding of industrial organization as a pursuit of certainty, although we should concede that many disagreements over beliefs stand in its way. We have just seen how theories that are appropriate for uncertainty, emphasizing imperfect information and risk, can help us be more specific in our disagreements and thereby can help us to resolve them; hence, the play on words in the title of this section. Although it is not really possible to review all the work that has been carried out, either on the subject of risk or of imperfect information, we shall try to show how the work can change our interpretation of events.

We now have well established ways for interpreting behaviour under risk using properties of utility functions,[12] and the implied behaviour appears reasonably consistent with psychological knowledge about behaviour under risk.[13] There are disputes about how to represent risk and still get by with tolerably weak restrictions on utility functions, but these disputes are not over matters so crucial as to prevent use by industrial organization researchers of simple and effective representations of risk. We also have ways to represent the riskiness of economic outcomes, mainly by a statistical measure like the variance, although other moments of the probability distributions of economic variables may also be important.[14]

Risk-bearing by the consumer implicitly has been the aim of much work on risk, but applied work has come mainly in the area of products liability.[15] Here again, both risk and imperfect information play a role. Recent analyses of the subject have been very exacting, and they yield useful implications about how to draw liability rules.[16] Consumers may not always search for information when it is imperfect, and we still need more knowledge of consumer behaviour in

---

12. See Arrow (1971), Borch (1968), Friedman and Savage (1948), Von Neuman and Morgenstern (1947), and also Pratt (1964). A textbook treatment is available in Levy and Sarnat (1972).
13. See Sherman, *Oligopoly*, (1972).
14. See Tsiang (1972). Probability analysis is reviewed in McCall (1971).
15. See McKean (1970), and Oi (1973).
16. Insurance is a related subject that has received broad treatment recently; see, e.g., Mossin (1968).

response to risk.[17] But when consumers search for information, by following Stigler (1961) the performance of industries can be explored more thoroughly with theories of search and risk-averse behaviour.

As Arrow (1971) has shown particularly well, lack of information can reach a point where markets will fail. When risks are important it is easy for two parties in a potential transaction to have different amounts of information. For example, a potential insurance purchaser may know he is an unusually safe risk, while the firm that is his potential insurer is left to rely on broad averages for judging all risks. Rather than pay rates based on the broad averages in such a situation, the safest risks in each category may withdraw from the market. The broad averages will then rise, and insurance rates will rise as a result, causing still more of the better risks to leave the market. Indeed, as Akerlof (1970) illustrates, self selection by the better-than-average risks (whether it be more healthy individuals or more reliable used cars) can have the perverse effect of ending market transactions.

Aside from consumers' responses to risk and imperfect information, the most studied economic agent is the business firm. Considerable attention has been given to risk in the firm, after a formal push from Frank Knight (1921), but it has often been covered only in a suggestive and descriptive *ad hoc* way rather than as an integral part of the analysis. Modern analytical efforts probably began with Ed Mills (1959) for the monopolist under risk. Richard Nelson (1961) put forward a remarkably convenient market model combining risk and imperfect information with competition, which was since elaborated by Massell (1969). Hayne Leland (1972) provides a recent morphology of models of the firm that include risk. These models may still be too parsimonious for empirical work, but it seems possible to tease general hypotheses from them, and they have been applied to regulated monopolies.[18]

Over the past twenty-five years the market responses to risk have been worked out, particularly in the capital market context, in considerable detail.[19] The capital-asset-pricing model shows, for instance, how investors who can hold diversified portfolios might assess risk and measure it, and the implications of this model for business firm organization and behaviour are manifold. Relying on a market-value maximizing goal, defined using profit risk and employment risk in a capital-asset-pricing model, Richard Schramm and I (1974 and 1976) have rationalized observable advertising policies, and administered-pricing policies, too. Many other industrial organization questions about firm behaviour, from

---

17. See Kunreuther (1976) for evidence that consumers exposed to the risk of disaster do not tend to inform themselves adequately.
18. See Brown and Johnsen (1969), Marchand (1973), and Visscher (1973).
19. This work can be traced to Markowitz (1952), with important developments since then by Sharpe (1964), Lintner (1965) and Mossin (1966).

warranty policies (Oi (1973)) to vertical and conglomerate mergers (Sherman (1972), Williamson (1971)) cannot even be posed well unless risk and imperfect information are explicitly considered.

The analysis of labour markets is not comparable to that of capital markets because a worker does not have an investor's diversification opportunity. But implications for employment stability as well as profit stability in the capital-asset-pricing model certainly seem worth examining.[20] Labour market institutions, such as the fixed-wage contract, appear to have been adopted largely in response to employment risk and possibly to transaction costs.[21] It is not yet clear whether market structure affects the distribution of risks among consumers, workers, managers, investors, or others, but it seems almost sure to have an effect. For some evidence already links the magnitude of fluctuations in production-worker hours, a risk borne by workers, with industry concentration.[22]

Theories of job search in the absence of perfect information also have been worked out in detail, and they yield testable implications.[23] While search does not yield an adequate explanation for unemployment in market economies, there appears to be some purposeful search by the unemployed that is efficient, and a full understanding of labour markets requires the consideration of the degree of available information.[24] Little work has combined job search by workers with the hiring behaviour of firms, but in that effort market structure also may turn out to play an important part.[25]

In any market where parties enter into contracts rather than negotiate constantly, Spence (1974) has demonstrated that imperfect information itself will affect actions. Employers, for instance, may have to rely on statistics in judging the potential productivity of applicants for permanent positions. Unless constrained they may rely for their own efficiency on what he calls indices, such as race and sex. Or they may rely on what he calls potential signals, such as education, which from the standpoint of employers are like indices but which the aspiring employee can alter. If he or she wishes to be judged more productive he or she can spend more years in school, thus 'signaling' greater productivity. Spence shows that if education is less costly to more productive workers and

20. See Grossman (1977) and Schramm and Sherman (1974). For development of a model to deal with the lack of a diversification opportunity in labour markets see Mayers (1974).
21. See Grossman (1975) and Townsend (1976).
22. Much work can be related to this question of industry organization and employment risk. For a recent empirical study see D. Stanton Smith (1971).
23. See Stigler (1961), McCall (1970), Feinberg (1976), and Filey (1976). The value of consumers' time is of interest even apart from search. See Becker (1965) and Visscher (1975).
24. For a general survey of market models with imperfect information see Rothschild (1973); and for other analyses see Grossman and Stiglitz (1975 and 1976), Johnsen (1976), Porter (1976), and Salop (1976).
25. For an example of equilibrium models see Wilde (1976).

employers act on signals they can reach an equilibrium in which they expect more productivity with more education, even though the education may not have exactly the effect they presume.

As might be expected, the signalling notion has implications not only for employee and employer actions, but also for the organization and operation of business firms. Indeed, a number of issues related to industrial organization should be approached with an eye for possibilities due to signalling. Spence mentions advertising, credit markets, conspicuous consumption, product quality and guarantees, and even promotion within organizations. Johnsen (1976) examines signalling aspects of advertising in some detail. In light of this signalling view, Adam Smith's concern for the institutions, practices and understandings on which market operations rest shows how aware he was that efforts to mislead can arise. More general theories of hierarchies, based partly on information considerations, are currently in the making,[26] and may help our understanding of industrial markets as well as of large firms.

Some other promising work recently has brought out and tested the implications of different forms of property rights.[27] While it has not been based heavily on risk and imperfect information, those elements have played an interesting role in the work. For instance, Kenneth Clarkson (1972) derived theoretically and showed empirically that private, profit-oriented hospitals differ from public ones in the variance of input mixtures that are used to produce the same services. Careful attention to various contract forms will probably yield more implications for determining who bears which risks. There is considerable evidence, too, that rewards for alternative actions will influence behaviour, even when interdependence of a prisoner's dilemma type exists.[28] Opportunities and their consequences, with the relation between them influenced perhaps by contract terms or other restraints, thus can serve to predict behaviour in oligopolistic or non-market situations as well as in competitive markets.

Institutional forms have been analyzed and explained by Oliver Williamson and others using knowledge from organization theory as well as economics.[29] Such theories can be blended well with the traditional corporate control issue, which began as we noted with the empirical findings of Berle and Means. By looking carefully at the main forms of corporate control in the USA and their implications for managerial behaviour, William McEachern (1975) has been able to reconcile a number of previously conflicting findings relating control to

26. See, e.g., Williamson (1975 and 1976), and the review by Preston (1975).
27. For a review of such work see Furubotn and Pejovich (1972).
28. See Sherman, *Oligopoly*, (1972).
29. See Williamson (1964, 1970, and 1975), Cyert and March (1963), and Alchian and Demsetz (1972).

managerial compensation and financial performance. And he paid attention to risk, too. John Palmer (1973) brought market structure explicitly into these analyses theoretically and then empirically, and showed it to be important. The promise of further work here, combining financial risk theory and organizational knowledge in industrial organization, appears to be considerable.

The main questions of industrial market performance may be more difficult to settle. On theoretical grounds we know that if we look at rate of return as a measure of performance we must look at risk as well, but results of Sherman and Tollison (1972) indicate that the omission of risk probably did not bias early empirical studies. We now must concede that some determinants of market structure, such as advertising, may also be part of the market performance result, so a form of simultaneous equations analysis may be in order.[30] The appropriate form for such analysis will almost certainly follow, though, from elaborations of other findings about large organizations and the working of markets in the presence of risk and imperfect information. Thus theorizing to deal with risk and imperfect information, besides being productive in separate areas of research, should also improve methods of analysis.

So more is going on than merely adding risk and information conditions to a deterministic theory, as a few final examples can show. Yves Balasko (1974) conceives of the tariff-setting task as an information-giving one and develops public enterprise pricing in a way that goes beyond just adding an information ingredient. Similarly, Townsend (1976) shows how transaction costs and uncertainty can affect the design of efficient contracts. Concern for risk and risk attitudes can also influence the design of antitrust penalties, as Breit and Elzinga (1973) have argued. And more complicated simultaneous equation, structure-performance models arise not just from concern for risk in economic theory but from its use in econometric analysis as well.[31] Thus, part of the promise for better industrial organization research comes from improved methods of analysis, and part comes from strengthening the theory itself.

5. Coherent theory for industrial organization

I did not examine systematically here all theory used earlier in industrial organization. After this brief review, though, one could claim the main theory

30. See Comanor and Wilson (1974), Mueller (1967), and Neumann (1974). Consideration of risk alone does not appear to upset single equation findings which ignored risk; see Sherman and Tollison (1972). Theoretically sound measures can also improve empirical soundness; see Cowling and Cubbin (1972) for an example.
31. See Butters (1976).

that had been used was neoclassical micro-theory, or no theory at all. When it relied on theory the empirical work often could be tied only tenuously to it, for that theory was not rich enough, either in institutional detail or in the variables it included, to fit the world. Recent theoretical work in risk and imperfect information now gives promise of elaborating the neoclassical theory, however. Besides offering new hypotheses in industrial organization the more complete theory can better discipline our claims as it provides a more unifying basis for empirical research.

Now a new wave of research can be anticipated in industrial organization, based on a theory that is more powerful because it omits less. Risk and imperfect information obviously are important in the world; the neoclassical theory that was used when industrial organization research began did not consider them importantly and that omission has limited its usefulness in the past. In other respects the neoclassical theory organizes economic thinking about markets well, and the addition of risk and information considerations need not detract from that orderliness. Academic methods can be stronger in posing issues and aiming research, and we should find ourselves less often being asked to respond to public concerns about which our theory has little to say. Indeed, there is reason to believe that future economists will understand public issues more clearly than we who occasionally, at our worst, could only chastise the world for not fitting U-shaped cost curves.

References

Akerlof, George A. (1970), The Market for 'Lemons': Quality, Uncertainty and the Market Mechanism, *Quarterly Journal of Economics*, 84 (August), pps. 488–500.

Alchian, Armen, A., and Harold Demsetz (1972), Production, Information Costs, and Economic Organization, *American Economic Review*, 62 (December), pps. 777–95.

Arrow, Kenneth J. (1971), *Essays in the Theory of Risk Bearing*, Chicago: Markham Publishing Co.

Azariadis, C. (1975), Implicit Contracts and Underemployment Equilibria, *Journal of Political Economy*, 83 (December), pps. 1183–1202.

Bain, Joe S. (1956), *Barriers to New Competition*, Cambridge, Mass.: Harvard University Press.

Balasko, Yves (1974), 'On Designing Public Utility Tariffs with Applications to Electricity,' Working Paper IP-218, Center for Research in Management Science, University of California at Berkeley, October.

Baumol, William J. (1967), *Business Behavior, Value, and Growth*, rev. ed., New York: Macmillan Co.

Becker, Gary S. (1975), *Human Capital*, 2nd ed., New York: National Bureau of Economic Research.

Becker, Gary S. (1965), A Theory of the Allocation of Time, *Economic Journal*, 75 (September), pp. 493–517.

Berle, Adolph, and Gardiner Means (1968), *The Modern Corporation and Private Property*, revised ed., New York: Harcourt, Brace, and World, (original ed., New York: Macmillan, 1932).

Blair, John M. (1972), *Economic Concentration*, New York: Harcourt Brace Jovanovich.

Borch, K. H. (1968), *The Economics of Uncertainty*, Princeton, N.J.: Princeton University Press.

Breit, William and Kenneth G. Elzinga (1973), Antitrust Penalties and Attitudes Toward Risk, *Harvard Law Review*, 86 (February), pps. 693–713.

Brown, Gardiner, and M. Bruce Johnson (1969), Public Utility Price and Output Under Risk, *American Economic Review*, 59 (March), pps. 119–28.

Butters, Gerard R. (1976), A Survey of Advertising and Market Structure, *American Economic Review* 66 (May), pps. 392–97.

Caves, Richard E. (1970), Uncertainty, Market Structure and Performance: Galbraith as Conventional Wisdom, in J. W. Markham and G. F. Papanek, eds., *Industrial Organization and Economic Development*, Boston, Mass.: Houghton-Mifflin Co.

Caves, Richard E. (1976), The Determinants of Market Structure: Design for Research, in Jacquemin and de Jong (1976).

Chamberlin, Edward H. (1962), *The Theory of Monopolistic Competition*, 8th ed., Cambridge, Mass.: Harvard University Press.

Clarkson, Kenneth (1972), Some Implications of Property Rights in Hospital Management, *Journal of Law and Economics*, 15 (October), pps. 363–84.

Coase, Ronald H. (1937), The Nature of the Firm, *Economica*, 4 (November), pps. 386–405.

Comanor, William S., and Thomas A. Wilson (1974), *Advertising and Market Power*, Cambridge, Mass.: Harvard University Press.

Cournot, Augustin (1927), *Researches into the Mathematical Principles of the Theory of Wealth*, New York: Macmillan Co., translated by N. T. Bacon and Irving Fisher from 1838 original.

Cowling, Keith, and Cubbin, John (1972), Hedonic Price Indexes for UK Cars, *Economic Journal*, 82 (September), pps. 963–78.

Cyert, Richard M., and James G. March (1963), *A Behavioral Theory of the Firm*, Englewood Cliffs, N.J.: Prentice-Hall.

Demsetz, Harold (1973), Industry Structure, Market Rivalry, and Public Policy, *Journal of Law and Economics*, 15 (April), pps. 1–9.

Feinberg, Robert M. (1976), Theoretical Implications and Empirical Tests of the Job Search Theory, unpublished Ph.D. dissertation, University of Virginia.

Flaherty, Marie-Therese (1976), Industry Structure and Cost-Reducing Investment: A Dynamic Equilibrium Analysis. A paper presented at NBER-NSF Seminar on Theoretical Industrial Organization at Carnegie-Mellon University, 20 March 1976.

Friedman, Milton, and L. J. Savage (1948), The Utility Analysis of Choices Involving Risk, *Journal of Political Economy*, 56 (August), pps. 279–304.

Furubotn, Erik, and Pejovitch, Svetozar (1972), Property Rights and Economic Theory: A Survey of Recent Literature, *Journal of Economic Literature*, 10 (December), pps. 1137–62.

Goldschmid, Harvey J., H. Michael Mann, and J. Fred Weston, eds. (1974), *Industrial Concentration: The New Learning*, Boston, Mass.: Little, Brown and Co.

Grossman, Sanford J., and Joseph E. Stiglitz (1975), On the Impossibility of Informationally Efficient Markets, presented at Econometric Society meetings at Dallas, Texas, in December.

Grossman, Sanford J., and Joseph E. Stiglitz (1976), Information and Competitive Price Systems, *American Economic Review*, 66 (May), pps. 246–53.

Grossman, Herschel I. (1975), The Nature of Optimal Labor Contracts: Towards a Theory of Wage and Employment Adjustment, Working Paper, Brown University, March.

Grossman, Herschel I. (1977), Risk Shifting and Reliability in Labor Markets, Scandinavian Journal of Economics.

Hart, P. E., ans S. J. Prais (1956), The Analysis of Business Concentration, *Journal of Royal Statistical Society*, 119, pt. 2, pps. 150–91.

Hirshleifer, Jack (1971), The Private and Social Value of Information and the Reward to Inventive Activity, *American Economic Review*, 61 (September), pps. 561–74.

Jacquemin, Alex P. (1972), Market Structure and the Firm's Market Power, *Journal of Industrial Economics*, 20 (April), pps. 122–34.

Jacquemin, Alex P. and Henk W. de Jong (1976), *Markets, Corporate Behavior, and the State*, The Hague: Martinus Nijhoff.

Jenny, F., and A. P. Weber (1976), Profit Rates and Structural Variables in French Manufacturing Industries, *European Economic Review*, 7 (February), pps. 187–206.

Johnsen, Thore (1976), Equilibrium Models with Advertising as a Signalling Device. A paper presented at NBER-NSF Seminar on Theoretical Industrial Organization at Carnegie-Mellon University, 19 March 1976.

Knight, Frank H. (1931), *Risk, Uncertainty and Profit*, New York: Hart Schaffner and Marx.

Kunreuther, Howard (1976), Economic Analysis of Low-Probability Events. A paper presented at American Economic Association meetings at Atlantic City, N.J., September 18, 1976.

Leland, Hayne E. (1972), Theory of the Firm Facing Uncertain Demand, *American Economic Review*, 62 (June), pps. 278–91.

Letwin, Shirley R. (1965), *The Pursuit of Certainty*, London: Cambridge University Press.

Levy, Haim, and Marshall, Sarnat (1972), *Investment and Portfolio Analysis*, New York: John Wiley and Sons.

Lintner, John (1965), The Valuation of Risky Assets and the Selection of Risky Investments in Stock Portfolios and Capital Budgets, *Review of Economics and Statistics*, 47 (February), pps. 13–37.

McCall, John J. (1970), The Economics of Information and Job Search, *Quarterly Journal of Economics*, 84 (February).

McCall, John J. (1971), Probabilistic Microeconomics, *The Bell Journal of Economics*, 2 (Autumn), pps. 403–433.

McEachern, William A. (1975), *Managerial Control and Performance*, Lexington, Mass.: D. C. Heath and Co.

McKean, Roland N. (1970), Products Liability: Trends and Implications, *Chicago Law Review*, 38 (Fall), pps. 3–63.

Mansfield, Edwin (1962), Entry, Gibrat's Law, Innovation, and the Growth of Firms, *American Economic Review*, 52 (December), pps. 1023–51.

Marchand, Maurice (1973), The Economic Principles of Telephone Rates under a Budgetary Constraint, *Review of Economic Studies*, 40 (October), pps. 507–15.

Markowitz, Harry (1952), Portfolio Selection, *Journal of Finance*, 7 (March), pps. 77–91.

Marshall, Alfred (1920), *Principles of Economics*, 8th ed., London: Macmillan.

Mason, E. S. (1939), Price and Production Policies of Large-Scale Enterprises, *American Economic Review*, 29 (March), pps. 61–74.

Massell, Benton F. (1969), Price Stabilization and Welfare, *Quarterly Journal of Economics*, 83 (May), pps. 284–98.

Mayers, David (1974), Portfolio Theory, Job Choice, and the Equilibrium Structure of Expected Wages, *Journal of Financial Economics*, 1 (February), pps. 23–42.

Means, Gardiner C. (1932), *Structure of the American Economy*, Washington, D.C.: National Resources Committee.

Mills, Edwin (1959), Uncertainty and Price Theory, *Quarterly Journal of Economics*, 73 (February), pps. 116–30.

Mossin, Jan (1966), Equilibrium in a Capital Asset Market, *Econometrica*, 34 (October), pps. 768–83.

Mossin, Jan (1968), Aspects of Rational Insurance Purchasing, *Journal of Political Economy*, 76 (July), pps. 553–68.

Mueller, Dennis C. (1967), The Firm Decision Process: An Econometric Investigation, *Quarterly Journal of Economics*, 81 (February), pps. 58–87.

Nelson, Richard R. (1961), Uncertainty, Prediction, and Competitive Equilibrium, *Quarterly Journal of Economics*, 95 (February), pps. 41–62.

Neumann, Manfred (1974), Profitability, Uncertainty, and Market Structure. A paper presented at Nijenrode Conference, August 1974.

Oi, Walter Y. (1973), The Economics of Product Safety, *Bell Journal of Economics*, 4 (Spring), pps. 3–28.

Palmer, John (1973), The Profit Performance Effects of the Separation of Ownership from Control in Large US Industrial Corporations, *Bell Journal of Economics*, 3 (Spring), pps. 293–303.

Phlips, Louis (1971), *Effects of Industrial Concentration: A Cross-Section Analysis for the Common Market*, Amsterdam: North-Holland Publishing Co.

Porter, Michael E. (1976), Interbrand Choice, Media Mix, and Market Performance, *American Economic Review*, (May), pps. 398–406.

Pratt, J. W. (1964), Risk Aversion in the Small and in the Large, *Econometrica*, 32 (January), pps. 122–36.

Preston, Lee E. (1975), Corporation and Society: The Search for a Paradigm, *Journal of Economic Literature*, 13 (June), pps. 434–53.

Riley, John G. (1976), Information, Screening, and Human Capital, *American Economic Review*, 66 (May), pps. 254–60..

Rothschild, Michael (1973), Models of Market Organization with Imperfect Information: A Survey, *Journal of Political Economy*, 81 (November), pps. 1283–1308.

Salop, Steve (1976), Information and Monopolistic Competition, *American Economic Review*, 66 (May), pps. 240–45.

Scherer, F. M. (1970), *Industrial Market Structure and Economic Performance*, Chicago: Rand McNally and Co.

Schramm, Richard and Roger Sherman (1974), Profit-Risk Management and the Theory of the Firm, *Southern Economic Journal*, 40 (January).

Schramm, Richard and Roger Sherman (1976), Advertising to Manage Profit Risk, *Journal of Industrial Economics*, 24 (June).

Schultz, T. W. (1961), Investment in Human Capital, *American Economic Review*, 51 (March), pps. 1–17.

Schwed, Fred (1955), *Where are the Customers' Yachts?*, New York: Simon and Schuster.

Sharpe, William F. (1964), Capital Asset Prices, *Journal of Finance*, (September), pps. 425–42.

Sherman, Roger (1974), *The Economics of Industry*, Boston, Mass.: Little, Brown and Co.

Sherman, Roger (1972), *Oligopoly*, Lexington, Mass.: D. C. Heath and Co.

Sherman, Roger (1972), How Tax Policy Induces Conglomerate Mergers, *National Tax Journal*, 25 (December), pps. 521–30.

Sherman, Roger, and Robert Tollison (1972), Profit Risk, Technology, and Assessments of Market Performance, *Quarterly Journal of Economics*, 86 (August), pps. 448–62.

Shubik, Martin (1970), A Curmudgeon's Guide to Microeconomics, *Journal of Economic Literature*, 8 (June), pps. 405–34.

Simon, Herbert A., and Charles P. Bonini (1958), The Size Distribution of Business Firms, *American Economic Review*, 48 (September), pps. 607–17.

Smith, Adam (1937), *An Inquiry into the Nature and Causes of the Wealth of Nations*, Edited by Edwin Cannan, New York: Modern Library, Inc.; first published in 1776.

Smith, D. Stanton (1971), Concentration and Employment Fluctuations, *Western Economic Journal*, 9 (September), pps. 267–77.

Spence, A. Michael (1974), *Market Signaling*, Cambridge, Mass.: Harvard University Press.

Stigler, George J. (1961), The Economics of Information, *Journal of Political Economy*, 69 (June), pps. 213–25.

Townsend, Robert (1976), Efficient Contracts with Costly State-Verification. A paper presented at NBER-NSF Seminar on Theoretical Industrial Organization at Carnegie-Mellon University, 19 March 1976.

Tsiang, S. C. (1972), The Rationale of Mean-Standard Deviation Analysis, Skewness Preference, and the Demand for Money, *American Economic Review*, 62 (June), pps. 354–71.

Vernon, John M. (1972), *Market Structure and Industrial Performance*, Boston: Allyn and Bacon.

Von Newman, John, and Oskar Morgenstern (1947), *Theory of Games and Economic Behavior*, 2nd ed., Princeton, N.J.: Princeton University Press.

Visscher, Michael (1973), Welfare-Maximizing Price and Output with Stochastic Demand, *American Economic Review*, 63 (March), pps. 224–29.

Visscher, Michael (1975), The Value of Consumer Waiting Time in the Supply of Goods. Ph.D. dissertation, University of Virginia.

Weiss, Leonard (1971), Quantitative Studies of Industrial Organization, in Michael D. Intriligator, ed., *Frontiers of Quantitative Economics*, Amsterdam: North-Holland Publishing Co.

Wilde, John (1976), Labor Market Equilibrium under Sequential Search. A paper presented at NBER-NSF Seminar on Theoretical Industrial Organization at Carnegie-Mellon University, 19 March 1976.

Williamson, Oliver E. (1970), *Corporate Control and Business Behavior*, Englewood Cliffs, N.J.: Prentice-Hall.

Williamson, Oliver E. (1964), *The Economics of Discretionary Behavior*, Englewood Cliffs, N.J.: Prentice-Hall.

Williamson, Oliver E. (1971), The Vertical Integration of Production: Market Failure Considerations, *American Economic Review*, 61 (May), pps. 112–23.

Williamson, Oliver E. (1976), The Economics of Internal Organization: Exit and Voice in Relation to Markets and Hierarchies, *American Economic Review*, 66 (May), pps. 369–77.

Williamson, Oliver E. (1975), *Markets and Hierarchies: Analysis and Antitrust Implications*, London: Collier-Macmillan.

II. THE DOMINANT FIRM IN RELATION TO MARKET STRUCTURE

William G. Shepherd

The dominant firm is an unsolved puzzle of industrial organization. A sizable number of dominant firms in large industries manage to retain high market shares and high rates of profit, despite the absence of large technical economies of scale. This has baffled scientific analysis, and it has put antitrust and regulatory policies in awkward positions. It has sown discord among us, setting 'Chicagoans' against others in the field.

In researching this dominant-firm problem for some years, I have come to regard it as deeply rooted in certain images and methods of the field of industrial organization. From a revised set of images and a comparative-static approach, much of the apparent puzzle is resolved. This involves going beyond the conventional paradigm of the field – the 'structure-behavior-performance triad' – and analyzing the rate of change in high market shares.

My discussion here extends the research findings in my paper for the first Nijenrode Conference and draws several implications. In a conference paper such as this, I have felt freer to explore ideas rather than record all possible footnote references. I hope the reader will treat the paper kindly, in that same exploratory spirit.

I begin with the setting of the firm and its inner incentives for growth. Then I explore its main choices and constraints. This includes discussion of the rate of change in the firm's market share, as a general matter and in specific countries. There are three kinds of implications from the analysis, which section 2 presents. One is for the structure-behavior-performance triad. A second concerns the motives of the firm. A third implication is for public policies toward market power.

1. The firm and its setting

The basic unit of analysis is the firm. Its boundaries and activities are concrete and known. There is a single main focus of its motives and decisions. The two alternative units of analysis are the group and the industry. Both of them usually have indistinct boundaries. Both usually contain units with mutually conflicting interests. Therefore the motivation and choices are more difficult to define for the group and the industry than for the firm.

(i) *Basic choices of the firm*

The firm has two basic roles: (1) as *owner* (the finance and control of the firm), and (2) as *producer* (the conversion of inputs into outputs, which are then sold).[1]

I will stress the first role here, since it is basic to the firm's motives and performance. The second, or 'industrial,' aspects can be regarded as a set of technical constraints on the firm's ability to generate profits for its owners. The firm 'solves' the industrial production problem simply as a means of reaping net income. Choices of input mixes, output levels, and prices are little more than by-products of the firm's main choices dealing with market shares and long-run profits.

The firm makes ongoing choices within a set of external constraints, including 'the' market and the degree of competition. Other firms do the same. Together, these choices determine the balance and shifts among dominant and lesser firms (including 'entrants'). The firm is aware of a range of competing firms of varying sizes. Figure 1 illustrates a standard situation for a dominant firm. Each firm attaches various probability levels to the possibility of adverse impacts from each other firm. The dominant firm's expected impacts from actions by its large rivals will normally be greater than those from lesser firms and 'potential entrants.' The firm then maximizes its present value subject to the limits set by all of the expected impacts.

Each firm's outcome will depend on its position in the market. Obviously, a lesser firm can only expect a rigorously competitive outcome, since it is a small seller facing strong competition. A firm with a large share can expect a sharply different outcome.

The firm chooses among future profit levels and market positions. There are two parts in determining the outcomes.[2] First, the firm's market position does influence its long-run profits, as shown in Figure 2. Second, the firm's future market position is itself a choice variable. As shown in Figure 3, the firm usually has a medium-run trade-off along the possibility frontier relating profit rate and changes in market share. It can 'invest' in an increase of market share, or liquidate

---

1. This distinction is familiar from the literature of business management. See, for example, Irvin M. Grossack and David D. Martin, *Managerial Economics: Microtheory and the Firm's Decisions* (Boston: Little, Brown and Co., 1973).
2. Further discussion of this is given in W. G. Shepherd, *The Treatment of Market Power* (New York: Columbia University Press, 1975), Chapters 2 and 4.

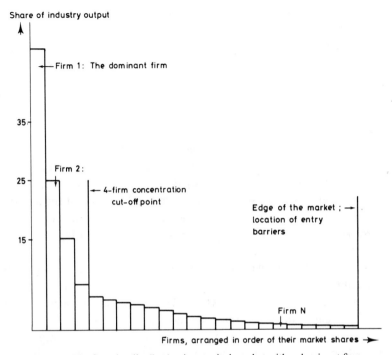

Figure 1. The firm size distribution in a typical market with a dominant firm.

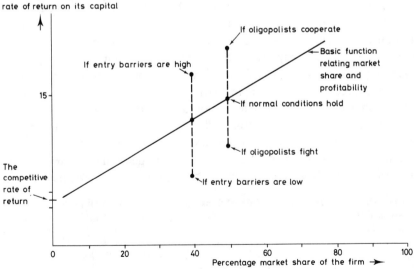

Figure 2. The basic relationship between market share and profit rate.

some of its market share. This comparative-static analysis helps one explore why high market shares arise, as well as what later effects a given market share may have. The time-path of each firm's market share and profitability is influenced by the firm's preferences and its $\pi \Delta M$ possibility frontier. Each firm's conditions may differ from the others'.

(ii) *Origins of dominant positions*
Dominant-firm positions arise from a number of different causes. Chance, personality and historical accident are often important.[3] There are two standard parts to the processes which create dominant firms. One is by industry growth: an industry is born with one firm holding a patent or other device, which helps that firm stay on top as the industry grows. A common belief is that the first firm in being can maintain dominance if the economies of scale remain large compared to the market's size. The other part of the process is by a firm rising within a given market, by chance or by a series of choices as in Figure 3.

After some years' study of many dominant firms, I think that no single cause is predominant.[4] Many cases mingle several of the causes in some degree. Perhaps the most common case is the firm which obtained an advantage at or near the industry's origin and has retained dominance since. In the USA, obvious examples include IBM, General Motors, Eastman Kodak, Campbell Soup, Coca-Cola and Gillette.[5] Achieving a new dominance in a mature industry is much rarer, unless horizontal merger is encouraged from outside by public agencies (as has happened since 1960 in some West European countries).

The 'industry's' technology is probably much less important in most cases, as a determinant of structure, than the literature has suggested. In fact the concept of 'the industry's' technology if often more precise than is appropriate. Production methods often change rapidly as time advances, so that no unique set of conditions determines a clear set of cost curves common to all firms competing in a market. Moreover, especially in industries with only one or a few main firms, each firm may have a distinctive technology. Each firm's existing capacity may largely be fixed, and different from others, and its combination of present engineering approaches and product mixes may also be different.

Even if the industry's technology provides clear, identical cost curves for all firms, economies of scale may be limited to small size ranges. The mainstream

3. This is evident from the histories of actual firms and markets. Also see Oliver E. Williamson, *Markets and Hierarchies: Analysis and Antitrust Implications* (New York: Free Press, 1975), especially Chapter 11.
4. See *Treatment, op cit.*; W. G. Shepherd, 'The Elements of Market Power,' *Review of Economics and Statistics*, February 1972, pp. 25–37; M. W. Klass and W. G. Shepherd, eds., *Regulation and Entry* (East Lansing, Michigan: Institute of Public Utilities, 1976).
5. See Tables 1 to 3 below for a listing of some dominant firms in US industries.

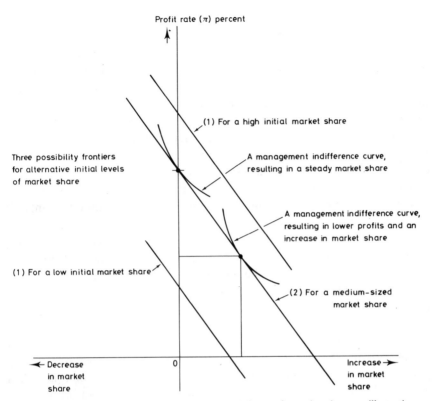

Figure 3. The possibility frontier for profit rate and changes in market share: an illustration.

research findings in our field have suggested that most dominant firms are well above 'minimum efficient scale.' This interpretation is still disputed by a few 'Chicago' oriented colleagues and by the firms themselves. Yet the burden of scientific proof lies mainly the other way. After all, most dominant firms have viable competitors which are very much smaller than themselves. This alone indicates that minimum efficient scale is small, or that there is no unique industry-wide technology/ or both.

6. Among many others, see Joe S. Bain, *Barriers to New Competition* (Cambridge, Mass.: Harvard University Press, 1956); F. M. Scherer, Alan Beckenstein, Erich Kaufer, and Richard D. Murphy, *The Economics of Multi-plant Operation: An International Comparisons Study* (Cambridge, Mass.: Harvard University Press, 1975); and C. F. Pratten, *Economies of Scale in Manufacturing Industry*, Occasional Paper 28 (Cambridge: Cambridge University Press, 1971).

    On 'Chicago' views, see Warren J. Samuels, ed., *The Chicago School of Political Economy*, Division of Research, Graduate School of Business Administration (East Lansing, Michigan: Michigan State University, 1976), especially the chapter by David D. Martin. The present Chicago view is, of course, much more optimistic than that of the original Chicago group, including Frank H. Knight, Henry C. Simons and Jacob Viner.

(iii) *The process of erosion*
Not surprisingly, there appears to be a general process eroding high market
shares. Some observers think that this rate of decay is high: that is the nub of what
is currently known as the 'Chicago' view. More probably it is a gradual rate, with
some high and low exceptions (see below). Our main task is to explain those
unusual cases where high shares are maintained and yet high profit rates are also
earned. One explanation is high entry barriers. Small firms often are fully in the
market and yet do not expand, even though they are as efficient as the large firm.
In some cases the dominant firm holds key patents, but these are a small minority
of cases. Often the dominant firm's own pricing actions and other tactics are
confining the competitors, as we will see shortly. Such actions are not the basic
sort of barriers which Bain explored. They are manipulated by the dominant firm
in order to restrain its existing rivals.

I will take it, in what follows, that neither entry barriers nor technical
economies of scale are satisfactory general explanations of maintained, profitable
dominant-firm shares. The explanation instead rests on (1) pecuniary gains from
dominance, and (2) the inner pressures on the firm to grow. I will now discuss
these.

(iv) *Pecuniary gains from dominance*
Pecuniary gains arise mainly from price discrimination and reductions in input
prices. Price discrimination is perhaps the most critical single factor. It has fallen
into relative neglect since the 1940s, even though leading US antitrust decisions
during this period (especially *United Shoe Machinery* in 1954) have recognized its
importance.[7] Instead, the field has turned much of its attention toward
'oligopolists' limit-pricing strategies': in that context, there is no dominant firm
and no price discrimination at all.

Roughly speaking, the field followed E. H. Chamberlin's lead rather than Joan
Robinson's after 1934. Price discrimination has been relegated mainly to the
public utility literature and peripheral Robinson-Patman issues of 'predatory'
pricing. It should now be placed firmly at the centre of the analysis of dominant
firms.

Most dominant firms face a variety of customer groups with varying demand
elasticities.[8] Systematic price discrimination enables the firm to extract maximum profit. Dominant firms often arrange their basic strategies in order to

7. See especially Carl Kaysen, *USA* v. *United Shoe Machinery Corporation* (Cambridge, Mass.:
Harvard University Press, 1955). The *locus classicus* is Joan Robinson, *The Economics of Imperfect
Competition* (London: Macmillan, 1934).
8. My discussion reflects study of the pricing by IBM, Xerox, automobile firms, Procter & Gamble
and other industrial firms, and by private and public corporations·in such 'utility' sectors as
electricity, gas, telephone service and railroads.

enhance discrimination. For example, product lines are designed and advertised so as to keep customers separable. The firm's own sales force is made a strong, direct link to customers (as is done by IBM and Xerox). Or possibly, a system of weak, passive dealers is used to bypass mass retailers (as in automobiles).

Price discrimination is also used systematically by dominant firms to exclude competition by small firms and possible newcomers. Selective price cuts are made to meet the smaller firms' efforts to expand or launch new products. The dominant firm covers the range of submarkets, while it confines the others to narrow lines.[9] This differs from classic 'predatory pricing,' for it need not aim to eliminate the competitors altogether. Nor need it involve pricing below cost. It also differs from vertical price 'squeezes.' Yet it often 'squeezes' small firms selling complementary products (e.g., as with peripheral computer devices, or cameras and film, or automobiles and parts) by changing the price relationships which permitted them to be viable. These pricing patterns are often reinforced by product strategies and advertising tactics.

To this extent, the dominant firm can maintain a large market share and also remain highly profitable. Its price structure can become at least as complex and interrelated as many 'utility' price structures: recent examples include IBM's and Xerox's current pricing, compared to gas or even electricity prices. Consider the matter in reverse, also. Many 'utilities' have evolved toward less complex cost and demand conditions, which would permit them to change from monopolies into loose-oligopoly status. In evaluating this from either direction, the role of price discrimination can be decisive.

J. M. Clark's earlier stress on 'overhead costs' is appropriate in this context.[10] Most of the stable, profitable dominant firms have large elements of overhead costs, which make price discrimination (1) inevitable, (2) extensive, and (3) difficult to measure and challenge. Where allocable marginal costs are low in many directions, the scope for discrimination is large. Yet issues like these have been neglected because of the preference for analyzing limit pricing by interdependent oligopolists.

Cheaper inputs are the other 'market power' source of profits for dominant firms. I need not elaborate this familiar idea. Yet I do think it is usually less important quantitatively than price discrimination is, in generating profits and reducing competition. Volume discounts tend to be less than proportional with the size of orders. Also, in order to get large discounts the firm often must exercise

9. IBM is a good example: see Gerald Brock, *The United States Computer Industry* (Cambridge, Mass.: Ballingen, 1975), and W. G. Shepherd, *Market Power and Economic Welfare* (New York: Random House, 1970), Chapter 15.
10. J. M. Clark, *Studies in the Theory of Overhead Costs* (New York: Macmillan, 1922); see also W. A. Robson's splendid *Overhead Costs* (London: Allen & Unwin, 1948).

strong monopoly power. Yet a dominant position in market X may provide little or no such power in buying from market Y.

(v) Pressures for maintaining dominance

The dominant firm is under several pressures for growth which usually impel it to exploit price discrimination and cheaper inputs fully, in order to maintain or increase its market share. One such pressure is overhead costs. They provide low marginal costs, within the limits or current and planned capacity. Thus, most of IBM's lines share common R&D and sales-network costs. Once these fixed, shared costs are committed, then marginal costs are low in most product lines and for most individual sales. The inducement for higher sales is strong, and it naturally yields price discrimination in some degree.

Another pressure for growth is shareholder expectations, reinforcing managers' preferences. Both groups tend to favor growth, often to the point of tolerating dubious or unprofitable investments in order to add growth. Much diversifying fits this category, as when firms' managers feel they must 'do something' with investable funds by branching into other markets, when optimal growth in their own primary markets is low.

A third pressure for growth arises from the accrual of internal resources in the firm, as discussed by Penrose.[11] As dominant firms adjust, they generate transferable resources (especially among upper-level personnel) which are available for growth. This is closely akin to the familiar 'learning curve,' whereby average costs fall over time as even the simplest production tasks are mastered.

These three conditions tend to make the possibility set in Figure 3 flatter than it would otherwise be. This in turn tends to tilt the choices toward a greater retention or enlargement of the dominant firm's market share.

In summary, dominant firms are under pressures to exploit their opportunities to maintain market share and accrue profits. Even when technical scale economies and Bain's type of entry barriers are absent, price discrimination and cheaper inputs can provide ample opportunities for this purpose.

The dominant firm simply makes its main choices along the profit-market share functions shown in Figures 2 and 3. Any interdependence or strategy issues between it and its rivals may be mere variations around the main relationships. Likewise, new entrants may be a trivial concern. Such oligopoly and barrier factors would only modify the mainstream choice conditions illustrated in Figures 2 and 3. The firm need not be maximizing its market share indeed, in most cases, it will be optimizing profitability and market share over the long run. The optimal time-path of market share may trace out a rise, a decline, a series of

11. Edith T. Penrose, *The Theory of the Growth of the Firm* (Oxford: Basil Blackwell, 1959).

shifts, or a constant level (Darius Gaskins has explored some of these possibilities).[12] The outcomes reflect both external conditions (including unexpected changes) and 'the firm's' own preferences.

(vi) *Rates of change in high market shares*
Research on the actual rates of change of high market shares has just begun. One can test for general processes, across the entire cross-section of industries. One can also identify the 'leading' cases (i.e., dominant firms in major industries) and evaluate their changes. I have attempted both approaches, to a modest degree.[13]
It appears probable that (1) the 'general' rate of decay in industrial markets in an economy such as the US is moderate, at about one point of market share per year, and (2) the rate of decline in major US dominant firms has declined since the 1930s. The latter point is shown by Tables 1 and 2.

For the first period, the year 1910 is a better starting date than, say, 1900, because in 1900 many of the trusts were brand new and obviously fated for a sharp decline. By 1910 most of this transient shrinkage had run its course (e.g., in sugar and tin cans). Also, 1910 is squarely in the first wave of 'trust-busting' cases, and so it is a good point for evaluating what was tried and achieved with those actions. For Table 2, the logical date is 1948. It avoids the special conditions of the 1930s, and it is at the onset of the post World War Two 'modern' industrial period. The 1910–35 and 1948–73 periods therefore provide two 25-year intervals for comparing early and recent industrial experience with market power.

The main lesson seems reasonably clear. The 'natural' decline of leading dominant firms was much more rapid in 1910–35 than in 1949–73. I have used a single approximate index of market power in the effort to test this. The index is the predicted profit rate of the firm, based on estimates of its market share and the 'height' of entry barriers into its markets.[14] A 100 per cent market share indicates an expected profit rate of 25 points; a high entry barrier adds about two more points.

During 1910–35, four of the 20 firms in Table 1 were touched by strong policy influences. Three – Standard Oil, American Tobacco, and duPont – underwent division, while Western Electric continued under its official antitrust exemption. The remaining 16 firms declined an average of 4.6 points in the 'market power

12. Darius W. Gaskins, 'Dynamic Limit Pricing: Optimal Pricing under Threat of Entry,' *Journal of Economic Theory*, 1971, pp. 306–22.
13. See Shepherd, *Treatment of Market Power, op. cit.*, from which the next several pages are adapted.
14. The index is explained in *Treatment of Market Power, op. cit.* It is based on the coefficients from the econometric model of market structure given in *Treatment* and in 'The Elements of Market Structure,' *op. cit.* To illustrate, a firm with a market share of 50 per cent and high entry barriers would be predicted to have a profit rate of about 20 per cent (see Table 3 for more examples). This predicted rate is the 'index' of market power.

Table 1. Changes in market position, leading dominant firms, 1910–1935.

Firm	Degree of market power 1910 (est. %)	Esti- mated assets, 1909–10 ($ mil.)	Degree of market power 1935 (est. %)	Change in market power 1910–35 (est. %)	Specific policy cause of change?
United States Steel	22.0	1804	17.0	− 5.0	(Informal antitrust effects?)
Standard Oil (New Jersey)	27.0	800	15.3	−11.7	1911 case
American Tobacco	27.0	286	13.3	−13.7	1911 case
International Harvester	25.5	166	15.0	−10.5	(Informal antitrust effects?)
Central Leather	21.0	138	6.0	−15.0	
Pullman	29.3	131	27.0	− 2.3	
American Sugar	21.0	124	14.7	− 6.3	
Singer Manufacturing	25.7	113	19.7	− 6.0	
General Electric	23.0	102	21.8	− 1.2	
Corn Products	21.0	97	17.3	− 3.7	
American Can	22.0	90	19.7	− 2.3	
Westinghouse Electric	20.5	84	19.3	− 1.2	
E. I. duPont de Nemours	29.5	75	13.5	−16.0	
International Paper	18.5	71	11.0	− 7.5	
National Biscuit	18.5	65	11.0	− 7.5	
Western Electric	33.0	43	33.0	0	Exemption in 1913
United Fruit	27.0	41	27.0	0	
United Shoe Machinery	31.7	40	30.5	− 1.2	
Eastman Kodak	29.5	35	29.5	0	
Alcoa	32.9	35	29.5	− 3.4	

Source:
W. G. Shepherd, *The Treatment of Market Power* (New York: Columbia University Press, 1975).

index.' This is equivalent to a shrinkage of nearly 20 points in market share. Perhaps some antitrust attempts that failed in the courts (e.g., International Harvester, US Steel) did in fact exert some downward effect, but that is difficult to appraise.

During 1948–73, seven of the 18 instances can be said to have been reduced by policy. For the other 11, the decline of market power was only 0.8 index points on average, corresponding to a market-share shrinkage of 3 points. These declines

Table 2. Changes in market position, leading dominant firms, 1948–73

Firm	Degree of market power 1948 (est. %)	Assets, 1948 ($ mil.)	Degree of market power 1973 (est. %)	Change in market power 1948–73 (est. %)	Specific policy cause of change?
General Motors	22.0	2958	21.8	− .2	
General Electric	20.5	1177	20.5	0	
Western Electric	33.0	650	32.6	− .4	Exemption
Alcoa	28.0	504	17.0	−1.1	Remedy of 1950
Eastman Kodak	27.0	412	27.0	0	
Procter & Gamble	19.5	356	19.5	0	
United Fruit	27.0	320	22.0	−5.0	Remedy
American Can	20.0	276	14.8	−5.2	Remedy of 1951
IBM	29.5	242	23.5	−6.0	Consent decree?
Coca-Cola	22.0	222	19.5	−2.5	
Campbell Soup	28.2	149	28.2	0	
Caterpillar Tractor	19.5	147	19.5	0	
Kellogg	19.5	41	18.3	−1.2	
Gillette	24.5	78	24.5	0	
Babcock and Wilcox	22.0	79	19.5	−2.5	
Hershey	25.8	62	23.5	−2.3	
duPont (cellophane)	30.5	65	22.0	−8.5	Lapse of patent?
United Shoe Machinery	29.2	104	18.5	−10.7	Remedy

Source: see Table 1.

were mainly among the lesser firms. The largest nine firms hardly changed at all, apart from specific policy effects.

During 1948–73, certain other firms rose to join the list, which stood in 1974 roughly as shown in Table 3 (it is not meant to be definitive or comprehensive). The newcomers are primarily IBM in computers, Xerox, aircraft, certain drug firms, and two major newspapers. Table 3 also indicates the relative permanence of these firms. This can be compared with the findings about the erosion of market shares and profit rates in the next section.

Why has the predicted rate of decline for the major dominant firms gone down in recent decades? There are several possible influences, but none of them seems

Table 3. Leading US dominant firms and their background, as of 1974.

Firm	Markets	Market share (%)	Barriers	Degree of market power	Present position dates back to about
General Motors	Autos, locomotives, buses	55	High	21.8	1927
IBM	Computers, type-writers	70	High	23.5	1954
Western Electric	Telecommunication equipment	98	High	32.6	1880s
General Electric	Heavy electrical equipment	50	High	20.5	1900
Eastman Kodak	Photographic supplies	80	Medium	27.0	1900
Xerox	Copying equipment	85	High	29.3	1961
Procter & Gamble	Detergents, toiletries	50	Medium	19.5	1940s
Boeing	Aircraft	45	High	19.5	1950s
McDonnell-Douglas	Aircraft	45	High	19.5	1968
United Aircraft	Aircraft engines	60	Medium	22.0	1950s
Coca-Cola	Flavoring syrups	50	Medium	19.5	1920s
Campell Soup	Canned soups	85	Medium	28.2	1920s
Gillette	Razors, toiletries	70	Medium	24.5	1910
Kellogg	Dry cereals	45	Medium	18.3	1940s
Times Mirror	Newspaper	70	High	23.5	1960
New York Times	Newspaper	75	High	23.5	1966

Source: see Table 1.

sufficient.[15] One reason may be a lessening of flexibility in financial markets. Banker-firm relationships are now of long standing for the older dominant firms, and the capability of capital markets to foster aggressive new competitors may have declined. Banking markets now appear to be more stable than they were during 1900–1920, especially as the role of merchant banks has dwindled. Only in the middle 1960s, during the brief run of some newer conglomerates, were certain banks willing to back newcomers. But that too has subsided, so the basic effects of financial markets on industry remain. As a result, existing dominant firms are

15. Richard Caves also has suggested that perhaps older dominant positions simply decline more slowly than newer ones. If true, that might account for some of the trends. Yet one would again need to ask why that occurs.

favoured. Though this favouritism may not affect the largest firms strongly, its tendency is to stabilize.

Another reason may be that antitrust limits on mergers may also have hardened market structure. Between 1958 and 1966, the limits became quite strict, so that mergers creating more than 10 per cent of any significant market were likely to be stopped.[16] But informal limits came earlier, especially with the passage of the Celler-Kefauver Act in 1949. After the 1920s, few mergers with a large horizontal impact occurred (except in banking). Therefore dominant firms have become freer from competitive challenge via mergers among lesser firms. The rise of Continental Can and Bethlehem Steel by mergers is not possible today. Internal growth is now virtually the only source of large changes in industry structure.

A third reason for the retention of high shares could be economies of scale. Yet the best evidence so far is that scale economies explain only a relatively small portion of most of the major dominant-firm positions. That is the clear lesson from survivor tests, despite their evident faults.[17] In another vein, Bain (in 1950) and Scherer et al. (in 1975), have made probes using 'engineering' estimates and the existing size arrays to indicate the optimal sizes and cost gradients. While these probes are not exhaustive, and they covered less than 30 industries, they do tend to affirm that scale economies are quite limited in most industries. The cost gradients, especially, are low, as Figure 4 shows. Thus, even at a size level only one-third of the inferred minimum optimal scale, the imputed cost levels are only slightly higher than at the minimum optimal scale.[18] However, because Bain and Scherer et al. did not include some of the leading cases of market power, there is a presumption (but not a proof) that the average cost curve flattens out at low sizes even in the main problem industries.

Finally, several specific kinds of barriers now exist, and might seem to cause an increasing rigidity of dominant-firm positions. Patents are important in drugs and photocopying equipment. Advertising-intensity influences soaps and cereals. Sales networks are important in automobiles, copiers, computers, drugs, and soup, among others. But these are simply a series of specific conditions, not a

16. They are reprinted in Clair Wilcox and William G. Shepherd, *Public Policies Toward Business* (Homewood, Ill.: Irwin, 1975), Chapter 8. I participated in the preparation of the final version of these guidelines. They were meant to codify existing practice, not to establish it anew.

17. This is discussed in my 'What Does the Survivor Test Show About Economies of Scale?' *Southern Economic Journal*, July 1967, pp. 113–22. But see also R. D. Rees, 'Optimum Plant Size in the United Kingdom Industries: Some Survivor Estimates,' *Economica*, November 1973, pp. 394–401.

18. F. M. Scherer, Alan Beckenstein, Erich Kaufer, and Richard D. Murphy, *The Economics of Multiplant Operation: An International Comparisons Study* (Cambridge, Mass.: Harvard University Press, 1975). See also C. F. Pratten, *Economies of Scale in Manufacturing Industry* (Cambridge: Cambridge University Press, 1971), and Leonard W. Weiss's chapter in P. D. Qualls and Robert T. Masson, *Essays on Industrial Organization in Honor of Joe S. Bain* (Cambridge, Mass.: Ballinger, 1976).

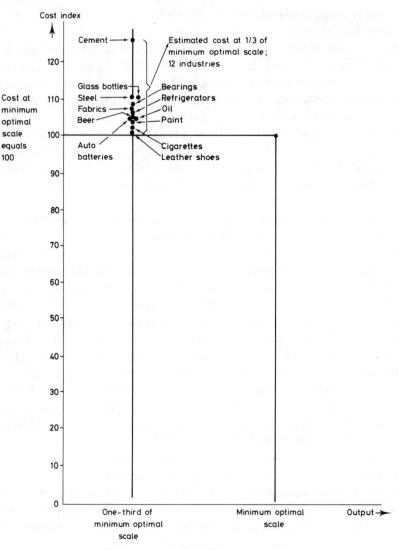

Figure 4. Most cost gradients are not steep

Source: Scherer, Beckenstein, Kaufer and Murphy, *op. cit.*, p. 80.

well integrated set of general factors. Nor is it clear that they are stronger than in earlier periods: patents and sales networks, for example, have long been important. Therefore they cannot yet be regarded as general explanations of the trend toward structural hardness, even though each one may need to be considered in specific treatments.

The rate of decline in other countries is virtually untouched by research so far. My rough comparisons suggest that the rate is higher in British and Japanese industry than in the USA.[19] Impressions from other West European countries are similar, but the issue needs much more work.

Regardless of the actual rates of change in recent decades, the concept is important. It and related comparative-static or 'dynamic' issues are, I think, the natural next stage for theory and testing in this field.

2. Several implications

In line with the analysis in section 1, several interesting lessons can be drawn:

(i) *The triad*
The familiar structure-behaviour-performance triad (as shown in Figure 5) is incomplete – even when 'determinants' are included (so that it becomes a quadriad!). My discussion in section 1 did not rely on the main concepts or logic of the quadriad.[20] Consider these concepts one by one:

(a) *The market has clear-cut edges.* My discussion is not so reliant on that. Instead, the market's edges, and possible barriers, are not crucial. My stress on market share does involve the concept of a market within which the share is defined. Yet many markets have submarkets or blurred edges, so that one can only define a range of probable market shares. Those focusing on barriers, by contrast, must rely on sharp market edges. Otherwise, one cannot speak clearly of barriers at the ends of the market, which separate those outside from those inside.

(b) *The determinants (especially the technology underlying economies of scale) are unique and common to all firms in the industry.* Instead, technology may vary among all firms and countries and shift rapidly.

(c) *The determinants influence structure and performance.* Instead, in most dominant-firm cases, economies of scale are not a close influence.

(d) *The oligopoly group is the main unit of choice, setting limit-prices in light of barrier conditions.* I find little content or plausibility in that approach. Rather, the individual firm is the main decision unit, and entry is usually of less concern to it than actual competition.

(e) *The structure causes the performance, within a degree of variation.* Instead, structure and performance evolve together as part of long-run choices.

19. See Shepherd, 'Structure and Behavior in British Industries, with US Comparisons,' *Journal of Industrial Economics*, (November 1972), pp. 35–54.
20. Scherer also offers a version of the triad: see F. M. Scherer, *Industrial Market Structure and Economic Performance* (Skokie, Ill.: Rand McNally, 1970), Chapter 1.

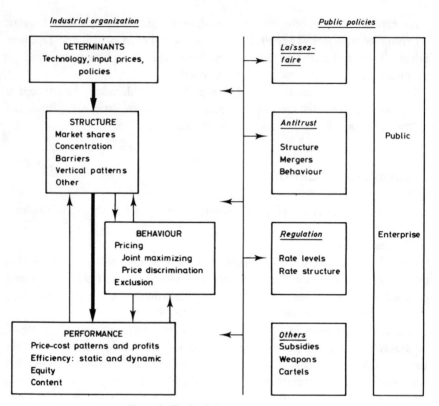

Figure 5. The basic format of the subject.

Some interesting patterns can be analyzed on a static basis. Yet comparative statics – or rates of change – are usually also important, even where, or especially where, the leading firm's share has been stable.

A comparative-static view offers the benefit of clearing up some fruitless debates among 'schools' in the profession. 'Structuralist' is seen to be a label with little meaning. The nub of the new 'Chicago' approach becomes the hypothesis that high market shares decline rapidly, rather than the more tortured view that structure does not matter. The comparative-static approach still requires complex analysis of behaviour, for price discrimination is a crucial topic.

The effort to define markets precisely and to estimate economies of scale becomes less critical. That is fortunate, for such efforts have proved frustrating (especially the effort to filter pecuniary elements out of the estimates of scale economies). The will-o'-the-wisp of 'oligopoly limit-pricing strategy toward entry' can be left as a secondary topic. Research could instead focus on definite choices by individual firms. Price discrimination would then be restored as a major topic. Concentration ratios could be demoted to their proper role as a broad descriptive statistic, with little analytical meaning. We could turn our research microscopes to where they belong, on individual-firm market shares and performance.

The shift in concepts and research would extend the field, rather than replace the quadriad. This is a modest change, with many fruitful research possibilities.

(ii) *The firm*

The nature of the firm is frequently said to be changing. Management control of large firms was the first modern revision.[21] That concept has, however, been diluted by more recent findings. 'Owner control' is more extensive than had been thought, and manager control seems to have had only weak effects – if any – on performance.

Currently, several other basic changes are said to be under way:

(a) The rate of profit is continuing its secular decline. The decline is said to be conspicuous when one allows for inflation's effect on the value of profits. One clear effect of the decline is a down-trend in 'real' common stock prices since 1950 (especially for medium-sized and smaller firms).

(b) Contractual rights and ownership claims are increasingly being diluted.[22] Companies' legal roles are markedly more vulnerable to *ex post* changes, by court action and new public regulations. The rules are more subject to change, both by public agencies and under challenge by private parties. New public controls and subsidies are increasingly decisive for the performance of many firms.

(c) Employee pension plans now hold large blocks of shares in many firms.[23] This is altering the nature of ownership and managers' perceptions of who they are accountable to. It may also shift workers' attitudes from alienation toward an identification with profitability.

To evaluate these and similar claims, one recalls that the firm is basically a transfer mechanism for resource claims. Profit is the main criterion which guides the setting of the resource flows and claims, but a growing list of other 'motives' may drain the margin of surplus available for profit. The political economy may impose specific claims on the firm's resources, in order to accomplish certain

---

21. A. A. Berle and G. C. Means, *The Modern Corporation and Private Property* (New York: Macmillan, 1932); E. S. Mason, ed., *The Corporation in Modern Society* (Cambridge, Mass.: Harvard University Press, 1960); and various more recent works by William J. Baumol, Robin Marris, J. K. Galbraith, Oliver E. Williamson, and Robert J. Larner.
22. 'The corporate form of organization is likely to disappear completely,' say Michael C. Jensen and William H. Meckling in 'A Theory of the Firm,' University of Rochester (mimeographed). They note various ways in which public agencies can now upset settled private-firm contractual claims or impose crippling rules on private firms.
23. Peter F. Drucker, *Pension Fund Socialism* (New York: 1976).

public purposes (or special interests!) via taxes, safety and pollution-control requirements, etc. Various public subsidies (in cash, in kind, or in 'tax expenditures') are also provided. The net effect could alter the firm's balance and perhaps its character.

Instead, the opposite result seems more probable. The basic motivation of the managers is to optimize the firm's margin of profit over the long run. This 'motive' is shared by most private firms – corporate and privately held. It is also shared by public firms of various sorts.[24] In each case, the enterprise manages a range of assets and resource flows. It has a market position. It is under various external constraints, and it gains revenues from market and other sources.

There has always been some 'public' dilution of the 'private' nature of private firms. Likewise, public firms have had important private-market aspects: market positions, profit (and/or cost-related) criteria, etc. Whether the public element is now increasing can be debated. In any case, the conditions seem not to be under radical change, and the same basic analysis is suited to both kinds of firms. Managers optimize along the basic possibility sets for profits and market share; only the shapes and positions differ from case to case. The effects on performance are largely the same for private and public firms. This approach fits such newer techniques as control theory, as well as the basic focus on market share which I have suggested above.

(iii) *Public policies*

Market dominance has come to be treated variously by antitrust, 'utility' regulation, and public enterprise. My line of analysis in this paper would lead to changes in emphasis and technique in these policies. First, it would restore the older concern with the firm's market share. The more recent tack in the USA since 1950 has been to try to reduce entry barriers.[25] Instead, reducing market share is the prime objective: or rather, the aim is to raise the rate at which market share declines toward the minimum required by technical economies of scale.

Also, the treatment should deal mainly with the firm's ownership and control role, rather than just its production role. This fits the extension from purely industrial analysis to include also the financial aspects, which I suggested in section 1. Policies can treat firms by altering the incentives and putting managers'

---

24. W. G. Shepherd and Associates, *Public Enterprise: Economic Analysis of Theory and Practice* (Lexington, Mass.: D. C. Heath-Lexington Books, 1976); and C. D. Foster, *Politics, Finance, and the Role of Economics: An Essay on the Control of Public Enterprise* (London: Allen & Unwin, 1971).
25. The emphasis on barriers can be seen in the *American Can* consent decree in 1950 and in the *United Shoe Machinery* decision of 1953, among others. I can attest from first hand that it has been important in Antitrust Division thinking since the 1960s at least. It has also become influential in plans for reforming the regulation of public utilities in the USA. For an evaluation of the possibilities, see Klass and Shepherd, *Regulation and Entry, ed. cit.*

controls to work, rather than just by forcing a restructuring of production in the teeth of managers' superior information and power.

These points apply to antitrust in the USA and elsewhere, to the regulation of 'public utilities,' and many public firms which have dominant positions. For US antitrust, the continuance of the main dominant firms has made structural action (under the Sherman Act, Section 2) seem out of balance with the 'tight' treatment of price-fixing and mergers. Section 2 actions have spoken of 'splitting up' dominant firms, but they have done little except try to make entry somewhat easier. As a result, since 1950 there has been little measurable effect. Even a small revival since 1968 has had little effect.[26] Judicial slowness and officials' mistakes explain some of the imbalance. Yet the main error is in trying to force industrial changes rather than using financial incentives.

How can public policies apply the proper conditions of choice to those managers and owners who set company policies? One possibility is a graduated tax on market share. The firm's rate of tax on net income would rise gradually, in proportion to its market share; in the USA, from roughly 40 per cent to about 60 per cent.[27] This approach would minimize the firm's resistance, and allow managers to continue to achieve any real economies of scale that may exist. If economies were high, the firm would choose to retain its high share and reap high profits. But the public would collect more tax on those profits. It would not reward X-inefficiency the way that many other treatments (including utility regulation) probably do. The firm would still have normal (perhaps even enhanced) incentives to minimize costs. Some firms would prefer to divide into two or more firms with lower market shares. That would reduce their tax liability. In many cases, shareholders would apply pressure to force managers to reduce share, in order to benefit the shareholders' interests.

One would apply the tax treatment at first only to the larger firms, perhaps the 100 largest (in manufacturing *and* other sectors). Where possible, divisions of companies would be treated separately, when they operate in separate markets. There would be problems in allocating costs and assets, of course. Yet those need not be fatal in most cases.

The method would be as applicable to regulated firms as to any others. In fact, the approach would be especially well suited in that area, for it would automatically capture much of the monopoly gains from the utility firms, and so the regulatory task of directly controlling that exploitation would be eased. One

26. There have been cases against IBM, cereals makers, Xerox and AT&T. The Xerox matter was settled in 1975 with a moderate relief, leaving Xerox's dominance intact. The other matters are in process, probably for many years more. At the end, no changes may occur.
27. This approach is explored for both industrial and utility markets in Shepherd, *Treatment of Market Power, op. cit.*, especially Chapters 6, 7 and 9.

would still need to apply some constraints on the firms' pricing, or perhaps provide rebates to the utility customers from the graduated-tax revenues. The graduated-tax treatment would induce utilities to yield up their monopoly shares as soon as those shares were no longer justified by large economies of scale.

Public firms could also be treated in this way. They too often attain and cling to pure- or near-monopoly positions, beyond what the true scale economies or other public purposes would justify. Regardless of the average rate of tax on their net income (at zero, positive, or negative – via subsidies), a graduated marginal rate could induce a yielding of excess market share by public firms.

The now-conventional policies attempt instead to force changes or constraints on managers, in direct opposition to their interests, controls and information. Shareholders, too, perceive the current treatments as a threat. It is little wonder that managers in both private and public firms have been able to fend off such weak attempts by officials in agencies which lack sufficient information about the firm's technical conditions.

Instead, one needs simply to revise the terms which managers are optimizing. The proper course is not to abandon the policy effort nor to shift it to such peripheral items as barriers or oligopoly-group strategies. Rather, the effort can be to alter the evolution of market share by a direct use of financial incentives: to work with the natural process of change rather than to go against the managers' and shareholders' interests and powers.

Instead, one needs simply to revise the terms which managers are optimizing. The proper course is not to abandon the policy effort nor to shift it to such peripheral items as barriers or oligopoly-group strategies. Rather, the effort can be to alter the evolution of market share by a direct use of financial incentives: to work with the natural process of change rather than to go against the managers' and shareholders' interests and powers.

Defining market share would still pose difficulties, of course. Yet these would probably be less crucial than the present blocks to antitrust policy. First, the market size and market share vary inversely; e.g., a firm may be defined to hold 90 per cent of a $ 100 million market or 60 per cent of a $ 150 million market. With the graduated tax rate, the actual tax paid might not vary by much. Second, only the tax is at stake, not the possibility of staggeringly large damage claims or the prospect of forced restructuring from outside. For both reasons, the firms' efforts to fight the definition of high market shares would be less intense than the present fierce resistance which is routine against US suits against dominant firms.

Such a new approach cannot perform miracles, of course, and it would cut across the present set of vested interests (both private and public) which have a stake in the present policies. But at least it could improve on the present ineffective 'treatments,' and reduce their real costs.[28] Some of my colleagues in public finance disapprove of this use of tax incentives, but I think the possible benefits may easily outweigh any bad effects on the tax base.

3. Conclusion

This brief summary omits much of the careful detail which would be needed before moving in the directions I have suggested. Yet it is important to re-think the main lines of the subject, so that our brick-by-brick research work is as productive as possible.

In recent decades, the tendency has been to fragment research, into several elements of structure and into sub-specialities. This is a good time to work toward re-unifying the analysis, by putting the focus on the firm, its market share, and the rate of change in that share. This would lead also to more unity among public policies, in treating the firm's choice of optimal profits in the long run. It may help us move from policies which seem dubious and costly toward others that fit the incentives and powers of the firm's managers.

28. For evaluations of these policies, see Wilcox and Shepherd, *Public Policies Toward Business, op. cit.*; Almarin Phillips, ed., *Promoting Competition in Regulated Markets* (Washington, D.C.: Brookings Institution, 1975); and Shepherd and Associated, *Public Enterprise, op. cit.*

III. THE OWNERSHIP AND CONTROL OF INDUSTRY

Steve Nyman and Aubrey Silberston

1. Introduction

Since Berle and Means (1932) wrote their pioneering work the ownership and control of large firms has been a continuing, if sporadic, interest of economists, and of industrial economists in particular. There now seems to be a consensus of opinion, or 'conventional wisdom,' that a majority of large firms are controlled by professional managers, that the proportion of large firms controlled by ownership interests is declining and that, in any event, there is very little difference in behaviour between manager- and owner-controlled firms. In this paper we suggest that the conventional wisdom is misleading to a considerable extent. It is based on too narrow a conception of the forms which ownership takes and on too simple a theory of the relationship between ownership and corporate behaviour.

We shall present new evidence on the extent of ownership control in British industry which shows that the extent of managerial control is more limited than has been thought and may not have an inexorable tendency to increase. However, the situation differs very much by industry and this may have affected the results of previous empirical studies on the relationship between control and behaviour. This differentiation by industry is of course of interest in itself and a topic that needs investigating. A further differentiation is that between different types of ownership control. Firms which are controlled by professional managers, by families, by other industrial firms, or by financial institutions may display very different behavioural characteristics. These differences have not been discussed much in the literature, nor have the ways in which the control of firms changed over time.

This work forms part of the Growth of Firms project at Nuffield College (financed by the Social Science Research Council) and is very much based on ideas and information gathered from intensive case studies of twenty large UK firms as well as less-intensive studies of the top 250 firms. We believe that it is this kind of study which is needed to bring out the continuing importance of ownership. In recent years a good deal of new work has been done elsewhere on this issue, much of it published outside conventional economic journals, and this too helps to throw light on data and hypotheses concerning the ownership structure of industry and its implications.

2. Previous studies

Two of the most widely used textbooks in Industrial Economics are those by George (1974) and Scherer (1970). George devotes only a few paragraphs to the question of the divorce between ownership and control in large UK firms and quotes the conclusion of Sargent Florence (1961) that 70 per cent of the large firms he studied were characterized by a divorce between ownership and control. George suggests that this is an overestimate of the extent of the divorce because of the stringent criteria used, and adds that ownership control is normal for smaller firms. Nevertheless he concludes that: 'a very important part of the private enterprise sector of the economy is characterized by management control' (p. 103).

Scherer devotes more space to the question of the ownership and control of industry – some four pages out of over five hundred. On the basis of Berle and Means' and Larner's (1970) data he suggests that managerial control has been increasing and quotes Larner's conclusion that by 1963 over 80 per cent of the largest 200 US Corporations were management controlled. However he admits that this may be an oversimplification, and that considerable power may be wielded by families and by financial institutions. Control of several corporations may also be exercized via interlocking directorates. Scherer concludes his review of the topic by saying:

'... our ignorance on this subject is great, and we can scarcely afford the complacent assumption that interlocking directorates and other corporate affiliations have not significant behavioural effects.' (p. 47)

The so-called 'divorce' between ownership and control has also been the starting point for recent managerial theories of the firm. Perhaps the most comprehensive discussion of these has been in *The Corporate Economy* edited by Marris and Wood (1971) which, however, contains no discussion of ownership and control in eleven chapters and three appendices. The authors rely on earlier works such as Marris (1964) which assume that most large corporations are managerially controlled, on the basis of evidence from Berle and Means, Gordon (1961), Larner and Sargent Florence.

The criteria which these and other writers have used to classify corporate control have differed, but in general they have mainly been mechanical. They have defined a percentage of the total votes which an individual or clearly defined group must own, to class a company as effectively controlled by a minority. Majority control of course, presents no problem. The relevant percentages as definitions of minority control are as follows .

20–50 per cent – Berle and Means
10–50 per cent – Larner
 5–50 per cent – Patman Committee (1968), Chevalier (1969)

In this study of the ownership of large UK companies Sargent Florence used several alternative criteria which a company had to satisfy to be considered owner-controlled. These were:

(A) that the largest single shareholder had 20 per cent of the votes or more;
(B) that the largest twenty shareholders had 30 per cent of the votes or more;
(C) that either A or B was satisfied, but these shareholders were companies, or, if persons, were connected;
(D) that the directors, between them, had 5 per cent or more of the ordinary shares. (Florence (1961), p. 111.)

For the UK, on the basis of the tests mentioned above, Florence identified thirty out of the ninety-eight largest companies as being probably owner-controlled or marginally so. Including a sample of smaller companies, he found that eighty-nine out of 268 were owner-controlled, or 33 per cent. He concluded that: 'Two thirds of the large companies in 1951 was thus probably not owner-controlled' (p. 85).

Furthermore he concluded that between 1936 and 1951 the trend towards a divorce of ownership from control was very clear (p. 186). He called the trend a 'managerial evolution' (p. 187).

On the basis of the criteria mentioned, Berle and Means classified 44 per cent of the largest 200 US firms in 1929 as under management control. Even after lowering the definition of 'minority control' to 10 per cent or more of the shares, Larner classified 84 per cent of the top 200 in 1963 as being management-controlled. He concluded that the 'managerial revolution,' in process in 1929, was now 'close to complete.'

Gordon's study, based on secondary analysis of the TNEC data, came to very similar conclusions for 176 out of the largest 200 US Corporations:

'The real revolution (in property rights) has already largely taken place; the great majority of stockholders have been deprived of their property through the diffusion of ownership and the growth in the power of management.' (Gordon (1961), p. 350.)

Gordon argues that the most significant figure for measuring the association between ownership and control is the ownership share of individuals or groups of individuals. Ownership by another corporation raises the question of who it is that controls that particular corporation. On this basis, Gordon suggests that ownership control was insignificant for utilities and railroads, where the largest shareholders were other corporations or financial institutions.

The TNEC report used the cut-off point of 10 per cent of the votes to define a dominant stockholding interest. They used less than 10 per cent only when there was evidence that the stockholding group had representatives in management. On this basis the TNEC concluded that, in 118 of the 176 corporations, control was exercized through ownership (see Gordon, pp. 40 and 41, for the TNEC results). However Gordon disputes the significance of this figure. He subtracts those corporations where the dominant stockholder is another corporation, and also those where a multi-family group is the dominant holder, especially as nearly two-thirds of the combined multi-family holdings total less than 30 per cent of the voting stock. On this basis he suggests that probably in less than one-third of the 176 corporations does a small compact group of individuals exercise control, i.e. 'possession of the power to select management' (p. 43). However he argues that active leadership does not necessarily go with substantial ownership. He concludes by saying that:

'Probably no more than a fifth, perhaps less, of the stock of the giant concerns is owned by those in a position to exercise a strong influence on management. Most important, however prevalent may be substantial minority holdings, the mere existence and size of these holdings tell us little or nothing concerning the extent to which stockholding groups actually participate in the function of business leadership. It is practically certain that those actively engaged in exercising the leadership function do not own, on the average, more than a small minority of the stock of the large corporations with which we are concerned. As we shall see in later chapters, corporation executives are today primarily responsible for the exercise of business leadership in the large corporation. To the extent that this is true, there can be no doubt that leadership and ownership are very largely in different hands.' (p. 45)

3. A critique of the conventional view

It is on the basis of the evidence of Berle and Means, Larner, Gordon and Florence that the current conventional wisdom is based. This views the typical large modern corporation as being run by professional managers with little proprietary relationship to their firm. Their actions are constrained, to the extent that they are, by product, labour and capital markets, and not by ownership interests, internal or external to the firm (see Marris 1964 and Galbraith 1967).

The methods and conclusions of these authors have been strongly challenged in recent papers by Fitch and Oppenheimer (1970), Zeitlin (1974) and Scott and Hughes (1976). These papers have not yet taken into the thinking of most economists, and they suggest that the current conventional wisdom is incorrect for the following main reasons:

(i) The suggestion by Gordon and others – most importantly Galbraith – that, even if we find interest groups owning large blocks of shares or having seats on the board of directors, this does not amount of business leadership, is not convincing. Fitch and Oppenheimer point out that the Board controls finance, capital expenditure, dividends and broad objectives, and that it chooses the Chief Executive. It controls operations by financial standards and does not need to concern itself with questions – considered by Galbraith to be the basis for management control – such as product technology. Evidence from intensive case-studies of large UK companies in our own research project supports this view.

(ii) Berle and Means, Gordon, and Larner's conclusion that there has been a managerial revolution is based on a particular approach to empirical data, or simply on a lack of relevant data. Gordon excluded from ownership control holdings by other corporations, even though this may clearly reduce managerial autonomy. Similarly Berle and Means excluded control by share-pyramiding, although this device actually reduces the percentage of shares needed for control.

The difference between the methodologies of Berle and Means, Gordon, et al. and Zeitlin, Fitch and Oppenheimer et al. may be partly explained by a difference of emphasis. The former group were more concerned with the disenfranchisment of the vast majority of shareholders and the ultimate location of control of large corporations. The latter group have been more concerned with the presence of ownership or external control from the point of view of any given large corporation. Thus Berle and Means excluded from their definition of owner-control, control by legal devices. They also classified companies according to their ultimate control. Thus if company A was minority-controlled by company B but the latter was management controlled, company A was also considered to be management controlled (Berle and Means (1932), p. 94), even though there was clearly an external locus of control.

Berle and Means classified 88 out of the largest 200 corporations as under management control in 1929. However, Zeitlin has pointed out that they actually provided no information on 44 of these, which they called 'presumably management controlled' (Zeitlin, p. 1081). Of the 43 (from a total of 106) industrial corporations classed as under management control, Berle and Means classified 39 as 'presumably under management control.' Of the 43 industrial

corporations, 36 were included in either the TNEC or National Resources
Committee (1939) studies. The former found a definite centre of control for 15 of
these and the latter a further 11. Perlo (1957) revealed another 7 of these
companies as being under the control of identifiable interests. (These studies are
reported by Zeitlin (p. 1084).) Thus only a very small number of industrial
corporations can be identified as under management control in the 1930's in the
USA.

(iii) To locate control in any given corporation, it is not adequate to set up
arbitrary statistical criteria such as the percentage of shares which must be owned
by the largest holder or the largest 20 holders. Rather a case-by-case approach is
necessary. Any individual firm may be related to other corporations, banks,
financial institutions and family owners *via* complex patterns of shareholdings,
interlocking directorates and kinship networks.

Using such an approach in a study which appeared at about the same time as
Berle and Means, Lundberg (1937) concluded that a small group of families, via
their control of the major banks, were still in control of the US industrial system.
More recently the Patman Committee suggested that banks were becoming
much more important as trustee holders of corporate stock and that control of a
corporation could be exercized with 5 per cent or sometimes even less of the total
shares. 147 out of the *Fortune 500* had more than 5 per cent of their shares held by
one of the 49 banks surveyed by the Patman Committee. Although these shares
are held by the banks for a variety of beneficial owners, there is little doubt that in
practice they provide the banks with potential control over a number of large
corporations. Furthermore, the largest banks are themselves very closely linked.
For the six largest New York City Banks in 1966, between 12 and 20 per cent of
their stock was held by the same six banks, and these proportions had markedly
increased since 1962. (Fitch and Oppenheimer, Part 1, p. 98.)

The importance of banks – although not necessarily as shareholders – has
increased a great deal in recent years as large corporations have increasingly relied
on external funds to finance expansion (Meeks and Whittington (1975)). Of
particular importance for the UK is the role of merchant banks in the issuing of
new equity, in the arranging of loans and the giving of general financial advice.
Many large UK companies have at least one merchant banker on the board. The
increase in the degree of external financing has also resulted in the rise of
institutional shareholders, such as pension funds and insurance companies. (See
Moyle, 1971.)

(iv) A very important means of control by interest groups has been interlocking directorates, and these have not been given sufficient attention in the past. Their importance is however stressed by both Fitch and Oppenheimer and Zeitlin. Particularly important again is the role of the banks. Of the 2,350 outside (i.e. non-executive) directorships of the largest 500 US corporations, 361 came from another of the top 500 firms and 491 from commercial and investment banks; for over 40 per cent of outside directors with three or more directorships, a bank was their principal employer (Zeitlin, p. 1104).

For the UK, Stanworth and Giddens (1975) have shown how the extent of interlocking directorships, between the top 50 industrial companies and the largest utilities and financial institutions, has increased markedly since 1900. Whitley (1973) has shown how for the largest 27 financial institutions in the UK, the directors not only interlock, but come from a common educational background, belong to the same social institutions and have many family connections. Family connections may spread both to financial institutions and large industrial corporations: Zeitlin has shown how families such as the Rockefellers and the Mellons are heavily involved in both spheres in the USA.

Another factor which has led to an underestimation of the extent to which ownership interests may dominate industrial corporations is the existence of nominee shareholders, about whom there is little information. Then there is the exclusion from lists of the largest companies of certain large private companies. These private companies are obviously owner-controlled, and in 1966 *Fortune* estimated that there were 26 private corporations that it believed would qualify for inclusion in the top 500 US list, and that there might be others which had escaped its notice. For the UK we have no such comparable data for firms which are not listed in the *Times 1000*.

There are at least two private companies which do not appear in the *Times 1000* but whose sales would warrant inclusion in the top 250, i.e. the Littlewoods organization controlled by the Moores family, and the Vestey organization.

This critique of earlier studies does not invalidate one of Berle and Means' central findings: that the vast majority of shareholders do not control the corporation which they own. Nor has it attempted to provide a solution to the debate on the legal rights of shareholders and the general role of ownership in the industrial structure, which was one of Berle and Means prime concerns. However it has suggested that the position taken by Galbraith, Marris and others – that most large corporations are controlled by managements with little proprietary interest in their companies – is not warranted by the evidence.

What is stressed here is that for many firms there is an effective locus of control connected with an identifiable group of proprietary interests. The exercise of this control may be actual or potential. In the last analysis, even a managerially-controlled firm is under the potential control of its shareholders, via a takeover bid, for example. So is a firm which is 'controlled' by a family holding of 5 per cent of the shares. It makes sense to call the latter firm owner-controlled, however, since the family is likely to exercise actual control unless it performs disastrously badly. It has considerable discretion in its behaviour, including the power which we regard as the key one: the power to change senior management.

It is less obvious that a firm can be 'owner-controlled' by a small shareholding held by another industrial company or by a financial institution, since in such a firm the managers may be able to exercise great discretion for considerable periods of time. However, control can be made actual, rather than potential, more readily and more speedily in this case than when there is no identifiable locus of control. The proprietary group may be reluctant to change the senior management but is able to do so with an ease denied to the shareholders of a managerially-controlled company. We share Zeitlin's view that:

'When the concrete structure of ownership and of intercorporate relationships makes it probable that an identifiable group of proprietary interests will be able to realize their corporate objectives over time, despite resistance, then we may say that they have "control" of the corporation.' (Zeitlin, p. 1091).

Since 'corporate objectives' have to be realized by the senior management of a company it is the power to select and change senior management that we consider to be the main indicator of control, rather than any specific company behaviour.

We are suggesting, therefore, a structural rather than a behavioural analysis, and emphasizing potential rather than observed control. This is important, since an analysis of observed power struggles in individual corporations, for example, will not disclose the numerous situations where control is exercised but never challenged.

4. Recent studies

The implication of this critique is that a full investigation of the extent of ownership control of industrial firms must take a case-by-case approach and investigate the wide range of factors discussed above. For the USA this has been partially done by Burch (1972) who systematically searched through business and financial journals over the period 1950–71 for evidence of control (reported in Zeitlin (1974)). One reason why he did this was that he believed and indeed showed, that stockholding reports to the Securities Exchange Commission had been deliberately falsified. His condition for classifying a firm as owner-controlled was that 4 to 5 per cent of the voting stock was owned by a family, group of families, or an individual, and that he found representation of a family on the board of directors over an extended period. For the top 300 he found that 45 per cent were probably under family control in this sense, 40 per cent probably under management control, and a further 15 per cent possibly under family control. He did not study control by financial institutions, but it is difficult to conclude, on the basis of this evidence, that most US corporations are managerially controlled.

Similarly Chevalier (1969) has looked at the 200 largest US manufacturing corporations in 1965 and included data gathered from the financial press. He defined 'minority-control' as a group or individual holding more than 5 per cent of the shares of a corporation. He also included a category of control called 'Dominant Influence' where 'There is a group, represented on the board of directors, which seems to wield a decisive influence on the corporation.' Included in this group were companies such as IBM where the Watson family was dominant but held only 3 per cent of the shares, and General Electric controlled by Morgan Guaranty via four interlocking directorships. Of the 200, he found that 69 corporations were controlled by individuals or families, 31 by banks and other financial institutions, and 20 by other groups. Thus only 80 could be said to be management-controlled. Chevalier believed some of these to be owner-controlled, but he lacked the necessary information to prove this.

Scott and Hughes' investigation, following Zeitlin's methodology for the largest Scottish registered companies, found the vast majority to be owner-controlled, *via* either large shareholding blocks or interlocking directorates. Most of these companies would not be very large in terms of the UK economy. However, Scott and Hughes have shown what can be achieved by looking very closely at large companies which on the surface appear to have no important proprietary interest. For example, Burmah Oil was ranked sixteenth in the 1975–6 *Times 1000*. In 1974 its board of directors owned only 0.09 per cent of the shares, and no single person or institutional investor owned a substantial percentage of the shares. Yet Scott and Hughes showed how six of the largest institutional holders in Burmah (two unit trusts, three investment trusts and an assurance company) were intimately linked *via* shareholdings, directorships, management and other associations. Most importantly, Burmah's six non-executive directors had six other directorships with four of these institutional holders. Burmah and one of the most important of these, the Murray Johnstone group, were founded by the same man, and Murray Johnstone's chairman was also chairman of Burmah until 1974 and is now deputy chairman. Similar studies for other UK companies which appear to be management controlled would probably produce similar evidence.

No comprehensive study of the ownership and control of large UK companies has been carried out since Florence's investigation of the 1951 position, referred to above. The following section describes a study we have carried out of the largest 250 companies in 1975. This goes some way, but by no means all the way, to utilizing the methodology implied above.

5. Ownership and control of the 'Top 250' UK firms

A comprehensive study of the pattern of proprietary interests in an individual company should, in our view, look at the following factors. Our aim in drawing up this list is to attempt to define circumstances in which an individual, or a group of individuals (whether incorporated or not), are probably able to exercise control over a firm, in the sense of being able to select its senior management.

(i)   The percentage of votes held by the largest shareholder and his identity;

(ii) The percentage of votes held by the largest twenty shareholders and their identities, the percentage of votes they hold in each others' companies and the extent of interlocking directorships among them;

(iii) The percentage of votes held by the board of directors and their families;

(iv) The presence on the board of directors of either the founder of a company, a member of his family or his descendants;

(v)   The other directorships of directors, and the relationship of these to major institutional shareholders;

(vi) The identities of the chairman and managing director, their career history and the manner by which they came to be appointed.

The last of these has not been explicitly mentioned by previous writers (except in Francis (1976)), but we believe it to be very important in deciding the location of control in any given company. Detailed studies of large companies co-operating with the Growth of Firms project have emphasized the power wielded by the chairman of the board of directors. Even if he is not the chief executive or a full-time executive, his control of board meetings, his contacts with major shareholders and his monitoring of company performance, normally make him the key person in appointing or dismissing senior management. The latter may make the operating decisions, but the Chairman in most cases has 'possession of the power to select management' (Gordon, p. 42). In some cases, of course, he may be a figurehead, and this power may lie with the managing director or chief executive. This may be the case in GEC, for example, where Sir Arnold Weinstock refused the position of chairman, but is clearly more powerful than the current chairman, Lord Nelson. However, how the chairman was appointed is clearly an important matter to investigate.

If the chairman is the founder of a company, or if he is a member of the founder's family or one of his descendants, then we may well be able to designate the firm's as 'family', even if the family are not large current shareholders. Similarly if the chairman has come to his position after a career as a merchant banker rather than as a full-time executive in the company, for example, and has been appointed after institutional intervention, then proprietary interests can be said in some sense to 'control' the company. We have come across more than one example of both these phenomena. It is, however, important to differentiate between these and other forms of control as they may well have very different implications.

A comprehensive study of the factors we have listed above for the largest 250 UK companies would be a very time-consuming exercise. To obtain at least some estimate of the extent to which large UK companies are effectively controlled by proprietary interests at present, we have looked at the following:

(i)   The percentage of votes held by a known individual, institution, or cohesive group;
(ii) The percentage of votes owned by the board of directors and their families;
(iii) The identity of the chairman and managing director, and their relationship to the firm's founder and his family.

Potential control is assumed to be present with a shareholding of more than 5 per cent.

This information has been gathered from *The Times 1000* (1975/76), *Moodies Investment Handbook* (July 1975), Company Annual Reports for 1974, and *Financial Times* articles in 1975 and 1976. We have defined the 'Top 250' as being all those companies ranked in the top 250 by the *Times 1000* by either net assets or sales (276 firms were actually involved). We have excluded all those companies wholly owned by foreign firms, and also those firms whose assets or sales were less than half those of the 250th by either assets or sales respectively. We also had to exclude two companies which appeared in the *Times 1000* but which were, in fact, subsidiaries of other firms appearing in the list – Carrington Viyella and Amalgamated Metal.

Table 1 presents a summary of our results. It can be seen that 55.5 per cent of our 'Top 250' firms have at least some proprietary interest and can be classified as 'owner-controlled' according to one of the factors we consider important.[1] We are aware that this use of the term 'owner-controlled' is not traditional in that we have included 17 companies which have family chairmen but with less than 5 per cent of the voting shares being held by any individual or known group. However, since the power of these chairmen is based on, at least, a former family ownership

1. Interested readers can obtain from the authors a list of the companies involved, their industrial and ownership classification, and the information which led us to place them in a particular category.

Table 1. Ownership control of the UK 'Top 250'* in 1975.

Percentage of shares held by a single institution or by the board of directors	Type of holder								
	I	F	D	C	G	M	O	N	Total
Unquoted company	3	–	8	1	1	–	–	3	16
Over 50 per cent	6	1	12	2	1	–	–	1	23
10 to 50 per cent	12	5	29	3	1	4	1	5	60
5 to 10 per cent	1	4	4	–	–	–	–	–	9
	22	10	53	6	3	4	1	9	108

Family chairman or managing director (but less than 5 per cent shareholding by individual or group)	17
Total owner-controlled	125
No known control	100
Total firms	225
Percentage owner-controlled	55.5

Notes: Types of holder: I = another industrial company; F = financial institution; D = director and their families; C = charitable trust; G = government or quasi-government agency; M = mixed control type; O = other control type; N = not classifiable due to lack of information.

of the company's shares, we feel justified in using the term. Also in some cases the family or board shareholding is only just below 5 per cent. Our use of the term is similar in this respect to that of Chevalier (1969).

It may be argued that nine of our 'owner-controlled' firms should be omitted from the analysis since they are majority-controlled by another industrial company, or are unquoted and controlled by another industrial company, i.e. they are really subsidiaries of other firms. However, of these nine, four are jointly controlled by two other firms and can thus be thought of as independent corporate entities. Another five are public companies in which foreign firms own more than 50 per cent of the shares, but since foreign control is not absolute, we have considered them still to be UK firms which should be included in the analysis.

The figure of 55.5 per cent quoted above is an underestimate of the extent of ownership control for the following reasons:

---

* For an explanation of how these firms were selected see Section 4 of this paper.

(i) There are an unknown number of private firms such as Littlewoods and the Vestey organization which are certainly large enough to come into the top 250 but for which sales or assets figures are not available. These firms are obviously owner-controlled.

(ii) For many individual companies large blocks of shares are held by nominees. Sometimes these are acting on behalf of many individuals, but they also act for companies, individuals or financial institutions who wish to remain anonymous. It is virtually certain that in some cases these nominee shareholdings would enable us to categorize a company as owner-controlled, if we knew the identity of the individuals concerned and their relationship to other shareholdings.

(iii) We have little data for the top 250 on shareholdings by other than the largest shareholders, on interlocking directorships, on family directors who do not bear the name of the firm, or on the career history and circumstances of appointment of all chairmen and managing directors. Knowledge of these would certainly add to the number of firms where there is a controlling proprietary interest.

This last point can be illustrated by work done on the Growth of Firms project. One of the firms co-operating with the project which appears on our list of firms in Table 1 with no known proprietary interest is Debenhams. (In 1974 the whole board of directors owned only 0.24 per cent of the ordinary shares.) However it appears that the current chairman of the company gained his position not through interests. In 1970, after a long period of very poor performance by the company, a group of institutional investors in the company (none of whom individually owned a significant percentage of the shares) placed Sir Anthony Burney on the board. In October 1970 he became chairman. His previous experience had been as a City accountant and he held a large number of directorships including Commercial Union Assurance, and several industrial companies. In 1972 he brought two non-executive directors with financial connections onto the board, and appointed a finance director from outside for the first time. In 1973 three of the pre-Burney directors left the company. In 1974 another of these left, and the chief executive was dismissed and a new one appointed. Thus of the board of 10 in 1970 only three remained in 1974. Financial interests had not only appointed a new chairman but he, in turn, had completely restructured the senior management and (as we shall describe later) greatly changed Debenhams' behaviour.

Another firm co-operating with the project is Associated Biscuit Manufacturers which we have classified as minority controlled by another industrial company. This is because of the shareholding of 12 per cent by Rowntree Macintosh reported by *Moodies*. However, we have discovered that Associated Biscuits is the result of a union (completed in 1960) of three family-owned companies. Nine out of the present fourteen directors are members of one of the founding families, and the families – even though shareholdings are quite widely spread – own well in excess of Rowntree Macintosh's proportion of the shares. Thus Associated Biscuits should probably rightly be reclassified as controlled by its directors and their families. This is not to deny that the role of Rowntree may be important in policy formation, but simply to point out that Rowntrees are not (as would at first appear) the primary ownership interest.

Thus the first part of the current conventional wisdom – that control of large corporations is by and large not in the hands of proprietary interests, is not true for the UK. However, as we can see from Table 1, there is a wide variety of proprietary interests. It is important to distinguish between different types of ownership control since, as we shall argue later, they may have a different impact on company behaviour. Of 125 companies classified as owner-controlled 70 are controlled via either the shareholding of their board of directors or through family chairmen or managing directors. Of the rest, 22 companies are controlled by other industrial firms, 10 by financial institutions and 9 by charitable trusts or government organizations. One interesting point to note is the relative lack of ownership by financial institutions. Of the 10 cases found, 4 were holdings of between 5 and 10 per cent by the Prudential Assurance Company. This is a very different situation from the USA where Chevalier found $15\frac{1}{2}$ per cent of his companies to be controlled by financial institutions: our figure is 4.4 per cent.

It is difficult to assess the impact of government agencies or charitable trusts, although we do know that the holdings of at least two of the latter must be very important sources of control or potential control. Some 18.5 per cent of Unilevers' equity is owned by the Leverhulme Trust, and 51 per cent of the voting shares of Great Universal Stores by the Wolfson Foundation. The Leverhulme Trust has five trustees – Lord Leverhulme, the current chairman and vice-chairman of Unilever, and two past chairmen of Unilever. The Wolfson Foundation is known to be controlled by Sir Issac Wolfson, chairman of Great Universal Stores.

The second part of the current conventional wisdom is that the proportion of large firms which are management controlled has been increasing over time. For the USA, this has been disputed by Fitch and Oppenheimer and by Zeitlin, who point to the increasing influence of financial institutions, particularly banks. They suggest that at some point families may have given way to professional managers but that the latter in turn have been forced to cede control to financial forces. Chevalier has compared the control position in the 85 corporations common to his 1965 study and that of Berle and Means for 1929. He found little change in the overall degree of ownership control but he did find a significant increase in the number of companies controlled by banks and other financial institutions.

For the UK it is difficult for us directly to compare our evidence for 1975 with that of Florence for 1951, since our methodology and research effort has differed widely. He found 30 per cent of very large companies to be owner-controlled, a substantially lower figure than our own for 1975. A rough calculation for Florence's categories A & D gives 41 per cent in 1975 for our whole sample as owner-controlled, and 37 per cent for the top 100 firms. On this bases, the figures suggest an increase over the period 1951 to 1975.

Other evidence used to suggest increasing management control of industry is the increasing dominance of very large firms in the economy, and the fact that larger firms are more likely to be management controlled. Table 2 shows that the latter does not appear to be true for the current UK 'Top 250.'

There is little evidence to show conclusively that management control of British industry is increasing. If anything the tendency may be the other way – towards a greater degree of ownership control, particularly by financial and other industrial interests. However, we have suggested above that the distinc-

Table 2. Ownership control and company size.

Rank in 'Times 1000' by turnover	Number of companies		Total	Percentage owner-controlled
	Owner-controlled	Management-controlled		
1–50	23	19	42	54.7
51–100	24	19	43	55.8
101–150	22	15	37	59.4
151–200	19	21	40	47.5
201–250	23	14	37	62.1
251–1,000	14	12	26	53.8
Total	125	100	225	55.5

tions between different forms of ownership may be just as important, in their behavioural consequences, as the distinction between owner and management control. This can best be looked at not cross-sectionally at one point in time, but as part of the evolution, or life cycle, of companies. We have therefore tried to develop a typology of stage of corporate control which we discuss in the next section.

A final important point about our research into the ownership of the 'Top 250' is that it has revealed very great industrial differences in the extent of ownership control. This is important partly because much empirical work on the relationship between ownership and control and company performance has

Table 3. Ownership control and industry.

Industrial group	Total number of companies in 'Top 250'	Number of companies owner-controlled
Food	15	12
Drink	7	5
Tobacco	3	1
Oil	4	1
Chemicals	12	3
Metal manufacture	6	4
Mechanical engineering	15	8
Electrical engineering	13	8
Vehicles	8	5
Metal goods (N.E.S.)	9	3
Textiles	6	3
Building materials	12	4
Paper, printing & publishing	7	4
Other manufacture	7	4
Construction	9	6
Transport	8	3
Retailing	17	12
Merchanting[1]	17	11
Miscellaneous services	7	7
Conglomerates[2]	23	10
Unclassified	20	11
Total	225	125

1. Wholesaling, merchanting and overseas commodities.
2. Companies with significant business in three or more industries, without 50 per cent or more in any.

looked at the question on an industry basis, ignoring the fact that industries differ widely in the extent to which they are owner-controlled. Table 3 shows the number of firms in each industry we have classified as owner-controlled. We can divide industries into groups, as follows:

Industries predominantly owner-controlled: Food, drink, metal manufacture, electrical engineering, construction, retailing, merchanting, miscellaneous services.

Industries predominantly non-owner-controlled: Tobacco, oil, chemicals, metal goods (n.e.s.), building materials.

The remaining industries appear to fall somewhere between these two extremes.

There must be many factors which account for these differences. It is apparent, for example, that industries which need very large individual capital investments, such as oil and chemicals, are mainly non-owner-controlled. A good many other influences are relevant, however: we hope to carry out further work on this question.

6. The stages of corporate control*

We have suggested above that to classify firms simply as owner or management-controlled does not do justice to the wide variety of ownership forms which we have encountered in the Growth of Firms case-studies. Such a classification may also serve to hide important differences in performance which are related to the ownership position. The different control situations we have found relate very much to the historical evolution of an individual company, and can best be described as stages of some kind of life cycle. This obviously begins with the foundation of the firm, which will then grow (since we are dealing mainly with large surviving firms) to be very large, remain small and independent or be taken over by a larger firm. Most of the 19 UK firms which have co-operated with the Growth of Firms project had their origins in the late nineteenth and early twentieth centuries. There appear to be three main modes by which they have been founded.

(i) By individuals or family groups who have been marginal to the existing social structure, i.e. people who have not been strongly connected to existing elite groups and who have had the ability and motivation to attain social advancement. These people include immigrants, Jews and Quakers, all of whom have been prevented in the past from entering occupations such as the law, politics and the civil service by various legal and other discriminatory practices. Table 4 shows the high proportion of UK firms founded by either Jews or Quakers.

(ii) By the defensive merger of several small business founded by 'non-marginal' men.

(iii) By foreign companies or businessmen, particularly Americans.

After its foundation there are several different paths which the control of the company may follow. Some of these are depicted in Diagram I.

The placing of any given company at a point in time will depend on the proportion of the shares held by particular groups and the career pattern and

---

* In this section we are very much indebted to the ideas of Arthur Francis. Diagram 1 is taken from Francis (1976).

circumstances of appointment of the senior management, particularly the chairman of the board. The mechanisms by which control may progress from the founding individual or group to another location have been described and rationalized in Francis (1976) and will not be discussed in detail in this paper. However we shall spend a little time discussing categories VI and VIII – control by Industrial or Finance capital.

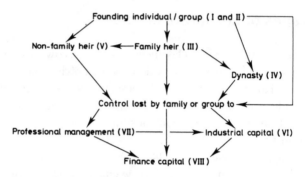

Diagram 1. Stages of corporate control.

'Industrial capital' is sometimes used to mean capital in the form of commodities i.e. bricks, mortar, stocks of materials and semi-finished goods and machinery, and 'finance capital' to mean capital in the form of money. Here we mean industrial companies and financial institutions respectively. Control may pass to industrial capital if the family prefer to have their interests looked after by other industrialists rather than by professional managers who may well have different objectives. It may also pass to industrial capital involuntarily as a substitute for a takeover bid. The presence of large blocks of shares held by industrial firms in each other may also indicate collusive practices, or simply technical co-operation. An example of such shareholding is British Insulated Callendars Cables, where General Cable Co., USA owns 10.8 per cent of the shares with an option to purchase a further 9 per cent BICC which in turn owns 20 per cent of General Cable Co.

Control by finance capital may appear in the form of large blocks of shares owned by financial institutions, such as pension funds or insurance companies, or in the form of a chairman or chief executive effectively appointed by financial institutions with interests in the firm. Banks do not normally own equity capital directly but they may manage such capital on behalf of nominees, pension funds etc. In addition, their control of credit may give them effective control for substantial periods of time. Control may pass to finance capital (possibly in the form of a new chairman with a financial background) if the family cannot find

Table 4. The founding and control of firms co-operating with the growth of firms project.

Company	Rank in 1975 'Times 1000' by turnover	Industry	Founder	Current control stage
Albright and Wilson	124	Chemicals	Quaker	VI
Associated Biscuits	187	Food	Quaker	IV
Baker Perkins	359	Mechanical Engineering	Quaker	IV
British Home Stores	144	Retailing	American businessmen	VII
Cadbury Schweppes	37	Food	Quaker (on Cadbury side)	IV
Debenhams	105	Retailing	English drapers	VIII
Dixons Photographic	367	Retailing	Jewish	I
EMI	64	Electrical Engineering	–	VI
GEC	12	Electrical Engineering	Jewish	I
ICI	4	Chemicals	German, Jewish, Swedish, Swiss	VII
ITT Consumer Products	(Not ranked)	Electrical Engineering	American subsidiary	–
J. Lyons	58	Food	Jewish	IV
Mothercare	363	Retailing	Iraqi Jewish	I
Sears Holdings	34	Retailing	Jewish	I
W. H. Smith	117	Retailing	English	I
Stone Platt	206	Mechanical Engineering	Defensive merger	VII
Tesco	61	Retailing	Jewish	III
Unilever	5	Food	English	VII
Vickers	97	Mechanical Engineering	Defensive merger	VIII

professional managers or other industrial capitalists they trust to look after their interests. It may also pass to finance capital if professional management or industrialist owners run into a profitability or liquidity crisis and need funds to survive. This was the case at Debenhams and was also the case at Vickers in 1970. Finance capital control appears to be much more prevalent in the USA (see Zeitlin, Fitch and Oppenheimer, Chevalier) and countries other than the UK. However, even in the UK it seems to be increasing, as industrial profitability has declined and equity investment by financial institutions has increased.

Finance capital has been shown in the diagram as the 'ultimate' form of control, since it might prove difficult (although not necessarily impossible), in contrast to the other forms, for it to be displaced once it has taken hold. In 1959, Berle for example, suggested that once the stages of majority, minority and management control has been gone through, a fourth stage of control, by fiduciary institutions, might be reached, through which dispersed stockholdings would once more become concentrated.

In the light of this analysis, we would not often expect to find professional or career managers in effective control, since their power base for gaining control is very small compared with families, other firms or financial interests. This is borne out by Table 4 which shows who founded the firms who have co-operated in the Growth of Firms project, and also who controls these firms at present. Thus of the 18 firms for which we have information only 4 can be classified as under professional management control.

7. The behaviour consequences of types of control

At least ten empirical studies have been published in the last fifteen years which have investigated the effect of the nature control on company performance. Almost without exception they have been based on the managerial models of the firm developed by Baumol (1962), Marris and others. These have suggested that owner-controlled firms should have higher rates of profit but lower rates of growth than management-controlled firms. Predictions have also been made about the effect of control on other measures of performance. Empirical studies have almost all been cross-sectional and based on categorizing firms as either owner- or management-controlled. A summary of their findings is shown in the Appendix. The only clear pattern which emerges from these studies is that without exception owner-controlled companies have a higher rate of profit than management-controlled companies.

However, of the seven studies in which this result was found, only two were statistically significant. In addition to these studies Palmer (1973) has suggested that we should only expect ownership type to affect performance where a firm has a substantial degree of market power. Thus he looked at the effect of ownership within three groups of large corporations classified according to the height of their industry barriers to entry. He found that owner-controlled firms had significantly higher rates of profit than management-controlled firms only in the group with high entry barriers.

Thus it may appear that while the nature of control has some impact on corporate behaviour, this impact is neither very strong, nor conclusively proven. This is believed now by a number of industrial economists, but we would argue that these studies have not revealed the true impact of ownership on company behaviour.

One problem with previous empirical studies, already discussed, is that they have a very narrow conception of the nature of ownership, of how it should be measured and what its effects are likely to be. The standard methodology has been to look at the proportion of shares held by various categories and to classify a company simply as owner- or management-controlled on this basis. We have already suggested that a much deeper kind of study is required to reveal the proprietary interests in a firm.

A second problem is that several of the studies cited in the Appendix have looked at the impact of ownership within particular industries. This is unfortunate, since, as Table 3 shows, some industries are much more owner-controlled than others. Thus, for example, it probably does not make much sense to compare two management-controlled retailers with two who are owner-controlled. The latter dominate the industry, and to a large extent determine the constraints within which the former must work.

Another defect of these studies is that they are cross-sectional, and thus cannot distinguish between the ways in which managerial motivation, as opposed to managerial efficiency, affect rates of growth. This argues for the use of longitudinal case studies.

Moreover, it may be impossible to infer managerial motivation from statistics of controlling ownership. The percentage of a firm's shares which its management owns may be very small, but the absolute value of those shares may be high, and may well induce shareholder-oriented behaviour. Nyman (1974) has looked at the relationship between the absolute value of directors' shareholdings in the top 100 UK companies, and the rates of growth and profit of those companies. The higher this value, the higher are the rates of growth and profit. This result is statistically significant, although ownership still explains only a small proportion of the variance.

Current empirical studies, by concentrating on the supposed link between ownership and performance, are therefore deficient in a large number of ways. That the measures of ownership may be inadequate is only one criticism. A more important defect is that the causal relationship between ownership and motivation is not explored, but simply taken for granted. Finally, the relationship between motivation and behaviour is not examined at all. To jump straight from 'ownership' to performance is therefore to ignore many of the most important aspects of the problem.

One of the most interesting things to have come out of our research is the great variety which ownership patterns can take. This was brought out by the consideration of stages of growth in the last section and also by Table 1. It is hardly surprising, in the light of this, that differences in performance cannot be inferred from ownership statistics. Even when a firm is effectively family-owned, for example, motivation and behaviour may differ according to which generation is in control. The founder of the firm may himself have followed one of a number of different policies, and may not have been interested in profit maximization in any simple sense of the term. His successors may have taken a different line, either because circumstances had changed or because their motivation was different – possibly weaker, as authors since Alfred Marshall have argued. Francis (1976) has only recently suggested that objectives in a family firm are very likely to change over time.

Once control has passed beyond the stage of the family of the founder, it may pass to other families, possibly those linked with prominent chairmen or senior management whose ownership stake is not large. Such families may still exhibit an 'ownership' attitude, since they have become so closely identified with the good name of the firm. Beyond this stage, there may be no clear family or group in effective control of the firm, but the management may still be greatly influenced by the latent (or open) powers of those who own the firm. What the American studies have shown is that the influence of financial institutions, even when their actual shareholdings are not large, may be of predominant importance. In our own research we have found examples both of the power exercized by other industrial firms and by financial institutions.

One simple differentiation of ownership which may affect behaviour is that between:
(a) Firms which are effectively owner-controlled by families, individuals or the board, giving those firms a large degree of discretion;
(b) Firms controlled by outside shareholders such as other firms or financial institutions, severely limiting management discretion;
(c) Firms with no centre of control, where management has significant discretion, within the limits set by the product and capital markets.

A historical case-study approach brings out clearly the wide variety of ways in which different types of owner may make their influence felt. It is impossible in this paper to give more than a brief impression of such case-studies, but we think it worthwhile to set down a few.

8. Historical case-studies

Fitch and Oppenheimer give a large number of examples of the power of financial institutions in American industry. They show that banks and other institutional investors have promoted mergers in some cases and blocked them in others. Such institutions were particularly active and influential in the conglomerate merger boom of the 1960's. One institution holding only six per cent of the shares of Polaroid pushed the company into expanding its sales goal, its advertising expenditure and the number of its trained personnel. At times institutional holders have acted to curb executive salaries.

Fitch and Oppenheimer provide many more examples of the power of financial interests, including the way in which they destroyed Howard Hughes' control over TWA. The authors' two most detailed case-studies show how financial interests built up one company in an expanding field and destroyed another in a declining industry. At Union Oil of California a need for external finance for expansion continually led the company into the arms of a series of financial interests from the 1880's to the present day. These interests repeatedly changed the top management, fought off takeovers and also fought among themselves. However they continued to build up the company, in an expanding and highly profitable field, from an insignificant Californian drilling operation to a major integrated firm producing for national and international markets.

Penn Central was one of the firms which Berle and Means chose to illustrate their thesis of managerialism on the basis of the wide dispersion of its shares. However by 1968, of the largest ten shareholders, nine were commercial banks, holding over 22 per cent of the shares. The largest holder was Morgan Guaranty with 3.4 per cent of the shares. Four directors of Penn Central were connected with Morgan, and altogether there were fourteen interlocking directorships with twelve banks. Years of neglect had led to a run-down of Penn Central's operations and diversification into more profitable fields such as amusement parks. When bankruptcy loomed, the outside directors voted as a block to fire the top executives and brought in a man with no railroad experience as president. The railway was then milked of its best assets and the company allowed to collapse into bankruptcy.

Fitch and Oppenheimer write from a Marxist viewpoint, but they document very fully their thesis that finance capital exercizes great power in American industry. They argue that finance capital acts to transfer capital from declining to expanding industries more quickly than the market mechanism would allow. They also suggest further consequences. One is that there is a relationship between financial control and reciprocal purchases between companies. Another is that financial institutions, both as holders of stocks and shares and as lenders of money, are interested in the profits accruing to themselves rather than in the overall profits of the firms over which they exercise so much control.

Turning now to Britain, it would be impossible in this paper for us to show the way in which different forms of control have influenced corporate behaviour in the companies the Growth of Firms project has studied. This will be reported in a further paper. However we return briefly to our example of Debenhams to show the influence of financial interests in one large British company.

Debenhams was founded as a drapery business in 1813 and gradually expanded as a chain of department stores until World War Two. It was under the control of the Debenham family until 1928 when control passed to professional managers who had risen through the retail hierarchy. After the war its expansion accelerated via the acquisition of a series of family-owned department stores throughout the country, until by 1965 Debenhams was operating 115 department stores as well as a chain of women's fashion shops and some small manufacturing interests. The chairman from 1956 to 1970 was John Beford, who had risen from being a Debenhams sales assistant. From the early 1960's the rate of return earned by Debenhams began to fall, until by 1969 the post-tax rate of return on equity capital had fallen to just over 3 per cent. To finance its activities the company had increasing resource to external finance, especially long-term loans and bank overdrafts. By 1969 these were taking almost 50 per cent of profits before tax and interest. The dividend was uncovered for the three years 1967–9.

In this situation some of the institutional investors in Debenhams began to put pressure on the management, and in 1970 John Beford gave up his position as chief executive and handed over to another career manager, A. J. Smith. In 1971 Beford retired, and Sir Anthony Burney became chairman, having had no previous experience of retailing. He immediately reorganized the top management structure and began the process of store rationalization which had been put off for at least ten years. The previous (career) management had been content to allow not only expansion, but the existence of obviously surplus stores. In 1972 and 1973 profits began to recover on the back of the retail boom.

In February 1972 United Drapery Stores made a takeover bid for Debenhams and two other retailers – Sears and Tesco – also showed interest in buying the company. These were all family-controlled firms, but it was obvious that once financial interests had control of Debenhams they were unwilling for control to pass into other hands. Sir Anthony Burney fought off the UDS bid – he had early masterminded the successful defence of Courtaulds against ICI – with a mixture of clever public relations, the use of his extensive network of City contacts, and the backing of the shareholdings of the institutions who had appointed him.

Following the unsuccessful bid, a stockbroker and the managing director of a financial company were appointed as non-executive directors of Debenhams

Information in the above paragraphs comes mainly from company reports and newspaper articles.

main board in July 1972. A well-known property developer joined the board of Debenhams (Property) Ltd., and carried out a revaluation of the company's property. Sir Anthony Burney gave up his directorships of ICI and Stone-Platt to free more of his time for Debenhams. A finance director was appointed from outside Debenhams, and in 1973 three of the old directors left the company. It was obvious that financial problems would return as soon as the retail boom had ended. A strategy with three prongs was adopted: the rationalization of the department store operation, involving closures and the generation of cash by selling properties; the transfer of capital into a more successful mode of retailing – specialized multiples; and the improvement of the operation of the remaining department stores.

During 1972 twenty-one department stores were closed and a number of other properties sold, and there is little doubt that more would have been sold if the property boom had not collapsed in 1973. During late 1972 Debenhams began to diversify its operations, especially into more successful forms of retailing, such as hypermarkets and specialist multiples. These acquisitions cost over £ 15 m in all and were financed by cash from property sales, by a massive increase in overdrafts and by other borrowings.

As regards the department store operation, top management was reorganized, the institution of central buying was completed and management consultants called in. During 1974 30 per cent of the labour force was made redundant. In May 1974 a new chief executive for Debenhams (A. J. Smith having resigned) was appointed from outside, but property and long-term planning were left under the direct control of the chairman. The new chief executive had had a successful retail career in both Marks and Spencer and British Home Stores, two of the most successful British retailing companies. Utilizing the methods he learned there, he is now increasing department store profitability, but diversification is continuing via acquisition of a US shoe retailer and a UK toy retailer within the last year. By the end of 1974 the number of department stores had fallen to 72, and only three of the 1970 directors remained. Their primary role has been to gain acceptance of the changes throughout the department store operation.

Thus the effect of finance capital's involvement in Debenhams, through the chairmanship of Sir Anthony Burney, has been to transform an unprofitable company, by raising money via the property market, by transferring resources from declining to expanding sectors, and by increasing the profitability of the main part of the business. It is very doubtful whether this would have happened had Debenhams' previous managers remained in control. It is also likely that the use of Debenhams assets and its corporate strategy would have been very different if the company had been taken over by an established retailer, such as Tesco.

9. Conclusion

We have tried to show in this paper that much of the current conventional wisdom regarding ownership and control is misconceived. Ownership interests control, in one way or another, the majority of large UK industrial companies, and the proportion of ownership control may well be increasing over time. At any event the picture of the large modern corporation painted by Galbraith, Marris and others applies to only a minority of large UK firms, and probably of large US firms also.

The growing importance of financial institutions has been one key development. These have always been important in European countries like Germany and France. Fitch and Oppenheimer, among others, have demonstrated their importance in the USA. Financial institutions, especially insurance companies and pension funds, have become increasingly large holders of industrial shares in a number of countries. These institutions are closely linked with the commercial and merchant banks, who wield additional power through their loan and new issue activity. The tradition of financial institutions in Britain has been to be passive in the affairs of the companies in whom they hold shares. Their increasing stake had made this role an increasingly difficult one to play, especially in view of the falling profitability of British industry generally in the 1960's and 1970's. Financial institutions have begun to intervene in the affairs of companies like Vickers, GEC, and, as we have seen, Debenhams. There is every reason to believe that the role of these institutions is likely to grow rather than to diminish.

An additional factor strengthening the importance of financial forces has been the growth of the takeover movement. Takeover raiders have been able to mobilize shareholders – and notably the financial institutions – in support of their activities. Where takeovers have failed this has often been because of the strength of opposition from the City. Takeovers have been an additional factor strengthening the position of the merchant banks, since these banks play a prominent role in takeover activity.

If we are right about the strength of ownership interests in British industry, and especially growing ownership by and through financial institutions, what are the consequences of this for managerial motivation and performance? The obvious answer seems to be that the forces making for greater profits have been much strengthened, although we would not claim that the firms concerned have been forced to 'maximize' their profits, whatever the term may be taken to mean. Nor would we claim that management-controlled companies are always forced to act as if they were owner-controlled since institutional intervention has occurred mainly in firms which have almost gone bankrupt after long periods of poor performance. The direction of capital accumulation in individual firms has been greatly changed in the course of this process. The Debenham story, and also the Vickers story, would seem to illustrate this. Fitch and Oppenheimer too present evidence that this is what has been happening.

A further question raised by Fitch and Oppenheimer, however, is how far policies are undertaken for the sake of profits for financial institutions rather than for the sake of industrial profits as a whole. There is no doubt that in the UK the activities of some takeover-bidders and property speculators have been motivated by short-run profit prospects rather than by regard for the long-run interests of the firms involved. Mergers have been promoted for financial rather than industrial reasons, and diversification has been the result of financial rather than industrial logic.

Having said this, it must be admitted that a good many of the takeovers and mergers that have taken place have probably been in the long-run interests of British industrial efficiency. In these cases financial profits and long-run industrial profits have gone hand in hand.

These conclusions are not of great originality as far as takeovers are concerned. If we are right about the growing importance of financial institutions in ownership, however, the considerations regarding the desirability or otherwise of takeovers may extend, so to speak, far more widely than at first appears.

There are a good many other things to be said about different aspects of the relationship between ownership and control. We have said little here, for example, about the implications of family ownership, or of ownership by other industrial companies: still far more important in aggregate in the UK than control by financial institutions. Nor have we said anything about the implications forms of ownership for the ways in which firms are organized, and how organizations change over time. We hope to discuss these, and a good many other relevant questions, in the course of our further work.

APPENDIX

Empirical findings of the relationship between control type and corporate performance

Author	Country	Sample	Variable(s)	Effect of Ownership control	Statistical significance
Florence (1961)	UK	223 firms, grouped in 8 industries	Retention ratio	Lower	–
Nichols (1969)	UK	Florence's 93 very large firms	Retention ratio	Lower	Worse than 5 per cent
Kamerschen (1968)	USA	Top 200	Profit rate	Higher	None
Monsen et al. (1968)	USA	From 'Top 500', 3 firms of each type in 12 industries	Profit rate	Higher	Significant for all industries
Hindley (1970)	USA	Steel and oil firms in 'Top 200'	(1) Growth of a dollar invested (2) Valuation ratio	(1) Less in oil, more in steel (2) Higher in oil, lower in steel	(1) None (2) None
Larner (1970)	USA	184 of 'Top 200'	(1) Profit rate (2) Variance of (1)	(1) Higher (2) Lower	(1) None (2) None
Radice (1971)	UK	89 firms in 3 industries	(1) Profit rate (2) Growth rate	(1) Higher (2) Higher	(1) Just worse than 5 per cent when growth constant
Elliott (1972)	USA	88 firms divided into below or above average growth for industry	Liquidity, leverage, growth, profit rate, etc.	Nothing significant except for liquidity-less	5 per cent
Boudreaux (1973)	USA	Same as Monsen et al.	(1) Profit rate (2) Variance of (1)	(1) Higher (2) Higher	Significant Significant
Holl (1975)	UK	183 of Florence's firms	(1) Profit rate (2) Growth rate (3) Variance of (1) (4) Skewness of (1) (5) Distribution ratio	(1) Higher (2) Lower (3) Greater (4) Greater (5) Lower	None

Bibliography

1. Baumol, W. J., On the Theory of the Expansion of the Firm. *American Economic Review*, 52: 1078–87, 1962.
2. Berle, A. A., *Power without Property*. New York, Harcourt Brace, 1959.
3. Berle, A. A. and G. C. Means, *The Modern Corporation and Private Property*, New York: Macmillan, 1932.
4. Boudreaux, K. J., Managerialism and Risk-Return Performance, *Southern Economic Journal*, XXXIX: 366–372, 1973.
5. Burch, Philip, H., *The Managerial Revolution Reassessed*. Lexington, Mass., 1972.
6. Chevalier, J. M., The Problem of Control in Large American Corporations. *Anti-trust Bulletin*, 14: 163–180, 1969.
7. Elliott, Control, Size, Growth and Financial Performance in the Firm. *Journal of Finance and Quantitative Economics*, 1972.
8. Fitch, R. and M. Oppenheimer, Who Rules the Corporation? Parts 1, 2 and 3. *Socialist Revolution* 4: 73–107; 5: 61–114; 6: 33–94, 1970.
9. Florence, P. S., *Ownership, Control and Success of Large Companies*, London: Sweet and Maxwell, 1961.
10. Francis, A., *Families, Firms and Finance Capital*. Forthcoming. Unpublished Working Paper, Nuffield College, 1976.
11. George, K. D., *Industrial Organisation: Competition, Growth and Structural Change in Britain*, London, Allen and Unwin, 1974.
12. Goldsmith, R. W. and R. C. Parmelee, *The Distribution of Ownership in the 200 Largest Non-financial Corporations. In Investigations of Concentration of Economic Power*. Monographs of the Temporary National Economic Committee, No. 29. Washington D.C.: Government Printing Office, 1940.
13. Gordon, R. A., *Business Leadership in the Large Corporation*. California, University of California Press, 1961.
14. Hindley, B., Separation of Ownership and Control in the Modern Corporation. *Journal of Law and Economics*, XIII: 185–222, 1970.
15. Holl, P., Effect of Control Type on the Performance of the Firm in the UK. *Journal of Industrial Economics*, XXIII: 257–271, 1975.
16. Kamerschen, D. R., The Influence of Ownership and Control on Profit Rates. *American Economic Review*, LVIII: 432–447, 1968.
17. Larner, R. J., *Management Control and the Large Corporation*. Cambridge, Mass.: Dunellan, 1970.
18. Lundberg, F., *America's Sixty Families*. New York: Citadel (originally published by Vanguard in 1937), 1946.
19. Marris, R. L., *The Economic Theory of Managerial Capitalism*. London: Macmillan, 1964.
20. Marris, R. L. and A. Wood (ed.), *The Corporate Economy*. London: Macmillan, 1971.
21. Meeks, G. and G. Whittington, Giant Companies in the United Kingdom, 1948–69. *Economic Journal*, 85: 824–843, 1975.
22. Monsen, R. J., J. S. Chiu and D. E. Cooley, The Effects of Separation of Ownership and Control on the Performance of the Large Firm. *Quarterly Journal of Economics*, 82: 435–451, 1968.
23. Moyle, J., *The Pattern Ordinary Share Ownership*, 1957–1970. Cambridge: Cambridge University Press, (UK), 1971.
24. Nichols, W. A. T., *Ownership, Control and Ideology*. London: Allen and Unwin, 1969.
25. National Resources Committee (NRC), *The Structure of the American Economy*. Washington, D.C.: Government Printing Office, 1939.
26. Nyman, S., *Directors' Shareholding and Company Performance – Empirical Evidence*. Unpublished Working Paper, 1974.
27. [Patman] Staff Report, *Commercial Banks and their Trust Activities: Emerging Influence on the American Economy*. Washington D.C.: Government Printing Office, 1968.

28. Palmer, J., The profit-performance effects of the separation of ownership from control in large US industrial corporations. *Bell Journal of Economics and Management Science*, Vol. 4, No. 1, Spring '73, 293–303, 1973.
29. Perlo, V., *The Empire of High Finance*. New York, International, 1957.
30. Radice, H. K., Control Type, Profitability and Growth in Large Firms. *Economic Journal*, 81: 547–562, 1971.
31. Scherer, F. M., *Industrial Market Structure and Economic Performance*. Chicago: Rand McNally, 1970.
32. Scott, J. and M. Hughes, Ownership and Control in a Satellite Economy: A Discussion from Scottish Data. *Sociology*, 10: 21–41, 1976.
33. Stanworth, P. and A. Giddens, The Modern Corporate Economy: Interlocking Directorships in Britain, 1906–1970. *Sociological Review*, 23: 5–28, 1975.
34. Whitley, R., Commonalities and Connections among Directors of Large Financial Institutions. *Sociological Review*, 21: 613–632, 1973.
35. Zeitlin, M., Corporate Ownership and Control: the Large Corporations and the Capitalist Class. *American Journal of Sociology*, 79: 1073–1119, 1974.

PART TWO

STAGFLATION AND INDUSTRIAL STRUCTURE

IV. INFLATION AND COMPETITION

Carl Christian von Weizsäcker

1. Introduction

There is a strong and well-established tradition in economic thinking which says that a policy of price stability could benefit greatly from a rigorous competition policy. In recent years, official bodies such as the German *Sachverständigenrat* or the US Council of Economic Advisers emphasized the importance of a procompetitive or antimonopolistic policy for the fight against inflation. The labour unions (in Germany and, I believe, elsewhere as well) demand strict government controls over the pricing of monopolistic and oligopolistic firms. Conspicuous price increases, such as those for automobiles, tend to be castigated as an evil outgrowth of monopolistic market power, and this even at a time when car manufacturers work at full capacity and still are not able to deliver as many cars as customers demand at the current price.

Whereas it cannot be denied that inflation and noncompetition are in some way related, the connection seems to be rather complex and not yet analytically fully understood. There is the danger that in the meantime the strong emphasis given by economists in official and semi-official positions in this connection lends support to those who want to use interventionist anticartel and antitrust policy for the purpose of regulating, increasingly, our economic activities and have the final aim of replacing market mechanisms by planned mechanisms. I therefore welcome the remarks made on this point by the German *Monopolkommission* in its evaluation of the proper use of Section 22 of the German Cartel Law. The Monopolkommission under the chairmanship of Professor Mestmäcker, is very critical of attempts to use the control of market power for purposes of putting large parts of industry under the sway of regulation and price control.

Moreover, the Monopolkommission stresses the need for a competition policy which operates quite independently from the consideration of short-term effects on the price level. Otherwise, rather than fostering competition in the long run, competition policy becomes an instrument of political opportunism destroying the very environment of independent and competitive business decisions it is supposed to generate or maintain. I support the view of the Monopolkommission, and the present paper is a contribution to the understanding of the issues involved here. As such, as it stands, it is a very preliminary contribution, and I shall welcome any comments from readers.

2. Relating monopolization to inflation

Let us start by rehearsing some of the well-known arguments. Friedman and others have argued against the connection of monopoly (or oligopoly) and inflation by pointing out the difference in dimensions involved. Inflation is a process of rising prices in time. Monopoly, if compared to competition, *ceteris paribus* implies higher prices in a comparative static framework and as such does not allow any inference about the rate of change of prices through time. Only a rising degree of monopoly through time – other things being equal – could contribute to the explanation of inflation in the sense that a constant or falling degree of monopoly would mean a lower rate of inflation.

But what does 'other things being equal' mean? We are aware of the difficulty of defining 'other things being equal' in a general equilibrium framework. In the present context, 'other things being equal' must mean the following: given the production technologies (return to scale etc.) in a comparative static framework, a higher degree of monopoly means (a) higher prices for consumers and (b) higher monopoly profits. Thus, one test for explaining part of inflation by a rising degree of monopoly would be rising monopoly profits. The evidence on rising monopoly profits is not very favourable on this hypothesis. Corporate profits as a share of GNP, profit margins, rates of return on equity capital, stockmarket valuation of corporate equity as compared to the national capital stock, all these indicators of profitability have declined over the last 15 years. All this is very unlikely to be consistent with a strongly rising share of monopoly profits in GNP.

Thus, whether or not the degree of monopoly has risen in Western economies, this explains little – if anything – of the rate of inflation. If the degree of monopoly has risen, other things (as relevant for this context) have not remained the same: perhaps economies of scale in product development, manufacturing, distribution etc. have become more important, so that a rising degree of monopoly went with a rising discrepancy of average and marginal cost or perhaps was even due to the rising importance of economies of scale. Under such circumstances it would be very difficult to argue that prices would have risen by a smaller amount, if only firms would have refrained from using the increased potential of large scale operations.

Alternatively, perhaps it is not true that the degree of monopoly in any meaningful sense has risen. The increased concentration in many industries on the national level may have been offset by increased competition from abroad, by increased customer mobility on the local level (increased availability of transportation for shopping) etc. But this issue is not really the one which I want to discuss in more detail. I just want to remind you that, it is fallacious to relate the level of monopolization to the rate of inflation. In my opinion, you can only relate the rate of change of the level of monopolization to the rate of inflation, but the empirical evidence seems to be negative with respect to this hypothesis.

3. Price rigidity and inflation

Although one quite frequently encounters lines of argument which do not seem to take into account the issues discussed in 2., this does not mean that it would be impossible to provide better arguments for a connection between noncompetition and inflation. They run as follows, and they are being used by more sophisticated economists. Monopoly and oligopoly imply a higher degree of price rigidity than true competition. The ideal type of competition in this respect is perfect competition, where suppliers are price takers. Any change in demand or supply conditions immediately moves the price to its new equilibrium level.

Oligopolistic price rigidity has been an amply covered field of research. The kinky demand curve and the administered price hypothesis have been with us for several decades. But even the profit maximizing pure monopolist tends to change his prices less frequently than price changes occur in pure competition. For, under conditions of uncertainty, the monopolist will not be certain whether any given change in demand is likely to be persistent or transitory, and he therefore does not know for sure which price reaction will be optimal. Given the administrative and goodwill cost of frequent price changes, he is likely to stay put, i.e. to keep his prices static until he can read and interpret the market signals better. Profit target pricing is an extreme case of monopolistic behaviour under uncertainty.

Price rigidity, the argument goes, is an obstacle to successful price stabilization, not because rigid prices directly contribute more to the rate of inflation, but because they make anti-inflationary monetary policies more expensive in terms of employment, output, and government popularity. At the same time, expansionary monetary policies, which in due course lead to inflation, have greater short run appeal, if prices react to changed demand conditions only with a substantial time lag. You can buy more short run output and employment by expanding money supply if prices are rigid rather than flexible. Since governments and politicians need short run success, since inflationary expectations are important (e.g. for wage negotiations) and usually are dependent on currently observed inflation rates, there is much more likely to be expansionary monetary policies with a long run inflationary effect, if prices are rigid rather than flexible.

In my opinion, the impact of price rigidity on inflationary policy is there and should realistically be recognized by economists and politicians alike. But it is an impact resulting from the interaction of market conditions and the political mechanism and not just from market conditions themselves. Moreover, I am not convinced that the lack of competition is at the core of price rigidity: I now turn to this issue.

4. Price rigidity and competition

The matter of concern is the substantial time lag between monetary measures and their impact on prices. Let us imagine a world in which all relevant markets are in a state of perfect competition and in which there are future markets for all commodities. Let us also assume that transaction costs on these markets can be neglected. Under such circumstances the time lag would be very small indeed. For people would look at the indicators of monetary policy and, having formed their opinion on which price level would in the long run correspond to the monetary indicators observed, they would speculate on the future and spot markets accordingly and thereby immediately drive the price level to the point which corresponds to the monetary policy. It would not be difficult to maintain an anti-inflationary policy. On the other hand, it would be impossible to pursue an employment policy by monetary of fiscal measures. The reason is clear: the world described does not exhibit involuntary unemployment. Greater government expenditure would just mean an increased preference for present goods (compared to future goods) and would drive up the rate of interest. The level of involuntary unemployment would remain the same: zero.

I mentioned speculation: speculation is a special form of anticipatory behaviour. Such anticipatory behaviour can speed up processes of adaptation and this is the reason why changes in monetary policy will have such a quick effect on the price level. In the context discussed here, speculation plays the particular role of bringing about changes in the price level without substantial changes of relative prices, something which even under conditions of perfect competition on all markets would not be possible without speculation. The course of relative prices would for example be influenced by the particular channels through which the quantity of money is changed, or other monetary variables are influenced.

It is important to recognize that only a small number of people who hold only a small fraction of national wealth do speculate in a big way. This does not affect the outcome in the model so far. Given a clear signal from the monetary authorities, speculators will be prepared to engage in a fairly substantial volume of speculative transactions. This will move absolute prices to their new appropriate level. The assumption of perfect markets implies that speculators are, not confronted with quantitative credit constraints, so that they can operate at the levels which they themselves find expected utility maximizing.

5. Price fluctuation and stability of relative prices

Let us now move away from the unrealistic model economy discussed so far. Let us assume that (1) for most commodities and services there do not exist well organized future markets, (2) that speculators – as well as other people – cannot borrow freely at the going market interest rate. We now can expect a much slower adaptation of the price level to new money supply conditions. Moreover, the process of adaptation will be characterized by changes in relative prices. Those commodities which are suitable objects of speculation will move faster than the other commodities.

But let us go a step further. Given otherwise perfect markets, we cannot be sure that under conditions (1) and (2) the system exhibits stability. The simple model of the cobweb is well known as an example of instability, if no forward markets exist and speculation does not operate. But, if relative prices tend to fluctuate substantially, we can expect a substantial deterioration of the efficiency in the economy. Otherwise, efficient producers of commodities and services may be forced out of operations due to bad luck in the relevant relative prices. Others are making big windfall profits, simply due to luck.

It is not at all clear that markets with price taking participants are superior in allocational efficiency under conditions of substantial uncertainty, if compared to markets with price making participants. Price making presupposes certain imperfections in the markets, but these very imperfections may also contribute to stability of relative prices. And stable relative prices are in an overwhelming number of cases good for allocational efficiencies. Relative prices ought to change in the long run, or, for seasonal reasons in a predictable periodic fashion. But essentially random fluctuations of relative prices are simply a detriment to allocational efficiency.

Price makers can have a stabilizing effect on relative prices, because they change their prices less frequently than these prices fluctuate on perfect markets. We shall investigate in more detail why price makers behave in such a way. Here, we only take note of this fact. Given that it contributes to a greater stability of relative prices, it also contributes to a greater time lag between monetary measures and their impact on the general price level. If the relative constancy of relative prices is obtained through the relative constancy of absolute prices, the general price level must exhibit substantial inertia, and this is what we observe.

6. The phenomenon of specialization or division of labour

In order to understand the positive role of price inertia (in terms of relative prices), we should discuss the phenomenon of specialization or division labour. The fantastic social productivity of specialization is common knowledge among economists since centuries. Two hundred years after the first printing of Adam Smith's *Wealth of Nations*, we still have not yet grasped all the implications and preconditions of the division of labour. Here I want to put forward two points:
(1) price inertia is an important means to save transaction costs under conditions of producer specialization;
(2) price inertia reduces the risks of specialization and thereby encourages more specialization.

If producer specialization prevails, there are many more buyers than sellers on any given market. Given that on a market the goodṣ or services in question are such that they cannot be traded via a Walrasian auctioneer, transaction costs may play an important role in understanding the market. Buyer and seller will have to agree on a particular price for the specific object of transaction. Substantial transaction costs can be saved, if a mode of transaction can be found in which the decisions to be taken (a) do not consume much time and (b) can be separated out from routine operations like packing, delivery etc. If the seller fixes the price at an equal level for all customers and lets the buyers decide how much to buy from this commodity or service, such a mode of transaction is found. The fact that one seller meets many buyers, makes it possible for him to keep a stock which is large in comparison with the average quantity demanded by any given buyer. It is therefore feasible for him to offer (within limits) any quantity the customer wants at the given price. Fixing the price in such a way means that no time is lost for the seller and the buyer in terms of price bargaining. It means that the seller is able to increase his volume of transactions substantially without having to delegate pricing decisions to subordinates.

But, of course, these advantages in terms of transaction costs do imply a certain price inertia in terms of the unit of account. The immediate impact of changed demand conditions will be on quantities: inventories will rise as demand declines, they will fall as demand rises. Only after some time will prices be changed to cope with the changed demand conditions. The time lag for the price reaction can be considerable, if for example the seller is uncertain about the nature of the demand change and if in general he is uncertain about the optimal price.

7. Specialization and risk

Specialization, while very efficient, involves risky investments. A person who gets a specialized training as a doctor or lawyer invests time and money in a risky venture. An entrepreneur specializing in a certain industry bears substantial risk, because the physical capital he owns, the specific labour force he hires, his own knowledge of the trade, and his business connections would be worth little or nothing if he decided to move out of the industry. Thus, his wealth will depend very much on the degree of relative prosperity of the industry he has specialized in. It is therefore natural to conjecture that in the long run the degree of specialization in an economy is inversely related to the average degree of riskiness of investments for any given degree of specialization. If more specialization means higher productivity, reducing the riskiness of specialization in itself is of value.

Inertia for the product prices in a specialized industry as a rule mean lower riskiness of investments if compared with perfect competition prices, which are short run marginal cost prices. If short-run marginal costs have the usual inverted L-shape, or are close to that shape, then the short run elasticity of supply is rather low, and so is the short-run elasticity of demand. This makes for substantial price fluctuations. The danger of loosing a large fraction of one's invested capital within a short period of time, is substantial. Given the uncertain prospects of the future, speculative counterforces may be too weak to dampen the price fluctuations. Price inertia, on the other hand, will change turn-over roughly in proportion to changes in demand. Revenue and, to a lesser degree, profits will be more stable.

It is well known that, in a static, one-period model, efficiency is greatest, if market price equals marginal cost. To the extent that sticky prices prevail, they will not always be equal to marginal cost. But it is easily seen that steep supply and demand curves imply only small welfare losses for any given deviation of prices from marginal cost. Indeed, if we use the usual consumers' surplus, producers' surplus approach, we obtain, for any given quantity sold, x_0, the market surplus R

$$R(x_0) = \int_0^{x_0} (p_D(x) - p_s(x)) \, dx$$

where $p_D(x)$ is the demand price and $p_s(x)$ the supply price of quantity x.

Then we obtain

$$\frac{dR}{dx_0} = p_D(x_0) - p_s(x_0)$$

If a certain price $\bar{p}$ is fixed by the supply side, then x_0 is given by the equation $p_D(x_0) = \bar{p}$. We thus obtain

$$\frac{dR}{d\bar{p}} = \frac{dR}{dx_0} \cdot \frac{dx_0}{d\bar{p}} = (p_D(x_0) - p_s(x_0)) \frac{1}{p_{D'}(x_0)}$$

Let $m = \dfrac{\bar{p} - p_s(x_0)}{\bar{p}}$ be the indicators of the difference between price and marginal cost. Then the difference between maximum surplus R^+ and actual surplus R can be approximated

$$R(\bar{p}) - R^+ = \tfrac{1}{2}R'(p) = \tfrac{1}{2}(\bar{p} - p_s)\frac{1}{p_{D'}} = \tfrac{1}{2}m\frac{p_D}{p_{D'}}$$
$$\approx \tfrac{1}{2}mp_D(x_0)(x_0 - x^+)$$

(The approximation is accurate for linear demand and supply curves).

The loss in total surplus for any given m thus is approximately fifty per cent of the loss in turnover, due to a reduced quantity sold compared to the optimum. Thus for given m the welfare loss is small, if the elasticity of demand is small, which usually is the case in the short run. The reduced riskiness of price inertia may thus be allocationally more important than this welfare loss.

8. Ruinous competition

The specialization argument just outlined may not be as familiar to the industrial organization economist as the ruinous competition argument, whose valid core (there exists of course much invalid, basically anticompetitive ideology about 'ruinous competition') can be formulated along similar lines. I believe that ruinous competition as a concept can only apply to economies in which capital markets or certain resource markets do not work according to the principles of perfect competition. Let me take the case of capital markets. Because it is not true that you can borrow as much as you want, ruinous competition can arise. For a firm, which cannot obtain the necessary funds to survive in a period of loss-creating competition, may be more efficient than another firm which has more capital at its disposal. The criterion of survival under these circumstances is not efficiency but capital availability. Ruinous competition would then be a state of affairs, in which firms have to give up which in terms of efficiency ought to have survived.

To the extent that price inertia helps to avoid situations of ruinous competition as just outlined, it may and probably will be allocationally superior to a situation of marginal cost prices. Ruinous competition as defined, is usually associated with a low short-run market elasticity of demand. Here the allocational loss of deviating from the marginal cost price is small, whereas the likelihood of preserving efficient production units in periods of low demand is much better with relatively stable prices. Another way to put it would be: With price inertia and the corresponding greater stability of revenue, the capital requirements of entry into such an industry are much lower and thus barriers to entry are lower than with marginal cost prices and the ensuing likelihood of ruinous competition.

9. Price competition

The service sector of the economy is an important and particularly good example for the theory outlined so far. Strong price fluctuations under conditions of perfect competition may under fortunate circumstances be dampened by anticipatory inventory policies which compensate demand fluctuations. But this is not possible in the service sector, where, as a rule, services cannot be stored. The service sector, and in particular industries providing services which in some way imply the presence of the customer, are characterized by substantial price inertia. Some of these industries are highly competitive by conventional standards (entry, degree of concentration, number of units). Price inertia here is not an indication of lacking competition. The 'administered price' for a haircut at my barber shop around the corner is at most an indication of the classic Chamberlinian case of monopolistic competition, where, as my barber would insist, the emphasis is on competition rather than monopoly.

Similar examples are restaurants, holiday resorts, retail shops etc. Those industries, although highly competitive, have a pricing mentality, which is very far away from marginal cost pricing. An interesting phenomenon in this context is the almost complete absence of peak load pricing in these industries, although there would be ample space for it. Why aren't there more restaurants around, which charge more for their meals at peak lunch and dinner times than at other times? Why don't we find more barbers and hairstylists who charge higher prices on Saturdays than on Thursdays? There is seasonal peak load pricing in the hotel and vacation resort industry. But there is no peak load pricing (to my knowledge) in retailing, although the uneven distribution of customer visits through the day significantly raises costs per sales dollar and/or reduces the sales volume.

Why is this so? It could be that the degree of pricing sophistication in those industries is rather low and that what is lacking is an innovator who would introduce these pricing schemes. It could be that the advantages are not worth the additional administrative effort. It could be (and in the case of certain restaurants this is likely) that countervailing economies of temporal concentration make peak load pricing unattractive. Or it could be that in personal service industries suppliers fear to antagonize their customers by charging more, just when the customers would most like to get served. Whatever the reasons are, the phenomenon of non-peak load pricing in these industries is an interesting indication of a form of price competition differing from the marginal cost principle.

Price competition in these industries does not take the form of daily price changes with the attempt to compensate fluctuation in demand. Price competition is of a more long-run nature and with some exaggeration takes the following form: firms set prices according to the full cost principle; as time goes on, new entrants who hope to have cost advantages or quality advantages, come into the industry and supply the services at more favourable prices. Those suppliers whose prices are too high, will loose many of their customers and, rather than reduce prices and incur losses, they quit the industry.

Even if strict full cost pricing were adhered to, price competition would operate in the long run, as long as entry is easy and because cost reductions will be transmitted to the customers via price reduction (or, in inflationary times, price increases below the rate of inflation). This long-run price competition is the price competition that really counts from the point of view of allocational efficiency. The substantial productivity increases, say, in the food retail industry, which we experienced in recent decades, have been induced by this price competition in the long run. There is no reason to believe that this process would have been any faster with price competition of the perfect competition variety.

10. Vertical integration

The vertical integration issue has similarities to the specialization and ruinous competition issue as discussed. Long lasting supplier-customer relations are quite common in business; indeed, for a very large fraction of the economy, they are the rule. Quite frequently they help or are indispensable to provide the product which the customer really wants. Without implying any altruistic behaviour on the part of the people involved, this business relation can be described as a relation of mutual trust. It enables substantial reductions of transaction and search costs on the part of the customer. Yet it is not inconsistent with competition on the part of the suppliers. It is the possibility for the customer to switch partners, which keeps the present supplier trying hard to satisfy his customer and thus maintaining his goodwill. Trust relations of this type, built upon good past performance, are probably one of the most efficient ways to provide good quality products. If embedded in a competitive environment, the supplier has no incentive to abuse his initially superior knowledge of the true quality of his product. The long run damage to his image and thus his ability to gain customers far outweighs the short-run advantage of selling something cheap for something dear.

But, of course, in many cases this kind of trust relation is not compatible with strongly fluctuating prices. Long-term contracts with prices fixed in advance are quite common. These contracts or corresponding informal understandings work like a mutual insurance, where the supplier is insured against the risk of particularly bad market conditions and the customer is insured against the risk of not being able to obtain an important input. The preference of both sides for such an ongoing business relation with relative price inertia does not by itself mean the absence of competition. It is just necessary for the economist to realize that competition is a long-run process, which cannot well be understood from a momentary picture of the industry.

A particular example, which points this out, is the market for rented houses and flats. There is no doubt that supply and demand conditions do have a dominating influence on the level of rents in the long run. On the other hand, we know three things about this market. There exist many instances in which the market has changed from a 'sellers' market' to a 'buyers' market' and vice versa. Contrary to textbook perfect competition, rent contracts are not drastically revised while such a switch takes place, partly due to long term contracts, partly due to the inconvenience which would be caused to the initiator of the contract change, if the other side would not agree to it, and partly due to goodwill considerations which are important both for the tenant and the owner. Thirdly, unless very special circumstances prevail, there is no reason to deny that the market for rental housing is competitive.

The modern literature on the economics of search behaviour and information provides an additional explanation for rather sticky rents under changed supply-demand conditions. Very large changes in rents would not be sustainable, due to the high long run elasticity of supply. But a rent contract is worthwhile for both parties only, if it lasts for a certain time. One of the two sides thus will be rather reluctant to sign a rent contract with an atypical rent level. Thus, quasi-speculative behaviour of the market participants will imply rent inertia with the burden of adaptation being put on the quantity side (the vacancy rate). Similar arguments are, of course, well known in the modern discussion of labour markets.

If the market for rented housing does not work properly (in most cases because of government intervention), then a frequently observed result is vertical integration: tenants turn into house-owners. Similarly, if the demand for trust and security which can be found in special business relations cannot be fulfilled, for example due to a mistaken competition policy, then the tendency for vertical integration becomes very strong. The informational and behavioural efficiency of close business relations will then be replaced by the corresponding advantages of dealing within the same economic unit. Competition clearly suffers from this development.

11. Price flexibility and anti-inflationary policies

The argument so far developed should not be understood to mean that there is no positive relation between the degree of competition and short-run price flexibility. There exist numerous cases in which actual prices paid react rather promptly on changed levels of demand for given productive capacities, if competition prevails. A cartelization of such industries, if it is effective, would introduce an extra element of pricing rigidity. I would strongly favour a policy against cartelization, but even here *not* for reasons of anti-inflationary policy. On the contrary: the increased price flexibility going with competition in certain industries makes anti-inflationary policies more difficult. Let me explain this.

The statement seems to contradict what I said above. But this contradiction is only apparent and not real. If price flexibility is a universal phenomenon, then it definitely helps anti-inflationary policies: price level expectations get easily transformed into the actual price level without transitory distortions of relative prices. But, if a large fraction of all prices is rather inflexible in the short run, even under conditions of competition, then this is not so clear. If the fraction of inflexible prices includes important cost components such as wages, and if firms do have large short-run fixed costs, then anti-inflationary policies will hurt the flexible price industries considerably. Even efficient firms (cf. the ruinous competition phenomenon) may be in danger. The consequence will be strong political resistance against anti-inflationary policies and pressure to allow cartelization (in German: *Krisenkartelle*). Thus, the unequal distribution of the burden of anti-inflationary policies will make these policies even more difficult to pursue as compared to a situation, where price inertia is a relatively universal phenomenon.

12. Conclusion

The aim of this paper is against false and therefore dangerous conceptions of competition. Actions and activities of economic units are strongly intertemporally connected. They only are properly analyzed, if one looks at their long-run effects. Production and associated economic activities are characterized by a substantial intertemporal complementarity of inputs and outputs. Thus, economic units can react fully on changed market signals only after substantial time lags. The test of the existence of competition is only appropriate, if this long-run view of economic action is maintained. Short-run price inertia is not a test for the absence of competition. On the contrary, given realistic conditions, short-run price inertia is likely to provide better market signals for economic units operating in a competitive environment.

Competition is not a good thing *per se*. It is only beneficial if the signals which guide the competitors are appropriate. To take a drastic example: the government needs a monopoly on the use of physical force. Legalizing competition in robbery and theft is certainly not beneficial to society. Economic theory must guide policy makers to select the appropriate signals and constraints for competitors. This probably is an everlasting research topic of economic theory. If competition is a long-run, evolutionary principle of social organization, then the causes of inflation, which lie in short-run price inertia, should not be a concern for competition policy. Its concern must be to keep open markets and industries to new entrants, to prevent undue concentration by mergers, to prevent cartelization, to prevent protectionist actions against foreign competition. This is difficult enough. It would hamper the healthy development of competition, if certain patterns of short-term price developments would be used as criteria for the presence or absence of competition. It is dangerous to emphasize short-run anti-inflationary benefits of competition policy, since they don't exist and it distorts the view of what competition really is about.

V. OLIGOPOLY AND INFLATION

Ernst Heusz

1. Introduction

The simple fact that prices under monopoly are higher than under competitive conditions has led some people to associate the continuous rises in price-levels during the postwar period with the existence of non-competitive markets. Numerous empirical studies on administered prices are based on this hypothesis. It was, however, the obvious flaw that monopolies do account for higher prices but not for their continuous rise. This phenomenon cannot be explained by conventional analysis of monopolized markets. If we still want to maintain this approach to inflationary processes, it has to be supplemented by taking into consideration additional factors that might close the gaps mentioned above. This will be attempted in two stages: after dealing with the problem on a rather abstract level using strongly simplifying assumptions, we shall try to show the relevance of our analysis to present-day reality in the final part.

2. A theoretical approach

Compared with the years between the two world wars, the post-World War Two period may be characterized not only by an unbroken rise in price-level but also by a continuous increase in productivity, the rate of which lies markedly above nineteenth century averages, even discounting the leaps in productivity experienced by those countries which after the war virtually had to start from the pre-industrial level. If since the early nineteen fifties we observe an average growth in productivity of 3 per cent, this may not be considered a *quantité négligeable* in the explanation of postwar economic development. Recalling that capital can be reduced to labour expended at an earlier date, any technical progress can justifiably be termed as labour-saving,[1] and we save ourselves the trouble of

1. In our context it is sufficient to reduce all costs to labour expense, that is to express the long chain of intermediary products making up goods for consumption or further production in terms of labour

differentiating between various types.[2]

Let us now consider a model-economy with only two markets for rather different products – housing and cars for example. Aggregate expenditure for both products always equals national income and remains constant irrespective of prices. In Walras' term we have therefore

$$x_1 p_1 + x_2 p_2 = Y \text{ or more general } \sum_{i=1}^{n} x_i p_i = Y \text{ [3]}$$

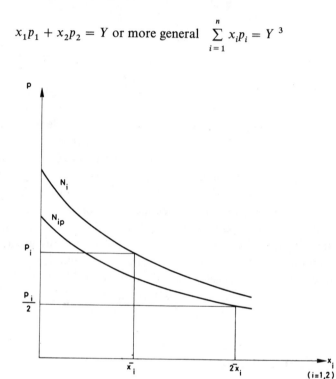

Figure 1

input. For simplicity's sake we shall – therefore – abstract from differential and contractual incomes on factors other than labour and centre our attention on gains accruing from non-competitive conditions.

2. Contemporary capital theory has its own approach to these problems which can be found, for example, in J. R. Hicks' *Capital and Time.*

3. The demand schedules implicit in Figure 1 are as follows:

$$x_1 = \frac{Y - bp_1 + bp_2}{2p_1}, \quad x_2 = \frac{Y - bp_2 + bp_1}{2p_2}$$

There are no economies of scale in the production of either product, so that, with perfect competition, the national income comprises wages only. The quantities $\bar{x}_1$ and $\bar{x}_2$ in Figure 1 stand for maximum capacity of production, that is to say, full employment. The prices corresponding to these quantities can be derived from the demand schedules N_1 and N_2. Through technical progress labour productivity is now doubled and hence, nominal wages remaining constant, unit costs are halved. Prices, accordingly, fall to $p_1/2$ and $p_2/2$ respectively, whereas quantities demanded are doubled. The demand schedules, however, have changed from N_1 and N_2 to N_{1p} and N_{2p}. This shift towards the origin is explained by the demand for one of the goods, not being related to its own price but also to the price of the other good, as may be derived directly from the demand schedules stated under note (3) above. Since aggregate expenditure remains unchanged, a reduction in prices by 50 per cent necessarily entails an increase in demand by 100 per cent which, of course, is necessary to sell the production at full employment level, doubled by technical progress.

If, alternatively, nominal wages are increased at the same rate as productivity, things are different. Since now there is no reduction in nominal costs and hence in prices, money supply has to be adjusted to double nominal national income.

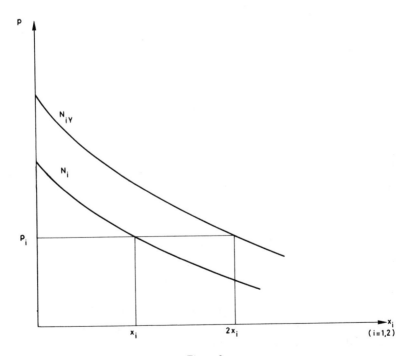

Figure 2

With prices p_1 and p_2 unchanged, demand shifts outward from the origin, new schedules being denoted by N_{1Y} and N_{2Y} respectively. This second alternative, where technical progress gives rise to higher nominal wages immediately, should be closer to present-day reality than the first. Let us now analyze the same situation under monopoly conditions:

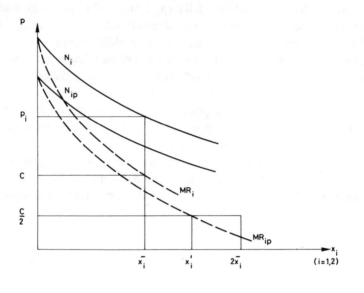

Figure 3

At the outset, demand schedules N_1 and N_2 are the same as shown in Figure 3. Since we now have marginal revenue = marginal costs, the wage rate is reduced to the level of C. Monopoly conditions account for a share of profits in national income which, using the Robinson-Amoroso relation, can be expressed as follows:

$$\frac{\bar{p} - \bar{p}\left(1 - \dfrac{1}{\eta}\right)}{\bar{p}} = \frac{1}{\eta}$$

It may be seen that the share of profits is inversely proportional to η. Since direct price elasticity normally decreases with the price (we have $\eta = \infty$ for a price prohibiting any demand and hence only a demand schedule parallel to the abscissa, as it presents itself to the seller under perfect competition, will prevent the elasticity from decreasing) technical progress resulting in lower prices would only be compatible with a given Y, if wage rates were reduced. If nominal wages remain constant, however, unit costs are reduced to $C/2$, but production will only be increased to x'_1 and x'_2 respectively which comes short of the new full employment level given by $2\bar{x}_1$ and $2\bar{x}_2$. The shift of demand schedules towards the origin due to the lower price of the other product will lessen the reduction of direct price elasticity, without however, fully compensating for the effect of the decrease in the goods' own price.

This result still holds in the case where an increase in productivity is immediately transformed into higher nominal wages and nominal unit costs remain unchanged. If nominal national income is now doubled, demand schedules will be shifted outward from the origin to N_{1Y} and N_{2Y} respectively, as shown above for the case of perfect competition, without, however, securing full employment (at $2\bar{x}_1$ and $2\bar{x}_2$).

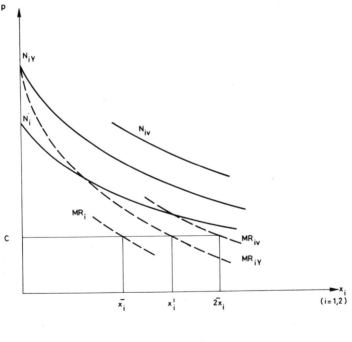

Figure 4

The explanation here is the same as in Figure 4. It makes no difference whether the increase in real income by technical progress is brought about by lower prices or higher nominal incomes. In either case there is a decrease in direct price elasticity of demand.[4] If full employment is to be warranted, a further increase in nominal income is needed until a horizontal line through $C/2$ intersects the total revenue-curves at $2\bar{x}_1$ and $2\bar{x}_2$ respectively. Corresponding demand schedules

4. For linear demand schedules the reduction in elasticity due to an increase in nominal income becomes immediately clear from graphical representation:

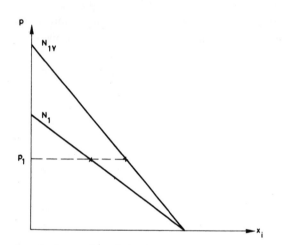

For obvious reasons the intersection of the demand curve with the abscissa $(p = 0)$ remains unchanged and the shift to the right pivots on this point. Thus, for the same price p_1 elasticity is evidently lower in N_{1Y} than in N_1.

The same may be shown in general terms algebraically: According to the Walras condition on page 90, we can write for the case that Y is multiplied with the factor m

$$F_1(p_1, \ldots, p_n, mY)p_1 + \ldots + F_n(p_1, \ldots, p_n, mY)p_n = Ym$$

and for the case that all prices are divided by m

$$F_1\left(\frac{p_1}{m}, \ldots, \frac{p_n}{m}, Y\right)\frac{p_1}{m} + \ldots + F_n\left(\frac{p_1}{m}, \ldots, \frac{p_n}{m}, Y\right)\frac{p_n}{m} = Y$$

and hence

$$F_1(p_1, \ldots, p_n, Ym)p_1 + \ldots + F_n(p_1, \ldots, p_n, Ym)p_n =$$
$$= F_1\left(\frac{p_1}{m}, \ldots, \frac{p_n}{m}, Y\right)p_1 + \ldots + F_n\left(\frac{p_1}{m}, \ldots, \frac{p_n}{m}\right)p_n$$

Evidently, demand schedules, therefore, change in the same way whether real income is increased by an overall increase in nominal incomes or by a general reduction in prices.

are N_{1v} and N_{2v} which at full employment quantities give prices higher than p_1 and p_2 respectively. From this we may conclude that in an economy with monopolized markets technical progress necessitates continuous price increases to assure full employment, these increases rising with the rate of progress in productivity.

3. Applying the analysis to present-day reality

It is sometimes useful to recall that theoretical analysis mainly aims at clearing up approaches which might serve to discover certain functional relationships. The purely deductive inquiry into the effects of technical progress under extreme market conditions was entered into for this purpose. Now we shall use the results to shed some light on reality. Let us begin with some remarks on market behaviour.

The most common approximation to the models of perfect competition and monopoly in reality are polypolistic and oligopolistic behaviour respectively. A great number of sellers and some degree of diversification among the products in a particular market are conducive of polypolistic behaviour. Under these conditions demand for a single product (product-demand) will be highly elastic with respect to its price, due to high cross elasticities with competing products. Hence, the opinion of each individual seller about the elasticity of demand for his own product is virtually independent of the elasticity of market-demand. This attitude is carried to an extreme in the model of perfect competition, where, no matter what the market price, product-demand, being represented by a parallel to the quantity-axis, is always infinitely elastic with respect to price. Polypolistic behaviour prevailing, a price reduction on account of increased productivity does not influence the price-elasticity of product-demand. Thus, in essence, the results for perfect competition arrived at above remain valid also for polypolistic markets.

As is well-known, the situation is different with respect to oligopolistic behaviour. Parallel price movements here lead to rigid price relations between the different products and thus influence from competitors' prices is virtually eliminated. The reaction of demand for a single product to a change in price will therefore be roughly proportional to that of market demand. Hence, oligopolists are confronted by the same price-elasticities as would be a monopolist and our analysis for monopolized markets, as outlined above, will also serve for the case of oligopolistic behaviour.

Let us turn to some manifestation of technical progress. In relation to our problem interest should be focussed on two types: The first and more spectacular type is the creation of entirely novel products which, at first, impress as technical marvels. Here the main advances in transport technique, that is, the substitution of horse-drawn carriages by railways, of railways by motorcars etc. may serve as an example. Almost all modern industrial products came into being by some similar revolutionizing developments. One should remember, however, that at the time those products made their debut in economic life, demand and markets for them had yet to be created. At this stage sellers' preoccupation is mainly with creating and developing demand for their products. They are more interested in the growth-rate of demand than in its price elasticity. This observation holds true for polypolistic as well as for oligopolistic markets. During the first tentative efforts of producing and selling a new product, costs of production and hence prices are still comparatively high. The difference between price and marginal revenue, therefore, is relatively small and price elasticity consequently high. Once a new product wins a foothold in the market a rapid development is characteristic both for production and demand. This is the time of substantial reductions in costs which result in lower prices, even if the market is not polypolistic. At this stage oligopolists too will enter into competition with price reductions and improvements of the product. This expansion of some new products frequently encroaches on the markets of older products (as, for example, kerosene ousting coal from heating), thus taking over the demand previously directed at the traditional goods.

Obviously, this is not the kind of technical progress underlying our analysis above. To provide an equivalent we will have to turn to the second type.

Considering the structural changes in agriculture – the oldest economic activity of man – during the last two generations (mechanization, universal use of chemical fertilizers, new methods of cultivation and husbandry), technical progress at a rate hardly inferior at least to the overall average of the economy becomes apparent. Other traditional industries, too, having long since passed their stage of rapid expansion, still undergo continuous technical progress, even if it is normally inspired from the outside.[5] The market for their products is more or less saturated, limits of demand stand out clearly. Here price elasticity becomes the central magnitude, giving the trade-off for quantitative expansion against price reductions. Technical change in this context was implied in our analysis above. Although this second type is less spectacular, its importance in western industrial economies presently at least equals that of the first type of technical progress.

5. Taking this point of view it is necessary to differentiate between endogenous and exogenous technical progress of a branch. We can observe that the rate of endogenous technical progress is decreasing with increasing age of industry. Such development, however, is not valid for the technical progress taken from outside.

Empirical observations will show price reductions resulting from technical progress of the first kind only (as, for example, for television sets after the war), whereas higher productivity due to technical progress of the second type is generally compensated by a corresponding rise in nominal wages. Thus, demand schedules are shifted to the right accordingly, as illustrated by N_{1Y}, N_{2Y} in the diagrams above. This, of course, means a continuously decreasing direct price elasticity so that there is a widening scope for price increases. Oligopolists, or rather the price leaders among them, will recognize this opportunity and use it. Whether they will strictly follow the rule marginal revenue = marginal costs or rather aim at maximal total sales as Baumol thinks likely, is only of secondary importance here. In the latter case sellers will try to settle for that price where elasticity of demand equals unity.

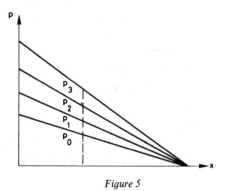

Figure 5

Prices would rise from p_0 to p_1 and so forth. The question as to which rule governs the marking up within the given scope is not really decisive. Whether it is cost-plus pricing or some other sort of calculation is a merely technical problem and should not be overrated by economists, however much it is stressed by men of business. Of much greater interest is the attitude of trades unions. They want to participate in the possibilities provided by the shift of demand (changing price-elasticity), and to a certain degree, are justified in doing so, if labour's share in national income is not to deteriorate. Wage negotiations may be interpreted as a struggle for the largest possible part in the margin thus given. To use the term cost-push-inflation in this context does not seem very much to the point. It is rather the oligopolistic structure of certain markets that makes it easy to give in to wage claims, since in the situation outlined above, it enables employers to pass higher costs on to prices without incurring substantial reductions in sales. There will be no such resistance as could be expected, if employers had their backs to the wall.

Some additional remarks are, however, required in respect to Western European industrial economies, especially the smaller ones. Here foreign competition restricts the scope of price rises in a majority of markets[6] thus weakening the position of employers as well as trades unions. The introduction of floating exchange rates has, however, brought about some modifications. Countries which, due at least partly to their own ill-advised economic policy, experience flight of capital have their currency underrated and hence prices of potential outside competitors are no real limitation to the scope for national oligopolistic policy. The same holds true for trades unions' wage claims. In the seventies, apparently Great Britain and Italy are undergoing this experience. The opposite situation is to be found in those countries that are on the receiving side. Here the influx of foreign capital enhances outside competition in a degree that may even enforce price reductions. Such seems to be the case with Switzerland where in 1976 inflation at a rate of 1 per cent was lowest in the western world.

It will be self-evident that the relationships between technical progress, price elasticity and market-structure we have dealt with so far are not intended as a comprehensive theory of inflation. The different rates of inflation in rather similar economies as France, Great Britain and West Germany clearly show the existence of more than one determinant of inflation. On the other hand, however, it should have become clear that with the number of oligopolistic markets increasing in every single economy the effects outlined in this paper may not be ignored. This part of the inflation problem cannot be dealt with by restrictive monetary policy alone.

If the quantity of money were to grow at the same rate as productivity with about 3 per cent per annum as Friedman proposed, oligopolistic market structures prevailing, we would have a similar situation as represented by N_{1Y}, N_{2Y} in Figure 4. Labour would be set free and could not be reemployed. Here competition policy is the only remedy. It has to create competitive conditions in oligopolistic markets, thus manoeuvring the respective firms in a position where the direct price elasticity of market demand cannot be their frame of reference. That is why Friedman's rule needs flanking support from competition policy.

On the other hand it would be wrong to believe, that the effects of an ill-advised monetary policy might be corrected by competition policy. If by unrestrained monetary expansion effective demand surpasses production possibilities, competitive markets are the first to answer such excessive demand with price

---

6. This is why national indices of concentration do not give a true picture of the competitive situation in the respective economies and can even be misleading as would be the case, if the higher degree of concentration in Switzerland were compared with that in the USA without any qualifications.

increases. As a rule oligopolists' reactions are much slower,[7] not to mention cartels whose sluggishness in responding to new situations is notorious. Careful differentiation in this respect is needed lest all empirical evidence comparing price movements on competitive and monopolistic markets should prove inconclusive and even misleading.

Independent from the causes of inflation actually dominating at the time, we find markets showing price increases best explained by our approach. This is the case with the US steel industry and, more recently, a similar development becomes apparent in the German automobile industry. Certainly, those are not the only instances, and it should be interesting to analyze other oligopolies from this point of view.

7. When in autumn 1973 petrol supply was threatened to be cut off and hoarding set in, demands for a more active competition policy against the multinational corporations was voiced in West Germany and, to a certain extent, heeded by the Federal Government. Clearly, this was an instance of barking up the wrong tree.

VI. STAGFLATION PROBLEMS IN A WORKERS' SELF-MANAGEMENT SOCIALIST ECONOMY: THE YUGOSLAV CASE

Branislav Šoškić

1. Introduction

Traditionally in Marxian and non-Marxian writings, a socialist economy has been considered to be a centralized planned economy with public ownership of the large-scale means of production. Only the private-enterprise economy, with private ownership of the means of production, could be considered to be a market economy. The amalgam of socialism with a decentralized market-oriented economy could not be conceived of in economic theory up to the thirties and in practice up to the fifties. It remained for Yugoslavia, after the break with Stalin, to attempt to combine socialism with a market-oriented economic system. Known as workers' self-management, this system is characterized by the autonomy of working organizations in individual enterprises, i.e., by their free economic decision-making as regards the amount and composition of production and investment, the pricing of their commodities and services and the distribution of their income.

Because it is decentralized and market-oriented, the Yugoslav economy has to face cyclical movements: including at some time falling economic activity, at others inflation; and more recently both of them together, known as stagflation. The problems presented in Yugoslavia by stagflation are in some respects different from those arising in more developed private-enterprise economies. It is with these problems that this paper is concerned.

2. Decisions on employment problems

Problems of employment cannot be solved in a self-managing socialist economy in the same way as in a centralized administrative socialist system. In a self-managed economy the starting point is the appraisal by the different enterprises of the prospects for the sale of their individual products, i.e., the level and composition of the effective demand. This will directly determine the level of production, but in a workers' self-managed economy the effect on employment is more complex. When effective demand rises, production will be expanded either immediately or after the stocks have been sold, which in turn will raise employment either immediately or after the elimination of a labour 'surplus.'

Matters stand differently when production is cut, since under workers' self-management a curtailment in output will ordinarily not result in a reduction of the labour force which is already employed. The self-managing character of decision-making, and hence in decisions on employment, compounded with the general principle of solidarity, have the effect of ensuring job security. While from a social point of view this is an important achievement of the socialist system, it has the effect of raising unit labour costs during periods of falling demand. Business organizations will not displace workers, if production is cut. They will accept the economically unreasonable solution of under-employment of the employed labour force, fully aware of what they are doing. The rise in unit costs of production will in turn create an upward pressure on prices, thereby lessening the enterprise's chances of selling its goods, impairing both domestic and export sales. The best way of avoiding such recession-induced increases in unit costs and prices would of course be to prevent recession in the first place.

In addition to the inflexibility in maintaining the level in the employed labour force introduced by job solidarity, the problem of employment in the Yugoslav economy has been complicated by two other factors. In the first place, the Yugoslav economy is still in the process of transition from exogenous to endogenous growth. In the relatively short period since World War Two, the share of the agrarian population declined from 78 to 37 per cent while substantial numbers of women continue to enter the labour force. Apart from the problems of creating employment for the former farm workers, the migration from country to town imposes new demands on society for housing, public utilities, education, health, culture and so on – problems which in Western countries used to be solved gradually over a much longer historical period.

In addition to the shift from the farm, there is the problem of guest workers. The high economic growth of advanced Western countries was made possible by a large-scale immigration of the labour force from less developed countries, including Yugoslavia. The need to make preparations for their return was highlighted by the economic recession experienced by West-European economies in 1974–75. Not only did jobs disappear but restrictions were imposed on the employment of guest workers. Moreover, workers employed abroad are generally in the prime of their lives. Through the job qualifications and skills they have acquired abroad, they can make an important contribution to the growth of the Yugoslav economy, if ways and means are found to accommodate them.

3. Policies to promote growth and employment

These policies cannot, of course, be considered apart from their effects on the general stability of prices. And, conversely, anti-inflationary policies should not be considered apart from their effects on growth and employment. If the inflation were of the classical demand type, i.e., an inflation which does not become manifest until the peak of economic activity when human resources and other factors of production (technical and available natural resources) are fully utilized, there would, theoretically, be no contradiction between measures to promote price stabilization and those to promote growth and employment.

Anti-inflationary measures to curb demand inflation, i.e., restrictive monetary and credit policies, more severe taxation and curtailment of public expenditures, would theoretically bring demand down to the level of the available resources. As capacity (both human and material) expanded, the appropriate rate of economic growth could be achieved by increasing overall effective demand through additional issues of money, easier credit for consumers and business enterprises, lower interest rates, more moderate taxation of consumers, reduced taxes for business organizations, and greater public expenditures (particularly for housing and public utilities, the building of schools, hospitals, cultural and other institutions, lines of transport, energy projects, etc.).

But this neat simplicity of the classical model becomes simply irrelevant when inflation develops in the face of slack economic activity. In recent years this has been the case of the Yugoslav economy as well as in other developed market economies. Previously unknown in economic theory or behaviour, this type of inflation makes restrictive monetary and fiscal policies worse than useless, since they produce unemployment without arresting inflation.

This is a special kind of inflation, which results when costs of production are raised under the pressure of the workers' trade unions (in private enterprise economies) or by way of self-managing decisions of direct producers (in Yugoslavia). It can also result when prices are raised as the consequence of autonomous, administrative decisions of enterprises and other authorities. In other words, the causes of this type of inflation must be sought in increases in costs and prices, particularly in monopolistic sectors of the economy.

Specifically, this type of inflation is generated by (1) monopolistic or oligopolistic conditions, (2) structural disproportions, including shortages of some products, (3) an excessive dependence on imports for some products whose prices have been sharply raised (e.g., petroleum), or (4) an increase in taxes that are passed on to the buyer. This type of inflation becomes particularly grave when the above-mentioned sources are to be found in industries producing energy, raw materials, tools and such vital commodities as food.

In a private-enterprise economy there are two rivals – producer-workers on the one hand, and managers and owners, on the other, with the former striving to maximize the proportion of total income to be used for wages and the latter the proportion to be accumulated (profits and the like). In this way a certain equilibrium is established between consumption and accumulation. In centralized planned economies, the relationship of personal incomes, i.e., consumption, to accumulation is controlled by central planning authorities, usually in favour of accumulation. There is no special force in the workers self-managing system which will constantly be striving to see that the largest possible portion is set aside for accumulation. Direct producers are both consumers and managers at the same time. As consumers, they would like to maximize personal incomes. As managers, running their own enterprises, they should secure the necessary amount for accumulation to be used as reinvestment. This double role of the direct producers often leads to decisions, which tend to favour personal incomes, i.e., consumption over accumulation.

This is particularly true where the majority of direct producers were formerly independent agricultural workers, not yet dependent on business enterprises who retain not only the habits and mentality of the farm but also some land which they continue to cultivate. Excessive distributions to consumption may also take place in enterprises that hold a monopoly or oligopoly position from which there is derived extra profit and rent. If there are no regulations, i.e., social and self-managing agreements nor any other stipulated standard regarding the income distribution, we may rightly expect that personal incomes will rise without an appropriate increase of labour productivity. Under the pressure of personal incomes, income is distributed thus to the benefit of consumption and to the detriment of accumulation, while the rate of economic growth is slowed down.

How should this basic problem be met? First of all, a well conceived incomes policy need not be accompanied by a comprehensive control on prices. An incomes policy should encourage enterprises holding a monopoly position to invest their extra profit and rent into funds for enlarging and modernizing their plant. Rather than employing fiscal and other measures to deprive enterprises enjoying a monopoly position of their extra profit and rent, it is better that they be induced to spend it on the expansion and modernization of production. By thus taking advantage of the principle of comparative advantage, the allocation of factors of production would become nearer to optimal, the rate of economic growth would be accelerated and exports would be promoted. The best way to find out whether the extra profit and rent are turned into personal incomes or into accumulation is by comparison with the average level of personal incomes for corresponding job qualifications in similar types of business enterprises within the same industry and region. Incomes that were conspicuously above those averages could be subjected to a system of differentiated and progressive taxation of personal incomes. Realizing that excessive distribution to income would simply be taxed away, the workers would seek to enhance their prospects for long-range job security by improving their plant's ability to compete. If properly formulated, such a policy would make for a higher technical equipment of labour, higher labour productivity and thus more rapid economic growth. Such a policy would also act as a restraint on inflation and would moreover be in accord with the socialist principle of distribution according to the quantity of the work done, moderating differences in distribution due to monopolistic privileges.

In order to overcome and moderate monopoly situations in the Yugoslav self-managing socialist economy we need not so much a prices policy but rather an anti-monopoly policy, a selective taxation policy and a policy of incomes and personal incomes.

In order to overcome and moderate structural disproportion and deficiency, a selective or rather a differentiated development policy is needed; first of all a stimulative credit (expansive) and fiscal (light) policy and also, for these industries, a beneficiary policy on foreign economic relations (foreign trade, investments, credits etc.).

The same measures have to be taken to curb the imported inflation, that is the dependence on imports, and reshape the composition of imports and exports. These measures must be applied in a stimulative way also to industries with comparative advantages.

In order to moderate the administrative effects which become manifest in higher costs of production (because of higher income contributions) and prices (because of increased turnover, taxes etc.) a selective and cautious approach should be recommended, which would favour industries producing articles of mass consumption, particularly food and other essential consumer goods, as well as investment goods necessary for their production.[1]

Such an economic policy against an inflation which arises in a situation of under-employment would not only slow down these aspects of the wage and cost-push inflation it would at the same time remove structural disproportions and thereby stimulate economic growth and employment.

Only after the above-mentioned measures have been taken and yielded their intended results should recourse be taken to the non-differentiated classical remedies; i.e., combatting unemployment through expansionary monetary and fiscal policies or combatting demand inflation through the reverse. The greatest error would be to try to use the classical remedies against an inflation that does

1. B. Šoškić, *Ekonomske doktrine* (Economic Doctrines). Beograd, Institut za ekonomska istraživanja i 'Savremena administracija,' 1975, p. 568 etc.

not arise from excessive demand. This would give us both a lower level of unemployment and a higher rate of inflation.

Unemployment and inflation are not the result of gaps in the self-managing economic system, even though improper solutions can (as has happened) aggravate the situation. While they can be moderated, these problems cannot be overcome once and for all, if one does not want to jeopardize the self-managing, free decision-making character of the economic system. In addition to the measures outlined above, what is needed is a combination of built-in stabilizers and specific actions to relieve identifiable bottlenecks. Among the built-in stabilizers would be the already-mentioned progressive taxation system which would bring about automatic changes in the incidence of taxes. A second stabilizer would be a self-managing agreement on personal incomes, which would prevent them from oscillating abruptly up and down in accordance with the general level of economic activity. And a third would be a system of payroll taxes to provide protection against unemployment and other social benefits. The yield of these taxes would increase during the upsurge of the economic cycle and fall during recessions and unemployment.

The built-in stabilizers need to be supplemented by direct measures against 'bottlenecks' which, if properly focused and taken at the right moment, can be highly effective.

The principal bottlenecks of production are those whose products appear as inputs or costs in many other economic activities, those which directly bring about certain types of cost-push inflation, or those which induce excessive imports and consequently imported cost-push inflation.

To be more specific, the production of food has become a bottleneck. High food prices tend to raise costs of production in all economic activities, generating cost-push inflation everywhere. And unfortunately, food is one of Yugoslavia's major imports, though prospects are good that it can become an export. Hence a high priority should be given to the financing and construction of grain elevators, refrigerator trucks, roads serving agricultural communities, etc. Similarly, a high priority must be given to the financing and construction of facilities producing energy and raw materials, also bottlenecks of the Yugoslav economy. Serving as inputs for most economic activities, they generate on their part a considerable amount of the country's cost-push inflation. Moreover, deficient output of energy and raw materials brings about a heavy dependence on imports, weakening the balance of payments on the one hand, and leaving ample scope to the import component of cost-push inflation.

Other important bottleneck areas in the Yugoslav economy are housing, public utilities, roads and other lines of communication. Due to their labour-intensive character, their expansion would absorb the labour force, particularly the unskilled labour force, which is plentiful, but unemployed or underemployed. That would create a wider scope for a more reasonable composition of employment in other fields and for the speedy return of workers from abroad. One might expect that the multiplier effect would become manifest in an increased production and employment in other fields, exceeding by far the primary additional production and employment.

4. Conclusion

It should be stressed that the economic policy against unemployment and inflation in a workers' self-management socialist economy is not and should not be aimed at the restriction of the market, as distinct from an economy which is administered from the centre. But to achieve continuing expansion, while avoiding the changes of demand inflation, will require a high order of skill in the framing of highly specific programmes tailored precisely to meet individual, identifiable problems. This is a challenge which I believe the Yugoslav worker's self-management system can and will meet.[2]

2. Problems of employment and inflation, from the aspect of the contemporary economic analysis and economic policy, have been considered in our book: *Production, Employment and Stabilization – a Contemporary Macro Economic Analysis*, 1970, 1972, 1974 (Proizvodnja, Zaposlenost i Stabilizacija – Savremena makro-ekonomska analiza). Some of these aspects have been considered also in our book: *Distribution of Incomes in a Market Economy – A Contemporary Micro-Economic Analysis*, 1971, 1972 (Raspodela dohodaka u trzisnoj privredi – Savremena mikro-ekonomska analiza). Both books have been published by the Institute for Economic Research and 'Savremena administracija,' Belgrade).

PART THREE

THE INTERNATIONAL ECONOMY
AND INDUSTRIAL ORGANIZATION

VII. INTERNATIONAL TRADE AND INDUSTRIAL ORGANIZATION: SOME STATISTICAL EVIDENCE*

R. E. Caves and J. Khalilzadeh-Shirazi

A modest trickle of research has now begun to fill the gap between traditional lines of research in the fields of international trade (general-equilibrium, normative, anti-empirical) and industrial organization (closed-economy, partial-equilibrium, atheoretical). International linkages can affect competition in domestic markets (Esposito and Esposito, 1971; Caves, 1974; Pagoulatos and Sorenson, 1976b), and competitive conditions in product markets can change the extent of an industry's participation in international trade (White, 1974; Pagoulatos and Sorenson, 1976a).

In this paper we report statistical evidence on the relationships between industrial organization and external trade in two countries, the United States and United Kingdom. The first section examines the structure and behaviour of US product markets that export substantially, face competing imports, or are sheltered from trade. It seeks to show how the bases of US comparative advantage are associated with the elements of market structure, and how exposure to trade alters market behaviour independent of the direction of trade. The second section reports on the effect of international linkages on the relation of profitability to market structure in the UK.

1. Trade structure and industrial structure in the USA

International market linkages can clearly affect the performance of industries, although the channels of influence are numerous and the qualitative predictions not always unique in sign. Import competition generally limits market power. So may export opportunities, but it depends on whether or not the exporting industry can dump abroad and prevent re-import. Multinational companies supply a source of potential entrants to industries with high entry barriers, but

* The authors are indebted to Michael Porter and Catherine D. Hayden for their comments and computational assistance. The views expressed in this paper are those of the authors and do not necessarily represent the institutions with which they are affiliated.

they themselves may be successful builders of barriers to deter other entrants. The elements of market structure – including exposure to international trade and investment – interact in determining how extensively the allocation of resources can be distorted. Therefore it is important to know how the international linkages of a nation's markets relate to the other elements of market structure.

The question is not only one of statistical correlations because the bases of national comparative advantage, determining the nature and extent of an industry's exposure to trade, are themselves related to key elements of market structure. A capital-abundant country's exports include manufactures that emanate from industries containing large enterprises and subject to absolute capital-cost barriers to entry, while its labour-intensive import-competing industries are less concentrated and smaller in scale of company and establishment.[1] A nation that leads in product-cycle innovations will have exporting industries marked by product differentiation – if the product cycle is seen as a sequence of innovative goods to satisfy (qualitatively) unchanging final uses.

This section explores some of these interrelations between trade structure and market structure for the USA. It employs an unusual data base, maintained by the PIMS programme of the Strategic Planning Institute, which contains many data on over 600 disguised 'businesses' – well-defined product lines – operated within a number of large US manufacturing enterprises. The data supplied by the business's managers include not only standard features of the structures of their markets but also many traits of market structure and behaviour on which data can otherwise be secured only with great difficulty.[2] The PIMS data include for each business its industry's exports expressed as a percentage of total shipments and imports as a percentage of domestic disappearance (shipments minus exports plus imports).[3] We proceeded by selecting from the 430 PIMS businesses engaged in manufacturing the following subsamples:

(i) *Export-oriented* (147 in number). Those for which industry exports as a percentage of shipments lies in (roughly) the upper third of the sample (the cut-off point is 9 per cent).

1. For example, Japan's comparative advantage in manufactures has turned around since World War Two, with the former export industries (labour-intensive, regionalized, and requiring relatively simple skills) now competing with imports, and the former import-competing industries (intensive in both physical and human capital, large-scale and concentrated) have become the leading exporters. See Caves and Uekusa (1976, chap. 2).
2. For a description of the PIMS data base see Buzzell, Gale, and Sultan (1975). The data generally pertain to the years 1970–1973.
3. In many cases these trade figures will be identical to official data published for industries at the four-digit level of disaggregation of the US standard industrial classification. The reporting business has the option, however, of designating its market not as national but as regional, regional in the USA and Canada, or wholly within Canada. The trade figures still pertain to shipments to or from foreign countries, and consequently will understate the trade exposure of regional industries.

(ii) *Import-competing* (146). Those for which industry imports as a percentage of domestic disappearance lies in (roughly) the upper third of the sample (the cut-off point is 5 per cent).

(iii) *Trade-exposed* (212). Those satisfying the requirements for either exporting or import-competing classifications. (The subsample size is smaller than the sum of the preceding two because 81 businesses' markets meet both criteria.)

(iv) *Sheltered or non-traded* (218). Those satisfying the requirements for neither export-oriented nor import-competing classifications.

We draw our inferences primarily from differences between mean values of variables among these subsamples and correlations of variables within them. Table 1 presents differences in means, with their statistical significance indicated, for those variables mentioned in the text.

Research, innovation, and product differentiation

Previous studies have found the USA to have a comparative advantage in research-intensive industries (Gruber, Mehta, and Vernon, 1967), and it is generally agreed to be at the forefront of product-cycle innovations. The relation between research activities and US comparative advantage is confirmed by the PIMS data. Both product and process patents (including trade secrets and other propietary information relating to production or operation) are rated important in a larger proportion of exporting than in import-competing businesses, although neither difference is statistically significant. One-third more of exporters' sales were accounted for by new products introduced in the preceding three years (significant at 1 per cent). The exporters consider their products to be in earlier stages of the product life-cycle, although not in significantly larger proportion, and fewer years have elapsed since their type of product was first sold (significant at 5 per cent). Product research and development outlays comprise a significantly larger fraction of sales for the exporting businesses, although there is no difference between levels of process R&D for the two groups. During the preceding eight years technological change occurred significantly more often for the exporting businesses. Model changes (or similar revisions of the product line) come slightly more often for the exporting businesses, though this difference is not statistically significant.

These results merely confirm previous research and the evidence of general observation. Somewhat more surprisingly trade-exposed businesses – imports as well as exports – are in some ways subject to more innovation than are producers not exposed to trade. Patents (both product and process) are significantly more important to trade-exposed businesses than to others, and technological change

Table 1. Significance of differences between mean values of selected variables, export-oriented minus import-competing and trade-exposed minus sheltered businesses

Variable	Export-oriented minus import-competing	Trade-exposed minus sheltered
Product patents important, proportion	0.03	0.13[b]
Process patents important, proportion	0.00	0.16[a]
New products, % of sales	3.73[a]	−0.76
Product life cycle, index	−0.16	−0.06
Age of product, index	0.27[b]	0.06
Product R & D, % of sales	0.46[b]	0.70[a]
Process R & D, % of sales	0.00	0.34[a]
Technological change occurred, proportion	0.11[b]	0.02
Model change frequency, index	0.05	−0.14[a]
Development time new products, index	−0.16	0.30[a]
Product typically customized, proportion	0.00	0.13[a]
Advertising, sales promotion, % of sales	−0.39	−4.06[a]
Media advertising, % of sales	−0.14	−2.51[a]
Sales-force outlays, % of sales	−0.60[b]	−0.79[b]
Auxilliary services important, proportion	0.24[a]	0.29[a]
Sales to households, percentage	−7.29[b]	−23.06[a]
Value added per employee, index	5.15[a]	0.23
Assets, % of sales	0.75	2.32
Finished goods inventories, % of sales	0.35	1.30[b]
Other inventories, % of sales	0.47	2.63[a]
Receivables, % of sales	0.68	1.94[a]
Age of reporting business, index	0.23[c]	0.10
Growth rate industry shipments 1963–72 (%)	1.01[c]	0.10
Net book value, % of gross book value	3.30[b]	−5.97[a]
Instability of industry shipments, index	0.02[b]	−0.08[a]
Capacity utilized (%)	−1.43	3.98[a]
Four-firm seller concentration (%)	0.04	5.84[a]
Reporting business's market share (%)	1.15	5.23[a]
Significant entry occurred, proportion	−0.01[b]	−0.02[a]
Market share instability, index	−2.68	3.72[a]
Pre-tax net income, % of capital	1.38	3.21[c]

Notes
Tests of significance were made on the assumption that the variances of the populations from which the subsamples are drawn are not necessarily equal.
Levels of significance are: a = 1 per cent; b = 5 per cent; and c = 10 per cent. In the case of variables measured by an index, neither the sign nor the magnitude of the difference between means can be given a direct interpretation.

has been somewhat more frequent. The development time for new products is significantly longer for trade-exposed than for sheltered businesses, suggesting a more intricate process of design and development. Average product age is slightly newer for all trade-exposed business than for sheltered businesses, although it is lower for import-competing than for sheltered businesses. That same pattern holds for stages of the product life-cycle: sheltered industries are farther along than are trade-exposed, although import-competing products are more mature than sheltered ones.

What these differences strongly suggest is the role of what has been called 'availability' in international trade: a significant volume of trade may consist of highly specialized articles that are produced only in a few locations around the world (Kravis, 1956; Grubel, 1967). That patents and product changes are generally more important in *both* the exporting and the import-competing industries of the USA, despite the manifest comparative advantage of the USA in innovative goods, strongly suggests that heterogeneous and distinctive goods are found to a greater extent in international trade than in sheltered circuits of commerce within national boundaries. The importance of availability and heterogeneity is supported by the fact that significantly more trade-exposed businesses indicate that their products are designed and/or produced to order for individual customers. The percentage of business reporting that their products are customized is about the same for import-competing as for exporting businesses.

The prevalence in international trade of distinctive goods marks the traded-goods sectors as subject to product differentiation. It is important to recognize, however, that differentiation resulting from the innate heterogeneity of a line of related products is for many purposes not the same thing as the differentiation associated with heavy sales promotion, in particular media advertising. Outlays by trade-exposed businesses on advertising and sales promotion as a percentage of sales are less than one-fifth those of sheltered industries (one-eighth, in the case of media advertising alone). The difference between sales-force outlays by trade-exposed and sheltered business is much smaller, consistent with the need of the trade-exposed producers of heterogeneous goods to employ direct representation to inform selected buyers of what they have available. Export-oriented businesses advertise somewhat less and spend less on their sales forces than import-competing business, but the differences are small and modestly significant.[4] Further evidence on the character of differentiation in trade-exposed sectors appears in the importance to buyers of auxilliary services

4. A possible reason for this difference is that exporters often sell to commission merchants abroad who employ their own sales forces and do their own advertising. In the case of sales-force expenditure, however, the data are supposed to include commissions paid to agents or brokers.

provided by the manufacturer. The buyer's reliance on auxiliary services ties him to the individual seller and provides a basis for differentiation. The proportion of trade-exposed PIMS businesses rating auxilliary services as important to the buyer is significantly higher than the proportion of sheltered businesses.

These differences between trade-exposed and sheltered businesses partly reflect the mixture of producer-good and consumer-good industries in the two sectors. Trade-exposed businesses supply only one-third as much of their output to final household users as do sheltered businesses, and among the trade-exposed businesses the import-competing businesses serve households to a larger extent than the export businesses. However, when we calculate differences in these same variables only for those businesses classifying themselves as making primarily producer goods, the resulting patterns prove identical to those described in the preceding paragraph, although with less dramatic differences between the trade-exposed and sheltered segments. Therefore the differences in information media utilized by businesses do seem to support our hypothesis that traded goods are differentiated through physical heterogeneity and distinctiveness, sheltered goods somewhat more through advertising and sales promotion.

Even if the differences in differentiation between traded and sheltered goods were explained away by their varying mixtures of producer and consumer goods, they would remain important for two reasons. First, the lesser prevalence of manufactured consumer goods in international trade is probably neither accidental nor confined to the USA. The weakness of consumers for organizing to combat tariffs on the goods they buy and the differences in national cultures that imprint themselves on the styles of consumer goods both favour the domestic producer for serving the domestic market for household goods, whereas neither force lends advantage to the domestic maker of producer goods. Second, the types of product differentiation we have considered ('heterogeneity' and 'branding') are not confined to the consumer-goods sector, nor is the distinction between them collinear with the producer/consumer distinction. It is obvious that product differentiation due to heterogeneity can prevail in producer goods, but that due to branding and advertising is often assumed absent from producer-good industries. That assumption is inappropriate and fails to recognize the theoretical basis of differentiation: an adverse benefit-cost ratio facing the buyer who would invest in information to improve his selection among competing suppliers. It often pay buyers of producer goods to inform themselves well about alternative sources of their key inputs, but for inputs purchased in small quantities or which they are technically ill-equipped to evaluate, they find themselves in the same position as the household buyer (Porter, 1976, chap. 5).

Factor intensity and trade position

Other characteristics of the PIMS businesses can be related to variables that hold more traditional interest in international economics. The orgy of computation that followed the announcement of the Leontief paradox (that American import-competing industries are more capital-intensive than American export industries) has still left the factor-intensity structure of US foreign trade somewhat unresolved. Are the export-oriented PIMS businesses less capital-intensive than their import-competing brethren? The data allow two approximations to the answer to this question...

First, value added (adjusted for any abnormal pre-tax profit on invested capital) per employee provides an indication of total capital services per employee, if not of the total capital stock. The figure is 20 per cent higher in the export businesses than in the import-competing businesses, and this difference is statistically significant at the 1 per cent level. Total assets as a percentage of sales, however, are only marginally higher in the export businesses, and the difference is not statistically significant. Values for the sheltered industries of both adjusted value added per employee and total assets as a percentage of sales are bracketed between the figures for the exporting and import-competing industries. Thus, these data give some support for a conventional interpretation of US factor-abundance, although they of course pertain to manufacturing and not to the whole economy, and they take no account of the factor intensities of the businesses' inputs.[5]

The capital structures of PIMS businesses confirm some of our expectations about the effects of participation or exposure to international trade. Longer elapsed times between shipment of goods and their receipts, and the use of supplier credit as a competitive device, both show their effects. Trade-exposed businesses hold significantly larger inventories of finished goods (as a percentage of sales revenue) than do sheltered businesses (export-oriented and import-competing businesses do not differ). The same pattern holds for inventories of raw materials and work-in-progress, with the differences between trade-exposed and sheltered businesses highly significant. The extension of trade credit is commonly said to be an important form of competition in international trade, and that practice coupled with the lengthier delivery time implies that receivables as a percentage of average revenues will be higher for trade-exposed businesses than for others. That pattern is confirmed, with the difference between trade-exposed and sheltered businesses highly significant.

Two other features of capital structures relate to patterns of trade. The relation

---

5. See Baldwin (1971) and previous studies cited therein.

between the US comparative advantage and the product cycle implies the exporting businesses are newer and operate overall in faster-growing markets, and the PIMS data confirm both differences. Therefore the physical capital of import-competing businesses should be older and more fully depreciated, and the difference in ratios of net to gross book value of capital stock is in fact significant at 5 per cent. Somewhat surprisingly, sheltered industries have newer capital stocks than trade-exposed industries. If traded-goods markets are subject to more instability and disturbances than domestic markets, we would also expect that the trade-exposed businesses (assuming that they operate in imperfectly competitive markets) would be able to achieve a lower utilization of their production capacity than businesses in sheltered sectors. Neither the premise nor the conclusion, however, turns out to be correct. The interannual stability of industry sales is significantly higher for the trade-exposed than for the sheltered sectors, and so is the average percentage of their capacity that is utilized. The higher utilization of capacity by the trade-exposed businesses may also reflect differences in competitive conditions, because unter-utilization can be associated with incomplete collusive agreements in certain market structures (Esposito and Esposito, 1973). Our data offer support for this hypothesis.[6] Higher utilization may also result because order backlogs vary, rather than sales, in the trade-exposed producer-good businesses.

Trade structure, market conduct and performance

Now we can turn to the implications of these differences in trade position for the market structure and performance of the industries involved. It is commonly observed that large businesses in a given sector tend to export larger portions of their output than small businesses. A sufficient basis for this pattern is higher fixed costs of information associated with selling in international markets. Their greater height seems a reasonable empirical assumption, although they can sometimes be avoided by the use of joint selling agents (such as Japan's general trading companies). Therefore, export industries may be more concentrated because heavier fixed costs of information (and perhaps economies in the pooling of risks, as well) increase the optimal sizes of firms. In addition, the scales of export enterprises which face relatively competitive world markets are less

6. We examined the correlations among our trade-exposed and sheltered businesses between the business's capacity utilization, on the one hand, and its profitability and market share, on the other. Capacity utilization is more highly correlated with both profit (difference significant at 11 per cent) and share (significant at 5 per cent) in the trade-exposed businesses. This we would expect if all three variables are influenced mainly by unobserved differences in commercial success, whereas a lack of correlation is consistent with imperfections in competition in the sheltered industries.

constrained by downward-sloping demand curves (whether market or firm-specific) than are firms in a domestic market. And, given any imperfections in the market, we expect to find the sizes of both plants and enterprises bearing some relation to the sizes of the markets in which they operate.[7]

These propositions about differences between exporting and sheltered enterprises logically apply as well to import-competing companies relative to sheltered ones, because exposure to an international market should have the same qualitative effect whether the industry turns out to be a net exporter or to face net imports. Hence, when seller concentration is measured conventionally in the national market, we expect the concentration of both exporting and import-competing industries to be higher, *ceteris paribus*, than in sheltered industries. The *ceteris paribus* qualification is important, especially for the USA, because the influence of higher levels of capital intensity and labour skill in the exporting sectors dispose them toward larger size companies and higher concentration than in the import-competing industries.

These predictions about concentration are in fact confirmed by the PIMS businesses without controlling for these probable differences in productive structure. There is no difference between the mean four-firm concentration ratios of exporting and import-competing businesses,[8] but both are significantly higher than the average for sheltered businesses. The reporting business's own market share is also higher in the trade-exposed businesses. These results are consistent with conclusions reported by Pagoulatos and Sorenson (1976a).

There may also be some connection between barriers to entry and exposure to international trade, although we cannot secure a clear-cut theoretical prediction. On the one hand, the entrant to a trade-exposed industry is less likely to face scale-economy entry barriers because of the international span of the market. On the other hand, the advantages of the large-size firm resting on informational and risk-bearing considerations tend to favour companies of large absolute scale and thereby elevate capital-cost barriers to entry. This effect may be further supplemented by a tendency for trade-exposed businesses to be more extensively vertically integrated with other parts of the enterprise to which it belongs.[9] Our data suggest that the export-oriented industries are surrounded by higher

---

7. A good deal of empirical evidence supports this hypothesis; see Bain (1966, chap. 3); Saving (1961); Eastman and Stykolt (1967, chap. 3); and Pryor (1972). There are possible causal connections running from concentration to proportion of output exported, but White (1974) shows that they are indeterminate in sign.

8. Concentration is measured from sales and not adjusted for the systematic difference in the sizes of markets.

9. The PIMS businesses indicate the extent to which they buy from components of the parent company and sell to its other components. In each case the trade-exposed businesses indicate significantly greater integration than the sheltered businesses.

barriers to entry. The proportion of these businesses reporting the entry of a major competitor (five per cent or more market share) in the past five years is significantly smaller than that of sheltered businesses, and entry has occurred in a significantly smaller proportion of trade-exposed businesses than sheltered ones.[10]

We can now pursue these differences in the structures of industries to their behaviour and performance. Because the PIMS businesses operate on the average in relatively concentrated industries, it is appropriate to look for indications of the degree to which they have achieved a stable oligopolistic consensus, and such evidence apparently reposes in the variations among markets in the stability of the market shares of leading sellers. With other influences controlled, a less tight-knit oligopoly is associated with greater instability of market shares.[11] We expect instability of shares to differ in a somewhat complex way among our groups of industries. A high level of imports should be quite hostile to the maintenance of a stable oligopolistic consensus because it is difficult to bring the importers into the bargain. Whether exporters face a similar constraint on their ability to collude, however, probably depends on whether or not they can effectively segment their domestic from their international markets. A segmented market elevates the effective level of concentration in the domestic market, and the more price-elastic foreign market can serve as a vent to absorb any variations in output. On the other hand, if exporters cannot segment their markets, the same argument applied to them as applies to import-competing businesses.[12]

Market-share instability for the PIMS businesses is measured by the sum of absolute percentage-point changes in shares between three consecutive pairs of years for the industry's four leading businesses. This index weakly supports the segmentation hypothesis about export markets, for it is higher in import-competing than in exporting industries. The difference is significant only at the 11 per cent level of confidence, but the *interannual* instability of industry sales, which should increase the instability of market shares, is significantly less for the importing-competing than for the export-oriented industries. Controlling for its influence would surely elevate the difference in their market-share instability levels to the conventional range of statistical significance. Market-share instability

10. The propensity of the exporting businesses for backward vertical integration also leaves them exposed to the threat of entry by other companies through vertical integration forward. The fraction of exporting businesses reporting that their suppliers had integrated forward is higher than the fraction of sheltered businesses (significant at 10 per cent).
11. See Caves and Porter (1976). This relation was found to be nonlinear, with instability rising as seller concentration fell from high to medium levels, then declining as concentration fell too low for oligopolistic interdependence to be recognized.
12. See Caves (1974, pp. 4–16); Caves and Porter (1976).

is significantly less for sheltered than for trade-exposed businesses, which suggests that the former enjoy more stable mutual understandings.

When we come to profitability, as an indicator of market performance, these elements of structure[13] and conduct leave us with few clear-cut predictions. The trade-exposed businesses exhibit higher concentration but face rivals in broader markets. The exporting industries are probably surrounded by higher entry barriers than others, though, and display less market-share instability than the import-competing businesses. The average rate of pretax profit on average investment earned by export businesses during 1970–1973 was in fact 1.4 percentage points higher than that of import-competing businesses; not statistically significant. Trade-exposed businesses in general, though, averaged 3.2 percentage points more profit than sheltered businesses, and the difference is weakly significant.[14]

More interesting than these mean differences in profitability is the sensitivity of trade-exposed businesses to the conventional structural determinants of profitability. If the structural parameters of the domestic market are inappropriate indicators of any market power possessed by the trade-exposed businesses, we can expect little success in explaining their profits statistically. We have not performed the indicated regression analysis, but we can report significantly lower zero-order correlations in the trade-exposed businesses between profitability and either seller concentration or market growth. In the next section we present and extend a regression analysis that delves into the influence of trade exposure on market power and profitability.

2. Trade and market power in the UK

In this section we develop the role of exports among the determinants of price-cost margins in the manufacturing industries of the UK, building on a previous study (Khalilzadeh-Shirazi, 1974; Caves, Khalilzadeh-Shirazi, and Porter, 1975). That study found that imports appear to limit market power. Expressed as a percentage of industry output, they bear a weakly significant negative relation to price-cost margins – a result that agrees with analyses of US data by Esposito and

13. The PIMS data also allow us to control for certain other elements of market structure, notably buyer concentration. Here we found no important differences among the groups of businesses.
14. The variance of profitability among the trade-exposed businesses is greater than among the sheltered ones, as the 'availability' hypothesis suggests, but the difference is not significant. The mean profit difference is not due to exchange-rate movements because the trade-exposed businesses reported an insignificantly greater price-cost squeeze than the sheltered businesses. The price-cost squeeze is measured by the percentage increase in selling price minus percentage increase in direct cost.

Esposito (1971) and Pagoulatos and Sorenson (1976b). More surprisingly, exports as a percentage of industry output were found positively related to price-cost margins, with the relation significant at the 10 per cent level.

This positive influence of exports stands as something of a puzzle because market power and exports can be related in so many ways, as we indicated above. If export opportunities weaken oligopolistic interdependence, essentially by flattening the demand curve that faces the individual seller, they should be negatively related to profitability. On the other hand, if exporters typically can segment their less-competitive domestic market from the more competitive international market and elevate price collusively above the international level, export opportunities raise profitability through the gains from price discrimination. The use of discrimination itself tends to inflate the share of output exported (Caves, 1974; White, 1974). And the phenomena of availability and international product differentation, discussed above, suggest that rents will accrue to industries whose distinctive varieties attain substantial export sales. Thus, both discrimination and availability imply a positive association between exports and profit margins, with both increased by the successful practice of discrimination or differentiation or both.

Finally, export opportunities may affect technical efficiency (and possibly, though not necessarily, profitability) by increasing the sizes of plants and enterprises and thereby increasing the proportion of output that emerges from efficient-scale production units. The research reported in this section seeks to sort out these various hypotheses.

Exports and scale of establishments

Because the details are available elsewhere, we shall explain the basic investigation of UK price-cost margins briefly. The dependent variable was the gross return on sales in 1963, with gross return measured as the sales value of output minus materials and fuel purchases, salaries, wages and related expenses, and outlays for purchased services (repairs and maintenance, advertising, insurance, etc.). The independent variables are:

$CR5$ Weighted average five-firm concentration ratio
K/Q Capital-output ratio (per cent)
GR Percentage growth of sales between 1958 and 1963
PDD Dummy variables indicating product differentiation
IMP Imports as a percentage of industry output
EXP Exports as a percentage of industry output

CDR   Value added per worker in smaller plants divided by value added per worker in larger plants

MES8 Estimated minimum efficient plant scale as a percentage of industry output, for those industries in which CDR is less than 80 per cent, zero otherwise.

Equation 1 of Table 2 presents the study's basic findings for a sample of sixty industries.

An incidental result of our analysis was to show that exports and scale economies are closely associated. This emerges (Equation 2) when we drop the variables MES8, replacing it with variable CDR that indicates the apparent cost disadvantage of small plants but does not reflect the size of larger (and presumably efficient-scale) plants relative to the market. The change increases the size and significance of the regression coefficient of EXP, strongly suggesting that the positive influence of exporting opportunities on profits in the UK operates partly through increasing the scale of plants. The resulting efficiency rents may be preserved in long-run profits, though their continuance is of course not necessary. This interpretation agrees with Scherer's finding (1975, p. 396) for his twelve industries that the sizes of leading plants 'increase much more than proportionately with increases in exports as a percentage of domestic production.' The associated inflation of price-cost margins presumably consists in part of a differential efficiency rent that might not be competed away where product differentiation is present or scale economies very important.

We found evidence (above) from US data suggesting the pervasiveness in international trade of differentiation associated with the heterogeneity and distinctiveness of an industry's products. To check further into the relation between differentiation and trade we subdivided the sample of UK industries into producer-good and consumer-good groups. Differentiation in our present sense can and clearly does occur in producer-good as well as consumer-good industries, but the consumer-good industries of countries like the UK and US that are successful on world markets probably all exhibit differentiation in this sense. If many goods move in international trade because of availability and international product differentiation, we should expect price-cost margins to be more sensitive to the share of output exported for consumer-good than producer-good industries. Equations 3c and 3p estimate our model for these two groups of industries separately. The coefficient of EXP is very small and insignificant in Equation 3p, whereas in Equation 3c, it is much larger than in the equation for the whole population (Equation 1), although only slightly more significant.[15]

15. The contrast between the subsamples is further supported by the difference in the correlations between MES8 and EXP, 0.74 in consumer goods and −0.05 in the producer-goods industries. If

Table 2. Regression analysis of determinants of price-cost margins, sixty UK manufacturing industries.

Equation no.	Constant	CR5	MES8	CDR	K/Q	GR	PDD	IMP	EXP	R^2	$\bar{R}^2$
1.	4.58	0.062[a] (2.59)	0.811[b] (2.35)		0.078[b] (2.09)	0.067[a] (2.51)	2.69[b] (2.39)	−0.055 (0.81)	0.080[c] (1.38)	0.533	0.470
2.	6.70	0.064[a] (2.55)		−2.52 (0.51)	0.074[b] (1.87)	0.065[b] (2.32)	3.29[a] (2.78)	−0.079 (1.12)	0.130[b] (2.33)	0.486	0.416
3c.	4.46	0.090[a] (2.75)	0.593 (1.20)		0.088[b] (1.91)	0.009 (0.27)	0.84 (0.55)	−0.026 (0.27)	0.204[c] (1.45)	0.739	0.638
3p.	6.30	0.027 (0.68)	−1.51 (0.87)		0.099[c] (1.58)	0.087[b] (2.24)	5.36[b] (2.36)	−0.133 (1.28)	0.016 (0.21)	0.535	0.410

Notes

Coefficients in parentheses are t-ratios.

Levels of significance (one-tailed tests) are: a = 1 per cent; b = 5 per cent; c = 10 per cent.

Thus there is some evidence for two propositions:
(i) the UK's comparative advantage appears to lie in consumer-good industries that earn a premium abroad on their distinctive products;
(ii) the sort of product differentiation congenial to international trade remains more prevalent in consumer-good than producer-good industries. (In both respects the structure of the UK's trade seems to differ from that of the USA.) Further support for both propositions appear in the coefficients of IMP in Equations 3c and 3p; although both are insignificant, the magnitude and near-significance of the coefficient in Equation 3p suggests that producer-good industries on the average have less of a differentiation advantage with which to defend themselves against foreign competition.

Export market and oligopolistic interdependence

So far we have attributed the positive relation between UK exports and price-cost margins partly to product-differentiation rents, partly to the effect of exports on the sizes of plants. Is there no support for the hypothesis that export opportunities reduce the effective recognition of mutual interdependence among oligopolists, and thereby reduce the profitability of concentrated industries? If the sixty industries in our sample are divided into their more- and less-concentrated halves (the dividing line fortuitously is $CR5 = 50.0$), the coefficient of EXP drops in magnitude and grows insignificant in the more concentrated industries, but does not become negative.

We pursued this question further by changing the specification shown in Table 2 to estimate separate coefficients on EXP for the concentrated ($CEXP$) and unconcentrated ($UEXP$) industries in the full sixty-industry sample. The equation for the full sixty-industry sample is:

$$PCM = 4.13 + 0.071^b CR + 0.893^b MES8 + 0.081^b K/Q + 2.73^b PDD$$
$$ (2.25) \qquad (2.24) \qquad (2.11) \qquad (2.40)$$

$$+ 0.065^b GR - 0.051 IMP + 0.053 CEXP + 0.090^c UEXP$$
$$ (2.36) \qquad (0.74) \qquad (0.61) \qquad (1.43)$$

$$R^2 = 0.534$$
$$\bar{R}^2 = 0.461$$

consumer-good industries' successes with international differentiation increase their profitability, it should be partly through increasing the sizes of plants belonging to the larger and more successful sellers. UK exports originate to quite a marked degree in the larger companies; see Khalilzadeh-Shirazi (1974, note 18).

If the export market deters effective recognition of mutual dependence in concentrated industries, we should expect a lower – preferably negative – coefficient for $CEXP$. In the equation it is lower than that of $UEXP$, though still positive and insignificant.[16] Although the difference between the two coefficients is not significant, the direction of the difference in both size and significance is consistent with the dampening of oligopoly behaviour by export opportunities exerting some negative pull on the forces otherwise producing a positive relation between exports and profitability.

3. Summary and conclusions

This paper has presented two independent studies of the relation between industrial organization and international trade in the USA and UK. For the USA we have demonstrated a contrast between the character of product differentiation found in the industries significantly exposed to trade (whether via export opportunities or import competition) and that found in industries sheltered from trade. Differentiation in the trade-exposed industries is associated with the intrinsic heterogeneity of the goods in question, a finding that supports the role of availability in determining the volume and pattern of trade. Differentiation in sheltered industries, by contrast, depends more on advertising and sales promotion. The contrast results partly but not entirely from the greater prevalence of consumer-goods industries in the sheltered sector of US manufacturing. Our analysis of US data also demonstrates a number of connections between the pattern of comparative advantage and the structures of markets.

We also extend a study of market structure and profitability in UK manufacturing industries in order to disentangle various hypotheses about the effect of export opportunities on market structure and performance. We find some support for three hypotheses:

(i) export opportunities relax the constraint of market size on the scale of manufacturing establishments;

(ii) UK exports seem to lean toward differentiated consumer goods that yield rents to their sellers;

(iii) in highly concentrated industries, export opportunities may reduce the effectiveness with which oligopolistic interdependence is recognized and exploited.

---

16. As a qualification, $CEXP$ is affected by multicollinearity although $UEXP$ is not.

References

Bain, J. S., *International Differences in Industrial Structure*. New Haven: Yale University Press, 1966.

Baldwin, R. E., Determinants of the Commodity Structure of US Trade, *American Economic Review*, 61, 126–146, 1971.

Buzzell, R. D., B. T. Gale, and R. G. M. Sultan, Market Share – A Key to Profitability, *Harvard Business Review*, 53, 97–107, 1975.

Caves, R. E., *International Trade, International Investment, and Imperfect Markets*, Special Papers in International Economics, No. 10. Princeton: International Finance Section, Princeton University, 1974.

Caves, R. E., J. Khalilzadeh-Shirazi, and M. E. Porter, Scale Economies in Statistical Analyses of Market Power, *Review of Economics and Statistics*, 57, 133–140, 1975.

Caves, R. E., and M. E. Porter, Market Structure, Oligopoly, and the Stability of Market Shares, Harvard Institute of Economic Research, Discussion Paper No. 478, 1976.

Caves, R. E., and M. Uekusa, *Industrial Organization in Japan*. Washington: Brookings Institution, 1976.

Eastman, H. C., and S. Stykolt, *The Tariff and Competition in Canada*. Toronto: Macmillan, 1967.

Esposito, F. F., and L. Esposito, Excess Capacity and Market Structure, *Review of Economics and Statistics*, 56, 188–194, 1974.

Esposito, L., and F. F. Esposito, Foreign Competition and Domestic Industry Profitability, *Review of Economics and Statistics*, 53, 343–353, 1971.

Grubel, H. G., Intra-Industry Specialization and the Pattern of Trade, *Canadian Journal of Economics and Political Science*, 33, 374–388, 1967.

Gruber, H., D. Mehta, and R. Vernon, The R&D Factor in International Trade and International Investment of United States Industries, *Journal of Political Economy*, 75, 20–37, 1967.

Khalilzadeh-Shirazi, J., Market Structure and Price-Cost Margins in United Kingdom Manufacturing Industries, *Review of Economics and Statistics*, 56, 67–76, 1974.

Kravis, I. B., 'Availability' and Other Influences on the Commodity Composition of Trade, *Journal of Political Economy*, 64, 143–155, 1956.

Pagoulatos, E., and R. Sorenson, Domestic Market Structure and International Trade: An Empirical Analysis, *Quarterly Review of Economics and Business*, 16, 45–60, 1967a.

Pagoulatos, E., and R. Sorenson, International Trade, International Investment and Industrial Profitability of US Manufacturing, *Southern Economic Journal*, 42, 1976b.

Porter, M. E., *Interbrand Choice, Strategy, and Bilateral Market Power*. Cambridge: Harvard University Press, 1976.

Pryor, F. L., An International Comparison of Concentration Ratios, *Review of Economics and Statistics*, 54, 130–140, 1972.

Saving, T. R., Estimation of Optimum Size of Plant by the Survivor Technique, *Quarterly Journal of Economics*, 75, 569–607, 1961.

Scherer, F. M., *et al.*, *The Economics of Multi-Plant Operation: An International Comparisons Study*. Cambridge: Harvard University Press, 1975.

White, L. J., Industrial Organization and International Trade: Some Theoretical Considerations, *American Economic Review*, 64, 1013–1020, 1974.

VIII. LARGE INDUSTRIAL FIRMS OF THE ATLANTIC COMMUNITY: PRODUCTION METHODS, ASSET FINANCE, PROFITABILITY, AND GROWTH

William James Adams

1. Introduction

A firm's nationality has long been considered a determinant of its conduct and performance. The ethos of French businessmen has been maligned since the beginning of this century.[1] So has the vigour of British entrepreneurs.[2] More recently, American firms have been held up as models for the rest of the world.[3] They are said to develop technology more actively, produce goods more cheaply, market goods more compellingly, finance a greater proportion of assets internally, respond to market forces more rationally, and remunerate share-holders more munificently than do their rivals abroad.

Several European governments evidently believe these allegations. Lamenting the poverty of domestic entrepreneurial genes, they have sought to insure the survival of native enterprise in world markets via massive industrial re-organization at home.[4]

Not everyone takes for granted these cross-national differences in corporate quality. Caves (1971) has argued that direct foreign investment dampens international disparities in an industry's profitability. If the barriers to resource mobility across industries exceed their counterparts across countries, then rates of return might vary more among industries than among countries. So might other corporate characteristics.

Now that companies on both sides of the Atlantic publish detailed financial accounts, it is possible to test some of these hypotheses empirically. In this

---

1. See the essays by Christopher, Landes, and Sawyer in Earle (1951). See also Kindleberger (1964).
2. See Caves (1968).
3. The *locus classicus* is Servan-Schreiber (1967). For a quantitative analysis, see *Compagnie Lambert pour l'Industrie et la Finance* (1967, 1968).
4. See McArthur and Scott (1969), the European Economic Community (1970), Nême and Nême (1970), and Warnecke and Suleiman (1975).

chapter I shall deal with three questions current in the comparative business literature. First, do firms comparable in product mix employ the same production methods in all developed countries? Second, do firms in the same line of business achieve the same profitability in all developed countries? Finally, do firms in some countries lack internal investment funds to such an extent that company growth is impeded?

The data employed to answer these questions are described in Section 2, the statistical results are reported in Sections 3 and 4, and conclusions are presented in Section 5.

2. The data

The variables

Differences among firms in production methods can be analyzed in terms of factor proportions, factor productivities, or factor cost.[5] I shall employ each of these indicators here. Factor proportions are measured by the amount of tangible fixed assets per employee (K/E).[6] Factor productivities are measured by the value of output per dollar of tangible fixed assets (PQ/K), and the value of output per employee (PQ/E).[7] Unit labour cost is represented by total labour compensation as a percentage of output value (LC/PQ).[8]

Profitability could be measured as book income per shareholder equity $(BKPRFT)$ if all firms employed the same accounting procedures.[9] To the extent

5. An alternative approach consists of estimating the production function associated with a particular line of business and then evaluating the extent to which parameters differ in value across countries. Given the data available, such a procedure would convey an erroneous sense of precision. See Pryor (1972).

6. Table 1 presents an exact definition of each variable. Included in tangible fixed assets is the value of tools and dies used in production. Note that the units in which K/E is expressed are thousands of dollars per employee. The figures reported for most non-American companies thus had to be converted into dollars. I employed the average rate of certified noon buying in New York, for cable transfers prevailing during the calendar year of a company's report. (The rates were taken from the *Federal Reserve Bulletin*, December, 1975, page A75.) Utilization of such rates could bias international comparisons such as those made in this paper because international differences in purchasing power are not taken into account. The direction of bias depends on the ways in which each sample company is affected by foreign trade and investment. Fortunately, most variables employed in this study are pure numbers, so that exchange rates never had to be applied to the raw data.

7. By value of output is meant sales revenue plus inventory increase. To the extent that sample firms differ in terms of production stage or vertical integration, value added would be preferable to output value.

8. Total labour compensation includes social contributions and bonuses as well as wages.

9. Actually, even this condition does not suffice to guarantee international comparability. See Adams (1976).

that firms differ in depreciation and reserve allocation methods on the basis of their nationality, however, book profitability may not provide unbiased estimates of cross-country differentials in the rate of return.[10] For this reason, I gathered data on cash flow as well as book profitability (CFPRFT). Cash flow profitability reflects the amount of total revenue left inside the firm once all external claims have been paid.

To analyze the quantitative impact of cross-national variations in the treatment of cash flow, I constructed three additional profitability variables. The first two – depreciation per shareholder equity (DE/EQ) and other reserve allocations per shareholder equity (AP/EQ) – simply decompose the difference between cash flow and book profitability into two categories. The third – depreciation per tangible fixed assets (DE/K) – represents the rate at which a firms depreciates its capital stock. The more conservative is the firm's accountant of the more obliging is its tax authority, the higher this rate is likely to be.

The manner in which a company chooses to finance its assets is monitored in terms of the amount available for internal finance, the proportion of assets actually financed via equity, and the proportion of assets actually financed via debt. Cash flow per tangible fixed assets (CF/K) measures the availability of internal funds, shareholder equity per total assets (EQ/TA) registers actual recourse to internal funds,[11] and financial debt per total assets (FL/TA) reflects actual employment of loan capital.[12]

The alleged virtue of internal finance is that it facilitates growth of the capital stock.[13] To measure such growth, I collected data on annual rates of change in the value of a firm's tangible fixed assets ($\dot{K}/K$). To explore the more general argument that internal finance promotes growth of the firm, I also collected data on annual rates of change in a firm's sales revenue ($\dot{S}/S$).

International differences in production methods or asset finance do not constitute *per se* evidence that entrepreneurship is deficient somewhere in the world. Structural and behavioural differences among firms could be caused by

10. Arthur Andersen (1974) suggests that accounting practices do vary systematically across countries.
11. Shareholder equity includes paid-in preference capital and provisions, as well as paid-in ordinary capital and reserves. Ideally, equity finance would be decomposed into finance from new subscriptions and finance from reinvested funds. The data at my disposal do not permit such a distinction.
12. Financial debt includes short- as well as long-term loans not originating from trade, government, or labour sources.
13. In a world endowed with perfect capital markets, Modigliani and Miller (1958) have demonstrated the logical impossibility of such an effect. However, real capital markets, especially in Europe, fail to allocate investible funds on a marginal efficiency basis (McArthur and Scott, 1969; Hodgman, 1974). Therefore, access to internal funds *could* permit expanded investment opportunities.

corresponding differences in market opportunities. As a result, I obtained information on the wage and interest rates facing each firm. As a measure of the former, I used total labour compensation per employee (LC/E). As a measure of the latter, I used financial cost per financial debt (FC/FL).[14] The ratio of these two variables represents relative factor prices (w/r).

Corporate production methods, profitability, and growth, are all sensitive to the business cycle. If the timing of business cycles varies among countries, then observations based on a single year may not reflect accurately the structural impact of nationality. For this reason, I gathered four years of financial data for each firm. The variables described above are thus temporal mean values of four years of company experience.[15] Since the company reports current at the time this project began covered the year 1974, 1971 through 1974 became the sample period.

The sample

In order to test the hypotheses set forth in Section 1, sample firms must be heterogeneous in both nationality and line of business. I had intended to represent (in addition to the United States) all developed countries which placed at least five firms on the 1974 *Fortune* list of large corporations outside the United States. Twelve countries qualified: Belgium (BG), Canada (CN), France (FR), Germany (GY), Italy (IY), Japan (JP), the Netherlands (NE), Spain (SP), Sweden (SW), Switzerland (CH), the United Kingdom (UK), and the United States (US).[16] Of these, Japan, Spain, and Switzerland had to be excluded due to deficiencies in their company financial data.

In choosing among lines of business, I had intended to represent all industries which placed at least ten firms among the top 100 on *Fortune*'s 1974 list of large corporations outside the United States. Five lines of business qualified: motor vehicles (AUTO), chemicals (CHEM), electrical and electronic equipment (ELEC), iron and steel (FERR), and petroleum (PETR).[17] Unfortunately, the

---

14. Three defects in this interest rate variable should be noted: It presumes that firms never issue obligations at a discount; it focuses on past rather than future interest rates; and it measures the nominal, as opposed to the real, price of capital.

15. Unfortunately, financial data covering all years could not be obtained for all companies. In 84 of 96 cases, the variables do constitute averages taken over all four sample years. In eight cases, the variables constitute averages taken over three of the four sample years. In three of the remaining five cases, the 'averages' relate to a single year of observation.

16. The only other country to place five or more firms on the *Fortune* list was Australia.

17. A firm is considered to be in a particular line of business if industries classified within that line account for at least two-thirds of consolidated firm sales. Seventy-four of the 100 largest industrial

Table 1. Variable list.

	Label	Definition	Proxy for
1.	K/E	tangible fixed assets per employee ($ thousands)	factor proportions
2.	PQ/K	value of output per dollar of tangible fixed assets	capital productivity
3.	PQ/E	value of output per employee ($ thousands)	labour productivity
4.	LC/PQ	labour compensation per $ 100 of output value	unit labour cost
5.	LC/E	compensation per employee ($ thousands)	wage rate
6.	FC/FL	financial expense per $ 100 of financial debt	interest rate
7.	w/r	(LC/E)/(FC/FL)	relative factor prices
8.	DE/EQ	depreciation on tangible fixed assets per $ 100 of shareholder equity	role of depreciation in cash flow profitability
9.	AP/EQ	cash flow revenue other than profits and depreciation on tangible fixed assets per $ 100 of shareholder equity	role of appropriations in cash flow profitability
10.	BKPRFT	book profits per $ 100 of shareholder equity	book profitability
11.	CFPRFT	cash flow per $ 100 of shareholder equity	cash flow profitability
12.	DE/K	depreciation charged per $ 100 of tangible fixed assets	depreciation rate
13.	EQ/TA	shareholder equity per $ 100 of total assets	equity as a source of finance
14.	FL/TA	financial debt per $ 100 of total assets	financial debt as a source of finance
15.	CF/K	cash flow per $ 100 of tangible fixed assets	internal funds available for capital investment
16.	$\dot{S}/S$	percentage increase in sales over previous year	growth rate of output
17.	$\dot{K}/K$	percentage increase in tangible fixed assets over previous year	growth rate of capital stock

last of these had to be omitted due to special problems associated with interpretation of oil company financial accounts.[18]

Three criteria were employed to select the firms with which to populate each country-business cell: listing in one of the *Fortune* directories for 1974, consolidated sales in excess of $ 500 million during 1973, and freedom for control by another manufacturing corporation.[19] The sales criterion excludes small and medium-sized firms from the sample. Such exclusion prevents confusion of nationality and scale effects on other corporate characteristics. The independence criterion prevents inclusion of subsidiary companies in the sample. Because parental decisions govern their behaviour, subsidiaries do not offer independent observations of corporate structure and performance.

Ninety-six firms satisfy all selection criteria. Their names appear in the appendix. The number of them inhabiting each country-business cell is reported in Table 2.

Table 2. Number of sample firms per geographic area and type of business.

Area	Auto	Chem	Elec	Ferr	Total
N.AMER	6	13	14	13	46
US	6	13	14	11	44
CN	0	0	0	2	2
EUROP	11	13	13	13	50
EEC6	8	10	6	10	34
FR	2	2	2	1	7
GY	4	3	3	6	16
IY	2	2	0	1	5
NE	0	2	1	1	4
BG	0	1	0	1	2
EFTA	3	3	7	3	16
UK	1	3	4	2	10
SW	2	0	3	1	6
Total	17	26	27	26	96

firms outside the United States specialize in one of these five lines of business. The largest number of firms among the top 100 representing any other line of business was four (food, nonferrous metals, and mining).

18. For the purpose of determining each sample firm's line of business according to the criterion established in note 17, the following industry definitions were employed: automobiles ISIC 2843; chemicals, ISIC 351 and 352 (excluding 3529); electrical equipment, ISIC 383 (excluding 3839); and steel, ISIC 3710.

19. A firm is considered free from the control of manufacturing corporations if less than 10 per cent of its equity is owned by them. Most sample firms are free from control by financial corporations as well.

3. Statistical results

Estimation procedure

Tables 3 and 4 present the mean value of each variable among firms grouped by line of business and by nationality. Significance[20] of the business and country groupings is best assessed within the framework of Equation 1.[21] The reason is simple. Coefficients a_2 through a_{12} pertain

$$Y = a_1 + a_2\text{CHEM} + a_3\text{ELEC} + a_4\text{FERR} + a_5\text{EUROP} +$$
$$+ a_6\text{EEC6} + a_7\text{CN} + a_8\text{FR} + a_9\text{IY} + a_{10}\text{NE} +$$
$$+ a_{11}\text{BG} + a_{12}\text{SW} + e \qquad (1)$$

to variables which assume a value of 1 if the firm belongs to the relevant group, 0 otherwise. Therefore, an F-test on the hypothesis that $a_2 = a_3 = a_4 = 0$ reveals whether or not firms differ on the basis of business line; a t-test on the hypothesis

Table 3. Variable means by line of business.

Variable	Auto	Chem	Elec	Ferr	All
K/E	7.9	21.0	4.4	21.4	13.9
PQ/K	5.1	2.1	6.2	2.3	3.8
PQ/E	37.7	41.7	24.7	38.6	35.1
LC/PQ	27.8	25.7	34.1	29.4	28.7
LC/E	9.6	10.6	9.1	11.2	10.3
FC/FL	9.3	8.1	9.0	8.2	8.6
w/r	1.2	1.5	1.3	1.5	1.4
DE/EQ	17.9	15.7	9.9	15.2	14.3
AP/EQ	3.9	3.8	3.0	2.2	3.2
BKPRFT	3.7	7.3	9.7	5.6	6.9
CFPRFT	25.5	26.7	22.6	23.0	24.4
DE/K	18.6	13.2	17.3	10.0	14.4
EQ/TA	37.4	43.9	44.2	40.7	42.0
FL/TA	24.0	29.9	20.5	28.6	25.9
CF/K	30.1	24.4	44.4	16.9	29.0
Ṡ/S	12.8	20.0	15.1	21.6	17.8
K̇/K	9.1	7.1	11.6	6.2	8.5

20. Whenever this term appears, its statistical connotation should be inferred.
21. One-way analysis of variance in the sample taken as a whole would fail to control for the other explanatory factors. One-way analysis of variance within particular sample subsets is inefficient statistically.

Table 4. Variable means by geographic area.

Area	K/E	PQ/K	PQ/E	LC/PQ	LC/E	FC/FL	w/r	DE/EQ	AP/EQ	BKPRFT	CFPRFT	DE/K	EQ/TA	FL/TA	CF/K	Ś/S	K̇/K
All	13.9	3.8	35.1	28.7	10.3	8.6	1.4	14.3	3.2	6.9	24.4	14.4	42.0	25.9	29.0	17.8	8.5
N.AMER	16.8	4.0	41.9	30.5	12.6	7.5	1.9	9.6	0.5	10.7	20.8	13.3	52.6	21.9	30./	18.2	7.5
US	15.8	4.1	41.8	30.5	12.6	7.5	1.9	9.7	0.5	10.6	20.8	13.6	52.4	22.2	31.3	18.1	7.5
CN	38.4	1.2	45.8	32.1	13.1	7.3	1.9	7.9	1.5	12.5	21.9	6.7	56.6	14.5	19.0	18.8	7.0
EUROP	10.9	3.7	28.1	27.1	7.9	9.6	0.9	18.7	5.6	3.4	27.6	15.5	32.3	29.5	27.3	17.5	9.4
EEC6	12.9	3.4	31.3	27.2	8.2	9.9	0.9	23.2	5.8	1.2	30.2	16.7	28.1	32.2	22.8	16.1	7.0
FR	8.6	4.1	29.7	23.5	8.4	13.0	0.6	22.9	5.4	6.7	35.0	17.7	24.7	31.1	27.5	20.1	13.1
GY	10.2	4.1	31.9	28.2	8.4	9.5	1.0	25.1	2.4	3.4	31.0	18.9	27.7	30.6	24.3	11.0	5.4
IY	28.2	2.1	31.5	27.1	7.1	6.6	1.3	28.1	20.3	−20.6	27.8	13.6	20.1	47.0	13.7	21.4	10.3
NE	15.1	2.3	30.3	27.8	8.1	11.3	0.8	14.6	2.4	9.0	26.0	11.6	36.1	22.0	21.1	21.6	3.9
BG	17.9	1.9	33.4	26.9	8.8	9.8	1.0	13.9	3.9	3.4	21.2	13.8	46.8	32.7	21.2	20.5	1.9
EFTA	6.9	4.2	21.6	26.4	7.0	8.9	0.8	9.0	5.2	7.9	22.1	13.0	41.1	23.8	36.8	20.1	14.1
UK	6.0	3.9	16.2	27.4	5.5	8.2	0.7	9.6	4.0	9.2	22.8	12.5	41.4	26.4	36.4	17.1	9.4
SW	8.2	4.6	29.5	25.7	8.2	10.1	0.9	7.9	7.2	5.8	21.0	13.8	40.5	19.5	37.4	25.2	22.0

Variable

Table 5*. Statistical significance statistics associated with estimation of equation 1.

Dependent variable (Y)	Regression		Variance among business		$\hat{a}_5$ EUROP		$\hat{a}_6$ EEC6		Variance within EEC6		$\hat{a}_{12}$ SW		$\hat{a}_7$ CN	
	N	R^2	F	s.s.	t	s.s.	t	s.s.	F	s.s.	t	s.s.	t	s.s.
1. K/E	91	66	31.1	***	-3.1	**	0.6		5.5	***	1.7		3.0	**
2. PQ/K	96	67	48.2	***	-0.8		0.9		1.5		-0.6		-1.3	
3. PQ/E	91	65	19.0	***	-7.9	***	3.6	***	0.1		3.3	**	0.1	
4. LC/PQ	70	32	5.6	**	-0.7		-0.2		0.4		-1.0		0.2	
5. LC/E	66	75	8.1	***	-7.6	***	2.9	**	0.8		2.4	*	-0.4	
6. FC/FL	94	44	1.5		0.9		1.5		7.1	***	1.5		0.1	
7. w/r	66	72	2.8		-6.0	***	1.4		1.5		1.2		-0.3	
8. DE/EQ	96	69	3.0	*	0.1		7.0	***	5.7	***	-0.5		-0.7	
9. AP/EQ	96	48	0.6		1.9		-0.5		12.5	***	1.3		0.5	
10. BKPRFT	96	62	1.0		-0.8		-2.1	*	20.2	***	-1.0		0.8	
11. CFPRFT	96	27	1.0		0.6		2.4	*	1.5		-0.2		0.4	
12. DE/K	96	49	16.5	***	-0.9		3.9	***	2.7	*	-0.1		-0.6	
13. EQ/TA	96	67	0.8		-3.6	***	-3.6	***	4.3	**	-0.1		1.0	
14. FL/TA	96	45	5.5	**	1.5		1.0		5.2	***	-0.1		-1.7	
15. CF/K	96	50	20.3	***	0.8		-1.5		0.7		-0.4		0.1	
16. S/S	93	43	10.3	***	-0.3		-2.4	*	3.9	**	3.1	**	-0.8	
17. K/K	93	29	1.3		0.6		-1.1		1.5		3.2	**	0.2	

* The initials 's.s.' stand for statistical significance. One, two, and three stars denote statistical significance at the 0.05, 0.01, and 0.001 levels. All t-tests are two-tailed.

Table 6*. Coefficient estimates for equation 1.

Dependent variable	Constant $\hat{a}_1$	CHEM $\hat{a}_2$	ELEC $\hat{a}_3$	FERR $\hat{a}_4$	EUROP $\hat{a}_5$	EEC6 $\hat{a}_6$	CN $\hat{a}_7$	FR $\hat{a}_8$	IY $\hat{a}_9$	NE $\hat{a}_{10}$	BG $\hat{a}_{11}$	SW $\hat{a}_{12}$
1. K/E	8.5 (2.1)	14.9 (2.5)	-1.6 (2.4)	13.7 (2.4)	-8.2 (2.6)	1.8 (3.1)	16.2 (5.3)	2.2 (3.5)	21.6 (4.6)	2.5 (4.1)	1.5 (5.4)	6.4 (3.8)
2. PQ/K	5.4 (0.4)	-3.0 (0.5)	1.0 (0.4)	-2.8 (0.5)	-0.4 (0.5)	0.5 (0.6)	-1.4 (1.0)	-0.5 (0.6)	-1.6 (0.7)	-1.3 (0.8)	-0.7 (1.1)	-0.4 (0.7)
3. PQ/E	45.7 (2.4)	2.0 (2.9)	-13.9 (2.7)	-0.3 (2.7)	-23.6 (3.0)	12.3 (3.5)	0.4 (6.1)	-0.3 (4.0)	-2.8 (5.3)	-1.5 (4.6)	-1.8 (6.2)	14.5 (4.3)
4. LC/PQ	30.6 (1.7)	-3.7 (2.0)	4.7 (2.3)	0.2 (1.9)	-2.1 (3.3)	-0.6 (3.4)	1.2 (5.5)	-3.5 (3.1)	0.6 (2.8)	0.4 (3.1)	0.6 (4.1)	-4.1 (4.1)
5. LC/E	13.4 (0.6)	-1.1 (0.7)	-2.7 (0.7)	0.3 (0.6)	-7.7 (1.0)	3.1 (1.1)	-0.6 (1.7)	-0.5 (1.1)	-1.8 (1.1)	0.4 (1.0)	0.4 (1.3)	3.0 (1.3)
6. FC/FL	8.1 (0.6)	-1.0 (0.7)	-0.0 (0.7)	-0.9 (0.7)	0.6 (0.7)	1.3 (0.8)	0.1 (1.5)	3.5 (1.0)	-2.8 (1.1)	2.0 (1.2)	0.7 (1.6)	1.6 (1.1)
7. w/r	1.9 (0.1)	-0.1 (0.1)	-0.3 (0.2)	0.1 (0.1)	-1.3 (0.2)	0.3 (0.2)	-0.1 (0.4)	-0.4 (0.2)	0.3 (0.2)	-0.1 (0.2)	0.0 (0.3)	0.3 (0.3)
8. DE/EQ	10.9 (1.5)	0.2 (1.7)	-3.7 (1.7)	-0.4 (1.7)	0.2 (1.8)	14.8 (2.1)	-2.7 (3.9)	-2.0 (2.4)	2.1 (2.7)	-10.4 (2.9)	-11.9 (3.9)	-1.3 (2.7)
9. AP/EQ	-0.6 (1.4)	1.5 (1.6)	1.7 (1.6)	0.4 (1.6)	3.4 (1.8)	-1.1 (2.1)	1.7 (3.8)	2.8 (2.3)	18.0 (2.6)	-0.5 (2.9)	1.3 (3.8)	3.5 (2.7)
10. BKPRFT	10.0 (1.7)	1.3 (1.9)	1.5 (1.9)	-1.2 (1.9)	-1.6 (2.1)	-5.0 (2.4)	3.6 (4.4)	2.8 (2.7)	-24.3 (3.1)	4.9 (3.4)	-0.0 (4.5)	-3.2 (3.1)
11. CFPRFT	20.4 (2.5)	3.0 (2.9)	-0.6 (2.9)	-1.2 (2.9)	2.0 (3.1)	8.6 (3.7)	2.7 (6.7)	3.5 (4.1)	-4.2 (4.6)	-6.0 (5.1)	-10.7 (6.8)	-0.9 (4.7)
12. DE/K	17.1 (1.3)	-4.8 (1.5)	-0.2 (1.5)	-8.3 (1.5)	-1.5 (1.6)	7.3 (1.9)	-2.1 (3.4)	-2.7 (2.1)	-5.8 (2.4)	-6.9 (2.6)	-2.7 (3.5)	-0.3 (2.4)
13. EQ/TA	52.2 (2.5)	1.9 (2.8)	0.3 (2.8)	-1.9 (2.9)	-11.1 (3.1)	-13.1 (3.6)	6.3 (6.6)	-3.7 (4.0)	-8.3 (4.6)	7.5 (5.0)	18.7 (6.7)	-0.4 (4.6)
14. FL/TA	17.7 (2.5)	8.0 (2.8)	0.5 (2.8)	8.0 (2.9)	4.5 (3.1)	3.8 (3.6)	-11.2 (6.6)	1.5 (4.0)	16.2 (4.6)	10.1 (5.0)	-1.3 (6.7)	-4.4 (4.4)
15. CF/K	33.1 (3.4)	-6.4 (3.9)	11.8 (3.9)	-14.7 (4.0)	3.4 (4.3)	-7.7 (5.0)	0.6 (9.1)	-0.8 (5.6)	-9.6 (6.3)	-3.8 (6.9)	2.9 (9.2)	-2.5 (6.4)
16. S/S	13.0 (1.9)	7.4 (2.2)	1.7 (2.1)	9.7 (2.2)	-0.7 (2.2)	-6.3 (2.6)	-3.9 (4.7)	8.5 (3.3)	10.5 (3.3)	9.0 (3.6)	6.0 (4.8)	10.4 (3.3)
17. K̇/K	7.1 (2.2)	-0.2 (2.5)	2.6 (2.5)	-1.4 (2.5)	1.6 (2.6)	-3.2 (3.0)	1.3 (5.5)	7.0 (3.9)	5.2 (3.8)	-1.7 (4.2)	-2.7 (5.6)	12.2 (3.8)

* Standard errors appear in parentheses under coefficient estimates.

that $a_5 = 0$ determines whether or not European firms differ from North American firms; a t-test on the hypothesis that $a_6 = 0$ discloses whether or not firms from the original EEC countries[22] differ from their EFTA counterparts; a t-test on the hypothesis that $a_7 = 0$ tells whether or not Canadian firms resemble American firms; an F-test on the hypothesis that $a_8 = a_9 = a_{10} = a_{11} = 0$ reveals whether or not Common Market firms differ one from another on the basis of nationality; and a t-test on the hypothesis that $a_{12} = 0$ discloses whether or not Swedish firms resemble their EFTA cousins in Britain.

I estimated Equation 1 with each Table 1 variable dependent. The statistical tests associated with each regression are reported in Table 5. The coefficient estimates can be found in Table 6. Let us examine in turn the effects of business line, continent of domicile,[23] trading bloc of domicile, and nationality *per se*.

Effects of business line

Since production functions differ among businesses, so well might production methods. According to Table 5, the value of each production indicator differs significantly among lines of business. Table 6 reveals that after controlling for their nationality, chemical and ferrous firms deploy substantially more capital per employee than do automotive and electrical firms. As a result, capital productivity is especially low in the chemical and ferrous lines, while labour productivity is especially low in the electrical line. Unit labour cost differs less significantly among businesses than do factor proportions or productivities. The reason is that in the electrical business, low wage rates partly compensate for low labour productivity. Nevertheless, unit labour cost is especially high in electrical firms and especially low in chemical firms.

Unlike production methods, factor prices do not appear to vary among business lines. Neither interest rates nor relative factor prices differ significantly among business lines once corporate nationality is taken into account. Only in the case of labour compensation for employee does one line of business differ significantly from the rest. The low value of LC/E associated with electrical firms can be attributed to low labour productivity in them.

Type of business does not seem to affect corporate profitability, either. After

---

22. Britain spent the first two sample years affiliated with the EFTA and the second two associated with the EEC. For the purposes of this study, I have assigned Britain to the Free Trade Association. Hence the term 'original'.

23. Wherever possible, I have used consolidated financial accounts. The more has a firm engaged in direct foreign investment, the more does any impact of nationality reflect the locus of ownership rather than operations. Hence the term 'domicile'.

controlling for nationality, both book and cash flow rates of return tend to equality across business lines. Depreciation rates differ significantly among businesses because capital vintages and composition vary in that way. The low rate of depreciation observed among ferrous firms can be attributed to the age of capital they employ. The high rate of depreciation observed among automotive firms could reflect the rapid obsolescence of model-specific tools and dies.

The effects of business line on company finance are difficult to summarize. Although the amount of internal funds available for investment differs dramatically among business lines, actual recourse to equity finance does not. On the other hand, chemical and ferrous firms employ significantly more debt per dollar of assets than do their automotive and electrical counterparts. Thus line of business affects more the ratio of financial to commercial liabilities than the ratio of total liabilities to equity.

Although financial debt differs in importance among business lines, the rate of capital formation does not. This similarity is somewhat surprising since output is growing significantly faster among chemical and ferrous than among other sample firms. Automotive firms grew slowly during this period because consumers shied away from vehicle purchases after the gasoline price increases of 1973.

Europe versus North America

North American and European firms are supposed to behave and perform differently. In terms of production methods, Table 5 suggests that differences do exist. The capital and the output per worker associated with North American firms exceed the capital and the output per worker associated with European firms. In each case, the disparity is enormous. The difference of $ 8,200 in capital per employee amounts to 59 per cent of the sample mean value of K/E. The difference of $ 23,600 in output per employee corresponds to 67 per cent of the sample mean value of PQ/E. On the other hand, neither capital productivity nor unit labour cost differs significantly between the Old and New Worlds.

A plausible explanation of factor proportion and labour productivity differences between continents may lie in the pattern of factor prices. The wage rate associated with North American firms exceeds that associated with European firms. So does the ratio of wage rate to interest rate.

The extent of transatlantic differences among companies subsides once we examine the profitability variables. Neither book nor cash flow rates of return differ significantly between continents. Nor do the importance of depreciation and appropriations in cash flow, or the rate at which tangible fixed assets are depreciated. It is difficult to conceive how data could show more conclusively that large European firms taken as a group are no less profitable than are their North American rivals.

The similarity of firms on the two continents hardly fades when we turn to growth and its alleged impediments. The amount of internal funds available for investment does not differ between Old and New Worlds. Neither does the proportion of assets paid for with debt. Equity does finance a smaller proportion of assets in Europe than in North America, and the difference exceeds 25 per cent of the sample mean value of EQ/TA. Although North Americans employ equity finance to a significantly greater extent, their rates of capital formation and output growth do not differ significantly from those of Europeans.

The EEC versus the EFTA

The general similarity of North American and European firms does not imply that nationality fails to affect a corporation. European firms may differ one from another on the basis of trading bloc affiliation. Table 5 tells the facts of the matter.

In terms of production methods, the European trading blocs differ only in labour productivity. Affiliation with the original EEC is associated with $ 12,300 more output per employee than is affiliation with the original EFTA. This difference exceeds 33 per cent of the sample mean value of PQ/E. Nevertheless, unit labour cost does not vary significantly between the two blocs. Neither do factor proportions or capital productivity.

Labour remuneration, as well as labour productivity, is greater in the EEC than in the EFTA. However, both the rate of interest and relative factor prices appear invariant between the two European groups.

Although EEC firms differ significantly from EFTA firms in profitability, the direction of disparity is ambiguous. Measured in book terms, the rate of return associated with Common Market affiliation is 5 percentage points below that associated with Free Trade Association affiliation. This difference represents 72 per cent of the sample mean value of BKPRFT. Measured in cash flow terms, however, Common Market affiliation is associated with a profitability rate 8.6 percentage points above that associated with Free Trade Association affiliation. This difference constitutes 36 per cent of the sample mean value of CFPRFT.

The difficulty in ranking the two trading blocs in terms of profitability stems from the differences between them in depreciation practices. The rate of depreciation is significantly higher in the original EEC than it is in the original EFTA. So is the amount of depreciation charged per dollar of equity. In fact, the difference bloc affiliation makes in DE/EQ (14.8 percentage points) exceeds the sample mean value of that variable (14.3)! No wonder the ranking of the two blocs reverses once cash flow items other than profit are taken into account.

Turning to asset finance, the availability of internal funds for investment does not differ significantly between EEC and EFTA firms. Neither does the proportion of assets financed via debt. However, equity finances a significantly lower proportion of assets in the Common Market than it does in the Free Trade Association. The difference of 13 percentage points constitutes 31 per cent of the sample mean value of EQ/TA.

There is some evidence that Common Market firms grow less rapidly than do EFTA firms. Measured in terms of sales, the difference is significant, and its magnitude (6.3 percentage points) represents over 33 per cent of the sample mean value of $\dot{S}/S$. Measured in terms of tangible fixed assets, the difference is not significant.

Effects of nationality per se

If market prices and credit availability are still determined nationally, or if culture conditions entrepreneurship, then corporate anatomy might vary among individual countries. Equation 1 permits us to examine the extent to which nationality explains company differences within the Common Market, within the Free Trade Association, and within North America.

Within the Common Market, the variables most sensitive to nationality are the components of cash flow profitability. Italian firms report especially low book profitability and especially high appropriations. Benelux firms report especially low depreciation per dollar of equity. In the Dutch case, this is due to unusually low rates of capital depreciation.

Common Market firms also differ on the basis of nationality in terms of asset finance. Belgian firms rely especially heavily on equity while Italian firms resort . unusually frequently to debt. Dutch firms employ little debt relative to their Community rivals.

Production methods and rates of growth appear less uniformly heterogeneous across Common Market countries. Capital per employee is relatively high in Italy. Interest rates are especially low in Italy[24] and especially high in France.[25]

24. Low Italian interest rates could explain the high capital intensity of Italian production. Daniel Fusfeld suggests another explanation: physical capital is used extensively relative to labour in countries where human capital per employee is low. The Fusfeld hypothesis is not consistent with the difference observed between North American and European factor proportions.
25. The high rate of interest paid by French firms is noteworthy in the light of Hodgman's allegation (1974) that French monetary authorities use the price system insufficiently to curb excess demand for

French, Italian, and Dutch firms seem to be expanding sales more rapidly than are their German and Belgian counterparts. In all other respects, Common Market firms fail to differ on the basis of nationality.

These findings suggest that the Community has failed to develop a common capital market, since interest rates and asset finance proceed differently by country. They also suggest that accounting methods vary across Common Market countries since the components of cash flow but not their sum vary in that way.

Within the European Free Trade Association, nationality affects labour productivity, labour remuneration, and company growth. After controlling for business line, the typical employee of a Swedish firm generates $ 14,500 more in output than does his counterpart in a British firm. This difference represents 41 per cent of the sample mean value of PQ/E. Accordingly, perhaps, wage rates in Sweden exceed those in Britain. So do company growth rates, whether measured in terms of capital stock or in terms of sales. The difference associated with capital growth is the more pronounced. At 12.2 percentage points, the margin of Swedish superiority exceeds the sample mean value of $\dot{K}/K$.

Within North America, nationality affects only the capital intensity of production. Canadian firms provide their employees with more capital than do American firms. In all other respects, Canadian firms are carbon copies of their neighbours to the south.

4. Implications

According to the evidence presented in Section 3, nationality affects corporate characteristics in several important respects. Should the nationality effect be attributed to cross-country variance in market opportunities, or to corresponding variance in entrepreneurial quality? The purpose of this section is to determine the relative plausibility of these hypotheses.

The market opportunities hypothesis generates the following predictions:

1. Nationality would not influence factor proportions if relative factor prices were controlled.
2. Nationality would not influence labour productivity if factor proportions were controlled.

credit. Serious evaluation of Hodgman's hypothesis requires examination of interest rate changes over the business cycle. Nevertheless, to the extent that excess credit demand is chronic in France, average rates of interest over time can provide a preliminary examination of his position. The findings presented here do not support Hodgman's hypothesis.

3. Nationality would not influence wage rates if labour productivity were controlled.
4. Nationality would not influence the pattern of asset finance if the relative cost of finance sources were controlled.

The entrepreneurial quality hypothesis would predict the opposite in each case. In addition, it suggests (1) that differences among countries in factor proportions and productivities should be reflected in corresponding differences in corporate profitability, and (2) that differences among countries in the pattern of asset finance should be reflected in corresponding differences in corporate growth.

The predictions of each theory can be evaluated within the framework of Equation 2. For example, consider the proposition that nationality

$$Y = a_1 + a_2\text{CHEM} + a_3\text{ELEC} + a_4\text{FERR} + a_5\text{EUROP} +$$
$$+ a_6\text{EEC6} + a_7\text{CN} + a_8\text{FR} + a_9\text{IY} + a_{10}\text{NE} + a_{11}\text{BG} +$$
$$+ a_{12}\text{SW} + b_1X + e \qquad (2)$$

would not have the effects on factor proportions observed in Table 5 if factor prices were controlled. With $Y = \text{K/E}$ and $X = \text{w/r}$, t-tests on the hypotheses that $a_5 = 0$ and that $a_7 = 0$, and an F-test on the hypothesis that $a_8 = a_9 = a_{10} = a_{11} = 0$, would provide the relevant evidence. The results of such statistical tests appear in row 1 of Table 7.

Once relative factor prices are taken into account, European and North American firms cannot be distinguished on the basis of factor proportions. Neither can Canadian and American firms. On the other hand, Italian firms continue to deploy more capital per employee than do other Common Market companies.[26]

The impact of nationality on labour productivity actually increases when factor proportions are taken into account. According to row 2 of Table 7, where $Y = \text{PQ/E}$ and $X = \text{K/E}$, differences between continents, between European trading blocs, and within the EFTA fail to disappear. Moreover, differences among EEC nations and between Canada and the United States become significant. With factor proportions and business line controlled, the labour productivity ranking of sample countries is: the United States comfortably on top; Germany, Sweden, France, Belgium, the Netherlands, and Canada all a bit

---

26. To the extent that Italian firms operate in a more inflationary environment than do firms domiciled in other Common Market countries, this finding can be attributed to defects in the factor price variable. See note 14, point 3.

Table 7*. Statistical significance statistics associated with estimation of equation 2.

Y	X	Regression N	R^2	Variance among business F	s.s.	$\hat{a}_5$ EUROP t	s.s.	$\hat{a}_6$ EEC6 t	s.s.	Variance within EEC6 F	s.s.	$\hat{a}_{12}$ SW t	s.s.	$\hat{a}_7$ CN t	s.s.	$\hat{b}_1$ X t	s.s.
1. K/E	w/r	66	62	17.0	***	−1.0		0.2		4.0	**	1.0		1.1		0.9	
2. PQ/E	K/E	91	77	11.9	***	−7.0	***	3.9	***	3.2	*	2.8	**	−2.0	*	6.5	***
3. LC/E	PQ/E	66	81	4.9	**	−4.6	***	1.7		1.1		1.2		−0.1		3.8	***
4. DE/EQ	PQ/K	96	69	1.6		0.1		7.0	***	5.6	***	−0.5		−0.7		−0.4	
5. BKPRFT	K/E	91	56	4.7	**	−1.0		−2.2	*	6.0	***	−1.0		0.8		1.0	
6. BKPRFT	PQ/E	91	56	5.0	**	−0.2		−2.4	*	6.0	***	−1.2		1.2		1.2	
7. BKPRFT	Ŝ/S	93	65	1.9		−0.7		−1.4		22.1	***	−1.8		1.0		2.2	*
8. BKPRFT	K̇/K	93	65	0.5		−1.0		−1.8		22.6	***	−1.9		0.8		2.6	*
9. CFPRFT	K/E	91	33	1.8		0.3		2.6	*	1.8		0.1		0.6		−0.5	
10. CFPRFT	PQ/E	91	33	1.5		0.7		2.2	*	1.8		−0.2		0.5		0.5	
11. CFPRFT	Ŝ/S	93	35	1.8		0.8		2.9	**	2.8	*	−1.1		0.7		2.7	**
12. CFPRFT	K̇/K	93	32	1.2		0.5		2.5	*	1.7		−0.9		0.4		1.8	
13. DE/K	PQ/K	96	55	4.6	**	−0.7		3.8	***	1.6		0.1		−0.2		3.3	***
14. EQ/TA	FC/FL	94	67	0.8		−3.7	***	−3.8	***	3.5	*	−0.3		1.0		1.4	
15. EQ/TA	CFPRFT	96	70	1.4		−3.5	***	−3.0	**	3.7	**	−0.1		1.1		−2.9	**
16. FL/TA	FC/FL	94	47	4.1	**	1.5		1.4		3.8	**	−0.7		−1.8		−1.7	
17. FLA/TA	CFPRFT	96	45	5.4	**	1.4		0.9		5.2	***	−0.9		−1.7		0.4	
18. Ŝ/S	FL/TA	93	43	7.7	***	−0.4		−2.4	*	3.7	**	3.2	**	−0.7		0.7	
19. Ŝ/S	CF/K	93	44	10.2	***	−0.5		−2.1	*	4.4	**	3.2	**	−0.8		1.6	
20. K̇/K	FL/TA	93	30	1.0		0.7		−1.0		1.6		3.1	**	0.1		−0.6	
21. K̇/K	CF/K	93	32	0.1		0.5		−0.8		1.7		3.3	**	0.2		1.6	

* The initials 's.s.' stand for statistical significance. One, two, and three stars denote statistical significance at the 0.05, 0.01, and 0.001 levels. All t-tests are two-tailed.

off the pace; Britain well off the pace; and Italy beyond sight of the pace. This ranking accords well with Denison's evidence (1967) concerning the residual factor in national economic growth. It also harmonizes with popular perceptions of business vigour in Atlantic Community countries.

Labour cost per employee does appear tied to labour productivity. As row 3 of Table 7 suggests, control for labour productivity eliminates the wage differentials between European trading blocs and within the EFTA. However, European firms are less generous than North American firms in terms of labour remuneration, even when labour productivity is taken into account.

In order to assess the impact of market opportunities on asset finance patterns, it is necessary to consult data on the relative costs associated with internal and loan funds. Because financial markets rarely allocate investible funds strictly on the basis of market prices, such relative costs are difficult to measure – especially in an international context. Cognizant of their limitations, I shall employ the rate of interest paid on debt (FC/FL) and cash flow profitability (CFPRFT) as alternative explanations of the proportion of total assets financed via equity or debt. The first constitutes one indicator of the cost associated with debt finance, while the second can be interpreted as an indicator of the facility of internal finance.

The results of estimating Equation 2 with EQ/TA and FL/TA dependent, and FC/FL and CFPRFT independent, appear in rows 14 through 17 of Table 7. Neither market opportunity variable affects the impact of nationality on the extent of equity finance. Significant differences persist between continents, between European trading blocs, and within the EEC. Similarly, neither market opportunity variable affects the impact of nationality on the extent of debt finance. Significant differences persist among Common Market firms.

The evidence so far examined bears more directly on the market opportunities hypothesis than on its entrepreneurial quality counterpart. In order to test the latter, we must examine the extent to which good performance is in fact linked to the production and finance choices made by sample firms. One set of tests involves profitability as the performance criterion and production characteristics as explanatory variables. These are reported in rows 5, 6, 9, and 10 of Table 7. The other set of tests involves growth as the performance criterion and asset finance patterns as explanatory variables. These are reported in rows 18 through 21 of Table 7.

The impact of nationality on corporate profitability cannot be attributed to production methods. Even with factor proportions or labour productivity controlled, a firm's rate of return depends on its country of domicile. In fact, neither aspect of production methods affects profitability once business line and nationality are taken into account.[27]

The rate at which a firm grows depends on neither the availability of internal funds nor the proportion of assets actually financed via debt.[28] Not only do EEC and Swedish firms grow faster than do other firms, in spite of their low reliance on internal finance; but such firms would not grow any faster were they to rely less heavily on debt.

5. Conclusion

The purpose of this chapter has been to identify and explain certain differences among large industrial firms in the Atlantic community. The differences considered were those measurable with financial accounting data. As a result, major areas of potential diversity were ignored.[29] A general appraisal of corporate heterogeneity must thus await more extensive research. Meanwhile, several particular observations can be made.

Firstly, nationality affects book profitability more than cash flow profitability. The conclusion I draw from this finding is that companies heterogeneous in nationality cannot be compared without allowance for cross-country variation in accounting methods.[30] My reasoning proceeds as follows. Cash flow finances both dividends and corporate investments. Since book profit is subject to income tax while depreciation and appropriations are not, firms desire to declare as profit only those funds to be distributed as dividends. If dividend payout rates or fiscal depreciation-appropriations allowances vary among countries, so will the propensity to report true profits as such. Tax rules certainly differ internationally

---

27. Zero-order Pearson correlations between production methods and profitability are also insignificant:

	K/E	PQ/E
BKPRFT	0.04	0.19
CFPRFT	−0.02	−0.06

28. The relevant zero-order Pearson correlations are:

	CF/K	FL/TA
$\dot{S}/S$	−0.12	0.14
$\dot{K}/K$	0.29**	−0.12

Although the correlation between growth in capital stock and availability of internal funds is significant at the .01 level, it is also extremely small.

29. Examples which come readily to mind include market position, integration pattern, innovativeness, and industrial democracy.

30. *Fortune*, a major purveyor of bottom line financial data, agrees. 'Since accounting and reporting requirements continue to vary widely among countries, *Fortune* does not compare various companies' returns on sales and stockholder's equity; the comparisons would be misleading.' *Fortune World Business Directory* for 1974, page 1.

and dividend payout practices probably do as well.[31] As a result, profitability comparisons involving firms heterogeneous in nationality should not be made on the basis of 'bottom line' data alone. I suspect the comparisons based on other variables should not be so made, either.

Secondly, nationality affects corporate structure more than corporate performance. In terms of structure, factor proportions vary between continents, within the Common Market, and within North America; the allocation of cash flow among depreciation, appropriations, and book profit varies between European trading blocs and within the Common Market; and the relative importance of debt and equity in corporate finance varies between continents, between European trading blocs, and within the Common Market. In most cases, the proportion of variance explained by nationality, in conjunction with business line, exceeds 60 per cent.

In terms of corporate performance, however, the impact of nationality is much less pronounced. Cash flow profitability varies only between European trading blocs, and the proportion of variance in CFPRFT explained by business line and nationality is under 30 per cent. These results suggest that nationality cannot be used to predict the performance of large industrial firms in the Atlantic community with the precision often implied in the popular business literature.[32]

Thirdly, when nationality does affect corporate performance, it is not because European firms differ from North American firms. The two continents cannot be distinguished on the basis of cash flow profitability. Nor can they be distinguished on the basis of company growth. Only when labour productivity is regressed on corporate nationality with factor proportions and business line controlled do American firms appear superior to their Old World counterparts. European firms are 'challenged' more by each other than by their rivals overseas.

---

31. With respect to the tax authority situation, see Arthur Andersen (1974). With respect to dividend payout, stock market structure is likely to determine corporate behaviour. Where shares are held primarily by households, firms may have to report high profits if they wish ever to issue new shares. Where shares are held primarily by financial holding companies, owners have access to information better than that found in company accounts. Window-dressing profits are not required. Moreover, financial holding companies probably prefer more retained earnings relative to dividends than do households.

32. If corporate growth is considered a performance variable, then nationality is a more important determinant of performance than the text suggests. The same would be true if labour productivity given factor proportions is considered a performance variable.

References

Adams, W. J., 'International Differences in Corporate Profitability.' *Economica*, 43 (November), 367–370, 1976.

Arthur Andersen & Co., *Accounting Standards for Business Enterprises Throughout the World*, 1974.

Caves, R. E. (ed.), *Britain's Economic Prospects*. London, George Allen and Unwin, 1968.

Caves, R. E., 'International Corporations: The Industrial Economics of Foreign Investment.' *Economica*, 38 (February), 1–27, 1971.

Compagnie Lambert pour l'Industrie et la Finance. *L'Emploi des Capitaux dans les Entreprises en Europe et aux Etats-Unis*. Appendix to the company's annual report for 1967, 1967.

Compagnie Lambert pour l'Industrie et la Finance. *L'Emploi des Capotaux dans les Entreprises en Europe et au Etats-Unis*. Appendix to the company's annual report for 1968, 1968.

Denison, E. F., *Why Growth Rates Differ*. Washington, Brookings, 1967.

Earle, E. M. (ed.), *Modern France*. Princeton, Princeton University Press, 1951.

European Economic Community, Commission. *La Politica Industriale della Communità*. Bruxelles, 1970.

Hodgman, D. R., *National Monetary Policies and International Monetary Cooperation*. Boston, Little, Brown, 1974.

Jacquemin, A. P., *Economie Industrielle Européenne*. Paris, Bordas, 1975.

Jacquemin, A. P., and M. Cardon, 'Size Structure, Stability, and Performance of the Largest British and EEC Firms.' *European Economic Review*, 4 (December), 393–408, 1973.

Jacquemin, A. P., and W. Saez, 'A Comparison of the Performance of the Largest European and Japanese Industrial Firms.' *Oxford Economic Papers*, 28 (July), 271–283, 1976.

Kindleberger, C., *Economic Growth in France and Britain*, 1852–1950, Cambridge, Harvard University Press, 1964.

McArthur, J. H. and B. R. Scott, *Industrial Planning in France*. Boston, Harvard University Graduate School of Business, 1969.

Modigliani, F. and M. H. Miller, 'The Cost of Capital, Corporation Finance and the Theory of Investment.' *American Economic Review*, 48 (June), 261–297, 1958.

Nême, J. and C. Nême, *Economie Européenne*. Paris, Presses Universitaires de France, 1970.

Pryor, F. L., 'The Size of Production Establishments in Manufacturing.' *Economic Journal*, 82 (June), 547–566, 1972.

Servan-Schreiber, J., *Le Défi Americain*. Paris, Denoël, 1967.

Warnecke, S. and E. Suleiman (eds.), *Industrial Policies in Western Europe*. New York, Praeger, 1975.

Appendix

Identity of sample firms

Automotive firms
1. General Motors
2. Ford
3. Chrysler
4. American Motors
5. Signal Companies
6. White Motor
7. Renault*
8. Peugeot
9. Volkswagen

10. Daimler Benz
11. Klockner Humboldt
    Deutz
12. BMW
13. Fiat*
14. Alfa Romeo*
15. British Leyland
16. Volvo
17. Saab

Chemical firms
1. Du Pont
2. Union Carbide
3. Dow
4. Monsanto
5. Allied Chemical
6. Celanese
7. American
   Cyanamid
8. Hercules
9. Rohm & Haas
   (US)

10. Ethyl
11. Diamond
    Shamrock
12. Stauffer Chemical
13. Pennwalt
14. Rhône Poulenc
15. Air Liquide
16. Hoechst
17. BASF
18. Bayer
19. Montedison
20. Snia Viscosa*
21. AKZO
22. DSM
23. Solvay
24. ICI
25. Courtaulds
26. British Oxygen

Electrical firms
1. General Electric
   (US)
2. ITT

* The financial data of this firm are unconsolidated.

3. Westinghouse
4. RCA
5. Whirlpool
6. Raytheon
7. Motorola
8. Texas
   Instruments
9. Zenith

10. Emerson Electric
11. McGraw Edison
12. Magnavox
13. Sunbeam
14. Hoover
15. CGE
16. Thomson Brandt
17. Siemens
18. AEG

19. Bosch
20. Philips
21. General Electric
    (UK)
22. Thorn
23. Plessey
24. EMI
25. ASEA
26. Ericsson
27. Electrolux

Ferrous firms
1. US Steel
2. Bethlehem Steel
3. Armco Steel
4. National Steel
5. Republic Steel
6. Inland Steel
7. Lykes Youngstown
8. Allegheny Ludlum
9. Wheeling
   Pittsburgh
10. Kaiser Steel
11. Cyclops
12. Stelco
13. Dofasco
14. Denain Nord Est
    Longwy

15. Thyssen**
16. Krupp***
17. Flick****
18. Salzgitter
19. Rheinstahl
20. Klöckner
21. Italsider
22. Estel
23. Cockerill*
24. British Steel
25. Tube Investments
26. Granges

   * The financial data of this firm are unconsolidated.
  ** August Thyssen Hütte AG.
 *** Friedrich Krupp GmbH.
**** Verwaltungsges. für Industrielle Unternehmungen Friedrich Flick GmbH.

IX. IMPORT QUOTAS AND INDUSTRIAL PERFORMANCE

Walter Adams and Joel B. Dirlam

With the internationalization of markets and the progressive liberalization of world trade, the threat of foreign competition has revived the age old cry for protectionism: to protect the nation's balance of payments; to protect domestic labour from import-induced unemployment; to protect domestic industry from the unfair competition of low-wage countries. These arguments are especially appealing in times of recession, and political office seekers are not loath to embrace them, especially in election years.

To an industry constrained to live in a free trade environment, and striving for survival, profitability, and growth, foreign competition is a serious challenge. It is a disruptive force which undermines the market control of oligopolized industries and the cartel-like price maintenance schemes prevalent in many competitive industries. It causes instability by undermining 'mutual dependence recognized,' by promoting defection among cartel partners, and by encouraging entry. Foreign competition is the nemesis of 'orderly marketing' and hence becomes a prime target for neo-mercantilist governments and the interest groups which manipulate them.

In recent years, import quotas – mandatory or voluntary – imposed unilaterally, or after bilateral or multilateral negotiations, have become a favourite tool of protectionism. In the USA the scenario is roughly as follows: imports increase and capture a growing share of the domestic market. The industry affected, exercising coalescing (rather than countervailing) power, is joined by its trade union in demanding protection from foreign competition. Complaints are filed under the antidumping, escape clause, countervailing duty, or similar statutes. In case of failure, which is more common than not, legislative action is then requested to impose mandatory restraints on the 'injurious' or 'potentially injurious' imports. Diplomatic channels are used to advise exporting countries that such mandatory restraints are likely to be imposed, unless they practice 'voluntary' self-limitation. The typical result is the 'voluntary' quota which, however, rarely constitutes a final solution.

If the quota applies to cotton textiles, the import problem will shift to wool or man-made fibres. If the quota applies to steel, the product mix of the imports will shift from lower priced to higher priced steel products. If the quota restrains one country (e.g. Japan), new producers (e.g. Hong Kong, Taiwan, or Korea) will enter the protected (high price) market. Bilateral negotiations must yield to multilateral negotiations. Global import controls over an entire industry or an industry segment must be refined and rendered increasingly specific. Moreover, exporting countries, responsible for monitoring their side of the bargain, are obliged to reorganize their export trade – to encourage collective action among competing companies and to promote the formation of export associations (i.e. export cartels). These newly formed producer groups must allocate quotas and divide markets and, in the process, they inevitably raise prices to the importing country. They are also constrained to negotiate with counterpart associations in other exporting countries to develop a *modus vivendi* for competition in the import market.

Finally, under the auspices of their respective governments, and under the threat of legislated trade restrictions, the exporting firms and the domestic industry are encouraged to work out orderly marketing agreements, designed to prevent injury or potential injury to industry and labour in the importing country. These orderly marketing agreements, of course, are little more than a euphemism for international cartels organized and operated by special interest groups with the connivance of governments. They are the politico-economic prototype of neo-mercantilist Statecraft. They create a private government, an *imperium in imperio*, immunized from the disciplinary control of competition, and yet not subject to public regulation aimed at insuring acceptable (not to say, progressive) performance.

It is our thesis that import quotas are the first step toward international cartels, and that the cartelization of trade in one product eventuates in controlling world trade in related products. We recognize, of course, that nations must be allowed to defend themselves against massive attacks of dumping, and that they should have the right to grant adjustment assistance to industries and workers suffering import-related hardships. But public policy should not embrace solutions to the import 'problem' like quotas and/or orderly marketing arrangements which do not provide adequate mechanisms for regulating industry performance or protecting the public interest.

In exploring this thesis, we shall first present a brief sketch of typical import quotas by the USA in the post World War Two era. Then we shall analyze in depth the most recent US import quota – on specialty steel – and what it might portend as a precedent. Next, we shall examine the standards used by the ITC for determining import injury and the relief appropriate thereto. Finally, we shall comment on import quotas and orderly marketing agreements as proper instruments of public policy.

1. Some representative US import quotas

In the USA, the principal quantitative import restrictions have been applied to textiles, steel, certain agricultural commodities, vessels engaged in US coastal trade, and, between 1959 and May 1973, to petroleum and petroleum products.[1]

Textiles. The first textile quotas were imposed in 1935. These were voluntary quotas worked out pursuant to 'friendly' agreement with Japan. After World War II, pursuant to negotiations initiated by President Eisenhower, Japan announced a five-year programme of voluntary export restraints, to start on January 1, 1957. Two weaknesses of these voluntary restraint arrangements soon became apparent:

1. While Japan limited its exports other low-cost producers (like Hong Kong) entered the US market.

2. While cotton textile imports were controlled, other textiles (like wool and man-made fibres) were not, and hence entered the US market in increasing quantities.

To deal with this situation, the contracting parties to GATT, meeting in Tokyo in 1960, adopted a definition of market disruption caused by imports. They deemed such disruption to occur when the following elements appear in combination:

1. a sharp and substantial increase or potential increase of imports of particular products from particular sources;

2. these products are offered at prices which are substantially below those prevailing for similar goods of comparable quality in the market of the importing country;

3. there is serious damage to domestic producers or threat thereof;

4. the price differentiatials referred to in paragraph 2 above do not arise from governmental intervention in the fixing or formation of prices or from dumping practices.

In July 1961, at a conference of principal textile importing and exporting countries, a Short Term Arrangement for Cotton Textile Trade (STA) was negotiated to cover the period October 1, 1961 to September 30, 1962. This was followed by a five-year long-term arrangement (LTA), based on the principle of 'market disruption' quoted above, which allowed importing countries, despite the general GATT rule against quotas, 'to limit imports of specified cotton textiles which it found were disrupting or threatening to disrupt its markets.'

1. For a comprehensive survey, see US Tariff Commission, *Nontariff Trade Barriers*, Part II, Vol. 5, Chapter VIII, Report to the Committee on Finance of the US Senate, TC Publication 665, Washington, DC, April 1974. For a critical analysis, see Robert E. Baldwin, *Nontariff Distortions of International Trade*, Washington, DC: The Brookings Institution, 1970.

Table 1. Quantitative limitations on U.S. import trade in cotton textiles, as of April 1, 1972, under the Long-Term Arrangement Regarding International Trade in Cotton Textiles (LTA)

Type of limitation	Country of origin	Number of LTA categories involved[1]	Limitations on import trade		
			For 12-month period beginning	Aggregate quantity (million equivalent square yards)	Limitation controlled by
Controls under authority of Article 3 of LTA.	Barbados	39	May 28, 1971	.4	USA
Controls under authority of Article 3 of LTA.	Ceylon	60	Aug. 3, 1971	1.0	USA
Controls under authority of Article 3 of LTA.	Costa Rica	53	Oct. 1, 1971	1.3	USA
		61	do	.4	
Controls under authority of Article 3 of LTA.	Israel	62	Oct. 5, 1971	1.4	Israel
		63	do	.6	
Controls under authority of Article 3 of LTA.	Mauritius	39	Aug. 25, 1971	.2	USA
Controls under authority of Article 3 of LTA.	Nicaragua	9	Nov. 30, 1971	.8	USA
		22	Apr. 29, 1971	1.0	
Bilateral agreements under authority of Article 4 of LTA.[2]					
2nd year of 5-year agreement	Brazil	All	Nov. 1, 1971	78.8	Brazil and USA
1st year of 4-year agreement	Colombia	All	July 1, 1971	40.0	USA
3rd year of 4-year agreement	Czechoslovakia	All	May 1, 1971	2.8	Czechoslovakia and USA
1st year of 5-year agreement	El Salvador	All	Apr. 1, 1971	5.1	El Salvador and USA
1st year of 4-year agreement	Greece	All	July 1, 1971	10.9	Greece
1st year of 5-year agreement	Haiti	All	Oct. 1, 1971	4.5	Haiti and USA
2nd year of 3-year agreement	Hong Kong	All	do	454.4[3]	Hong Kong
2nd year of 5-year agreement	Hungary	All	Aug. 1, 1971	4.5	Hungary and USA
2nd year of 4-year agreement	India	All[4]	Oct. 1, 1971	120.8	India
2nd year of 2¾-year agreement	Italy	7	Jan. 1, 1972	2.3	Italy
2nd year of 3-year agreement	Jamaica	All	Oct. 1, 1971	27.3	Jamaica
1st year of 1½-year agreement	Japan	All[5]	Jan. 1, 1972	453.5	Japan

2nd year of $4\frac{3}{4}$-year agreement	Korea	All	Jan. 1, 1972[6]	36.8	USA
2nd year of 4-year agreement	Malaysia	All	Sept. 1, 1971	21.0	Malaysia and USA
6th year of 7-year agreement	Malta	All	Jan. 1, 1972	16.2	Malta and USA
1st year of 5-year agreement	Mexico	All	May 1, 1971	98.1	USA
2nd nine months of $1\frac{3}{4}$-year agreement	Nansei-Nanpo	All	Oct. 1, 1971[6]	11.7	Nansei-Nanpo
2nd year of 4-year agreement	Pakistan	All	July 1, 1971	89.2	Pakistan and USA
1st year of 5-year agreement	Peru	All	Oct. 1, 1971	5.0	Peru and USA
5th year of 6-year agreement	Philippines	All	Jan. 1, 1972	60.2	Philippines and USA
3rd year of 5-year agreement	Poland	All	Mar. 1, 1972	7.1	Poland and USA
2nd year of 4-year agreement	Portugal	All	Jan. 1, 1972	119.2	Portugal and USA
2nd year of 5-year agreement	Rep. of China (Taiwan)	All	do	94.5	Rep. of China and USA
Do	Romania	All	do	9.4	Romania and USA
2nd year of 4-year agreement	Singapore	All	do	47.1	Singapore
2nd year of 5-year agreement	Spain	All	do	51.4	Spain
1st year of 5-year agreement	Thailand	All	April 1, 1972	15.0	Thailand and USA
8th year of 9-year agreement	Turkey	All	July 1, 1971	3.9	Turkey
2nd year of 3-year agreement	United Arab Republic	All	Oct. 1, 1971	55.1	United Arab Republic
2nd year of 5-year agreement	Yugoslavia	All	Jan. 1, 1972	24.5	Yugoslavia and USA

Notes

1. Import data for textiles wholly of or in chief value of cotton have been grouped into 64 categories of products. These categories are used by the USA in administering the provisions of the LTA and in reporting trade activity in each group. All categories from all countries are subject to limitation whenever market disruption exists; categories listed are those on which limitations were actually in force as of April 1, 1972. In those cases where an aggregate limitation applies to all categories from a country, smaller limitations apply to each category.

2. Many bilateral agreements for countries listed superseded numerous restraints under article 3 of the LTA. Where applicable, the aggregate quantities shown for each country reflect increases (usually by 5 per cent per 12-month period) above limitations imposed during the first agreement year and further annual increases are authorized until each agreement is terminated or expires.

3. Includes wool textile products, other than apparel, in the amount of 0.2 million equivalent square yards, and man-made fibre textile products, other than apparel, in the amount of 2.1 million equivalent square yards. Imports of apparel of wool or man-made fibres are controlled under a separate bilateral agreement.

4. Imports of certain uniquely and historically traditional Indian products are not limited by the agreement.

5. Not all items in all 64 categories are under restriction.

6. Nine-month period.

Source

Compiled by the International Trade Commission from official records of the US Department of Commerce.

Renewed in 1967 and 1970, the LTA was succeeded on January 1, 1974 by a new multifibre agreement under GATT covering trade in cotton-textiles, wool, man-made fibres, and blends thereof. Table 1 shows the US quotas on cotton textiles under the LTA. Table 2 shows the US quotas on wool and man-made fibres under LTA. Table 3 shows the textile restrictions of other countries during the period 1962–1972.

The annual cost to consumers of US import quotas on textiles has been estimated at $ 2.5 billion (1972) and $ 4.8 billion (1976). The estimate is based on the cautious assumption that import quotas raise textile prices by a mere 5 to 10 per cent.[2]

Meat. This quota is a prime example of the quantitative restrictions imposed on the importation of agricultural commodities into the USA.[3] Under the Meat Import Act of 1964, annual imports of fresh chilled or frozen meat of cattle, goats, and sheep (except lambs) were not to exceed 725.4 million pounds, adjusted upward or downward by the same percentage that domestic commercial production changed in comparison with the 1959–1963 base period. No limitations on trade were required until imports exceeded a so-called trigger point – 10 per cent above the basic limitations.

In 1968, 'voluntary' import quotas on meat were set at an annual level of 1 to 1.2 billion pounds for a three-year period ending in 1971. A 'voluntary' quota totaling 1,238 million pounds was established for 1972, on a country-by-country basis, ranging from 600.4 million pounds for Australia to 2.6 million pounds for Haiti.

The annual cost of these quotas to US consumers is estimated at $ 600 m.[4] It is noteworthy that this burden is borne largely by low-income groups, since most of the imported meat is of the low-grade variety going into hamburger and processed meat products. It is also noteworthy that the export price of meat to the USA is 10 to 20 per cent higher than the export price to other countries, partly because of the fear of intensified political pressure by domestic producers if imports were to exercise greater downward restraint on prices in the US market.

---

2. Ilse Mintz, *US Import Quotas: Cost and Consequences*, Washington, DC: American Enterprise Institute for Public Policy Research, 1973, pp. 10 and 47–76.
3. Other examples of 'agricultural' quotas are the restraints embodied in the International Coffee Agreement of 1968, the International Cocoa Agreement of 1973, the mandatory quotas legislated under the Sugar Act of 1948 as amended (which have been estimated to cost US consumers $ 580 to $ 700 million a year, or roughly 32 to 39 per cent of the total annual US expenditure on sugar), the mandatory quotas on wheat, raw cotton, peanuts, and certain dairy products legislated by a series of amendments to the Agricultural Adjustment Act dating back to 1939, the bilateral agreement in 1972 between Mexico and the USA setting an import quota on frozen strawberries and strawberry paste, and a 'voluntary' quota by Mexico on the shipment of fresh strawberries to the USA.
4. Mintz, *op. cit.*, p. 75.

Table 2. Quantitative limitations on US import trade in textiles of wool or man-made fibres pursuant to bilateral agreements,[1] as on April 1, 1972

Products restrained	Country of origin	Limitations on import trade		Limitation controlled by
		For 12-month period beginning	Aggregate quantity (million equivalent square yards)	
Apparel of wool[2]	Hong Kong	Oct. 1, 1971	40.0	Hong Kong
Apparel of man-made fibres[2]	Hong Kong	Oct. 1, 1971	210.0	Hong Kong
Textile products, of wool	Korea	Oct. 1, 1971	12.7	Korea and USA
Textile products, of man-made fibres	Korea	Oct. 1, 1971	344.3	Korea and USA
Textile products, of wool	Japan	Oct. 1, 1971	42.8	Japan
Textile products, of man-made fibres	Japan	Oct. 1, 1971	954.7	Japan
Textile products, of wool	Malaysia	Sept. 1, 1971	.1	Malaysia
Textile products, of man-made fibres	Malaysia	Sept. 1, 1971	5.4	Malaysia
Textile products, of wool	Rep. of China	Oct. 1, 1971	4.7	Rep. of China and USA
Textile products, of man-made fibres	Rep. of China	Oct. 1, 1971	467.5	Rep. of China and USA

Notes
1. Agreements with Hong Kong, Korea, and Republic of China (Taiwan) are for 5 years beginning Oct. 1, 1971; the agreement with Japan is for 3 years beginning Oct. 1, 1971; and the agreement with Malayisa is for 4 years beginning Sept. 1, 1970.
2. Limitations on wool and man-made fibre products other than apparel are included under the bilateral agreement with Hong Kong negotiated under the authority of the Long-Term Arrangement Regarding International Trade in Cotton Textiles (LTA) effective Oct. 1, 1970.

Source
Compiled by the US International Trade Commission from official records of the US Department of Commerce.

Table 3. Limitations imposed on textile trade between foreign countries during the period *1962–1972*.

Importing country	Exporting country	Restricted product
Australia	Hong Kong	Cotton drills, cotton denims, and knitted shirts
Austria	Egypt, Japan, India, Israel, Pakistan, Mexico, Korea, several Communist countries	Various products
Benelux	Japan	Cotton, wool, and man-made textiles
	Hong Kong	Cotton shirts, woven nightwear, handkerchiefs, bedlinens, household linen, and terry cloth
	India, Pakistan	Cotton textiles
	Several Eastern European countries, USSR	Wool and man-made fibre fabrics and man-made fibre clothing
Canada	Israel, Portugal, Greece, Colombia, Mexico, Spain, Egypt, Brazil, Korea, Hong Kong, India, Taiwan, Mainland China	Cotton yarn
	Hong Kong, Japan, Taiwan, Macao, Korea, Malaysia, Singapore, Poland, Romania, Trinidad/Tobago	Certain fabrics, made-up goods, and apparel (of various fibres)
Denmark	Egypt, Japan, Korea	Various products
European Community	Japan, India, Pakistan, Hong Kong, Taiwan, Egypt	Various products
France	Japan, India, Pakistan, Hong Kong, Korea, Egypt Argentina, Australia, Brazil, Burma, Ceylon, Chile, Cuba, Czechoslovakia, Dominican Republic, Haiti, Hong Kong, India, Indonesia, Israel, Japan, South Korea, New Zealand, Nicaragua, Pakistan, Peru, Poland, South Africa, Uruguay	Various products
West Germany	Japan, India, Pakistan, Taiwan, Egypt, Korea	Textile products of wool or man-made fibres
	Japan, Taiwan, South Korea, Singapore, India, Pakistan, Egypt, Yugoslavia, Bulgaria, Czechoslovakia, Hungary, Romania, Poland	Various products Man-made fibres and wools

Country	Countries affected	Products
Italy	Japan	Various products
	USA, Spain, Egypt, Hong Kong, Taiwan, India, Pakistan, Yugoslavia	Grey and bleached fabrics
	Albania, Czechoslovakia, East Germany, Poland	Wool products
	Bulgaria, Hungary, Romania, USSR	Certain man-made fibre products
Finland	Some Eastern countries	Various products
Norway	Japan, Korea, Hong Kong	Yarn, fabrics, certain knitted fabrics, cotton undergarments, shirts and nightwear; wool jackets, sweaters and cardigans; man-made fibre anoraks, shirts, sweaters, jackets
	Japan, Bulgaria, Poland, Romania, Czechoslovakia, Hungary, USSR, South Korea, Portugal, Macao, Hong Kong	Wool and man-made fibres
	Bulgaria, Czechoslovakia, East Germany, Hungary, Poland, Romania	All textile fibres
Sweden	Japan	All textiles
	Portugal, Macao	Wool and man-made fibre textiles
	Singapore	Shirts
	Korea	Certain wool and man-made fibre apparel
	Bulgaria, Czechoslovakia, East Germany, Hungary, Poland, Romania, USSR	Various products
	Hong Kong	Wool and man-made fibres plus other various products
United Kingdom	Hong Kong	Various products, including polyester/cotton fabrics
	Japan, Bulgaria, Czechoslovakia, Hungary, Poland, Romania, The Peoples Republic of China, USSR, East Germany	Wool and man-made fibre products
	India, Ireland, Israel, Japan, Malaysia, Spain, Yugoslavia, certain Eastern Area countries, Pakistan, Taiwan	Various products

Source
Compiled by the US International Trade Commission from various GATT documents.

Table 4. Japanese voluntary quantitative export controls on products, other than textiles and steel, by country of destination, as of July 1971[1]

Articles	Countries of destination
Bicycles	USA, Canada, and Mexico
Stainless steel knives, forks, and spoons	Benelux
Radios of six or more transistors	USA, Australia, Austria, Belgium, Canada, Denmark, W. Germany, Finland, France, Greece, Hong Kong, Ireland, Italy, Luxembourg, Malaysia, Netherlands, Norway, New Zealand, Panama, Portugal, Rep. of Korea, S. Vietnam, Singapore, Spain, Sweden, Switzerland, Taiwan, Thailand, and the UK
Silk fabrics	All countries, except Iran, Iraq, Nansei Islands, Okinawa, South America, and Africa
Zoris (footwear) made of rubber sponge	USA, and Canada
Umbrellas	USA, W. Germany, France, Italy, Belgium, Netherlands, and Luxembourg
Umbrella ribs and stretchers	USA, France, Italy, W. Germany, Belgium, Netherlands, and Luxembourg
Baseball or softball gloves and mitts	USA, Canada, and Hawaii
Badminton rackets and frames	USA, Italy, France, W. Germany, Belgium, Netherlands, and Luxembourg
Ceramics (tableware, kitchen utensils, personal effects, ornaments, smokers' supplies, toys, stationery)[2]	All countries, except UK, Iran, Iraq, Nigeria, S. Rhodesia, and Nansei Islands
Glazed ceramic wall tile[2]	USA and Benelux
Ceramic mosaic tiles	USA, W. Germany, and Canada
Flatware[2]	All countries, except Iran, Iraq, Nigeria, S. Rhodesia, and Nansei Islands
Iron and steel wood screws	USA, Norway, Sweden, U.K., Denmark, Ireland,

	Benelux, France, W. Germany, Switzerland, Portugal, Spain, Italy, and Austria
Frozen swordfish	USA and Canada
Iodine and iodine products	All countries, except Nansei Islands
Household sewing machines	USA and Canada
Canned mandarine oranges	USA, UK, Canada, Belgium, W. Germany, Netherlands, Luxembourg, France, Italy, Sweden, Norway, Ireland, Switzerland, and Denmark
Fresh mandarine oranges[2]	Canada
Tuna, canned in brine	USA
Fresh or frozen tuna	American Samoa, British and French New Hebrides, Malaysia, and Dutch St. Martin Island
Batteries with manganese layer	France, Italy, W. Germany, Belgium, Netherlands, Luxembourg, Switzerland, and Sweden
Polyvinyl chloride leather	Australia
Knives (kitchen, pocket, hunting, and carving)[2]	UK
Apples[2]	Taiwan, Hong Kong, Macao, S. Vietnam, Thailand, Malaysia, Singapore, and the Philippines
Polychloride resins[2]	All countries, except African countries (other than the UAR and Rep. of S. Africa), USA, and Nansei Islands
Rubber shoes (excluding rubber beach sandals) and shoes made of textiles with rubber soles	Benelux

Notes
1. In addition to the items listed above as having voluntary quantitative export controls, the following items have both export and domestic shipment controls: cellophane, high quality paper, coated paper, rolled light metal products, selenium, malleabele cast iron joints, shovels, scoops, western-style farm implements, gas pipes, fence tube, ferro-chromium, ferro-manganese, dry batteries, 8 mm film, editing machines, TV receivers, sulphur, paint, explosives, caustic soda, methanol, acetic acid, soda sulphine, and certain polyethylene resins.
2. In addition to quantitative restrictions, other factors are controlled, such as price, design, evidence of bona fide importer, and type of transaction.

Source
Prepared by the US International Trade Commission, based on Department of State Airgram No. A-567 from American Embassy in Tokyo dated July 21, 1971.

Finally, it is noteworthy that the President twice directed the suspension of the quotas – on June 26, 1972 for the balance of that year and on January 29, 1973 for the balance of that year. On both occasions, the action was taken to slow down the rapid rise in domestic meat prices, thus indicating official recognition of the inflationary consequences of quota restrictions.

Petroleum. First introduced as 'voluntary' restraints in 1955, the import quotas on petroleum and petroleum products were made mandatory in 1959, and eventually suspended in May 1973. Their imposition was based on legislation authorizing the restriction of imports which would endanger the national security. They limited imports east of the Rocky Mountains to 12.2 per cent of estimated production. West of the Rockies (District V), the crude-products quota was set at 'the difference between estimated demand for the calendar year and estimated US and Canadian supplies produced or shipped into District V.'

Between 1959 and 1973, these quotas were the capstone of a government-sanctioned and government-subsidized cartel which permitted the major oil companies to exercise comprehensive horizontal and vertical control of the US market. The effects of the quota were predictable:

1. They helped maintain a non-competitive, artificially high price for crude. In 1969, for example, Middle Eastern oil (in the absence of quotas) could have been sold at $ 2.10 per barrel delivered at the US East Coast ports, whereas the quota-protected price was $ 3.42 per barrel. Thus, the US was developing resources at a social cost of $ 3.42 per barrel that had a social value of only $ 2.10 per barrel.[5]

2. The artificially high price for oil stimulated exploration and an uneconomic rate of development of a depletable resource. Producers were induced to search for oil in marginal areas, to develop marginal (i.e., high cost) reservoirs, and to produce from marginal (i.e., high cost) wells.

3. The artificially high price also stimulated the creation of excess domestic capacity. As Alfred E. Kahn put it, 'if you hold price far above the cost of efficient producers and raise after-tax returns on investment in any industry above those of other industries, then so long as entry is free, capital will pour in. And if, when this produces excess capacity, you protect profits by cutting back production and maintaining price, then capital will keep coming in.[6]

4. The artificially high price of petroleum in the USA had an injurious effect not only on the ultimate consumer, but also on those American industries which used it as a raw material and then had to sell their finished products in competitive world markets. Major American chemical companies have estimated that

---

5. US Senate Antitrust and Monopoly Subcommittee, Hearings on Governmental Intervention in the Market Mechanism, Part I, 91st Congress, 1st session, 1969, p. 306.
6. *Ibid.*, p. 136.

domestic oil prices on the East Coast in 1969 averaged $ 1.25 per barrel more than elsewhere in the world; this amounted to 3 cents a gallon, or 60 per cent above the world price. This quota-protected price differential, they pointed out, can be critical, if not fatal, in petrochemical production where, in many cases, raw material costs account for more than 50 per cent of the cost of basic products. Professor Wayne Leeman has well summarized this aspect of the problem:

'So the oil we keep out of the United States benefits our most important competitors. Manufacturers in Japan and Western Europe buy energy, industrial heat, and petrochemical feedstocks at prices which give them a competitive advantage over US producers. And they have this competitive advantage partly because import quotas give US firms only limited access to cheap foreign oil and partly because oil shut out of the United States depresses the prices they pay.[7]

5. The quotas were not in the best interests of the national security – the ostensible justification for their imposition. They depleted, rather than conserved a vital national resource. Thus, instead of importing low-cost foreign oil while still accessible, in order to conserve US domestic reserves for such time as foreign oil became inaccessible, the USA under the quota programme acted in precisely contrary fashion. As a result, the quotas served neither the national security nor the nation's economic self-interest.

The national cost of the oil import quotas has been estimated at $ 1.5 to $ 2 billion annually, and the total user cost at about $ 5 billion annually (which represents roughly 40 per cent of the annual value of domestic oil production).[8]

The pervasiveness of quotas. Perhaps, the pervasiveness of quotas is best gauged by viewing them from the perspective of a single exporting nation. This is done in Table 4 which shows the 'voluntary' restraints on products other than textiles and steel to which Japan's world trade was subject as of July 1971. Since then, of course, other restrictions – both mandatory and voluntary – have been added.

2. The political economy of protectionism: a case study of steel

For decades, the steel industry in the USA has been afflicted by the typical maladies of a tight oligopoly. Entry has been at a minimum, or non-existent. Innovation has been slow, hampered by the bureaucratic dry-rot which tends to accompany monopoloid giantism. Price policy has been directed at uniformity

7. *Ibid.*, p. 274.
8. Mintz, *op. cit.*, pp. 9–10.

and inflexibility, except in an upward direction; and, while the leadership role has rotated among the oligopolists, the level of product prices has been anything but market-determined. Moreover, until 1959, the industry had little to fear from foreign competition, so that the members of its co-fraternal, close-knit group felt it safe to follow concerted, tacitly collusive, and consciously parallel price and product policies. Occasional mavericks might from time to time disturb the industry's quiet life but, like others before them, they eventually became members of the club.

Into this well-ordered preserve, where the rules of the game were understood and observed by all parties, surged a rising tide of imports, initiated by the long strike of 1959. Once the industry grasped the fact that these imports were not a temporary phenomenon, and that they were not only securing a US franchise but, more important, disturbing accustomed price relationships and procedures, and indeed undermining the very foundations of the oligopoly, US steelmakers organized themselves for a massive counter-offensive. On one front, they sought relief from the import pressure of the 1960's, by forging a major technological revolution, substituting the oxygen converter for the outmoded open-hearth furnaces, introducing vacuum degassing, and making a (belated) start on continuous casting. On the other front, they tried to interdict imports by administrative action under existing trade legislation.

The first volley in this campaign was fired in an escape clause proceeding, but the standards of the Trade Expansion Act of 1962 were too stringent to permit a finding of import-caused injury as a result of negotiated tariff concessions. The domestic producers then turned to the Anti-Dumping Act of 1921 but, here again, they were frustrated; under the terms of this statute, conveniently exhumed for the purpose at hand, separate complaints had to be brought against each exporting country alleged to be guilty of a violation. However, the Tariff Commission found that if the major exporter to the USA (e.g. Japan) could not be shown to be guilty of dumping, then the other exporting countries (e.g. EEC members) selling in the same market could not be convicted for what was only a good-faith meeting of competition. Moreover, the Commission accepted evidence that the injury each exporting country might have inflicted was slight and that, given the rigid price structure prevailing in the USA, any injury which the domestic industry might have sustained was in any event self-inflicted.

Following those defeats, the US industry launched a major campaign on a new front. It began to marshall political support for amending the Trade Expansion Act in order to obtain quota protection. Beginning as early as 1967, a succession of Bills surfaced in Congress providing for statutory limits on steel imports. Other industries which, with the rapid growth of international trade in the 1960's also faced intense foreign competition for the first time, joined forces with the steel interests. These protectionist efforts peaked when Representative Burke, the Massachusetts champion of the embattled footwear industry, and Senator Hartke, the indefatigable spokesman for Indiana's steel industry, submitted an omnibus Bill which included mandatory import quotas on a number of products. By 1968, the forces supporting legislative quotas had gathered such strength that the State Department panicked. To undercut support for Congressional quotas, the Department (with Administration blessing) persuaded the major steel exporting countries – Japan and the members of the EEC – to enter into a Voluntary Restraint Agreement (VRA). Under the Agreement, steel imports from Japan were limited to 5.8 million tons and from the EEC to 5.8 million tons annually, compared with their then current levels of 7.5 million and 7.3 million tons, respectively. The Agreement also provided for an annual growth factor of 5 per cent in the allowable quotas. Scheduled to go into effect on January 1, 1969, the Agreement was described approvingly by the Chairman of the powerful Ways and Means Committee of the US House of Representatives as a 'welcome and realistic step.'

Within three years, the domestic industry found the VRA unsatisfactory. Quotas had not been established for specific products, nor for individual exporting countries (other than Japan). Moreover, both the Japanese and Europeans claimed that fabricated structural steel and cold-finished bars were not included in the VRA limitations. Because the VRA quota was expressed in tonnage terms, they rapidly expanded their shipments of stainless steel and other high-value products to the US market – despite their promise to 'try to maintain approximately the same product mix and pattern of distribution' as before the accord was signed. The effect of this upgrading in imports, combined with the inevitable increase in the price of imported steel, was that the total value of steel imports was as high in 1970 as in 1968 – in the face of a 25 per cent decline in the volume of imports during the same period.[9]

As a result, the three-year extension of the Agreement – announced by the White House on May 6, 1972 – contained specific tonnage limitations on three categories of specialty steels (stainless, too, and other alloys), and set the quotas at less than their 1971 import level. In addition, fabricated structural steel and cold-finished bars were specifically included in the Agreement. Also, the participants agreed to maintain their product mix and their customary geo-graphic distribution pattern. Finally, a $2\frac{1}{2}$ per cent (instead of the former 5 per cent) annual increase in the allowable imports was to be applied to the global tonnage allocated to Japan and the EEC.

9. Leonard W. Weiss, *Case Studies in American Industry*, 2d ed., New York: Wiley and Sons, 1971, p. 193, cited in Mintz, *op. cit.*, p. 83.

To enforce the extended VRA, the USA installed a monitoring system to be administered by the Treasury and the Customs Service. The exporting countries not only had to agree among themselves to observe the VRA, but also had to set up machinery for the producers within each country to arrive at mutually satisfactory export quotas to the US market. In other words, Japanese and European steel producers, under US pressure, were obliged to set up cartels in order to arrange for their share of the US market, and thus engage in activity that is suspect, if not illegal, under the Treaty of Paris. More important, however, the connivance between the domestic industry, the State Department, and foreign steel producers to limit imports triggered an antitrust suit by Consumers Union which charged that the VRA constituted a *prima facie* conspiracy under the Sherman Act. The court's decision, while ambiguous in many respects, was clear enough to persuade all concerned that the VRA should not be renewed when it expired in May 1975.[10]

The steel industry now placed its hopes in a new strategy – one that did not require its members to incur any risks of antitrust violations. In December 1974, the new approach paid off when Congress enacted the Trade Reform Act which directed the International Trade Commission to provide relief (including quotas) for industries injured by rising imports and – incorporating earlier provisions of the Trade Expansion Act of 1962 – allowed the Treasury to impose countervailing duties to offset export assistance. The industry did not hesitate long before availing itself of the new weaponry. US Steel, joined by other producers, filed a complaint with the Treasury charging that the remission of the TRA by EEC exporting countries constituted an unfair trade practice. This foray was unsuccessful, the Treasury rejecting the complaint on technical grounds. A second action, however, by the specialty steel producers, succeeded, when the International Trade Commission ruled that the domestic firms were indeed injured by rising imports, and recommended to the President the imposition of quotas on four categories of specialty steel products.

Stating that quotas are an inflexible and relatively undesirable remedy for the supposed injury, the President gave Japan, the EEC, and Sweden 90 days to enter into voluntary 'orderly marketing agreements' with US negotiators before approving the Commission's recommendation. Under the threat, the Japanese gave in, signing a VRA on the final day of the ultimatum. The other countries, however, spurned the proposed arrangement. Quotas were imposed, as threatened, with the Japanese benefiting, and the EEC losing, as compared to the

10. *Consumers Union of US Inc.* v. *William P. Rogers et. al.*, Civil Action No. 1029–72, Memorandum Opinion, Declaration, and Order of the US District Court for the District of Coumbia, January 8, 1973.

original Commission recommendations. Table 5 summarizes the essential features; the details of the quotas are analyzed below.

Table 5. Stainless and specialty steel import quotas (tons), United States.

Exporter	Recommended by ITC, 1976–77	Quotas imposed by the president 1976–77	1977–78	1978–79	Imports 1975	Average imports 1970–74
Total	146,000	147,000	151,500	155,900	153,900	152,000
EEC	34,000	32,000	33,000	33,900	28,700	29,000
Japan	63,500	66,400	68,400	70,000	78,000	66,000
Sweden	23,500	24,000	24,700	25,500	22,800	—

At every stage of the proceeding, the political power of the steel industry was brought to bear on the decision makers. Senator Schweiker of Pennsylvania, admitting that he was unfamiliar with the relevant economic data, testified as an industry witness for the Specialty Steel Committee. So did Mr. I. W. Abel, President of the United Steel Workers. And after the ITC decision was announced, the President of Allegheny Ludlum Steel, the industry spokesman, 'truculently' threatened to go to Congress to override the President if he did not approve the quotas recommended by the ITC[11] – only to have his threat echoed by Senator Ribicoff as he presided over the Senate Finance Committee's oversight hearings on US foreign trade policy. The chain of events was an object lesson in political economy.

What, then, were the economic consequences of the steel industry's manoeuverings on behalf of import quotas?

First, the succession of anti-dumping complaints, countervailing duty charges, mandatory quota threats, the VRA, and the import injury case (followed by a separate proceeding for so-called round stainless steel wire industry) must have had a chilling effect on the intensity of import competition. Import sales were probably reduced, simply to avoid the appearance of an 'excessive' inflow during the period when remedies were being considered. The success of the specialty steel producers in securing quota relief, for example, may have had inevitable side effects on the importation of carbon steels.

11. At a press conference shortly after the ITC decision, a journalist asked Mr. Richard P. Simmons, President of Allegheny-Ludlum Steel, about prices: If the President imposes quotas to protect his industry from foreign competition, would Mr. Simmons support wage and price controls to protect the consumers from his industry? Mr. Simmons replied that he opposes wage and price controls, and that he puts his faith in the free market. Said the *Washington Post*, in an editorial comment: 'But a country under import quotas is not everybody's idea of a free market.' (March 8, 1976, p. A 18.)

Second, there is hard evidence that the VRA has increased steel prices and raised costs to American industry and consumers. Thus, according to one study, between January 1960 and December 1968, a period of nine years, the composite steel price index rose 4.1 points – or 0.45 points per year, indicating the moderating effects which surging imports had on domestic prices. In the four years between January 1969 and December 1972, while the VRA was in effect, the steel price index rose 26.7 points – or 6.67 per year. Put differently, steel prices increased at an annual rate 14 times greater since the import quotas went into effect than in the nine years prior thereto.[12] Another study shows that the products which had been subjected to particularly hard import pressure prior to the VRA, evidenced greater price increases than other steel products after the VRA became effective, again highlighting the anticompetitive effects of the quotas.[13] Yet a third study, that took into account the overall price rise and was calculated on certain assumptions about differentials between domestic and imported prices and foreign supply elasticities as well as the loss in tariff revenues, estimated that steel quotas imposed a burden of about $ 386 million annually on the USA.[14] Other less conservative estimates, put the annual cost burden of VRA in the $ 500 million to $ 1 billion range.[15]

Third, the use of quotas, or threat of quotas, to moderate the intensity of competition from foreign steel, has profound implications for the battle against inflation. While it may be difficult to specify the precise quantitative importance of steel in the wholesale price index, there can be little doubt that price increases in steel trigger and 'justify' concomitant price increases in a host of other products, particularly in the durable consumer goods industries. In an economy where oligopoly and oligopolistic pricing are pervasive, public policy would be remiss in artificially insulating steel prices from the competive pressure of imports. As the Council on Wage and Price Stability recently pointed out:

'Throughout this report, the crucial role that import competition plays in moderating domestic steel price increases has been continually stressed ... While we must protect ourselves against unfair foreign competition, there is a tendency on the part of many industries to consider *all* foreign competition 'unfair.' Domestic firms cannot be allowed to take advantage of their market power to raise prices [perversely] during periods of weak demand and then expect the Government to protect them from the consequences.'[16]

12. Cited in Comptroller General of the USA, 'Economic and Foreign Policy Effects of Voluntary Restraint Agreements on Textiles and Steel,' *Report B-179342*, Washington, DC, March 31, 1974, p. 23.
13. Unpublished manuscript by Richard Fanara.
14. Stephen P. Magee, 'The Welfare Effects of Restrictions on US Trade,' *Brookings Papers on Economic Activity*, 1972.
15. Cited in Comptroller General of the USA, *op. cit.*, p. 23.
16. US Council on Wage and Price Stability, *A Study of Steel Prices*, Washington, DC, July 1975, p. ii (Letter of Transmittal from George C. Eads, acting director of the Council.).

Fourth, quotas are contagious, especially in times of weak demand, and are reminiscent of the 'beggar-thy-neighbour' policies of the industrial nations during the Great Depression. Thus, while the USA imposed specialty steel quotas on the major exporting countries, the Europeans forced Japan to accept a 'voluntary restraint' agreement on steel shipments into the EEC. According to the *Japan Economic Journal* (December 30, 1975):

'The Ministry of International Trade and Industry has approved formation of a cartel proposed by six major steelmakers for voluntarily regulating their exports to the European Economic Community. By creating such a cartel ... the steelmakers intend to set a ceiling of their exports to EEC nations in calendar 1976 at 1,220,000 tons.'[17]

This commitment by Japan represents, as US steelmakers rightly point out, a 23.8 per cent reduction from the 1975 level.

Such bilateral agreements, reinforced by the mandatory quotas unilaterally imposed by the USA, are significant because they help lay the groundwork for comprehensive, multinational agreements controlling world trade in steel. Such agreements, of course, are the dream of influential members of the world steel community. As recently as July 1976, M. Jacques Ferry, President of the French Steel Industry Association, stated that 'a world steel pact is urgently needed to stave off chaotic market conditions.' Such a pact, he said, would 'involve major steel-producing countries agreeing to orderly marketing procedures, with rules for resorting to production controls and import restrictions when these are justified by previously agreed criteria on levels of investment, employment, deliveries and the like.' M. Ferry claimed 'considerable support from US steel circles for such a pact.' As a prelude to a world-wide entente, however, M. Ferry 'urged European Communities (EC) nations to conclude a defensive agreement either inside or outside the European Coal and Steel Community (ECSC) Treaty. The European agreement would provide for continuous cooperation between all EC steelmakers, who would abide by pre-agreed rules on production 'disciplines,' measures to prevent 'abnormal' price reductions, and meet other 'crisis' situations.'[18] In short, M. Ferry used the same arguments employed by the American steel industry, and by President Ford, to justify the imposition of steel import quotas in the USA to support proposals for establishing an international steel cartel. Success may yet crown such efforts.

Summarizing, then, the American steel industry in the past seven years has used all the weapons in its arsenal to choke off import competition. Its major thrust has been directed, not at tariff protection, but at quotas and 'orderly

17. Quoted in *Oversight Hearings, op. cit.*, p. 171.
18. "Worldwide Steel Pact Held 'Must'," *The New York Journal of Commerce*, July 9, 1976, pp. 1 and 6.

marketing agreements.' Such restrictions are attractive to the industry because they set an absolute maximum to allowable competition, and bring in their train disciplined, cartel-like behaviour by both domestic and foreign producers. They protect the existing industry structure and its accustomed way of doing things. They preserve the status quo, meaning the status quo of contained competition, which is the normal goal of a mature, not to say aged oligopoly like steel. From the industry's point of view, imports are a disruptive influence, because they seek to capture larger market shares by such unorthodox means as price cutting, and hence upset anticipations, introduce unpredictability, and threaten not only profits but a way of life. No wonder that the industry felt constrained to meet such a threat with a total response.

3. Imports, injury and relief: the question of standards

A central problem of quantitative restrictions is to determine when, if ever, they may be justified. We may assume, without the necessity for elaborate proof, that quotas imposed by legislation, or by executive fiat, will represent little but the application of naked political power. Our earlier recital of economically indefensible agricultural quotas and the long years of consumer exploitation by the petroleum quota, both established at the Presidential level, are cases in point. The ITC, however, according to the language and intent of the statutes it administers, is supposed to bring expert, neutral analysis to bear on the desirability of using quotas or similar quantitative restrictions to limit imports. Accordingly, we turn to an examination first of the Commission's procedures for determining the relation of imports to industry difficulties or 'injury,' and secondly to its justification for choosing quotas.

Before determining whether imports have substantially injured a domestic industry, the Commission is obliged to measure the seriousness of the injury. Without entering into details of the ITC reports[19] suffice it to say that the concept of industry injury by imports, in spite of its being imbedded in Article 19 of the GATT, still awaits explication in terms that make sense to an economist. After all, the very process of competition is bound to 'injure,' in some way, some of the participating firms, in that their expectations are disappointed, they fail to earn anticipated returns, or they are forced to lay off workers. In fact, we would feel that 'injury' could properly be found only when there has been damage to the long-run viability of an industry, rather than individual firms and then only when

---

19. See Table 1 in our working paper, 'The ITC and Import Relief Under the Trade Act of 1974.'

there has been unfair competition.[20] Nevertheless, Congress has expressed itself otherwise, and the statutory measures such as profit rates, employment, utilization of capacity, levels of inventory, carried over from earlier decisions of the Commission under the Trade Expansion Act of 1962, can be used as indications – though not exclusive ones – of the presence and extent of injury. To these, from time to time, the Commission appears to have added, falling prices.[21]

Given the statutory directions to rely on such economic variables, with their superficially attractive precision, one might suppose that the Commission would have been able to move toward consistent, quantitatively comparable findings of the presence or absence of serious injury. Yet, when one examines decisions under both the Trade Expansion Act and the 1974 Trade Act he confronts a host of problems in applying even these rudimentary tests. How should the relevant time periods be chosen? The Senate Finance Committee in reporting out the 1974 Act suggested that trends be pushed back no further than 1968, but in at least one case, non-rubber footwear, the Commission – or some Commissioners – compared 1975 import levels with those prevailing in 1960. Even if the base period begins with 1968, how should the effect of the 1974–1975 recession be taken into account? Then there are accounting problems. What should be the relative weight given to profits, sales and employment resulting from overall plant or enterprise operations as compared with those allocated – on a more or less arbitrary basis – to the product that happens to be selected by the petitioners as a cause of injury? How can the Commission manage to determine the extent of injury when the industry consists of a large number of different-sized firms, the large prospering, while the small ones are unable to achieve minimum levels of efficiency? Or, to take a contrary case, what sense does it make to devote ITC resources to assessing injury when the industry consists of a single US producer, whose total employment has dropped from 400 to 100?[22]

These conceptual problems only serve to introduce the Commission to still more puzzling questions of determining whether an injury has been serious.[23] Suppose that there has been a shift, over a meaningful time period, of several indexes in the same direction. How much unemployment; what percentage of

20. See Walter Adams and Joel Dirlam, 'Dumping, Antitrust Policy, and Economic Power,' Michigan State University *Business Topics*, Vol. 14, No. 2, Spring 1966, pp. 20–29.
21. We make no attempt here to distinguish between the standards set for existing injury, and those to be applied when there is a finding of *threat* of injury. The latter, in the statute, seems to put more emphasis on trends than the former; yet the legislative history of the Trade Act of 1974, and the application of preceding legislation – as well as economic common sense – should reject a finding of injury based upon a short time period.
22. Reference is to the Quimby Company, in the *Birch Plywood Doorskin* case, discussed in our paper cited in note 19.
23. See e.g. Tariff Commission Publication 145, 1964, p. 8.

under-utilization of capacity; and what decline in profits is 'significant'? Moreover, how is the Commission to arrive at a measure of normal profits that will be relevant to a specific industry? What profit rate should be earned by a declining industry? By a highly cyclical industry?

Assuming that the injury determination obstacle is surmounted, how can the Commission deal with causality? The Commission has usually eschewed an 'arithmetic' approach to ranking the causes of injury. Nevertheless, in some reports is resorted, perhaps in desperation, to the same quantitative evidence that supported the necessary prerequisite of rising import shares – that is, a rising import penetration ratio – to demonstrate that imports have been a substantial cause of injury. One can only characterize this type of argument, used in the *Specialty Steel* and *Footwear* reports, as a kind of analytical self-levitation. Ironically, one Commissioner, in the *Specialty Steel* case, after adopting the petitioners' own industry definition of a monolithic Specialty Steel industry embracing the major stainless steel and alloy tool steel products based his negative decision on declining import penetration.

Could the Commission extricate itself from this morass of inconsistencies, and what seems to be an almost random selection of tests for causality, by relying on more refined techniques, particularly the use of regressions or other analyses of variance? Injury indices could be correlated with imports, and with other independent variables. Although little reliance has been placed on such statistical tools, the Commission has not wholly rejected them; indeed, under pressure from the staff, and perhaps also from witnesses, it seems in recent cases to have been willing to at least refer to relationships between imports and the industrial production index and the level of output of the domestic petitioners. Yet many of the possible causes of injury, including style changes, inefficiency, and recession, and other factors such as variable and divergent delivery times by foreign and domestic suppliers, and the degree of substitutability of imports for domestic products, introduce measurement and specification problems calling for econometric expertise of the highest order. Even in the best of circumstances, and in spite of the Commission's power to require response, the underlying data are far from complete. Within a matter of weeks, the staff must prepare a questionnaire, conduct interviews, and prepare the basis for a decision. In these circumstances, it would be fatuous to look forward to a promised land where the Commission, with a stock of prefabricated computer models, need only plug the necessary data into simultaneous equations to arrive at the proper beta coefficients that will represent the relative importance of each variable, and especially imports, in affecting the health of a domestic industry.

Having reached an affirmative finding with regard to an import-caused injury, the Commission must then recommend appropriate relief. Apart from avoiding the procedural pitfalls strewn in its path by Congress[24] the Commission faces the delicate and crucial task of deciding which, of several types of relief, will be the most effective in reducing 'injury,' a task which the Commission rarely chooses to confront directly. As an expert body familiar with the industry on the basis not only of a current escape clause investigation, but also in many instances, earlier economic inquiry, the Commission has been selected as presumably qualified to devise a relief programme. Congress has not sought to limit its options. At a minimum, the ITC can recommend adjustment assistance, consisting of unemployment and other benefits to workers, and low-cost loans to firms suffering from import competition. Upward adjustments in tariff rates can be proposed, in specific amounts or, a more severe restriction, tariff rate quotas, may be recommended – that is, the application of two sets of tariffs, with higher rates applying after imports reach a minimum level. Finally, quotas – purely quantitative restrictions – may also be the remedy.[25] The Commission has been provided therefore with the means to tailor carefully its relief recommendations to the exigencies of the industry's position. No minimum relief period is set, but the maximum is five years, with a possible three-year extension. And relief that extends beyond three years must be phased down, although the degree of diminution is not specified.

In reaching its relief-making recommendations the Commission has provided little sustained or hard data that can be used to assess its rationale for the specific measures recommended. Rather, the recommendations seem to have been plucked from thin air, although they all have some tenuous relation to preceding import levels or existing tariff rates or quotas. The *Asparagus*, *Stainless Steel Flatware*, and *Footwear* cases are egregious illustrations.

In none of these cases did the Commissioners link the recommendations quantitatively to the supposed injury, its magnitude, or its origins. Remedies seem almost to be selected by chance. Nevertheless, could one have anticipated a more precise justification for specific relief? Not only is the role of imports inherently extremely difficult to assess, but it has, in most instances, not been

---

24. With only six Commissioners, it is possible that the Commission will be evenly divided, and even if a majority finds injury, there is no requirement that this majority be unanimous with regard to relief recommendations, so that the President may find himself faced by anywhere from one to six relief proposals!

25. The language of the Act provides merely that the Commission shall 'find the amount of the increase in, or imposition of, any duty or import restriction on such article which is necessary to prevent or remedy such injury...' (Sec. 201(d) (1)(A). Or, the Commission shall recommend adjustment assistance if such assistance 'can effectively remedy such injury' (Sec. 201(d)(1)(B). Each one of these remedies or a combination thereof, may be adopted by the President. It is unclear from the statute whether the Commission can recommend that the President seek to negotiate an orderly marketing agreement, although this option is made specifically available to him, as a substitute for relief proposed by the ITC.

clearly established by the Commission decision. The impressionistic character of causality, which ranges from a high level of importers' inventories, to the labour intensiveness of the domestic industry, or the low price of imports, would preclude a specific remedy. Small wonder, therefore, that the nexus between relief and causality seems conspicuous by its absence, and that the President has refused in every case except *Specialty Steel* to go along with the ITC's recommendations for relief, other than adjustment assistance.

Our final judgment on the capstone of the expert economic administration of the process – the remedy – must be, unfortunately, that it is still a long way from satisfying rigorous economic standards. Leaving to one side improvements in the Commission's internal procedures, we question whether it will ever be possible to arrive at recommendations for quantitative restrictions that are economically justifiable. Setting the level of pure quotas, or tariff rate quotas, with a view to remedying an injury, when the injury itself is, to say the least, elusive, may be compared to Lewis Carroll's *Hunting of the Snark*.[26] Small wonder that its findings are shot through with inconsistencies. But the irremediable weakness of its recommendations for quantitative relief must be found not in the Commission's structure nor even in its economic analysis but in the statutory assumption that somehow restrictions on imports will improve industry performance.

4. Import quotas and industry performance

Perhaps the ITC's difficulty in determining import-related injury or probable injury – as distinct from deficient industry performance – is best highlighted by the facts in the automobile dumping case. The complaint was filed by the United Automobile Workers which charged that the increased market share of imported automobiles – up from 15.2 per cent in 1970 to 15.9 per cent in 1974 to 20.3 per cent in the first half of 1975 – was 'at the expense of domestic sales'; that, discounting the effects of the US recession, there was still a loss of domestic sales to imports; and that the pricing of imported cars *caused* the resulting injury to the American automobile industry and its workers. The union demanded the imposition of dumping penalties and simultaneously asked Congress for quota protection against the import of compacts and subcompacts from Europe and Japan.

---

26. Lewis Carrol, *The Hunting of the Snark:* 'They sought it with thimbles, they sought it with care; / They pursued it with forks and hope; / They threatened its life with a railway-share; / They charmed it with smiles and soap.'

The complaint was dismissed 'provisionally,' after extended and bizarre manoeuvering by various instrumentalities of the administrative bureaucracy. To a disinterested observer it is apparent that such injury as the industry suffered was not caused by imports but rather due to deficient performance.

First, a primary factor explaining the industry's travails was the national recession which drastically reduced the demand for virtually all consumer durables, including automobiles.

Second, the success of the imports was partly attributable to the delayed response by US car manufacturers to a shift in consumer demand toward smaller, more fuel-efficient models. As of January 1975, according to the Council on Wage and Price Stability, *no* domestic cars obtained 20 mpg or more in the EPA city driving test, whereas 15 of 19 foreign compacts (small cars) and subcompacts obtained 20 mpg or better. In the highway driving rest, *no* US compact or subcompact car had a mileage rating of over 30 mpg whereas 14 of 19 foreign makes did.

Third, while foreign producers liquidated their large inventories of 1974 models at 1974 prices well into 1975, US manufacturers posted price increases of roughly 12 per cent on their 1975 models which went on sale in the autumn of 1974. This perverse pricing policy by US producers in the face of a deepening recession, combined with the realistic market-oriented price policy of their foreign competitiors, was an additional factor explaining the dramatic market penetration of the imports.

Fourth, the fact that imported compacts and subcompacts offered consumers a far wider range of price alternatives compared to their US counterparts, may also have given imports a competitive edge over domestic models.

In any event, as the Council on Wage and Price Stability told the International Trade Commission, the most important factors explaining the increased market share of foreign automobiles 'are the pricing policies of domestic producers and the inability of domestic manufacturers to respond rapidly to changing market conditions.' The Council warned the ITC that the imposition of special dumping penalties 'would likely result in an immediate increase in the price of. automobiles to the American consumer. Moreover, such penalties, or even the threat of penalties, could substantially check what has been perhaps the single most effective spur to competition in this highly concentrated industry. This, in turn, could lead to less competitive prices and a reduced level of innovation.'

One can only speculate on 'what might have been,' if either dumping penalties or import quotas had been ordered. Would this have intensified the sensitivity of the domestic industry to the vagaries of consumer tastes? Would it have given the lusty automobile oligopoly (which cast itself in the role of an infant industry) the needed respite to adjust to foreign competition without long-term production?

Would it have accelerated the introduction of revolutionary engines or the development of radically new body designs? Would it have spurred investment in US plants by foreign manufacturers, or discouraged the expansion by US multinationals in their foreign affiliates? What would have been the effect on X-efficiency and on the industry's traditional pricing policy? Neither a *savant-sans-cullottes*, nor an expert armed with computer models and multiple regressions would dare offer a definitive response.

Much the same conclusion can be reached with regard to footwear. A perennial supplicant for protection, the shoe manufacturing industry has, in the words of Commissioner Leonard, been almost 'studied to death' in the course of anti-dumping cases, escape clause proceedings and task force reports. As a concession to Congressman Burke, footwear was singled out by name in the Trade Act of 1974.[31]

To determine why the industry, or segments of it, are ailing, to assign the proper degree of responsibility to imports, and to distinguish those ills that derive from the inefficiency, lethargy, and obsolescent plants has presented the Commission with a monumental analytical task. Certainly the performance of the US shoe industry has left much to be desired. And imports have taken a substantial share of US markets. The shoe retailers insist that US manufacturers will not provide the models that attract customers. If during the decade or more that the industry has been under pressure, some firms have modernized and successfully met foreign competition, would three or five years of limitation on Italian and Brazilian shoe imports insure a change in industry mores, the employment of imaginative designers, and the recasting of plants and equipment? If, as the Commission insists, the low wages of foreign workers are responsible for some US firms' difficulties, is it likely that the interval can be used to depress wages in what is already a low-wage industry, unable to attract and hold semi- or unskilled workers? A reasonable hypothesis is that imports have hastened the exit of small, poorly managed firms. But it is impossible even with the most advanced techniques to conclude definitely whether quotas would merely have slowed up this process, at the expense of the consumers or provided a breathing space for a few firms to make a comeback.

Clearly, the problem of assessing quota-performance links is complex, if not insoluble. As US experience with the so-called independent regulatory commissions demonstrates, an administrative agency, in the absence of competitive yardsticks, does not know what constitutes 'good' performance; nor does it know how performance could be improved by changing an industry's structure; and, most important, even if it did, the agency would lack the regulatory arsenal to exact 'good' performance as a quid pro quo for protection from competition.

It is a truism that once competition has been abandoned, or significantly crippled – and this is a necessary consequence of import quotas – some surrogate for the competitive process must be devised to assure acceptable performance and to induce progressive performance. Otherwise, the restrictions imposed would not only be injurious to consumers, and detract from the general welfare, but would also fail to accomplish their only justifiable goal, i.e. to give temporary protection to an infant industry.

It would seem, and here again the US experience with regulation is enlightening, that there are only two systems of industrial organization, each with inherent shortcomings, which might be effective substitutes for competitive controls. One alternative is pervasive, dictatorial regulation, with an elaborate mechanism of rewards and penalties, reaching down to the management level, utilizing the most advanced techniques of management science, and capable of simulating the crucial elements of competitive structure and behaviour. The cost of such regulation, not only directly, but in terms of stifling entrepreneurial initiative, may suffice to condemn it. Another alternative, of course, is government ownership, again with the appropriate complement of efficiency-compelling and progress-inducing directives. In some circumstances, this solution appears to economize resources as compared to 'effective' regulation. However, when the industry in question is not a 'natural' monopoly, both regulation and nationalization (as Oskar Lange recognized long ago) almost inevitably tend to introduce bureaucratic rigidities and inefficiencies whose intensity will increase with the extent and detail of control.

One is driven to the conclusion, therefore, that import restrictions are to be embraced, if at all, only within a framework of comprehensive control, so that 'good' performance is not jeopardized by the attenuation of competition and its disciplinary incentives.

5. Conclusion

Short of total exclusion, import quotas are the most stringent and least flexible limitations on international trade. They are a favourite policy instrument of governments desirous of giving immediate and definitive relief to industries suffering from the discomfiture of foreign competition and its concomitant pressure on sales, prices, and costs. Although a theoretical case, akin to an 'infant industry' argument, can be made for temporary quotas, our examination of quotas in action shows that selecting the 'right' industry for the 'right' kind and the 'right' amount of protection, without excessive costs to the community, is in practice an intractable, if not insoluble problem. Quotas, it seems, are imposed or 'agreed to' in response to the political pressure of vested interests and without regard to the probability that the protected industry will, in the predictably foreseeable future, be able to stand on its own feet.

While we would condemn quotas as an undesirable form of protectionism, we are nevertheless mindful of three special cases sometimes cited to justify their imposition. First, it might be argued that if an efficient exporter (like Japan) is excluded by countries that have no reluctance to impose quotas, then other importing countries must, in self-defence, likewise check the newly augmented competitive pressures. Second, it may be said that, for some products, an inelastic demand and cyclical swings require a regulation of imports to prevent market disruptions. Third, a more general case for quotas is said to exist when a country has become so inefficient in almost all lines of production that imports threaten to destroy most of its basic industries. At present, Great Britain is said by some to be in this predicament.

With regard to the first problem – that is, how to cope with the 'focusing' of exports to a single, or a few countries, because they alone do not erect quantitative barriers – we suggest that this is a problem to be resolved by bargaining among the exporting countries. If, for example, Japanese steel is excluded from Europe and sold in the USA at lower prices than before, European producers would quickly find that they have lost their US markets to the Japanese steel they pushed out of their home territories. They would then be compelled to recognize the futility of unilateral quota restrictions. Moreover, in that event, the USA might (perhaps, justifiably) retalliate by imposing the same import restrictions on European exporters that the EEC has placed on Japan – with the understanding that the quotas would be removed as soon as the EEC reversed its position.

With regard to the second problem – the simultaneous occurrence of world-wide business cycles in the industrialized countries – it is doubtful that import quotas are the proper solution. Aside from the fact that protecting lethargic oligopolies from competition will not cure a world-wide recession – any more than did the 'beggar-thy-neighbour' tariffs of the 1930's – it may well be that in periods of stagflation import competition is one of the most felicitous, short-run public policies to check price increases which threaten to choke off an incipient recovery.

As to the third problem – i.e., when a nation's whole industrial structure is infected with high costs, low productivity, antiquated plant capacity, or similar disadvantages – international trade can be carried on only if the nation is willing to accept the realities of the situation. That is, it must forego a high level of consumption – it must stop living beyond its means – until it is capable of using its resources more efficiently. Excluding imports, without more, will do nothing to improve its productivity. Employment may rise, but this goal could be achieved by other, less deleterious techniques than quantitative exclusion of imports. Thus, Great Britain, where nationalized industries such as automobiles and steel have 'suffered' from substantial imports, cannot resolve the underlying problems of these industries simply by eliminating import competition. Nor can Great Britain hope to maintain a high level of competitive exports by pursuing a policy of import exclusion. In this case, the erosion of domestic markets by imports is a symptom of the disease, not the disease itself, and policy makers must distinguish between them in devising the appropriate cure.

In sum, the resort to quotas in an effort to relieve an industry from one form of competition must be condemned in all but very exceptional circumstances. One such circumstance is where a society has decided to abandon the regulatory mechanism of competition, and to substitute in its place centralized planning and direction of economic activity. In such an economy, quotas do have a place – as part of a total control system which relies on mechanisms other than competition to provide the 'right' incentives and 'right' operational rules to assure acceptable industrial performance. But short of a comprehensive revision of the whole economic system, and the economic calculus by which to appraise public policy, it is illusory to suppose that import restrictions *per se* can somehow restore or impart to individual industries, or to an entire economy, those qualities that will enable them to emulate the efficiency of their dreaded competitors.

X. UK INDUSTRY AND THE WORLD ECONOMY: A CASE OF DE-INDUSTRIALIZATION?

Ajit Singh

1. The phenomenon known as 'de-industrialization'

Over the last couple of years in the UK, there has been growing discussion of a phenomenon known as the 'de-industrialization' of the UK economy. Writing in his usual forceful manner, the then Secretary for Industry, Anthony Wedgwood Benn, observed in 1975:

The trend to contraction of British manufacturing industry which we are now suffering has gathered force in the last four years. If this trend is allowed to continue, we will have closed down 15 per cent of our entire manufacturing capacity and nearly 2 million industrial workers will have been made redundant between 1970 and 1980. During the five years 1970–74 there was a 7 per cent fall in employment in manufacturing in Britain, while it was still rising in most of our competitor countries. In this period the total number of manufacturing jobs lost through redundancy averaged about 180,000 a year and the net contraction of manufacturing employment averaged 120,000 a year. Only about one in three of the jobs lost through redundancy was effectively replaced by the creation of a new job in the manufacturing sector (Benn, 1975).[1]

Mr. Benn's concern with this process of de-industrialization has been echoed by both academic and Government economists. For example, Roger Bacon and Walter Eltis, in their recent widely publicized analysis of the ills of the UK economy, argue that the major problem during the last decade has not been the lack of growth of industrial productivity. The latter (with a growth rate of

The author wishes to thank A. D. Cosh, T. F. Cripps, J. L. Eatwell, A. Hughes, G. Meeks, A. Sen, and V. Woodward for helpful discussions or comments. An earlier version of the paper was given at the Nijenrode Conference on Industrial Organization at Breukelen, Holland, in August 1976, and it has benefited from comments made there, particularly by R. E. Caves, H. W. de Jong, P. E. Hart and C. C. Von Weiszäcker.
1. The theme was subsequently taken up by other Government ministers: e.g. the Chancellor of the Exchequer, Dennis Healey, in February 1976, 'The TUC and Labour party are united in believing that the steady contraction in our manufacturing industry is the main reason for our disappointing economic performance. This contraction must be halted and reversed' (quoted in Bacon and Eltis, 1976b).

approximately 4 per cent a year), in their view, has been quite respectable, both in terms of previous historical experience and by comparison with other industrial countries. They identify the central problem as the fall in the number of people employed in industry by 14 per cent over this period, and suggest that 'it is from this basic fact that the disastrous course the British economy followed in 1965–75 stems, and this was one result of the real structural maladjustment of the British economy that has occurred in these ten years and is still occurring.'[2]

The notion of de-industrialization as applied to an advanced industrial economy immediately raises a host of conceptual difficulties. Firstly, there is the simple, but by no means entirely trivial, question: What is so special about industry that one should be concerned about 'de-industrialization'? There has also been a considerable loss of employment from agriculture, but not much has been said, at least by economists, about de-ruralization. Secondly, it may well be that de-industrialization (particularly in the sense of loss of employment from the industrial sector) is a long-run structural feature of all advanced industrial countries: beyond a certain level of economic development or 'industrial maturity', it may not be possible to increase the proportion of the labour force employed in industry and Britain, for historical reasons, may have attained such a level of maturity earlier than some other advanced countries. Thirdly, and much more importantly, in an *open* economy, the so-called phenomenon of de-industrialization may be no more than a normal adjustment to changing domestic and world market conditions.

In fact an important purpose of this paper will be to argue that, in an open economy, the question whether de-industrialization can in any sense be regarded as implying 'structural maladjustment' cannot be properly considered in terms of the characteristics of the domestic economy alone. Such a proposition has a sensible meaning only in the context of the interactions of the economy with the rest of the world, i.e. in terms of its overall trading and payments position in the world economy. Thus one major aim of this paper is to provide a valid economic meaning for the concept of de-industrialization for the UK economy, to assess its empirical relevance and to indicate its economic consequences, if any. The second and related purpose is to articulate, to extend and to empirically examine an important line of argument which has been put forward to account for the phenomenon of de-industrialization: that, whether or not it is caused by, it is certainly made much worse by, Britain's increasing participation in the international economy under the existing institutional arrangements (namely free trade and free convertibility of currency).

---

2. Bacon and Eltis (1976a), p. 10. See also Bacon and Eltis (1975); Panic (1976); Department of Employment (1975); Moore and Rhodes (1976).

It is suggested that, for a number of reasons, Britain's industrial economy has been a weak relative to that of her main competitors. Consequently liberalization of trade has been detrimental to British industry since it has inevitably led to a much faster increase in imports of manufactured goods without a concomitant rise in exports.[3] This is an interesting and important hypothesis both from a theoretical standpoint and from the point of view of public policy. It raises a number of rather complex questions, which cannot all be dealt with here. However an attempt will be made at least to clarify the main points of the argument and to outline some of the evidence which bears on them.

The paper deals with a whole range of closely related but usually analytically distinct questions, which we shall discuss in the following order. We shall find it useful to start with the second set of issues, and ask precisely in what sense participation in the international economy can contribute to de-industrialization, or more generally be harmful rather than helpful to an economy. This question will first be examined at a preliminary level, from the point of view of economic history in section 2 and in more theoretical terms in section 3. Sections 4 and 5 revert to the first set of issues above and examine changes in the structural characteristics of the British economy in terms of its own history and in comparison with other countries. More specifically, these sections will discuss the significance of industry for the UK economy and the question whether there has been greater loss of employment or output in the manufacturing sector in the UK in recent years than elsewhere. In section 6, the notion of an 'efficient' economic structure is developed in terms of the interaction of the economy with the rest of the world, i.e. its overall trading and payments position. Empirical evidence bearing on this issue – whether and in what sense the observed loss of employment in the manufacturing sector in the UK really implies structural maladjustment in the economy – will then be discussed. This evidence also bears *inter alia* on the related question of whether continuing participation in the international economy is leading to a further deterioration of Britain's economic position and, more specifically, of its manufacturing sector. Section 7 will summarize the main conclusions.

---

3. See, for instance, Cambridge Economic Policy Group (1976), Chapter 1. Bacon and Eltis (1976a), incidentally, take a rather different view; they attribute de-industrialization to the rapid growth of employment in the 'non-industrial' sector of the economy, and particularly in the public services. A systematic examination of this hypothesis is outside the scope of this paper, but some of the evidence presented in sections 4–6 will have a bearing on it.

2. The effects of foreign competition on domestic manufacturing industry

It is somewhat ironic that an Indian economist like myself should be discussing the question of the de-industrialization of the UK economy. For one of the major issues in the economic history of India during the nineteenth century is the contention of a number of Indian historians that, unlike the West European countries, which during that century were undergoing the process of industrial revolution, for the Indian economy it was an age of de-industrialization or ruralization.[4] It is contended that, as a result of free trade and competition with imported machine-made goods from the UK, as well as other policies of the colonial Government, traditional Indian manufacturing industry declined during this period, without being replaced by modern industry on a sufficient scale, or by expansion in other sectors of the economy.

There was therefore a significant fall in the proportion of the labour force employed in manufacturing and a consequent increase in the agricultural population (which in turn is thought to have added to the difficulties of the agrarian economy). Thus A. K. Bagchi, in his carefully documented study of Gangetic Bihar, found that over the period 1809–13 tot 1901, the number of people dependent on secondary industry fell by about 45 per cent; the proportion of the population thus dependent declined from 18.6 to 8.5 per cent, with little evidence of modernization either in industry or in other economic sectors. For the country as a whole, Bagchi's evidence is much more tentative, but he concludes that for most of the nineteenth century the Indian economy experienced de-industrialization, in the sense that both the proportion of output contributed by industry and the labour force employed in industry declined significantly.[5]

However, the possible adverse consequences of free trade need not be confined to the less-developed countries. Even in the country which was first to industrialize and which many commentators would regard as having benefited

4. See the debate between Morris D. Morris, Toru Matsui, Bipan Chandra and T. Raychaudhuri, on the re-interpretation of nineteenth century Indian economic history, in *Indian Economic and Social History Review* (1968). See also D. and A. Thorner (1962), Chapter 6.
5. Bagchi (1967). See also Bagchi (1976), pp. 135–165. For theoretical support for the de-industrialization thesis, cf. Hicks (1969), who comments on the phenomenon in the following way: 'The English handloom weavers, who were displaced by textile machinery, could (in the end and after much travail) find re-employment in England; but what of the Indian weavers who were displaced by the same improvement? Even in their case there would be a favourable effect, somewhere, but it might be anywhere; there would be no particular reason why it should be in India. The poorer the country, the narrower will be its range of opportunities; the more likely, therefore, it is that it will suffer long-lasting damage, now and then, from a backlash of improvements that have occurred elsewhere' (p. 165).

substantially from international trade over the last two centuries, there have been frequent references to the detrimental effects of competition on domestic manufacturing industry. Time and again it has been argued – and, recent studies suggest, with ample justification[6] – that competition from the expanding industries of the countries which followed (e.g. Germany, France, Japan) was arresting the growth and development of British industry. In the last quarter of the nineteenth century, and in the period up to World War One, Britain's share of world exports fell and her imports rose steeply. It is estimated that the rate of growth of UK manufacturing exports fell from 4.8 per cent a year in constant prices in the period 1854–72 to 2.1 per cent a year during 1876–1910; her share in world exports of manufactures fell from 41.4 per cent in 1880 to 29.9 per cent in 1913, whereas it had increased in the earlier period. Not unlike the current situation of the UK economy, there was at the same time a sharp increase in import penetration of manufactures: between 1870–74 and the early years of the twentieth century, the share of imports of finished consumer goods in total consumption rose from 9.5 per cent to 20 per cent; the rate of growth of manufactured imports during 1883–1913 averaged 3.4 per cent a year.[7]

It has been pointed out that this major turn-round in the UK foreign trade position came about not because British wage costs were rising faster than in other countries,[8] but simply as a consequence of the industrialization and expansion of the economies of Britain's competitor countries. During the first half of the nineteenth century, while those countries were developing, British exports to them rose very fast, providing a powerful stimulus to her economic growth. But by the last quarter of the century, when such countries had reached a certain level of development, not only were British exports to them falling, but they were also able to compete with British exports in third markets (such as the USA) and eventually in Britain's own home markets. This is reflected in the following figures for the rate of growth of net exports of British manufactures (i.e. the difference between the growth rates of exports and imports) at constant prices (Lewis, 1967): 1836–53: 5.7 per cent, 1853–73: 2.9 per cent, 1873–1907: 1.5 per cent.

Thus although a whole complex of factors contributed to the observed decline in the rate of growth of British industry during the forty years preceding World

6. See for instance Conrad and Meyer (1965), chapter 5; Lewis (1967). Both focus on the period before World War One. For illuminating analyses of the relationship between foreign trade and economic growth for the British economy over the last century or more, see, in particular, Sayers (1965) and Matthews (1973).

7. See Conrad and Meyer (1965), Lewis (1967), and Aldcroft (1968) for sources for these figures.

8. Matthews (1973). Figures given by Phelps Brown and Brown (1968) suggest that during the last quarter of the 19th century, British costs fell relative to foreign costs.

War One,[9] it would be difficult to deny the very important role played by foreign competition in bringing it about.[10]

In this context, R. S. Sayers (1965) makes a useful distinction between the 'complementary' and 'competitive' aspects of economic growth elsewhere. This distinction is relevant in assessing the gains a country can make from foreign trade in a dynamic world, which is necessarily characterized by uneven development of productive potential over time and in different regions. Economic growth elsewhere[11] is 'complementary' to the extent that it raises demand for exports, but it becomes 'competitive' insofar as it leads to the development of alternative sources of supply. The essential point is that expansion of the world economy, although it may raise the demand for a country's products, also creates alternative sources of supply, which may compete with them in any market, including its home market. So, from the point of view of a particular country, the development of the world economy may be characterized by a changing balance between 'complementarity' and competitiveness'.

As far as the British economy is concerned, Sayers argues that 'competitiveness' was the dominant element after 1880 and, more particularly, in the interwar period. However, in the first fifteen years after World War Two there was a historically unprecedented increase in British exports: between 1945 and 1960 their volume grew by 250 per cent relative to the 1938 level. At least in the first decade after the war, this was largely because British industry had emerged relatively unscathed compared with that of her competitors, and was therefore able to greatly increase exports to the latter, as well as to third countries.[12]

9. The rate of growth of British industry (manufacturing and mining) declined from 2.7 per cent a year during the period 1853–75 to 2.1 per cent a year during 1873–1907. This led to an overall decline in the growth rate of GDP, in spite of the fact that the service industries grew faster during the latter period. See further Lewis (1967).
10. After a careful analysis of the various hypotheses concerning the slow-down in the growth of British industry during this period, Lewis (1967) comes to the conclusion that 'the major responsibility' must lie with the sharp decline in the growth of net manufactured exports as a consequence of foreign competition. In fact, he argues that protection against foreign manufactured imports (as was being practised by other countries) would have considerably benefited British industry. Conrad and Meyer (1965) also ascribe the decline in industrial growth to the deterioration in Britain's trading position in manufactures, which they suggest is 'best explained as a consequence more of external than of internal causes'. See also Matthews (1973), Sayers (1965) and Levine (1967).
11. This argument refers to the effects merely of economic expansion abroad; but one should also consider the nature of technical progress in other countries, which could also be biased either towards 'competitiveness' or 'complementarity', in the sense discussed above. This phenomenon is well known in the literature on the theory of international trade, although it is usually discussed in a different context. See Hicks (1959), Johnson (1962).
12. In fact, the UK was finally able to get her area and commodity pattern of trade into the right lines, i.e. into the faster growing European markets and into exports of the more advanced engineering and metal products.

Although the situation began to change as the West European countries and Japan rebuilt their industry, nevertheless, at least up to the early 1960s, the 'complementary' aspects of foreign growth seem to have been predominant.

The above discussion suggests that, even for a developed country, simply as a consequence of the changing pattern of development of the world economy, international trade can have undesirable consequences during certain periods; i.e. the 'competitive aspects' of economic expansion elsewhere can become dominant and create disequilibrium. It may be noted that the above analysis has been confined simply to one aspect of participation in the international economy – namely trade in goods and services. I have not discussed the precise mechanisms through which trade affects the growth and structure of the economy; nor have I considered other channels – for example the balance of payments, terms of trade etc. – through which involvement in the international economy can affect these variables for better or for worse. Nevertheless, this extremely brief and schematic examination of the historical effects of an aspect of international economic relations on a nation's economic growth does raise the question whether, as a consequence of the further development of the world economy and that of Britain's competitors, the 'competitive aspects' have again become dominant (perhaps cripplingly so) for the British economy during the last ten years.

3. Ways in which participation in the international economy could lead to de-industrialization

Those who argue that it is continuing participation in the regime of free trade and free convertibility of currency[13] which is mainly responsible for the deterioration of the British economy in recent years, and in particular for the loss of employment in the manufacturing sector, are not simply referring to the 'competitive' effects of growth abroad on the British economy. From a theoretical standpoint, there is a complex inter-relationship between foreign trade, international payments and economic growth, which for reasons of space cannot be fully discussed in this paper.[14] However, in order to clarify the empirical issues

13. Of course, it is not being suggested that trade and capital movements between the UK and other countries are completely 'free': the term is used in a relative sense and refers specifically to the increased liberalization of trade and capital movements which has taken place among the industrial countries during the 1960s, and, in the case of the British economy, particularly since her entry into the EEC.
14. There are a number of formal models which explore the relationship between aspects of trade, the balance of payments and domestic economic activity. (See for example, Bardhan (1965), Black (1970), Corden (1971), Krueger (1969), Oniki and Uzawa (1965), Stern (1973), Whitman (1970).) These can

involved in the line of argument indicated above, it will be useful to outline the most important ways in which participation in the international economy could possibly lead to a shrinking manufacturing sector, or 'de-industrialization'.

In discussing the international position of the economy, one must obviously consider not just its foreign trade, but also its balance of payments. There are three distinct, though related, channels through which the trade and payments position of an economy can affect its growth and industrial development: (a) through the level of demand; (b) through the structure of demand and, most importantly; (c) through investment.

Apart from its direct effect on specific industries, foreign competition clearly also has an indirect effect on the overall level of demand in the economy. The latter seems to have been important in the period before World War One and in the inter-war years. However, nowadays if there is, for example, a fall in the demand for exports, this need not necessarily mean a lower level of effective demand in the economy, since governments can, and do, use Keynesian fiscal and monetary measures to counteract such a shortfall. But the foreign trade position affects the balance of payments, which, under the present institutional arrangements, is a major constraint on the government's ability to maintain a high level of effective demand in the economy.

Successful foreign competition can affect the structure of demand and output by pushing a country out of those markets or industries which are technically most advanced or which have the highest potential for productivity growth.[15] Thus one reason for concern about the reduction in the relative or absolute size of the manufacturing sector is the belief that this sector of the economy is subject to dynamic economies of scale, so that its decline will reduce the potential for future economic growth (see further section 4 below).

The level and direction of investment may be affected in three different ways. First, the foreign trade position and the balance of payments affect the level of

be broadly classified into two types: (1) the short-run Keynesian or post-Keynesian growth models of the Harrod-Domar variety, which stress the role of demand factors, but usually neglect the feedback effects of investment on growth, productivity, and hence competitiveness and trade in the medium and long run; (2) the neo-classical models which do take into account the supply-side effects, but neglect the role of effective demand. Both types are invariably equilibrium models and are therefore not very helpful in explaining the real world of disequilibrium and change. This section has been much influenced by the less formal, but much richer analysis of Matthews (1973) and Kaldor (1970, 1971), as well as earlier work of Kindleberger (1962) and Myrdal (1957), which consider both the demand and supply side effects, and comment on the dynamics of the system in disequilibrium. Also useful in this context are the 'export-led growth' models of Lamfalussy (1963) and Beckerman (1962). See also Caves (1970) and Whitman (1967).

15. This is the familiar argument of spokesmen for many of the less-developed countries, that historically foreign trade has pushed them into 'unfavourable' patterns of production, for which terms of trade move against them in the long run, and for which growth potential is low. See for instance Kindleberger (1962).

aggregate demand, which in turn influences investment decisions.[16] Secondly, foreign competition may bring about a fall in the rate of profit, which will also influence the inducement to invest. Thirdly, if foreign economies enjoy a faster rate of growth or greater profitability, this may not merely mean less foreign investment in the UK. It may also result in the switching of investment abroad by UK companies (thus, incidentally, immediately exacerbating the balance-of-payments situation). This is an extremely important consideration for a country which, for historical reasons, has a tradition of investing abroad, and which has more large multinational companies than its competitors.[17] These companies are likely to be highly sensitive to differences in profitability and growth prospects.

The most important point to note here is that if the economy happens to be in disequilibrium, all these effects may work together in a cumulative and circular chain of causation, in the way suggested by Myrdal (1957), and thereby help to perpetuate the disequilibrium. For instance, a country in a weak competitive position and with balance-of-payments difficulties, will, because of the operation of these forces, have a lower rate of increase of effective demand, and hence a lower rate of investment, and a lower rate of technical progress and growth in productivity. It will thus be in an even weaker competitive position than before, especially as the same forces will be working in the opposite direction to improve the position of its more successful rivals.

On the above argument, the original source of the disequilibrium (i.e. how the economy has got itself into a weak competitive position and balance-of-payments difficulties in the first place) is not particularly important. The imbalance could have arisen from the kind of considerations discussed in section 2, i.e. because of the nature and pace of economic development abroad; this in fact is the most likely source. It could of course also be due to the choice of an incorrect exchange rate;[18] alternatively it could be due to weaknesses having gradually developed in the internal economy – say, on account of a deterioration in industrial relations or in the quality of entrepreneurship. These factors could have acted singly or together in producing the initial disequilibrium. But, whatever the cause, according to the theory of cumulative and circular causation, such an economy, if it continues to participate in international economic

16. Foreign trade may also affect investment from the supply side. Nurkse (1956) gives an interesting example of this phenomenon for the UK economy for the immediate post-war period. In the early and middle 1950s there was a severe capacity constraint in the engineering and metal products industries. The effect of this was to reduce investment generally, in order to allow exports of these commodities, which were essential for balance-of-payments reasons.

17. See George and Ward (1975); Jacquemin and de Lichtbuer (1973) and Singh (1975).

18. Many economists have argued that the UK had an over-valued exchange rate in the early 1960s. See for example Kaldor (1971). Moggridge (1969) makes a similar point with respect to the 1920's.

relations on the same terms as before, will suffer a continual contraction (or a reduction in its manufacturing sector, if it is competing mainly in manufactures).

The above result is in sharp contrast to that provided by orthodox theory, which suggests that if there is disequilibrium, market forces will automatically tend to correct it. It does not deny that the correction of disequilibrium of the kind discussed above will require changes in the terms on which the country participates in the international economy, and/or in its productive structure. But, by assuming complete wage-price flexibility, it argues that disequilibrium will induce changes in the exchange rate and other prices which will automatically bring these about.[19]

However, even assuming wage-price flexibility, whether market forces can restore equilibrium depends crucially on the nature and adequacy of the response of entrepreneurs in bringing about the required changes in the productive structure, as well as the magnitude of the relevant elasticities for exports and imports, and in a dynamic world on the speed of these adjustments. Now if, for institutional reasons, real wages and the exchange rate are not sufficiently flexible,[20] there cannot be any presumption that market forces will on their own be able to correct the disequilibrium. In such a situation, government action of one kind or another (fiscal and monetary policy, tariffs, wage-price controls, etc.) is required to bring about changes in the economic structure and the terms on which the country participates in the international economy, so as to prevent further deterioration of its economic position.

19. See Caves and Jones (1973), chapter 16, where the properties of such a model are analyzed. (Needless to say, they do not claim that it is realistic. In some variants of this model international capital movements also play an additional equilibrating role. See Mundell (1968).

20. The nature and degree of wage-price flexibility in the real world are essentially empirical questions. Frankel and Johnson (1976), however, provide a theoretical justification for the assumption of wage flexibility: 'That the monetary approach [to the balance of payments] largely assumes a fully employed economy is partly the result of the fact that in the context of a growing world economy in the long run the assumption of wage rigidity and variable employment becomes uninteresting; either employment expands into the full employment range and quantity adjustments yield to money, price and wage adjustments, or it contracts and people starve to death and go back to full employment numbers, or there is a revolution on Marxist lines, or more likely the public simply votes for the other political party than the one in power, since all of them promise to maintain full employment and the public expects them to do it'. They go on to add: 'More fundamentally, the assumption of normally full employment reflects the passage of time and the accumulation of experience of reasonably full employment as the historical norm rather than the historical rarity that Keynes's theory and the left-wing Keynesian mythology made it out to be'. This reads rather oddly at a time when unemployment in most advanced capitalist economies ranges between 6 per cent and 10 per cent, and when organizations such as the OECD are seriously concerned about the problem of rising long-term unemployment in the industrial countries.

4. The de-industrialization of the UK economy

In the light of the above historical and *a priori* discussion of the relationship between trade, the balance of payments and domestic economic activity, and how these may interact in certain circumstances to produce long-term economic contraction, we shall now consider the set of questions raised in section 1 concerning the de-industrialization of the UK economy in recent years. We shall examine empirical evidence about the nature and extent of this phenomenon, as well as the position of UK industry in the world economy.

However, before considering these questions there is a logically prior issue which must be discussed, namely: Why should one be so concerned with the fate of the manufacturing sector, while neglecting other sectors, for example, services? This is a particularly relevant question in the case of the UK economy, since it has been argued that its comparative advantage is now in services, rather than in manufacturing.[21]

The answer seems to me to lie chiefly in two major factors: (a) the relative contributions of manufacturing and services to UK exports and the balance of payments, and (b) structural characteristics of the manufacturing sector and its potential for technical progress and productivity growth. We shall briefly examine each of these in turn.

As far as (a) is concerned, it is, indeed, true that invisibles have traditionally made an important contribution to the UK balance on current account. There has usually been a positive balance on invisibles and a negative one on visible trade. However, since, for historical reasons, UK firms and citizens have been major investors abroad, much the greater part of the surplus on invisibles tends to be made up of net credit on interest, profits and dividend payments. Now, if the economy is in disequilibrium and an improvement in the balance of payments is sought, one cannot normally rely on a greater contribution from this source. An increased capital outflow will usually be required to generate greater dividends, profits and interest payments in the future, but this will *inter alia* worsen the balance of payments in the short and the medium term.[22] For this reason, as well as the issue of comparative advantage mentioned above, the relevant comparison is really between trade in manufactures and that in private services (tourism, sea

21. A. K. Cairncross argued this point strongly in a paper given at the S.S.R.C. conference on industrial economics in Oxford in December 1975. He did not, however, provide empirical evidence in support of the assertion. It is interesting to recall that similar suggestions were also made at the end of the nineteenth century. See Lewis (1967) and Levine (1968).

22. Cf. Reddaway (1968). In principle, it would be possible to increase the net contribution from this source by imposing controls on outflows of dividends etc., as is done by many less-developed countries. However, such a course is hardly open to the UK economy under the present institutional arrangements.

Table 1. The relative trade performance of manufacturing and services:[1] UK 1966–75

	Ratio of exports of manufactures to those of private-services (current values)	Trade ratio for manufactures[1]	Trade ratio for private services[2]
1966	2.37	0.31	0.08
1967	2.04	0.24	0.10
1968	2.10	0.21	0.13
1969	2.19	0.24	0.12
1970	1.98	0.23	0.12
1971	1.95	0.25	0.12
1972	1.87	0.16	0.12
1973	1.91	0.11	0.11
1974	2.04	0.09	0.13
1975	2.14	0.14	0.13

Source:
C.S.O. (1974), (1975), (1976a).

Notes:
1. 'Exports' and 'Imports' of private services are defined so as to include credits and debits in invisible trade on account of sea transport, civil aviation, travel and 'other services'. Other services include commissions etc. on imports and exports, telecommunications and postal services; films and television royalties received and paid; services rendered by and to UK enterprises; construction work overseas and financial and allied services, such as banking, insurance and merchanting. Interest received by UK banks and other financial institutions and profits of their overseas branches, subsidiaries etc. are not included, nor are interests paid to foreign banks, financial institutions and profits to their UK subsidiaries, branches, etc. See further C.S.O. [1976a].

2. The trade ratio is defined as $\dfrac{\text{Exports} - \text{Imports}}{\text{Exports} + \text{Imports}}$.

Its maximum value is $+1$ (indicating complete trade advantage) and its minimum -1 (indicating complete disadvantage). *Ceteris paribus*, a reduction in this ratio over time denotes a lack of competitiveness.

transport and civil aviation, city and financial services etc.).[23] Table 1 compares the relative importance, and very roughly the relative performance, of trade in these two sectors of the economy. The first thing to notice is that the value of manufactured exports usually runs at twice the level of gross credit from services and that this ratio has remained much the same over the last decade. Secondly, although a proper examination of the question of comparative advantage would take us too far away from the main subject of this paper, we note that in recent

23. We shall ignore the credits and debits on government services for the purpose of this discussion. Such services normally constitute a relatively small part of the total trade in services, and invariably show a deficit. However, activities of public corporations (such as British Airways) are included in the category of private services.

years the UK does appear to have performed relatively better in its trade in services than in manufactures. The trade ratio (which is used here as a rough indicator of trade performance) for services has remained more or less constant since 1968, while that for manufactures has fallen sharply since 1971.[24]

Can one conclude from this evidence that there is no need for concern about de-industrialization in the UK economy, and that more resources should in fact be allocated to the expansion of private services? Considering the balance-of-payments position alone, there are strong grounds for thinking that the latter course would at best produce no more than a marginal improvement. The main reason for this is that when trade in 'services' is examined at a more disaggregated level, it turns out that almost the whole of the surplus on these services is contributed by a category known as 'other services' (which includes the city's financial services, royalties etc.). The credits on sea transport, civil aviation and tourism are roughly matched by equivalent debits in each case, and there has been relatively little improvement in this situation over the last decade. On the other hand, there has been an enormous growth in the credits from the city's financial services (a seven-fold increase during the last decade), but their total gross value (about £ 700 million) in 1975 amounted to only a tenth of total service exports and to less than 5 per cent of exports of manufactures.[25] So, although there may be scope for further expansion of financial and possibly some other services, this is unlikely to have more than a minor impact on the overall trade balance. The continuing importance of the manufacturing sector for the balance of payments can therefore hardly be overstated. This is particularly so since even a marginal improvement in the latter, brought about either by the allocation of more resources to services or their more efficient utilization, could easily be more than offset if the trading performance of the manufacturing sector were to continue to deteriorate. (See further section 6).

The other major reason for giving special attention to the manufacturing sector is its significance from the point of view of the structure of the economy. Many people would accept that it is a dynamic sector with increasing returns and a high growth of productivity, especially compared with the service sector, where both the level and the rate of growth of productivity tend to be much lower.[26]

24. This ratio has many limitations. See Balassa (1967) and Panic and Rajan (1971). As a consequence, it is valid only to compare the movements over time in the values of such ratios, not to compare their absolute values for the two sectors in any specific year. See section 4 for a further discussion of other measures of trade performance for UK manufacturing industry.
25. C.S.O. (1976a). It is interesting to note that another item in 'other services' to show a large increase in gross value, particularly during the last three years, is that of 'commissions, etc. on imports'; in 1975, the credits on this item amounted to nearly half the gross value of the credits from the city's financial services.
26. In his careful analysis of the US service economy over the period 1929–65, Fuchs (1968) found that the annual average rate of growth of productivity in industry was 2.2 per cent compared with 1.1

Although on the basis of the evidence produced to show the validity of Verdoorn's Law, there may be some dispute about whether manufacturing is subject to 'dynamic economies of scale' in Kaldor's sense,[27] there is a great deal more solidly based relevant evidence concerning the dynamic role of the manufacturing sector in economic growth. For instance, Cripps and Tarling (1973), in their analysis of the growth process in advanced industrial countries during 1950–1970, have confirmed Kaldor's hypothesis that there is a close relationship between the rate of growth of a country's GDP and the growth of its manufacturing sector. This relationship is much closer than would be expected (since manufacturing is quite a large component of GDP) on purely statistical grounds; it is also closer than that observed between the growth of GDP and of other sectors of the economy. Therefore from the point of view of the future growth potential of the economy, a shrinkage in its manufacturing sector is clearly a cause for legitimate concern.

5. The nature and extent of the decline in UK manufacturing industry

It will be useful first to examine the decline in UK manufacturing industry in a historical perspective, i.e. in terms of long-run structural changes in the economy. Figure 1 shows the proportion of the labour force employed in manufacturing over the last hundred years, as well as the proportion of GDP contributed by this sector since 1907.[28]

Although such long-run comparisons inevitably involve statistical problems, Figure 1 demonstrates how difficult it is to sustain the thesis of 'de-industrialisation' for a mature industrial economy like that of the UK, when one considers changes over a period of a century. Indeed, the proportion of the labour force engaged in manufacturing activity was just about the same in 1970 as it was in 1871. This proportion certainly did not remain constant throughout, but if we abstract from cyclical fluctuations, its general level was much the same (perhaps slightly lower) in the inter-war period as in the fifty years before World War One. There was, however, a trend increase in manufacturing's share in the labour force

per cent in services. He concluded that such a difference in growth rates over a long period could not be accounted for in terms of the well-known problems of the measurement of the output of the service industry. Instead, on the basis of the usual production function analysis, he attributed nearly half the observed difference (0.5 per cent a year) to more rapid technological change or greater economies of scale in industry compared with services.

27. See Kaldor (1966, 1975); Rowthorn (1975a, 1975b).
28. Corresponding figures for the period before 1907 are not readily available, but rough comparisons can be made with the data given in Deane & Cole (1962), Table 37.

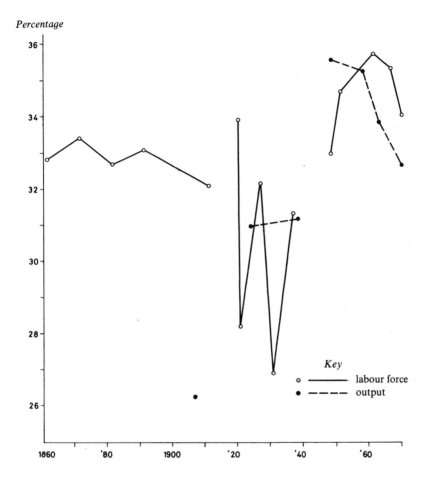

Percentage

Fig. 1. Share of manufacturing in the UK economy: labour force 1861–1970 and output (in current prices) 1907–1970.

Sources and notes

(a) The share of manufacturing in the labour force is measured by the numbers occupied in manufacturing as a percentage of the total working population. *Sources*: for 1861–1911, Feinstein (1972); for 1921–1970, London and Cambridge Economic Service (1971). The data plotted are for selected years (normally census, but also some intercensal years), excluding the two wars.

(b) The share of manufacturing in output is measured by its contribution to net output (i.e. gross domestic product) in the bench-mark years (which are usually the census of production years) 1907, 1924, 1938, 1948, 1958, 1963 and 1970. *Sources*: For 1907–1948, Feinstein (1972). For 1958 and 1963, C.S.O. (1970); For 1970, C.S.O. (1976c).

Fig. 1. Share of manufacturing in the UK economy: labour force 1861–1970 and output (in current prices) 1907–1970.

(of about 4 percentage points) between the mid-1930s and the early-1960s; it has since been slowly declining.[29]

As far as the proportion of output contributed by manufacturing is concerned, the picture is slightly different. Even when the share of manufacturing in net output is measured in current prices,[30] there was some trend increase between the period before World War One and the inter-war period (Deane and Cole, 1962). There was a relatively larger increase between the mid-1930s and the mid-1950s, but since then there has been a decline.

In order to examine in greater detail the more recent trends in the share of manufacturing in output and employment, figure 2 considers the period 1955–75. It also includes a series for overall unemployment as an indicator of cyclical fluctuations in the economy. The chart clearly shows that there has been a trend decline in the proportion of the labour force employed in manufacturing since the early 1960s, which accelerated in the late 1960s. Thus there was a larger fall in the proportion employed in manufacturing between the recession year 1972 and 1975 (i.e. the year before the cyclical trough was reached) than between the recession years 1968 and 1972. The latest figures show that in absolute terms, the numbers employed in manufacturing have decreased by nearly a million between 1968 and 1976; by 1976 the proportion employed in manufacturing had fallen to 32 per cent (Brittan, 1977).

However, if we consider the share of manufacturing in output at *constant* 1963 prices, the picture is rather different. We find a very slow secular increase in share until the latest downturn in the economy in 1973, since when it has fallen much more sharply than in previous recessions. On the other hand, if the contribution of manufacturing is measured in current prices (not shown in figure 2), there is clear evidence of a trend decline since the middle 1950s, which is demonstrated in the figure on the following page.

Next we consider the important hypothesis that de-industrialization as discussed above (i.e. a trend reduction in the share of manufacturing at least in the labour force, if not in output) is not simply a feature peculiar to the UK economy, but is a long-rung structural feature of all industrial economies.[31] The argument is simply that all advanced industrial economies beyond a certain stage of their development may be subject to similar structural changes, resulting in the

---

29. There was in fact a similar increase in manufacturing employment immediately following World War One, but it could not be sustained (see Chart 1). Cf. Deane & Cole (1962).

30. As the prices of manufactured products may in general be expected to fall relatively more than those in other sectors of the economy (because of the effect of greater productivity gains), manufacturing should show a larger increase in its share of GDP if its contribution is measured in constant prices.

31. For studies of long-run changes in the economic structure of the industrialized countries, see Kuznets (1971) and Fuchs (1968).

Percentage

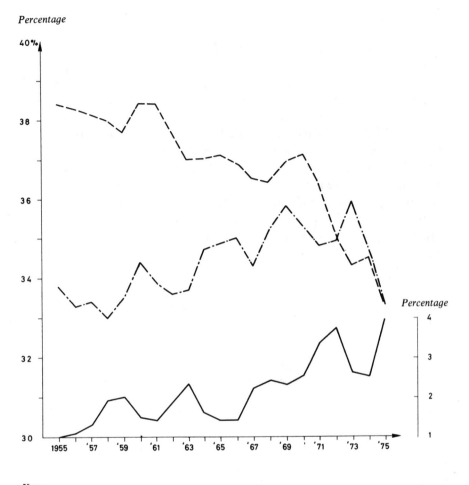

Key
— — — —   Share of employment in manufacturing (employees only)
— ·— ·—   Share of manufacturing in GDP (1963 prices)
————————   Percentage unemployed

Sources
Department of Employment Gazette, March 1975
OECD Manpower Statistics, 1954–1959
NIESR *Review*, May 1976
OECD National Accounts, 1950–1968, 1960–1970

Fig. 2. Share of manufacturing in the UK economy (employment and output) and percentage of
labour force unemployed 1955–1975.

transfer of labour from manufacturing to other sectors of the economy, and the behaviour of the UK manufacturing sector may therefore be no different from that of the rest. Evidence bearing on this hypothesis is set out in Tables 2 and 3, which compare the UK and a group of other industrial countries over the last two decades in terms of their growth rates of output and employment, as well as the proportions of the labour force employed in manufacturing and the shares of manufacturing in GDP (at constant prices).

Table 2A tells the familiar story of a UK growth rate in manufacturing lower than that of most other countries in every period. Table 2B is, however, much more interesting. Firstly, it shows that, although during the most recent period employment fell more in the UK than anywhere else, the UK was not the only country to suffer a reduction – the majority of countries did so. This was a notable break with experience up to the mid-1960s, when growth of output in manufacturing in every country was associated with rising employment. One plausible explanation is that, as a consequence of the liberalization of world trade and increased international competition, as well as the worldwide merger movement,

Table 2A. Growth rates of manufacturing output between cyclical peaks[1]: the UK and other industrial countries

	(Percentage per annum at 1963 prices)				
	Early 1950's to mid-1950's	Mid-1950's to early 1960's	Early 1960's to mid-1960's	Mid-1960's to late 1960's	Last peak to 1973[2]
Belgium	3.64	5.77	see note 3	4.89	8.34
France	4.88	4.40	6.87	5.86	6.55
Germany	11.30	7.99	6.12	5.53	3.82
Italy	7.57	6.61	9.59	6.81	5.07
Japan	13.81	14.59	11.46	13.14	7.26
Netherlands	6.24	5.94	5.63	7.06	5.56
Sweden	3.05	3.35	8.29	4.36	3.28
UK	3.76	2.81	3.28	2.78	2.95
USA	2.86	2.40	7.39	3.36	4.66

Notes:
1. Cycles do not necessarily coincide for all countries.
2. Except in case of Japan, where 1972 is the end-year.
3. Cycle for Belgium runs from 1957 to 1964, so figure in previous column runs from mid-1950's to mid-1960's.

Sources:
(a) Cripps, T. F. and Tarling, R. J.: *Growth in Advanced Capitalist Economies 1950–1970.*
(b) OECD: *National Accounts 1950–68; 1960–70; 1962–73.*
(c) OECD: *Manpower Statistics 1950–60; 1954–64.*
       Labour Force Statistics 1959–70; 1962–73

Table 2B. Growth rates of employment* in manufacturing between cyclical peaks[1]: the UK and other industrial countries.

	(Percentage per annum)				
	Early 1950's to mid-1950's	Mid-1950's to early 1960's	Early 1960's to mid-1960's	Mid 1960's to late 1960's	Last peak to 1973[2]
Belgium	0.42	0.82	see note 3	0.16	−0.08
France	0.51	0.37	2.19	0.44	1.21
Germany	5.82	2.93	1.75	0.65	−0.58
Italy	1.62	1.52	5.28	1.18	0.21
Japan	6.27	5.63	4.19	2.74	1.76
Netherlands	1.92	1.29	1.69	−0.13	−2.45
Sweden	0.93	0.21	5.96	−1.24	0.32
UK	1.17	0.73	0.49	−0.46	−2.78
USA	1.01	0.28	1.74	1.62	−0.43

Notes:
* employment refers to wage and salary earners only.
1, 2, 3. See notes to Table 2A.

Sources: Same as Table 2A.

a considerable amount of rationalization took place within the manufacturing sector. This enabled both output and productivity to grow, despite the fall in employment. It is a moot question whether this was a once-and-for-all fall, so that a further reduction in the manufacturing labour force would lead to a fall in manufacturing output. Secondly, Table 2B shows that, apart from the Netherlands, the UK was the only country for which employment in manufacturing fell between both the last two cycles. Also, relative to other countries, manufacturing employment in the UK fell further during the last period, as well as over the last two periods taken together.

Table 3A shows that, as far as the share of manufacturing in GDP is concerned, UK experience during the last decade has not been very different from that of other countries. This could, however, be misleading, since a lower manufacturing growth rate in the UK probably meant a relatively lower growth rate overall. Nevertheless, Table 3B indicates that between 1970 and 1973 the proportion of the UK labour force employed in manufacturing fell appreciably faster, although it still remained larger, than in many other countries. (The relatively larger proportion of labour force in manufacturing has traditionally been an important characteristic of the UK economic structure; it derives from the fact that historically this country has had a much smaller agricultural sector relative to other countries [Kuznets 1972].)

Table 3A. Share of manufacturing in GDP (at 1963 prices), at cyclical peaks from 1950 to 1970 and for years 1970 to 1973: the UK and other industrial countries

	Early 1950's	Mid- 1950's	Early 1960's	Mid- 1960's	Late 1960's	1970	1971	1972	1973
Belgium	n.a.	27.8	–	31.3	33.5	33.5	33.4	33.8	34.1
France	33.6	34.7	35.0	36.4	37.3	n.a.	n.a.	n.a.	n.a.
Germany	32.1	37.4	40.6	42.3	44.8	44.8	44.4	44.3	45.0
Italy	20.4	22.6	24.0	27.6	31.2	31.2	30.7	31.2	32.0
Japan	18.5	23.5	27.6	29.2	33.6	n.a.	n.a.	n.a.	n.a.
Netherlands	28.3	28.9	29.9	30.8	32.9	32.9	33.2	33.2	33.8
Sweden	26.4	25.6	25.4	30.6	31.6	31.6	31.7	32.6	32.7
UK	32.4	33.8	34.4	34.8	35.9	35.6	34.9	37.2	35.7
USA	28.7	28.5	27.7	29.7	29.9	28.3	28.1	29.2	30.7

Note: See notes at end of Table 2A.
Sources: Same as Table 2A.

Table 3B. Share of total labour force* in manufacturing, at cyclical peaks from 1950 to 1970 and for years 1970 to 1973: the UK and other industrial countries.

	Early 1950's	Mid- 1950's	Early 1960's	Mid- 1960's	Late 1960's	1970	1971	1972	1973
Belgium	35.1	35.2	–	35.4	34.1	34.1	33.7	33.2	33.4
France	n.a.	27.8	27.2	28.1	27.6	27.8	28.0	28.0	28.1
Germany	34.1	34.2	38.5	39.3	40.5	40.5	40.2	39.7	39.8
Italy	n.a.	22.8	26.3	29.2	31.7	31.7	32.0	32.1	32.2
Japan	n.a.	19.8	22.5	24.3	26.7	27.0	27.0	26.9	27.4
Netherlands	30.8	30.8	28.2	28.2	26.2	26.2	25.7	24.9	24.5
Sweden	n.a.	n.a.	n.a.	32.4	27.6	27.6	27.3	27.1	27.5
UK	39.3	40.1	37.5	36.5	36.3	36.4	34.0	32.8	32.3
USA	n.a.	26.2	26.6	27.7	27.2	26.1	25.1	24.9	25.3

Notes:
* Labour force refers to total civilian employment.
See also notes to Table 2A.

Sources: Same as Table 2A.

To sum up, the empirical evidence indicates that, since the late 1960s, Britain's manufacturing labour force has declined faster, both compared with her own experience over the previous two decades, and relative to that of other countries. With respect to the growth of real output in manufacturing, there is a trend of reduction in it when compared with past UK experience, but not when it is compared with its previous performance in relation to other countries.

Finally, to complete the picture, we shall briefly examine the implied movements in the growth of productivity in the UK and in other industrial countries. Although the rate of growth of manufacturing output in the UK during the last decade was lower than in the previous ten years, a fall in manufacturing employment has meant that there has been no reduction in the rate of growth of productivity. Output per man hour in manufacturing during 1965–1975 grew, if anything, at a slightly higher rate (about 3.5 per cent a year) than during the period 1955–1965 (about 3 per cent a year).[32] However, since 1973 there have been signs of stagnation in productivity growth. This is in contrast to the previous recessions, when a 'shake-out' of labour led to improved productivity performance. Relative to other countries, the UK's productivity growth was still low, but there appears to have been a slight narrowing of the gap in recent years (Ray 1976).

The question now arises as to how we should assess the above evidence from the point of view of the structure of the economy. Loss of employment in the manufacturing sector (or, for that matter, in any sector) is clearly undesirable and socially and economically wasteful, if it leads not to redeployment elsewhere, but only to increased overall unemployment. However, as far as the efficiency and growth potential of the manufacturing sector are concerned, it could be argued that the loss of manpower was in fact a positive feature, in that it reduced previous overmanning without adversely affecting productivity performance. Thus, unless the evidence of loss of employment is supplemented by other data, and, more importantly, unless there is a clear notion of what constitutes an 'efficient' economic structure, one cannot conclude that the recent de-industrialization of the UK economy implies any structural maladjustment of the economy, actual or potential.

6. Trends in the UK's price competitiveness and trading position

The debate about 'de-industrialization' reflects more than a concern with the general problem of unemployment. Mr. Benn and others do, indeed, refer to a structural problem, but it is one which needs to be more precisely delineated. The crucial issue here is: what does one mean by an 'efficient' manufacturing sector in an open economy such as the UK? We saw in section 4 that the manufacturing sector is the major source of foreign exchange earnings on current account. More importantly, we have seen that it is potentially the main means through which an

32. See Bacon & Eltis (1976a) and NIESR (1976).

improvement in the balance of payments could be sought sufficient to correct the existing disequilibrium. Therefore, given the normal levels of the other components of the balance of payments, we may define an efficient manufacturing sector as one which (currently as well as potentially) not only satisfies the demands of consumers at home, but is also able to sell enough of its products abroad to pay for the nation's import requirements. This is, however, subject to the important restriction that an 'efficient' manufacturing sector must be able to achieve these objectives at socially acceptable levels of output, employment and exchange rate.[33] These qualifications are essential, since otherwise at a low enough level of real income or employment, almost any manufacturing sector might be able to meet such criteria of efficiency.

In operational terms, a structural problem can arise in this sense, if for example the manufacturing sector, without losing price or cost competitiveness, is unable to export enough to pay for the full employment level of imports. Some evidence of this phenomenon in the UK is found in Table 4. The table (columns 3 and 4) shows that since the mid-1960's the UK has had an increasing price advantage relative to its main competitors (owing to progressive devaluations of the currency). This is true whether such advantage is measured in terms of relative changes in the export prices of manufactures, or in terms of the more appropriate variable of 'efficiency wages,' i.e. relative movements in the indices of unit labour costs measured in a common currency (dollars). In spite of this, there appears to have been a trend deterioration in the underlying current balance, which is reflected in the fact that even in 1975 there was a large deficit on current account, when nearly 4 per cent of the labour force was unemployed. By contrast, in 1970–71 there were sizeable surpluses, which were achieved at a lower rate of unemployment and with less favourable relative prices. The Cambridge Economic Policy Group, on the basis of their model of the British economy [CEPG (1976)], estimate that at full employment the current account deficit in 1975 would have been of the order of £ 4,000 million.[34]

The UK therefore seems to be becoming increasingly unable to pay for its current import requirements by means of exports of goods and services and property income from abroad. In section 4 we saw that there has been little, if any,

33. Output, employment and the exchange rate are clearly interrelated. Variations in the exchange rate, however, also influence the distribution of income and the rate of domestic inflation; it is in relation to the socially acceptable levels of the latter parameters that the exchange rate is used here as an operational surrogate.
34. Nearly half of this huge projected deficit is due to the sharp deterioration in the UK terms of trade after 1972 – see further below. The full employment deficit, at constant pre-1972 terms of trade, is estimated by CEPG to be £ 2000 million in 1975 – still a large figure. Their calculations suggest a serious deterioration in full employment current balance since 1965 even when terms of trade are held constant.

Table 4. UK current balance, unemployment and indices of price and cost competitiveness, 1963–1975.

	Current balance (£ 000 millions)	Percentage of labour force unemployed	Index of price competitiveness[1] (1970 = 100)	Index of cost competitiveness[2] (1970 = 100)
1963	0.34	2.30	101.3	(average
1964	− 0.89	1.65	101.9	1963–67)
1965	− 0.06	1.43	105.2	109.0
1966	0.23	1.46	106.6	
1967	− 0.67	2.31	105.8	
1968	− 0.59	2.41	99.7	
1969	0.93	2.42	98.7	
1970	1.39	2.56	100.0	100.0
1971	1.81	3.35	100.9	
1972	0.20	3.68	99.3	
1973	− 1.22	2.58	92.2	
1974	− 4.53	2.53	90.5	87.6
1975	− 1.71	3.94	n.a.	87.0

Notes:
1. The index of price competitiveness is the ratio of UK to weighted average export (dollar) prices for major competitors in respect of manufactured goods.
2. Index of unit manpower costs: UK/weighted competitors' ratio ($) 1970 = 100.

Sources:
CEPG (1976); *Economic Trends*, CSO, May 1976; Kaldor (1976).

deterioration in the trading position of services over the past decade. Furthermore, as far as net income from interest, profits and dividends from abroad is concerned, there has been a trend increase in the contribution from this source during the last three years.[35] The disequilibrium in the current account is, therefore, basically due to a marked deterioration in the visible trade account since 1972.[36]

A disaggregated analysis of visible trade shows that there have been two major factors responsible for this situation. Firstly, after having remained more or less constant for a number of years, the terms of trade have moved sharply against the UK since 1972, and especially since the oil price rise in 1973. This has led to a

35. The net balance on interest, profits and dividend payments increased from an average of a little over £ 500 million during 1969–72, to over £ 1000 million during 1973–75 (CSO 1967a).
36. The movements in the visible balance since 1970 have been as follows (CSO 1976a):

	1970	1971	1972	1973	1974	1975
visible balance: (£ million)	− 25	280	− 702	− 2334	− 5220	− 3204

much higher import bill for food, raw materials and fuel (in spite of lower volumes of these imports as a consequence of the recession in the last two years). Secondly, and quite independently, as seen in section 4 (Table 1), instead of compensating for this rise by an improvement, the trading performance of the manufacturing sector has greatly deteriorated since 1972. An analysis of the commodity and area pattern of the trade in manufactures (Woodward, 1976b) shows that the main reason for the poor trading performance of this sector is the large and continuing decline in recent years in the UK's manufacturing trade balance with the advanced industrial countries. At constant 1970 prices, the trade balance in manufactures with these countries moved from a positive figure of more than £ 950 million in 1970, to a negative figure of £ 251 million in 1975.[37] (During the same period, the corresponding balance with the rest of the world (including the oil exporting countries) increased from £ 1956 million to £ 2794 million).

Further evidence of the deteriorating trading position of the UK manufacturing sector is provided by detailed studies of the recent behaviour of imports and exports which have been carried out by my colleagues in Cambridge, and others elsewhere. I shall merely summarise below the main relevant findings.

1. Moore and Rhodes (1976) show that there has been a sharp increase in the degree of import penetration of manufactured products in the UK home market over the period 1969–74 – an increase far greater than that found for a group of selected industrial countries. This was in contrast with the evidence for the period 1963–70, when it was found that the level of and increase in import penetration by manufactured goods in the UK were much the same as in other countries.

2. Woodward (1976A) shows that, unlike in the past, in 1975 import penetration in the UK domestic market continued to increase even in a recession year. An analysis by broad categories of imports shows that this was largely due to increased penetration by competitive manufactures. Such imports fell by only 2 per cent in 1975, while the size of their domestic market fell by about 5 per cent, resulting in a significant increase in market penetration.

3. On the exports side, in spite of improvements in the UK's price competitiveness, it continued to lose ground in its share of exports to other industrial countries. Between 1964 and 1974, the UK share of industrial countries'

---

37. Kaldor (1976) similarly observes: 'The most striking evidence of the deterioration of our position during the last 10 years resides in the fact that whereas in 1966 we had a net export surplus in our trade in manufactured goods with [6 leading industrial countries] of £ 142m, 10 per cent of exports, in the first 6 months of 1976, we had an import surplus of manufactures of £ 1550 millions (in terms of annual rates) or 20 per cent of our exports. This was in spite of the fact that in 1966 we had near-full employment whereas in 1976 the economy has been in recession.'

exports fell by more than 50 per cent, whilst most of its competitor countries either maintained or improved theirs. In 1975, as a consequence of the world recession, the UK's share increased slightly (from 8.8 to 9.3 per cent). Such an improvement is, however, normal for the UK economy in a recession year. In the first three quarters of 1976, as world exports picked up, the share declined again. Furthermore, as Godley (1976) points out, if the figures for the second and third quarters of 1976 are compared with the whole of 1975, although there has been a recovery in world trade and a fall in the pressure of demand at home, it turns out that the volume of manufactured exports has risen less than that of manufactured imports (by 8 per cent as compared with 10 per cent).

4. Important econometric evidence concerning the income and price elasticities of UK trade also suggests an underlying disequilibrium in manufacturing. In their well-known study of trade elasticities for fifteen industrial countries over the period 1951–66, Houthakker and Magee (1969) found that the UK and USA had income elasticities of demand for their imports which were much greater than the foreign income elasticities of demand for their exports. The UK had an income elasticity of demand for imports of 1.66 as compared with the foreign income elasticity of demand for her exports of 0.66. Japan, on the other hand, had asymmetrical elasticities in the opposite direction, so that it would have a persistent tendency towards surplus as world income rises over time. The UK and USA would have a similar tendency towards deficit – a result much in accord with what has actually happened.

Houthakker and Magee's study has been criticized for the poor quality of their data and for certain statistical shortcomings (e.g. serial correlation in residuals) (Morgan, 1970; Stern et al, 1976). Nevertheless a number of subsequent investigations have by and large confirmed their estimates of relative elasticities in the UK and in other countries,[38] especially with respect to income and price elasticities of demand for UK imports. Despite the statistical difficulties involved in the measurement of such aggregate elasticities as those for the manufacturing sector as a whole, the evidence from these studies is impressive and significant. Thus the Economic Commission for Europe estimated that over the period 1953–67, the UK's elasticity of change in the value of imports to a change in the volume of GDP (a kind of hybrid income elasticity) was 5.7, compared with 3.4 for France, 2.6 for Sweden and 4.3 for West Germany [Worswick, 1971]. Similarly Taplin (1973) found that over the period 1953–70, the UK had the highest income elasticity of demand for manufactured imports among the 26

38. See, for example, Magee (1975), which brings together various estimates of income and price elasticities for UK imports and exports.

developed countries which were members of the Council of Mutual Assistance.[39] In a more recent study of the period 1957–72, Panic (1975) has found that the UK's income elasticity of demand for manufactured imports is 3.09, compared with 2.14 for West Germany and 2.19 for France. On the other hand the UK's price elasticity of demand for manufactures is lower than in the other two countries.[40]

How does one explain the high income elasticity of demand for UK manufactured imports? It cannot be attributed to peculiarities in the UK's pattern of demand, since these tend to be much the same in all advanced industrial countries. Nor can it be claimed that UK costs have risen faster than those in other countries; as we saw earlier, measured in a common currency, this has not been so since at least the mid-1960's (see also Ray, 1976). Nor can other familiar explanations, such as greater specialization of production in the UK be sustained. The UK's higher income elasticity for imports certainly stems from deficiencies in industrial structure, which responds rather ineffectively to changes in domestic demand; it is, however, interesting that such weaknesses are not revealed in static comparisons with the industrial structures of other countries. A recent study (Panic, 1976) shows, for instance, that the structure of manufacturing industry in the UK is not much different from that of West Germany (measured in terms of the sectoral distribution of outputs and factor inputs). On the basis of a number of surveys of individual industries undertaken by the National Economic Development Office, Panic argues that the main reason for the UK's high income elasticity of demand for imports is to be found in the lower quality, design and general performance of its products relative to other countries.[41] These in turn are thought to be related to the lower rate of growth of UK industry; the faster growing, more dynamic economies are able to achieve greater technical progress and make product improvements in all the above-mentioned directions, which suggests a 'vicious circle' type of explanation.

The above evidence of unfavourable price and income elasticities goes some way towards explaining why, in spite of increasing cost and price advantages, the trading performance of the manufacturing sector continues to deteriorate.[42] The

39. The UK elasticity was 2.61, compared with 1.77 for Japan and 1.69 for the Netherlands.
40. Other studies also report relatively low price elasticities for UK manufactured imports. See Worswick (1971). A number of recent estimates of price elasticities of total UK imports are given in Magee (1975), Table 1.
41. The same factors may account for the relatively low income elasticity of world demand for UK exports.
42. Without such advantages (as a consequence of exchange rate depreciation), the trading position of the manufacturing sector would probably have deteriorated even further. However, exchange rate depreciation alone may not be able to correct the underlying structural disequilibrium (see section 3); alternatively, such a large further depreciation may be required as to be socially unacceptable.

main question is: how can the underlying disequilibrium be corrected? If attempts at changing the pattern of domestic demand are ruled out, the only alternative is to alter the productive structure so as to make it more responsive to domestic and world demand. The chief instrument for such transformation must be investment. However, it turns out that, whatever index is used, the UK's investment record in recent years has been disappointing. On the basis of a detailed analysis of the manufacturing sector, Woodward (1976b) shows that, whereas between 1954–6 and 1963–65 manufacturing investment at constant prices grew by 39 per cent, between 1963–65 and 1972–74 it grew only by 19 per cent. More recent statistics show that during 1970–75 net investment in manufacturing at constant prices was running at about four-fifths of the levels reached in the previous five years. Further, over the period 1964–72, manufacturing investment as a proportion of GDP was on average lower in the UK than in most competitor countries (the USA being a notable exception). There is also some indirect evidence that, relative to large firms elsewhere, large UK manufacturing firms may be investing more abroad than at home. According to the UN data, the value of production abroad by UK multinationals in 1973[43] was more than twice the value of their exports from the UK; for the Japanese and West German multinationals, the corresponding proportions were 0.38 and 0.37 respectively (Holland, 1976).

To the extent that it is argued that a faster rate of growth of UK manufacturing industry is necessary to correct trade disequilibrium (see page 133 above), it is not just the rate of investment which is relevant, but also how effectively investment is utilized. Statistical evidence on the relative efficiency of the utilization of investment in the UK, as compared with other countries, is mixed.[44] On the other hand, casual observation suggests that, owing to the nature of worker-management relations in this country, the UK's relative performance in this respect also may well be poor. However, it could be argued that, if there were a faster rate of growth and higher employment, it would lead to greater cooperation between the two sides of industry and hence better utilization of resources.

To sum up, the evidence outlined above suggests that there are structural weaknesses in the manufacturing sector of the economy, which make it increasingly difficult for it to meet foreign competition in either home or overseas markets. It is these facts, when considered in conjunction with the reduction in the labour force in manufacturing, which make 'de-industrialization' a matter of

43. Because of the high concentration in UK export trade, these multinationals account for the bulk of the country's manufacturing exports. The rapid growth of their production facilities abroad is very much a post-war phenomenon.
44. See, for example, Woodward (1976); Purdy (1976).

serious concern. In view of the sluggish rate of investment, low growth and high unemployment, it is difficult to see how these structural weaknesses can be remedied. The evidence suggests that, left to itself, the situation may continue to deteriorate in the manner postulated by Myrdal's theory. Structural weaknesses in the productive sphere may continue to lead to growing inroads by competitive imports, poor export performance and hence balance-of-payments difficulties and low growth.

Finally, it is important to recall that the whole of the discussion of this section has assumed 'normal' levels of other components of the balance of payments. But there is at least one component of visible trade (minerals, fuels, etc.), which may be expected to show an enormous improvement over the next few years, as a consequence of the development of North Sea oil. Depending on the size of the surplus, the country could in principle then have a balance-of-payments equilibrium at full employment, and at desired levels of real income and exchange rate, even if the trading position of the manufacturing sector continued to decline. This is, however, not a sustainable position in the long run, since, unless the manufacturing sector improves, it may not be able to pay for the full employment level of imports at a later stage, when the oil flow runs out. The situation in this respect could become somewhat like that in the period before World War One. As Lewis (1967) points out, during 1870–1914 the balance-of-payments surplus (owing at that time to remittances from abroad) saved Britain from having to make the changes in her productive structure necessary to meet the growing foreign competition in manufactures. But after World War One, the flow of property income from abroad dropped sharply, and the UK then had to face the necessity of 'earning a living through successful competition in manufacturing, both in her home market and abroad; and this problem she had not solved after forty years of grappling with it' (Lewis, 1967).

7. Implications of the above analysis

It has been argued in this paper that liberalization of trade and free capital movements are not always necessarily beneficial for a country. Because of the uneven development of the world economy and of the productive potential of different regions, there may be many periods when participation in the international economy under such arrangements can lead to disequilibrium and be seriously harmful to a country's economy. The detrimental effects can work in a number of ways – most importantly through the level of demand, the structure of demand and through investment. Once the economy is in disequilibrium, for whatever reason, continued participation in international economic relations on the same terms as before may produce a vicious circle of causation. As a consequence, a country in a weak competitive position may have balance-of-payments difficulties, which lead the government to have a lower level of demand, which leads to lower investment and hence lower growth of productivity and continuing balance-of-payments difficulties. There may be no automatic market mechanism to correct the disequilibrium.

The de-industrialization of the UK economy which has occurred in recent years has been only in the sense of loss of employment from the manufacturing sector. This loss has been greater than in other industrial countries, and also as compared with the trend rate of decline in the UK itself during the last two decades. Between the recession years of 1968 and 1976, employment in manufacturing fell by nearly 1 million workers; the proportion employed in manufacturing decreased from 36 to 32 per cent. There has, however, been no reduction in manufacturing output, although there was a slowdown in its rate of growth. Because of falling employment, the rate of growth of productivity has not declined during the last decade as a whole, but there is evidence of stagnation since 1973. It has been argued here that the observed loss of manufacturing employment, as well as these other features of the relative performance of the manufacturing sector, cannot, by themselves, be regarded as an indication of structural maladjustment of the economy or an 'inefficient' manufacturing sector.

I have suggested that the concept of an 'efficient' manufacturing sector in an open economy must be considered in broader terms. To the extent that manufacturing may constitute the major source of foreign exchange earnings for a country, an 'efficient' manufacturing sector must also be able to provide (currently and potentially) sufficient net exports to meet the country's overall import requirements at socially acceptable levels of output, employment and exchange rate. It is in this important sense that, in spite of the growth in productivity, there is evidence that the UK manufacturing sector is becoming increasingly inefficient. The evidence suggests a structural disequilibrium, whereby the trading position of the manufacturing sector in the world economy continues to deteriorate, in spite of increasing cost and price competitiveness. De-industrialization is a symptom or a consequence of this 'inefficiency' or of disequilibrium, rather than its cause; this disequilibrium needs to be corrected if the manufacturing sector is not to decline further.

The main policy implication of the above analysis is that important changes in the structure of UK manufacturing production are required in order for it to be able to compete successfully in world markets and in its own home market. The question as to what is the best or even the most feasible way of bringing about such changes raises extremely complex issues. An adequate analysis of these will require a separate paper, and must therefore be left for another occasion. All that one can say in general is that the choice of preferred policy instruments (devaluation, import controls, cuts in public expenditure, planning agreements with large firms etc.) will depend on one's view of the workings of the economy (i.e. the appropriate empirical model) and on political values and judgments.

Bibliography

Aldcroft, D. H. (ed.), 1968, *The Development of British Industry and Foreign Competition, 1875–1914*, London, Allen and Unwin.

Bacon, R. W. and Eltis, W. A., 1975, 'Stop-go and de-industrialization', *National Westminster Bank Quarterly Review*, November.

Bacon, R. W. and Eltis, W. A., 1976a, *Britain's economic problem: too few producers*, London, Macmillan.

Bacon, R. W. and Eltis, W. A., 1976b, 'Too few producers: the drift Healey must stop', *Sunday Times*, 14 November 1976.

Bagchi, A. K., 1967, 'De-industrialization in Gangetic Bihar 1809–1901 and its implications' in Barun De et al., *Essays in honour of S. C. Sarkar*, New Delhi, People's Publishing House.

Bagchi, A. K., 1976, 'De-industrialization in India in the 19th century: some theoretical implications', *Journal of Development Studies*, January.

Bardhan, P. K., 1965, 'Equilibrium growth in the international economy', *Quarterly Journal of Economics*, August.

Beckerman, W., 1962, 'Projecting Europe's growth', *Economic Journal*, December.

Benn, Anthony Wedgwood, 1975, 'Tony Benn writes about industrial policy', *Trade and Industry*, 4 April 1975.

Black, J., 1970, 'Trade and the long-run growth rate', *Oxford Economic Papers*, March.

Brittan, S., 1977, 'De-industrialization revisited', *Financial Times*, 26 January.

Cairncross, A. (ed.), 1971, *Britain's Economic Prospects Reconsidered*, London, Allen and Unwin.

Cambridge Economic Policy Group, 1976, *Economic Policy Review*, 2, Cambridge, Department of Applied Economics, March.

Caves, R. E., 1970, 'Export-led growth' in W. A. Eltis et al. (eds.), *Induction, growth and trade: essays in honour of Roy Harrod*, Oxford, Clarendon.

Caves, R. E. and Jones, R. W., 1973, *World trade and payments*, Boston, Little Brown.

CSO, 1970, *The Index of Industrial Production and other related Output Measures*, London, HMSO.

CSO, 1974, *United Kingdom Balance of Payments 1963–73*, London, HMSO.

CSO, 1975, *United Kingdom Balance of Payments 1964–74*, London, HMSO.

CSO, 1976a, *United Kingdom Balance of Payments 1965–75*, London, HMSO.

CSO, 1976b, *Economic Trends*, London, HMSO, November.

CSO, 1976c, *National Income and Expenditure, 1965–75*, London, HMSO.

Conrad, A. H. and Meyer, J. R., 1965, *Studies in econometric history*, London, Chapman and Hall.

Corden, W. M., 1971, 'The effects of trade on the rate of growth', in J. N. Bhagwati et al. (eds.), *Trade, Balance of Payments and Growth, Papers in International Economics in Honour of Charles P. Kindleberger*, Amsterdam, North Holland.

Cripps, T. F. and Tarling, R. J., 1974, *Growth in advanced capitalist economies*, Cambridge University Press, Cambridge, UK.

Deane, Phyllis and Cole, W. A., 1962, *British Economic Growth: 1688–1959*, Cambridge University Press, Cambridge.

Department of Employment, 1975, 'A view of industrial employment in 1981', *Department of Employment Gazette*, May.

Feinstein, C. H., 1972, *National Income, Expenditure and Output of the United Kingdom, 1855–1965*, Cambridge University Press, Cambridge, UK.

Frenkel, J. A. and Johnson, H. G., 1976, *The monetary approach to the balance of payments*, London, Allen and Unwin.

Fuchs, V. R., 1968, *The Service Economy*, New York, National Bureau of Economic Research.

George, K. D. and Ward, T. S., 1975, *The Structure of Industry in the EEC: An International Comparison*, Cambridge University Press, Cambridge, UK.

Godley, W. A. H., 1976, 'What Britain needs is growth – but it must be the right kind', *The Times*, 1 November.

Hicks, J. R., 1959, *Essays in World Economics*, Oxford, Clarendon Press.

Hicks, J. R., 1969, *A theory of economic history*, Oxford, Clarendon Press.

Holland, S. 1976, 'The socialist alternatives', *The Economist*, 3 April.

Houthakker, H. S. and Magee, S. P., 1969, 'Income and price elasticities in world trade', *Review of Economics and Statistics*, May.

Indian Economic and Social History Review, 1968, Debate on the re-interpretation of 19th-century Indian economic history, *Indian Economic and Social Review*, March.

Jacquemin, A. and de Lichtbuer, M. C., 1973, 'Size, structure, stability and performance of the largest British and EEC firms', *European Economic Review*, December.

Johnson, H. G., 1962, *Money, trade and economic growth*, London, Allen and Unwin.

Kaldor, N., 1966, *Causes of the slow rate of economic growth of the United Kingdom*, Cambridge University Press, Cambridge, UK.

Kaldor, N., 1970, 'The case for regional policies', *Scottish Journal of Political Economy*, November.

Kaldor, N., 1971, 'Conflicts in national economic objectives', *Economic Journal*, March.

Kaldor, N., 1975, 'Economic growth and the Verdoorn law: a comment on Mr Rowthorn's article', *Economic Journal*, December.

Kaldor, N., 1976, Letter to *The Times*, London, 9 November.

Kindleberger, C. P., 1962, *Foreign trade and the national economy*, New Haven, Yale University Press.

Krueger, A. O., 1969, 'Balance-of-payments theory', *Journal of Economic Literature*, March.

Kuznets, S., 1971, *Economic Growth of Nations*, Cambridge, Mass., Harvard University Press.

Lamfalussy, A., 1963, *The United Kingdom and the Six: an Essay on Economic Growth in Western Europe*, Homewood, Ill., Richard D. Irwin.

Levine, A. L., 1967, *Industrial retardation in Britain 1880–1914*, London, Weidenfeld and Nicholson.

Lewis, W. A., 1967, 'The deceleration of British growth 1873–1913', Princeton, mimeographed.

London and Cambridge Economic Service, 1971, *The British Economy: key statistics 1900–1970*, London, Times Newspapers Ltd.

Magee, S. P., 1975, 'Prices, Income and Foreign Trade', in Peter B. Kenen (ed.), *International Trade and Finance, Frontiers for Research*, Cambridge University Press, Cambridge, UK.

Matthews, R. C. O., 1973, 'Foreign trade and British economic growth', *Scottish Journal of Political Economy*, November.

Moggridge, D. E., 1969, *The Return to Gold, 1925*, Cambridge University Press, Cambridge, UK.

Moore, B. and Rhodes, J., 1976, 'The relative decline of the UK manufacturing sector', *Economic Policy Review*, 2, Cambridge, Department of Applied Economics, March.

Morgan, A. D., 1970, 'Income and price elasticities in world trade: a comment', *Manchester School*, December.

Mundell, R. A., 1968, *International Economics*, New York, Macmillan.

Myrdal, G., 1957, *Economic Theory and Under-developed Regions*, London, Duckworth.

NIESR, 1976, *National Institute Economic Review*, London, November.

Nurkse, R., 1956, 'The relation between home investment and external balance in the light of British experience', *Review of Economics and Statistics*.

Oniki, H. and Uzawa, H., 1965, 'Patterns of trade and investment in a dynamic model of international trade', *Review of Economic Studies*, January.

Panic, M. (ed.), 1976, *The UK and West German manufacturing industry, 1954–1972*, London, National Economic Development Office.

Panic, M. and Rajan, A. H., 1971, *Product changes in industrial countries' trade: 1955–68*, London, National Economic Development Office.

Phelps Brown, E. H. and Browne, M. H., 1968, *A century of pay*, London, Macmillan.

Purdy, D., 1976, 'British capitalism since the war: part 2, decline and prospects', *Marxism Today*, October.

Ray, G. F., 1976, 'Labour costs in OECD countries, 1964–75', *National Institute Economic Review*, November.

Reddaway, W. B., et al., 1968, *Effects of UK Direct Investment Overseas*, Cambridge, CUP.

Rowthorn, R. E., 1975a, 'What remains of Kaldor's Law', *Economic Journal*, March.

Rowthorn, R. E., 1975b, 'A reply to Lord Kaldor's comment', *Economic Journal*, December.

Sayers, R. S., 1965, *The vicissitudes of an export economy: Britain since 1880*, Sydney, University of Sydney.

Singh, A., 1975, 'Take-overs, economic natural selection and the theory of the firm', *Economic Journal*, December.

Stern, R. M., 1973, *The balance of payments*, London, Macmillan.

Stern, R. M., Francis, J. and Schumacher, B., 1976, *Price-elasticities in international trade*, London, Macmillan.

Taplin, G. R., 1973, 'A model of world trade', in R. J. Ball, ed., *The International Linkage of National Economic Models*, Amsterdam, North-Holland.

Thorner, D. and A., 1962, *Land and labour in India*, London, Asia Publishing House.

Whitman, M. V. N., 1967, *International and interregional payments adjustment: a synthetic view*, Princeton, Studies in International Finance, No. 19.

Whitman, M. V. N., 1970, *Policies for internal and external balance*, Special Papers in International Economics, 9, Princeton, Princeton University.

Woodward, V., 1976a, 'No cause for optimism over imports', *The Times*, 23 June.

Woodward, V., 1976b, *Government Policy and the Structure of the Economy*, Cambridge, DAE, mimeographed.

Worswick, G. D. N., 1971, 'Trade and payments' in Cairncross (1971).

PART FOUR

MONOPOLY AND ECONOMIES OF SCALE

XI. MONOPOLY WELFARE GAINS AND THE COSTS OF DECENTRALIZATION*

Lennart Hjalmarsson

1. Introduction

One of the most well-known results from the standard micro theory is that competition is more efficient than monopoly. This result seems to be taken for granted in the antitrust policy of most countries. Even if most economists do not question the result, a fervent discussion about the quantitative degree of welfare losses due to monopoly has taken place in recent years. The analysis is largely based on losses of consumer surplus. The social welfare loss (the deadweight loss) arising from monopoly refers to the net reduction of consumers' surplus, i.e. the excess of the loss of consumers' surplus over the monopolist's gain in profits, the latter being regarded as a transfer of income from the consumers. Thus the concept of welfare losses or welfare gains utilized for this purpose totally neglects the distributional consequences of changes in resource allocation. The neoclassical approach to this issue is outlined in Figure 1. It produces an unambigous loss of social welfare from market power and constitutes a forceful case in favour of an antitrust policy (see Rowley 1973).

The analysis of monopoly welfare losses is largely based on traditional static price theory. The purpose of this paper is to put forward some dynamic efficiency aspects of monopoly in connection with economies of scale. In doing so I will utilize the capacity expansion model developed in Hjalmarsson (1974), which makes it possible to compare the costs of two different cases of capacity expansion for a branch: (1) when the capacity expansion takes place with only one, multiplant, monopoly firm, (2) when the capacity expansion takes place in a branch producing the same output but with two or more multiplant firms. The difference in costs is then to be compared with the results of Williamson (1968-a), (1968-b) and (1969) concerning the welfare trade-off between higher prices due to changes in monopoly power and cost savings due to economies of scale.

Thus the analysis set out here emphasizes the cost level in production.

* The author wishes to thank Harold Dickson, Leif Johansen and Ajit Singh for their valuable comments.

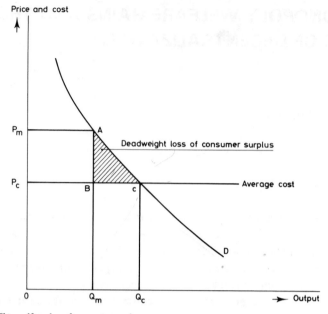

Figure 1. The welfare loss from monopoly.
c denotes competitive and m monopolistic output and price.

However, in the light of recent empirical investigations on the importance of economies of scale in most manufacturing branches (see Pratten 1971), cost aspects seem to have been rather neglected in the debate on antitrust policy and industrial concentration.

This paper is also a further development of the paper by Førsund and Hjalmarsson (1974) where various aspects of static and dynamic efficiency are treated. However, the problem of the number of firms in a branch is not considered there. Before proceeding to the analysis, a brief literature review may be of value.

2. Literature review

The first economist to use the concept of economic surplus to quantify the welfare effects of monopoly was Harberger (1954). In his study (based on profit data from the late 1920's) he shows that the benefits of eliminating monopoly in the United States in 1953 would have raised national income no more than $\frac{1}{13}$ of 1 per cent. In another study Schwartzman (1960) recomputes the benefits of eliminating monopoly by comparing Canadian monopolized industries as against counterpart competitive US industries, and vice versa, in order to determine the excess price attributable to monopoly. He arrived at a similar result: the calculated welfare loss for the USA 1954 amounted to less than 0.01 per cent of national income.

Recently, Leibenstein (1966) and Comanor and Leibenstein (1969) argued that departures from competitive norms such as result under monopolistic pricing are likely to be relatively inconsequential and that they hardly seem worth worrying about (Leibenstein p. 395).

(Instead, Leibenstein introduces the concept of X-inefficiency, but the existing evidence is patchy and a great deal of research is necessary before confident conclusions may be drawn as to its importance.)

A study of Worcester (1973) uses data for the 500 largest industrial firms in USA for each year 1956 through 1969. He finds estimates ranging over the 14 years (for the whole economy) between 0.203 per cent and 0.440 per cent of national income with an average of about 0.329 per cent. The data also offer some evidence that the amount of welfare loss attributable to the 500 largest firms has been declining during the 14 years preceding 1970.

In another study Siegfried and Tiemann (1974) attempt to identify those specific mining and manufacturing industries which are responsible for the greatest proportion of the welfare losses arising from imperfect market structures. The results of their analysis show that the bulk of the welfare loss due to monopoly (1963) is concentrated in relatively few industries. Five industries – plastic materials and synthetics; office and computing machinery; and motor vehicles – account for the vast majority of the welfare loss, namely 67 per cent of the estimated welfare loss. On the other hand the estimate of total welfare cost of monopoly is 0,0734 per cent of the national income.

However, there exist dissenters. Stigler (1956) and Bergson (1973) criticize the theoretical approaches adopted in empirical studies, and Kamerschen (1966) indicated in an empirical study that welfare losses due to monopoly pricing might be appreciably greater than Harberger and Schwartzman had found. Monopoly welfare losses were estimated at 1.03 to 1.87 per cent of the national income, depending on which of a number of estimates is considered.

3. Williamson's trade-off approach

The analyses of monopoly losses are usually based on constant average cost curves independent of market structure, in spite of the fact that empirical investigations have reported the existence of considerable economies of scale for most manufacturing branches. See Haldi and Whitcomb (1967) and Pratten

(1971). In 1968, however, the welfare trade-off between cost savings from economies of scale and the loss of consumer surplus was analyzed by Williamson (1968-a) and formalized within a social welfare function framework. Williamson restricted his analysis to the case of a merger which simultaneously provided cost savings and a price in excess of the competitive level. Figure 2 depicts Williamson's trade-off approach.

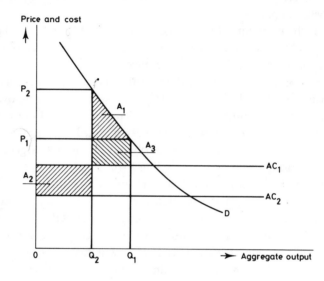

Figure 2. The Williamson trade-off.

It depicts the case of a proposed merger which would introduce market power into a previously more or less competitive market situation. The horizontal line labeled AC_1 represents the level of average costs of the two (or more) firms before combination, while AC_2 shows the level of average costs after the merger. The price before the merger is given by P_1 and is equal to $k \cdot AC_1$ where k is an index of pre-merger market power and is greater than or equal to unity. The price after the merger is given by P_2 and is assumed to exceed P_1 i.e. the price is assumed to be higher than in the pre-merger case in spite of the scale economies. In such circumstances a welfare trade-off is required between the loss of consumers' surplus, A_1, and area A_3, due to the higher price and the cost savings gain to the producer, A_2 (see Figure 2).

The area A_1 is given approximately by

$$\tfrac{1}{2}(P_2 - P_1) \cdot (Q_1 - Q_2), \text{ or } \tfrac{1}{2}\varDelta P \cdot \varDelta Q \text{ and } A_3 \text{ by}$$

$$(k - 1)AC_1 \cdot \varDelta Q \text{ while } A_2 \text{ is given by } \varDelta AC \cdot Q_2.$$

The net economic effect will be positive if the following inequality holds:

$$\varDelta AC \cdot Q_2 - [\tfrac{1}{2}\varDelta P + (k - 1) \cdot AC_1]\varDelta Q > 0$$

Dividing the inequality through by $P_1 \cdot Q_2$ where $P_1 = k \cdot AC_1$ yields:

$$(*) \quad \frac{\varDelta AC}{AC_1} - \left[\frac{k}{2}\frac{\varDelta P}{P_1} + (k - 1)\right]\frac{\varDelta Q}{Q_1} \cdot \frac{Q_1}{Q_2} > 0$$

Substituting $\eta(\varDelta P/P_1)$ for $\varDelta Q/Q_1$ we obtain (see Williamson 1969, p. 956):

$$(**) \quad \frac{\varDelta AC}{AC_1} - \left[\frac{k}{2}\frac{\varDelta P}{P_1} + (k - 1)\right]\eta\frac{\varDelta P}{P_1} \cdot \frac{Q_1}{Q_2} > 0$$

where η is the elasticity of demand.

Calculations are presented in Table 1.

Table 1.

$\frac{\varDelta P}{P_1} \times 100$	$\eta = 2$			$\eta = 1$			$\eta = \tfrac{1}{2}$		
	$k = 1,00$	$k = 1,05$	$k = 1,10$	$k = 1,00$	$k = 1,05$	$k = 1,10$	$k = 1,00$	$k = 1,05$	$k = 1,10$
5	0,3	0,8	1,4	0,1	0,4	0,6	0,1	0,2	0,5
10	1,1	2,2	3,3	0,5	1,0	1,7	0,2	0,5	0,8
20	4,4	6,8	9,3	2,0	3,1	4,2	1,0	1,5	2,0
30	10,4	14,3	18,3	4,5	6,2	7,9	2,1	2,9	3,7

Percentage cost reductions $[(\varDelta(AC)/(AC_1)) \times 100]$ sufficient to offset
percentage price increases $[(\varDelta P/P_1) \times 100]$ for selected values of η.
(Sources: Williamson 1969, p. 957 for $k = 1.00$ and $k = 1.05$ and own computations for $k = 1.10$)[1]

1. The computations are based on the expression (*), since the substitution of $\eta(\varDelta P/P)$ for $\varDelta Q/Q$ is appropriate only for small percentage price changes. Moreover, a constant elasticity function is assumed in the relevant region. See Williamson (1968b).

The numerical calculations performed by Williamson support the following proposition (Williamson 1968a, p. 23): 'A merger which yields non-trivial real economies must produce substantial market power and result in relatively large price increases for the net allocative effects to be negative.'

In his further analysis Williamson advanced a number of qualifications. When time is introduced, Williamson (1968-a, p. 25) states that: 'Significant economies will ordinarily be realized eventually through internal expansion if not by merger. Growth of demand can facilitate this internal adjustment process; the necessity for part of the industry to be displaced in order that efficient size be achieved is relieved in a growing market.'

Thus although a merger may have immediate net positive effects, when allowance is made for the possibility of internal expansion these effects can eventually become negative. The cost savings persist but these could be realized anyway, and the deadweight loss could be avoided by prohibiting the merger. Then it is the discounted value of net benefits which are relevant.

Williamson's article was followed by a theoretical discussion of the importance, measure and sign of the welfare effect. See Prano and Nugent (1968), Ross (1968), Koo (1970) and Williamson (1968-b) and (1969).

Especially Ross emphasized that when time is introduced, scale economies would be achieved ordinarily in the absence of a merger simply by the internal expansion of existing firms, at least within a growing market. At the same time internal expansion in a growing market does not lessen the degree of competition.

4. The importance of economies of scale

The Williamson (1968-a) model is based on economies of scale. However, these scale economies are assumed to be constant through time. This assumption seems to differ from reality. In a vast study of economies of scale Pratten (1971, p. 303) states that: 'A number of writers have implied that the economies of scale do not change over time. Our studies suggest that the range of output to which they apply and the magnitude of the economies of scale are increasing.' This fact is very important in considering the relevance of Williamson's model. If economies of scale are increasing over time, Williamson's analysis underestimates the cost-savings and the net benefits from a merger. Moreover, economies of scale would not be achieved by the internal expansion of existing firms in a growing market. Cf. Williamson (1968-a, p. 25) and Ross (1968, p. 1371).

If economies of scale are present over the whole range of potential capacities of new plants, a technically optimal scale does not exist or is very large compared with demand. However, an economically optimal scale, which differs from the technically optimal scale, may exist anyway. In such a case, economies of scale must be treated as an endogeneous concept and not as an exogeneous concept. (The latter seems to be the rule in most analyses where economies of scale are present.) Optimal scale gets a rather different meaning from what is usual and the main point is not to achieve an optimal scale as in a comparative static analysis but to achieve an optimal path of capacity expansion. The plant capacities generated by such an optimal process of capacity expansion are all economically optimal even if they differ in size.

5. Empirical estimates of economies of scale

Usually, economies of scale relate to the effect on the average cost of production of different rate of outputs, per unit of time, of a given commodity, when production at each scale is as efficient as possible. This is the long run average cost curve of the firm, or the 'scale curve' – a more appropriate term. The scale curve holds at a given point in time and it assumes a given state of technological knowledge. (See Pratten 1971. Chapter 1). The shape of the scale curve is determined by the elasticity of scale, ε, or the scale factor $n = \frac{1}{\varepsilon}$ (see Frisch 1965).

Geometric relationships apply to many basic industrial processes. An exponential function therefore provides an appropriate basis for fitting cost-capacity data, and all data in Tables 2 and 3 below have been fitted to $C = aX^n$. The scale factor is the value of n in the equation $C = aX^n$ where C = Total Costs or Total Value Added, a = Constant, X = Scale (of physical output).

The results from the different empirical investigations on economies of scale do not suit our purpose perfectly. Pratten (1971) estimates scale curves existing at a given point in time and especially the difference in average cost and value added per unit between minimum efficient scale (m.e.s.) and 50 per cent of m.e.s. where m.e.s. is defined as that point on the scale curve above which any possible subsequent doubling in scale would reduce value added per unit by less than 10 per cent (Pratten, 1971, p. 26).

The results of Pratten are summarised in Table 30.1 of his book (1971) but they are also rearranged and discussed in a valuable article by Silberston (1972), where scale factors are also calculated but only for value added and only for the range of the scale curve between m.e.s. and 50 per cent of m.e.s. However, 'Over this range the scale curve would be expected to fall more slowly than over lower ranges of output, where the value of the scale factor might well be smaller than over the 50–100 per cent range.' Silberston (1972, p. 383). See also Haldi and Whitcomb (1967), Pratten (1971) and Ribrant (1970).

Considering that the scale curve changes over time (Pratten 1971, p. 303) we

Table 2. Estimates of economies of scale.

Product etc.	Source of data	Range of physical capacity		Scale factor n	Elasticity of scale: $\varepsilon = \dfrac{1}{n}$
Refinery	Ribrant p. 251	(4–6)	000 tons p.a.	0,74	1,35
Ethylene plants	Ribrant p. 265	(100–300)	000 tons p.a.	0,85	1,17
Ethylene plants	Ribrant p. 265	(50–200)	000 tons p.a.	0,80	1,24
Surphuric acid	Pratten p. 50	(100–1000)	000 tons p.a.	0,96	1,03
Dyes plants	Pratten p. 52	$(0{,}75 \times {-}1{,}5 \times)$		0,71	1,40
Polymer plants	Pratten p. 65	(4–80)	000 tons p.a.	0,92	1,07
Polymer plants	Pratten p. 65	(20–80)	000 tons p.a.	0,92	1,07
Beer-breweries	Pratten p. 74	(0,1–1,0)	million barrels p.a.	0,80	1,24
Beer-breweries	Pratten p. 74	(0,2–1,0)	million barrels p.a.	0,79	1,25
Bread-bakery	Ribrant p. 352	(0,9–1,8)	tons p.h.	0,78	1,27
Sugar refinery plant	Ribrant p. 360	(1,1–4,2)	tons p. 24 hs	0,91	1,09
Milk-diary	Ribrant p. 370	(10–40)	000 tons p.a.	0,64	1,55
Butchery	Ribrant p. 380	(2–8)	000 tons p.a.	0,82	1,21
Butchery	Ribrant p. 380	(2–4)	000 tons p.a.	0,71	1,40
Detergents plants	Pratten p. 86	10–70	000 tons p.a.	0,94	1,05
Detergents plants	Pratten p. 86	30–70	000 tons p.a.	0,96	1,03
Cement portland	Pratten p. 92	(0,1–2,0)	million tons p.a.	0,84	1,18
Cement works	Ribrant p. 209	(0,12–1,0)	million tons p.a.	0,74	1,38
Steel-Crude steel plants	Pratten p. 105	(0,25–10)	million tons p.a.	0,91	1,09
Steel-blast furnaces	Pratten p. 106	(265–400)	tons p.a.	0,74–0,51	1,34–1,93
Pulp plants	Wohlin p. 77	(67–268)	000 tons pna.	0,78	1,28
Newspaper pulp plants	Wohlin p. 77	(55–440)	000 tons p.a.	0,84	1,19

are rather interested in the long run scale curve i.e. the envelope of the different vintage scale curves. At least for small countries, with a limited market and relatively small economically optimal plant sizes, this long run scale curve seems to be the relevant 'choice of capacity' curve i.e. the curve representing the actual possibilities from which the firm has to choose when a new plant is to be established. The impression one gets from a cursory glance at plant capacity data for Sweden is that plant capacities for many branches are located on the steep part of the respective scale curves. On the other hand for large countries such as the UK and the USA, the largest plants seem to be located on the more flat part of the respective scale curves. If this hypothesis is correct small countries with small markets have larger possibilities and gains from exploiting economies of scale than large countries. Thus, for such branches one should expect a faster rate of productivity growth *ceteris paribus* for small countries than for large. I think this is a point worth further investigation.

I have not found any estimates of such long run scale curves. Instead I shall utilize data from Pratten (1971), Ribrant (1970) and Wohlin (1970) for a wide range of capacities including a greater part of the scale curve than the interval between m.e.s. and 50 per cent of m.e.s. Thus I have made some crude estimates in Table 2 of scale factors for total costs of specific branches. These estimates are from only two points of the scale curve (which are indicated in the table) – usually

Table 3. Estimates of scale factors

Value of the scale factor *n*	Installed plant equipment		Total operating cost	
	No. of estimates of *n*	Percentage	No. of estimates of *n*	Percentage
Under .40	66	9,9	4	12,5
.40– .49	96	14,5	1	3,1
.50– .59	143	21,6	5	15,6
.60– .69	142	21,5	3	9,4
.70– .79	90	13,7	10	31,3
.80– .89	60	9,0	9	28,1
.90– .99	29	4,4	0	0
1.00–1.09	18	2,7	0	0
Over 1.10	18	2,7	0	0
Totals	662	100,0	32	100,0

Source: Haldi and Whitcomb 1967.

one of the lowest or next lowest values reported and the m.e.s.-value. Thus the scale factors in Table 2 hold for the ranges of capacities denoted in the third column.

These estimates can be compared with those of Haldi and Whitcomb (1967). Table 3 summarizes 'estimates of the scale coefficient for a large assortment of common industrial equipment. In most instances the exponential or linear log function fits the data well throughout the observed range of capacities. Most of the underlying cost-size observations came from catalogues of industrial equipment.' Haldi and Whitcomb (1967, p. 374).

There are, however, no direct estimates of scale factors for total costs but the results are divided in items of industrial equipment with a median scale factor of about 0,62 and 0,73 for operating costs (including raw material costs). The scale factor for total costs is then an average of the different scale factors for equipment and operation.

The model developed in Hjalmarsson (1974) seems to be suitable for an analysis of the costs of decentralization in the case of economies of scale. This model can be interpreted as a capacity expansion model for a multiplant firm producing a homogeneous product. In this paper we consider a manufacturing branch, which can consist of one or more firms each with its own optimal process of capacity expansion and with determinate market shares constant through time.

Limited space allows only a brief description of the model: for a complete description one should refer to Hjalmarsson (1974).

6. The model

Consider an industry producing a homogeneous product which serves demand that grows at a constant rate of 100 g per cent per year. All demand is to be satisfied by domestic production and initially there is enough capacity, denoted by x_0, to meet the demand. Substitution possibilities are present in the production *ex ante* but fixed proportions obtain *ex post* (putty clay). (For a definition of the concept *ex ante* production function, see Johansen 1972.)

The *ex ante* function at the micro level exhibits increasing returns to scale and is a quasi concave function with capital equipment and one current input. On grounds of mathematical and computational simplicity a Cobb-Douglas function with neutral technological change has been chosen. The *ex ante* function can be written as

$$\bar{x}_t = f_t(\bar{v}_t, \bar{k}_t, t) = A_0 e^{\delta t} \bar{v}_t^\alpha \cdot \bar{k}_t^\beta, \alpha + \beta = \varepsilon > 1 \tag{1}$$

Where

$\bar{x}_t$ = capacity (measured by maximum output) of the new production unit which constitutes vintage t.

$\bar{v}_t$ = input of the current factor when the unit is operated at full capacity,

$\bar{k}_t$ = amount of capital invested in the production unit.

δ = rate of technical progress. This is assumed to be embodied.

The price of the current factor, initially denoted by q_0, is continuously increasing at a rate of 100 a per cent per year, and for capital, z_0 is the initial price and 100 b the percentage growth rate.

Plant life is assumed to be infinite. This assumption is less realistic when economies of scale exist which make it profitable to scrap old plants with high unit costs and build new plants, with low unit costs, somewhat larger. However, as far as can be seen, the results below are not biased by this assumption. For a more thorough discussion of this and the other assumptions below, see Hjalmarsson (1974).

The horizon is infinite and the discount rate is denoted by r.

The capacity utilization of a plant completed at a certain investment point is zero at first but grows correspondingly to demand until the next investment point, when there is no unutilized capacity. The assumption is made partly for convenience and is partly based on the following consideration: If the time period between two investments is not too long, we can regard it as an initial and adjustment period. During this period utilization of capacity grows continuously.

Two successive investment points are denoted τ_n and τ_{n+1}, $\tau_0 = 0$, $n = = 0, 1, 2, \ldots$ During the interval between two successive installations, input requirement is fixed at the full capacity level independent of the capacity utilization.

The assumptions above imply the following theorem:

An optimal policy consists of building successive plants at equidistant intervals of time. Proof in Hjalmarsson (1974).

The distance between two investment points is denoted by τ and $\tau_n = n\tau$, $n = 0, 1, 2, \ldots$

The minimum cost of the plant to be constructed at time point τ_n, inclusive of the cost of running it for ever at full capacity, discounted to point 0, is denoted by C_{τ_n} and is given by the expression

$$C_{\tau_n} = z_{\tau_n} e^{-r\tau_n} \cdot \bar{k}_{\tau_n} + \sum_{t=\tau_n}^{\infty} q_t e^{-rt} \cdot \bar{v}_{\tau_n} \tag{2}$$

The expression is to be minimized with respect to $\bar{k}_{\tau_n}$ and $\bar{v}_{\tau_n}$ under the 'capacity-demand' constraint

$$A_0 e^{\delta\tau_n} \cdot \bar{v}_{\tau_n}^{\alpha} \cdot \bar{k}_{\tau_n}^{\beta} = x_0 e^{g\tau_{n+1}} - x_0 e^{g\tau_n} \tag{3}$$

i.e. the capacity of a new production unit at point τ_n is equal to the growth in demand between the successive investment points τ_n and τ_{n+1}

Then C_{τ_n} can be written

$$C_{\tau_n} = H \cdot x_0^{1/\varepsilon} (e^{g(\tau_{n+1} - \tau_n)} - 1)^{1/\varepsilon} e^{\gamma\tau_n} \tag{4}$$

where

$$H = \left(\frac{1}{A_0}\right)^{1/\varepsilon} \cdot \left(\frac{\beta}{\alpha}\right)^{\alpha/\varepsilon} \left(1 + \frac{\alpha}{\beta}\right) \frac{z_0^{1-\alpha/\varepsilon} \cdot q_0^{\alpha/\varepsilon}}{(1 - e^{(a-r)})^{\alpha/\varepsilon}} \tag{5}$$

$$\gamma = \frac{\alpha \cdot a + \beta \cdot b + g - \delta}{\varepsilon} - r \tag{6}$$

From the theorem we have $\tau_n = n_\tau$. Then

$$C_{\tau_n} = Hx_0^{1/\varepsilon} (e^{g\tau} - 1)^{1/\varepsilon} e^{\gamma n\tau} \tag{7}$$

Summation over all n yields the total cost function for the whole future as a function of the time distance, to be denoted by $C(\tau)$. $C(\tau)$ includes the discounted stream of construction costs as well as operation costs:

$$C(\tau) = \sum_{n=0}^{\infty} C_{\tau_n} = Hx_0^{1/\varepsilon} \cdot \frac{(e^{g\tau} - 1)^{1/\varepsilon}}{1 - e^{\gamma\tau}} \quad \text{where } \gamma < 0, \; H > 0 \tag{8}$$

It follows that $C(\tau) \to \infty$ for $\tau \to \infty$ and $\tau \to 0$. A minimum does exist. If $\gamma > 0$, C_{τ_n} in (7) is strictly increasing and $\sum_{n=0}^{\infty} C_{\tau_n}$ does not converge.

The optimal time interval is obtained by minimizing $C(\tau)$ with respect to τ. Differentiating $\log C(\tau)$ with respect to τ and equating the derivative to zero we get the following first order condition:

$$\frac{1}{\varepsilon} \cdot \frac{g e^{g\tau}}{(e^{g\tau} - 1)} - \frac{\gamma e^{\gamma\tau}}{e^{\gamma\tau} - 1} = 0 \tag{9}$$

It can be shown that $C(\tau)$ has a unique minimum.

In the one-firm case the model generates a path of capacity expansion and a branch structure of the form shown in Figure 3 below. On the axes are input-coefficients and the size of the units are indicated by the area of the squares. If there exists several firms in the branch following the same rule of capacity expansion the branch structure is constituted by similar structures of the individual firms. Such a structure seems to be fairly realistic for many branches (see e.g. Johansen 1972, p. 247).

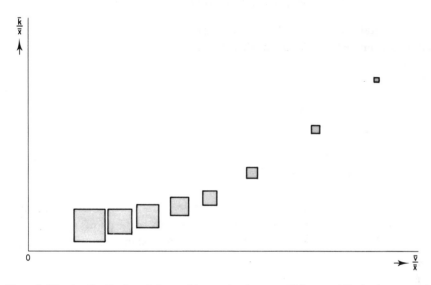

Figure 3. The size distribution of plants with regard to input coefficients and size in the monopoly firm case.

$C(\tau)$ is the discounted total cost as a function of the time interval, τ, of a process of capacity expansion for a branch with an initial capacity of x_0 and a growth in demand of 100 g per cent per year. Let us now assume that there exists only one firm in the branch and that it follows the rule of an optimal capacity expansion process as outlined above. Let us compare this development with that of a branch embracing two or more firms, each following the same rule of optimal capacity expansion and keeping their original market shares constant through time. The ratio of discounted costs, between the 'decentralized' process of capacity expansion and the monopolistic one, is denoted by m.

Since g and γ are assumed equal for all firms, both in the multifirm case and the monopoly firm case, so $\tau \cdot H$, too, is assumed equal for all firms, i.e. the same *ex ante* function holds in both cases and the same initial factorprices. If all firms begin their process of capacity expansion at the same moment, they will later invest on the same points of time. This assumption is probably less realistic and tends to overestimate the value of m. A cost minimizing development for a branch embracing m investing firms would show that the investments should be spread over time reducing the excess capacity. Maybe, this also is common in practice in many multifirm branches even if there seems to be a lot of exceptions as for example the European chemical and pulp and paper industries which seem to exhibit a very regular pattern of capacity expansion.

Let x_0^i be the initial capacity of firm no i ($i = 1 \ldots$); $\sum_i x_0^i = x_0$, which means that the total capacity equals that of the branch with single firm. From (8) one obtains a simple formula for the discounted cost ratio of the processes:

$$m = \frac{\sum_i (x_0^{i(1/\varepsilon)})}{x_0^{1/\varepsilon}} \tag{10}$$

From (4) it can then be seen that m is also the ratio between the costs of plants at every time of investment i.e. the costs of the plants to be constructed and operated in the multifirm case are m times those of the plant erected by the monopoly firm at the same investment point, when the capacity of the single plant belonging to the monopoly firm is equal to the aggregate capacity of the plants erected by the multifirm branch. This also means that the average cost in the multifirm case is m times as high as the cost in the single firm case.

However, if we still assume that the values of all the parameters are the same in both cases, different optimizing rules might be adopted by the firms in the multifirm case, and then formula (10) does not hold, because the time period between two investment points, τ, will now differ between firms and perhaps also for the same firm over time. If the number of firms are constant, such a development will probably result in higher costs compared with the case above where all firms follow a cost minimizing path of capacity expansion with constant market shares. In oligopolistic markets, strategic or other considerations may result in too large overcapacity and heavy advertising expenditures. Cf Ferguson Esposito and Esposito (1974), Sherman (1972) and Sutton (1974).

Thus we can distinguish two different aspects of efficiency here. The first is connected with the assumption of a constant elasticity of scale greater than 1, over the whole scale. In this case (with the assumptions above) formula (10) shows that the time does not bring anything essentially new into the analysis. The ratio m becomes independent of the time cycle τ. The same formula must hold, ceteris paribus, also when the assumption of putty clay is removed and a smooth capacity adjustment in pace with demand is possible. Inefficiency is here due to the number of firms and their market shares.

The second aspect is connected with the assumption of a putty clay production structure. When capacity expansion must take place step by step, the costs of different paths of capacity expansion become important. Inefficiency is here due to lacking coordination of investment decisions both with regard to the size of the plants and the time points of investments. See also Hjalmarsson (1973), Førsund and Hjalmarsson (1974) and Hjalmarsson (1974).

A third aspect of efficiency which is important, is that of differences in capital replacement criteria under different market structures; on the assumption that perfect competition plants are closed down and replaced when quasi-rents tend to zero (see Johansen 1972 and Hjalmarsson 1973). On the other hand a monopoly firm or a firm that is not a price-leader can adopt (and seems to adopt) another replacement criterion. The firm does not wait until the quasi-rent is zero but compares the unit costs in a new plant with unit operating costs of an old plant. Such a criterion tends to lower unit costs of a branch at a faster rate than the 'quasi-rent equal to zero' criterion. (The same point holds in the case of limited supply of resources.)

Thus in a certain sense a monopolist might be a more pure cost-minimizer than a perfect competition firm. This is quite opposite to the argument in the X-inefficiency theory where a monopoly firm does not care so much about the costs as a perfect competition firm (see Rowley 1973).

A fourth aspect of efficiency is of course that of transport costs which are heavy for many branches e.g. cement, timber, beer and milk. A total optimization usually might reduce these too.

Thus if m is calculated from formula (10) it tends to underestimate the benefits of a centralized development of capacity expansion.

The assumptions of constant elasticity of scale and a putty-clay production structure do not hold in Williamson's analysis, where the scale curve is assumed to be L-shaped (or U-shaped) and scale economies can be fully exploited in a growing market by a smooth adjustment of capacity in pace with development of demand.

From formula (10) it is easy to calculate m, and below the numerical calculations are limited to this aspect of efficiency.

7. Numerical computations and results

In the tables below the value of m is calculated for different values of ε and different numbers of firms with different market shares. The number of firms is denoted by n and $x_0 = 100$. Thus in Table 4 all firms are assumed to be equally large with equal market shares. In Table 5 the firms differ in market shares.

The tables show considerable differences in costs between the monopoly case and the multifirm case. These costs of decentralization increase when the elasticity of scale increases but decrease when the number of firms decreases.

Table 4. The value of m for different values of elasticity of scale when all firms have equal market shares.

n	x_i	1,10	1,20	1,25	1,30	1,40	1,50	1,75	2,00
2	50	1,07	1,12	1,15	1,17	1,22	1,26	1,36	1,41
4	25	1,13	1,26	1,32	1,38	1,49	1,59	1,81	2,00
5	20	1,16	1,31	1,38	1,45	1,58	1,71	1,99	2,24
10	10	1,23	1,47	1,58	1,70	1,93	2,15	2,68	3,16
20	5	1,31	1,65	1,82	2,00	2,35	2,71	3,61	4,47
25	4	1,31	1,71	1,90	2,10	2,51	2,92	3,97	5,00
50	2	1,43	1,92	2,19	2,47	3,06	3,68	5,35	7,07
100	1	1,52	2,15	2,51	2,89	3,73	4,64	7,20	10,00

Table 5. The value of m for different values of elasticity of scale when market shares differ between firms.

x_1	x_2	x_3	x_4	x_5	x_6	n	1,10	1,25	1,50
1	99					2	1,01	1,02	1,04
2	98					2	1,01	1,03	1,06
5	95					2	1,02	1,05	1,10
10	90					2	1,03	1,08	1,15
20	80					2	1,05	1,11	1,20
25	75					2	1,05	1,12	1,22
5	5	90				3	1,04	1,10	1,20
5	5	5	85			4	1,06	1,15	1,30
10	10	80				3	1,06	1,15	1,29
10	10	10	70			4	1,09	1,23	1,43
20	20	60				3	1,09	1,22	1,36
20	20	20	40			4	1,13	1,31	1,57
5	10	20	25	40		5	1,14	1,34	1,63
5	5	10	20	25	35	6	1,16	1,38	1,72
15	15	20	25	25		5	1,16	1,37	1,70

To gain further information about the relevance of these results we have to compare them with both actually estimated values of elasticity of scale in Table 2 and Table 3 and the Williamson trade-off results in Table 1.

The empirical estimates of elasticity of scale show great differences between branches and the whole range of elasticities from 1,10–2,00 is relevant. Comparing our estimates of cost reduction with the trade-off values of Williamson in Table 1, we find that lower average costs and monopoly welfare gains are likely to arise for a centralized process of capacity expansion compared to a decentralized one. In every case, very large price increases seem to be required in the monopoly case to offset the cost reductions due to centralization.

8. Some further empirical observations

In this section some empirical observations are presented to support the arguments put forward above.

1. In an interesting article Parry (1974) reports the findings of an investigation of unit costs in Australian chemical plants compared with unit costs in the same type but larger plants in USA and UK. The main point is the high unit costs in the comparatively small Australian plants compared with the costs of the larger overseas plants.
2. Through a merger of two independent firms a cement monopoly was established in Sweden in 1974. After the merger the monopoly firm developed a large and advanced programming model. From this model the firm determined the future optimal structure and structural development of the Swedish cement branch for twenty years ahead with regard to capital costs, operating costs and transportation costs. The impression is that the firm will behave as an almost perfect cost-minimizer with regard to future structure and structural transformation of the branch. (As a sharp contrast compare Renck (1966) which investigated investment appraisal and investment criteria in some Swedish firms.)
3. Another interesting example is the Swedish dairy industry which consists of twenty regional monopolies with altogether about 150 single plants. The Swedish dairies have a central service organization, which collects very detailed information from about fifty individual plants about production, labour input, capital and other inputs related to the different stages of the milk treatment process. These data are analyzed by the central organization so that the different plants can be compared with regard to efficiency. These efficiency calculations are regarded as a substitute for the market mechanism.

4. In a study of Norwegian tankers reported in Johansen (1972) Eide has shown that great differences in efficiency exist between old and small tankers compared with modern and large. But according to the newspapers a lot of very large tankers without contracts were laid up in Scandinavia during spring 1975 while at the same time many small inefficient tankers with long contracts were being utilized for the transport of oil. It seems that a central organization which could allocate the oil to be transported to the most efficient tankers would be highly profitable.

9. Qualifications and conclusions

Of course the model is too simplified and too strictly limited to homogeneous products to allow any strong policy recommendations concerning antitrust policy. Cf. Williamson (1968) and Rowley (1973). However, the computations of cost savings due to economies of scale are illuminating and strongly support the proposition of Williamson concerning the net allocative effect of merger in the case of homogeneous output. In some cases the estimates drawn from scale coefficients tend to underestimate rather than overestimate the importance of economies of scale on plant level and moreover it is highly probable that the capacity expansion in the multifirm case does not follow a cost-minimizing path when, as in oligopolistic markets, strategic considerations are important. In some branches transport costs are important and sometimes a total optimization may reduce these too, but in other cases they will impede a full utilization of economies of scale.

The analysis is limited to plant level. The effects on the firms' pricing policy of changes in market power is hard to evaluate and also the question of increasing X-inefficiency due to monopoly. However, it is not only the competitive firm and the monopoly firm that has to be compared but the whole industrial structure, structural development and rate of technological progress that follow with a special market form.

References

Bergson, A., On Monopoly Welfare Losses. *American Economic Review* 63 (5), 853–870, 1973.
Comanor, W. S. and H. Leibenstein, Allocative Efficiency, X-Efficiency and the Measurement of Welfare Losses. *Economica* 36, 304–309, 1969.
De Prano, M. E. and J. B. Nugent, Economies as an Antitrust Defence: Comment. *American Economic Review* 59 (5), 947–953, 1969.
Ferguson Esposito, F. and L. Esposito, Excess Capacity and Market Structure. *Review of Economics and Statistics* 56 (2), 188–194, 1974.

Frisch, R., *Theory of Production*, D. Reidel Publishing Co/Dordrecht-Holland, 1965.

Førsund, R. F. and L. Hjalmarsson, On the Measurement of Productive Efficiency, *Swedish Journal of Economics* 76 (2), 141–154, 1974.

Haldi, J. and D. Whitcomb, Economies of scale in Industrial Plants. *Journal of Political Economy* 75 (4), 373–385, 1967.

Harberger, A. C., Monopoly and Resource Allocation. *American Economic Review* 44, 77–87, 1954.

Hjalmarsson, L., Optimal Structural Change and Related Concepts. *Swedish Journal of Economics* 75 (2), 1973.

Hjalmarsson, L., The Size Distribution of Establishments and Firms Derived from an Optimal Process of Capacity Expansion. *European Economic Review* 5, 1974.

Johansen, L., *Production Functions*, North Holland Publishing Co., Amsterdam, 1972.

Kamerschen, D. R., Welfare Losses from Monopoly. *Western Economic Journal* 1966 (4), 221–36.

Koo, S-E., A Note on the Social Welfare Loss Due to Monopoly. *Southern Economic Journal* 37 (2), 212–214, 1970.

Leibenstein, H., Allocative Efficiency vs. X-efficiency. *American Economic Review* 56 (3), 392–415, 1966.

Parry, T. G., Plant Size, Capacity Utilization and Economic Efficiency: Foreign Investment in the Australian Chemical Industry. *Economic Record* 50 (2), 218–244, 1974.

Pratten, C. F., Economies of Scale in Manufacturing Industries, Department of applied economics *Occasional Papers No.* 28, Cambridge University Press, 1971.

Renck, O., *Investeringsbedoômning i några svenska foôretag.* (Investment appraisal in some Swedish firms) Nordstedt Stockholm 1966. (Second printing 1972).

Ribrandt, G., *Stordriftsfoôrdelar inom industriproduktionen*, SOU 1970: 30 Stockholm 1970. (Economics of scale in industrial production). (The Swedish Government Committee on the Concentration of Economic Power.)

Ross, P., Economies as an Antitrust Defense: Comment. *American Economic Review* 58 (5), 1371–1372, 1968.

Rowley, C. K., *Antitrust and Economic Efficiency*, Macmillan Studies in Economics London 1973.

Schwartzman, D., The Burden of Monopoly. *Journal of Political Economy* 68 (6), 627–630, 1960.

Sherman, R., *Oligopoly*. Lexington Books, D. C. Heath and Company Lexington 1972.

Siegfried, J. and T. Tiemann, The Welfare Costs of Monopoly: An Inter-Industry Analysis. *Economic Inquiry* 12 (2), 190–203, 1974.

Silberston, A., Economies of Scale in Theory and Practice. *Economic Journal* 82 (special issue), 369–391, 1972.

Stigler, G. J., The Statistics of Monopoly and Merger. *Journal of Political Economy* 64 (1), 33–40, 1956.

Sutton, C. J., Advertising, Concentration and Competition, *Economic Journal* 84 (1), 56–69, 1974.

Williamson, O. E., Economies as an Antitrust Defense: The Welfare Trade-offs. *American Economic Review* 58 (1), 18–36, 1968.

Williamson, O. E., Economies as an Antitrust Defense: Correction and Reply. *American Economic Review* 58 (5), 1372–1376, 1968.

Williamson, O. E., Economies as an Antitrust Defense: Reply. *American Economic Review* 59 (5), 954–959, 1969.

Wohlin, L., *Skogsindustrins strukturomvandling och expansionsmoôjlighet.* Industrins Utredningsinstitut, Stockholm 1970 with an English summary: Forest-Based Industries: Structural Change and Growth Potentials.

Worcester, D. A. Jr., New Estimates of the Welfare Loss to Monopoly United States: 1956–1969. *Southern Economic Journal* 40 (2), 234–245, 1973.

XII. ECONOMIES AS AN ANTITRUST DEFENSE REVISITED

Oliver E. Williamson

The merger of two firms is commonly viewed from an antitrust standpoint in terms of its anticompetitive effects on price. Sometimes, however, a merger will also result in real increases in efficiency which reduce the average cost of production of the combined entity below that of the two merging firms. The neglect, suppression, or even perverse interpretation of such economies was characteristic of antitrust enforcement in the early sixties and beyond. There are recent indications, however, that economies are now being valued more positively.

When I first addressed the question of economies as an antitrust defense in 1968,[1] I had misgivings over whether public policy would really benefit from explicit consideration of the issues. The alternative of keeping the economies defense in the background and relying instead on someone connected with the enforcement process to intrude whenever antitrust actions of a strongly efficiency impairing kind were contemplated had merit. After all, antitrust enforcement officials and the courts were not altogether insensitive to the benefits of efficiency considerations, and the potential operational problems of the courts entertaining an economies defense were not insignificant.[2]

Still, only six years earlier the Federal Trade Commission had stated that 'the necessary proof of violation of the statute consists of types of evidence that the acquiring firm possesses significant power in some markets *or* that its overall organization gives it a decisive advantage in efficiency over its smaller rivals.'[3] And although the 1966 language of the Supreme Court in *United States v. Von's Grocery Co.*[4] was somewhat more guarded, it scarcely dispelled the schizophrenic quality of *Brown Shoe Co. v. United States*[5] in which '[f]irst the Court says

1. Williamson, 'Economies as an Antitrust Defense: The Welfare Tradeoffs,' 58 *Am. Econ. Rev.* 18 (1968).
2. See text accompanying notes 10–14 *infra*.
3. *In re* Foremost Dairies, Inc., 60 F.T.C. 944, 1084 (1962) (emphasis supplied).
4. 384 U.S. 270 (1966).
5. 370 U.S. 270 (1962).

that the [Clayton] Act protects competition, not individual competitors, and in the next breath it says the Act protects higher-cost from lower-cost competitors.'[6]

Serving as I did as Special Economic Assistant to the head of the Antitrust Division of the U.S. Department of Justice during 1966–67 involved me in an operational way with the issues. Discussions with the career staff disclosed that possible economies associated with horizontal or vertical mergers were regarded with great skepticism and an exclusive focus on anticompetitive effects was common. The suggestion that economies might warrant affirmative consideration was apt to be dismissed on grounds that even small anticompetitive effects would surely swamp any possible efficiency benefits from such mergers. The conglomerate, moreover, was widely held to lack redeeming efficiency properties altogether: 'Doubtless some conglomerate mergers are harmless; some may even be useful. But the merger of unrelated activities seldom offers much prospect of efficiency.'[7]

Faced with what appeared to be a rather hostile climate towards economies considerations, I resolved my misgivings in favor of going ahead with the economies defense paper. To be sure, the partial equilibrium welfare economics apparatus upon which I relied to display the welfare tradeoffs is a blunt instrument which can be used in an intimidating way. To forestall the risk that subtle and complex policy issues might be resolved in an undiscerning manner, I specifically labeled the simple welfare economics model as 'naive' and went on to introduce a number of economic and extra-economic qualifications which must be considered.[8]

6. Posner, 'Antitrust Policy and the Supreme Court,' 75 *Colum. L. Rev.* 282, 306 (1975).
The tension running through the *Brown Shoe* Court's argument is illustrated by the following statement:

> Of course, some of the results of large integrated or chain operations are beneficial to consumers. Their expansion is not rendered unlawful by the mere fact that small independent stores may be adversely affected. It is competition, not competitors, which the Act protects. But we cannot fail to recognize Congress' desire to promote competition through the protection of viable, small, locally owned businesses. Congress appreciated that occasional higher costs and prices might result from the maintenance of fragmented industries and markets. It resolved these competing considerations in favor of decentralization. We must give effect to that decision (370 U.S. at 344).

7. Edwards, 'Economic Concentration, Part 1: Overall and Conglomerate Aspects,' *Hearings before the Subcommittee on Antitrust and Monopoly*, Committee on the Judiciary, U.S. Senate, 82nd Cong. 1964, at 46. But see Turner, 'Conglomerate Mergers and Section 7 of the Clayton Act,' 78 *Harv. L. Rev.* 1313 (1965). Turner, then head of the Antitrust Division, gave prominent attention in his article on conglomerates to possible efficiency consequences attributable to commonalities in marketing, manufacturing, and administration. But Turner failed to consider transaction cost economies of the kinds discussed in section IV and concluded that the possibility of other types of economies is necessarily 'slight' in a 'pure' conglomerate merger. *Id.* 1330.
8. See section II, part C.

A reexamination of antitrust enforcement eight years later reveals that the treatment of economies in antitrust enforcement has improved.[9] Although the economies argument has sometimes been used as a blunt instrument, officials charged with antitrust enforcement do not appear to have been intimidated. In the meantime, new issues of an economies related kind have arisen, which I attempt to address here. The revisitation of economies as an antitrust defense is in six parts. The operationality of an economies defense is examined in Section 1. The basic partial equilibrium model, including qualifications, is set out in Section 2. Next, the relevance of rent transformation arguments are treated in Section 3. Transactional efficiencies are discussed in Section 4, and the policy impact of the economies defense is assessed in Section 5. The conclusions appear in Section 6.

1. Operationality

The object is to evaluate the welfare implications of a merger which arguably increases market power but simultaneously yields real cost savings. Whether the standard partial equilibrium welfare economics model should be used to assess the merits of an economies defense in such instances turns partly on operationality considerations. Two problems arise in this connection; I shall refer to these as 'bounded rationality' and the pairing of opportunism with a condition of information impactedness.[10]

Bounded rationality refers to the computational and perceptual limits of human agents for dealing with complex events. Abstract theories for dealing with policy problems which require policy makers to possess powers of calculation and perspicacity that vastly exceed their objective limits may fail for lack of operationality. For example, my reliance on partial equilibrium rather than general equilibrium[11] analysis is, in a sense, a concession that an economies defense cannot be dealt with satisfactorily in all of its rich complexity. Suppose, however, that this is a reasonable concession to prospective operationality, so

---

9. See section V, *infra*.
10. I have had occasion elsewhere to develop a general framework for examining matters of institutional design. O. Williamson, *Markets and Hierarchies: Analysis and Antitrust Implications* (1975). Bounded rationality and opportunism/information impactedness are prominent features of that framework.
11. Partial equilibrium analysis involves an examination of one market while assuming that incomes, other prices, and production conditions ramain unchanged. Partial analysis is appropriate when changes in the particular market do not significantly affect the economy as a whole, which would in turn affect the relevant market. When changes in the relevant market do affect the general economy, a general equilibrium analysis, in which prices and quantities for all markets must be determined together, is usually appropriate.

that the economic analysis is not vitiated by reason of its partial equilibrium orientation. A further problem to be addressed is whether even partial equilibrium analysis can be usefully introduced into a judicial proceeding. Derek Bok's discussion of merger law and economics is relevant in this connection:

Lawyers have perhaps not always been explicit enough in articulating the peculiar qualifications which their institutions place upon the unbridled pursuit of truth, and this failure may in some measure explain the irritation with which their handiwork is so often greeted by even thoughtful economists. This problem cannot be solved, nor can the economist-critic be placated, by embracing more and more of the niceties of economic theory into our antitrust proceedings. Unless we can be certain of the capacity of our legal system to absorb new doctrine, our attempts to introduce it will only be more ludicrous in failure and more costly in execution.[12]

Fifteen years later, Richard Posner contends that legal capacities to deal with the economic complexities of merger law are severely limited: 'Rebuttal based on ease of entry, economies of scale, or managerial efficiency should not be allowed, because these factors, though clearly relevant to a correct evaluation of the competitive significance of a merger, are intractable subjects for litigation.'[13]

Whether the lack of sophistication by the courts is responsible for Posner's policy position is unclear. But suppose that the formal apparatus of partial equilibrium welfare economics poses no operationality problems for the courts. I submit that the courts might still decline to entertain a *full-blown* economies defense – whereby the economies and market power effects of a merger are expressly evaluated in net benefit terms – because of the hazards of opportunism/information impactedness.

Although the government and the defendant have roughly equal access to market share statistics, and can both present, interpret, and contest such data, the same is not true with respect to a purported economies defense. Here, the data are asymmetrically distributed to the strategic advantage of the defendant, whence an information impactedness condition can be said to exist. Not only can the defendant use its information advantage by disclosing the data in a selective way, but advocacy legitimizes such disclosure. Unless the government can demonstrate that the data are incomplete or significantly distorted, which may not be easy, the advocacy process is poorly suited for purposes of getting a balanced presentation of the evidence before the court.[14]

12. Bok, 'Section 7 of the Clayton Act and the Merging of Law and Economics,' 74 *Harv. L. Rev.* 226, 228 (1960).
13. Posner, *supra* note 6, at 313.
14. Note, however, that modern discovery practices may somewhat reduce the government's disadvantage. See, e.g., *Fed. R. Civ. P.* 26–37.

In consideration of these infirmities, ought the entire economies defense question be interred and attention turned to more practical matters? I think not, because simple sensitivity to economies in antitrust policy formation is enormously important. Such sensitivity is promoted by engaging in a dialogue with respect to an economies defense, even though full blown implementation of the specific tradeoff apparatus is never contemplated. This issue will be examined more thoroughly in Section 5.

2. Tradeoff analysis

2.1. General approach

Three postulates for doing applied welfare economics have been offered by Arnold Harberger:[15]
(a) the competitive demand price for a given unit measures the value of that unit to the demander;
(b) the competitive supply price for a given unit measures the value of that unit to the supplier;
(c) when evaluating the net benefits or costs of a given action (project, program, or policy), the costs and benefits accruing to each member of the relevant group (e.g., a nation) should normally be added without regard to the individual(s) to whom they accrue.

While this approach represents a rather narrow view of economics, it often constitutes a useful beginning. Other factors, to the extent that they are thought to be relevant, can usually be introduced separately.[16] Although the requisite expertise to make these subsequent adjustments will often be of an extraeconomic sort, economists need not disqualify themselves from any further involvement merely because the required adjustments are not purely economic ones. Indeed, since these 'other factors' will frequently fall outside the purview of any single discipline, decision-making responsibility falls on nonspecialists by default. Still, the lack of strictly professional qualifications ought to be noted.

A net benefit approach to the economies defense issue is to be contrasted with common admonitions that 'wherever noncompetitive markets exist, government should operate to lead them to the competitive solution.'[17] This latter position

15. Harberger, 'Three Basic Postulates for Applied Welfare Economics,' 9 *J. Econ. Lit.* 785, 785 (1971).
16. See text accompanying notes 33–36 *infra*.
17. Feldman, 'Efficiency, Distribution, and the Role of Government in a Market Economy,' 79 *J. Pol. Econ.* 508, 517 (1971).

appears to be consistent with a literal reading of Section 7 of the Clayton Act, which prohibits mergers 'where in any line of commerce in any section of the country, the effect of such acquisiton may be substantially to lessen competition, or to tend to create a monopoly.'[18] To be sure, the necessity to make hard choices is avoided by literal interpretations of passages of this kind. But ought the conflict between competition and merger economies always to be resolved in favor of competition, even if current and prospective competitive effects are slight and allocative efficiency is seriously impaired in the process?

One possible response when such tradeoffs appear would be to resort to regulation. Indeed, John Cable has argued that mergers which realize economies while enhancing market power should be permitted to occur, with the resulting combination made subject to price regulation.[19] The resulting prices would presumably be 'fair,' if not strictly competitive. There is a growing appreciation, however, that regulation involves severe costs of its own and hence should be extended only reluctantly. Thus, although Cable supports his proposal for price regulation with the observation that 'the kind of government intrusion into private decision-making which is envisaged is one for which there are existing precedents (and in the U.K. some considerable experience in recent years),'[20] I find the results of government price management efforts mainly dissuasive[21] – not least of all in the U.K.

A discussion of these issues, however, is beyond the scope of this paper. Accordingly, I will ignore the regulatory option and focus instead on the following two alternatives: (1) permit the merger, thereby facilitating the early realization of economies, with a resulting (possibly temporary) increase in monopoly power, or (2) prohibit the merger, thereby preserving competition but forcing the affected firms to achieve the economies independently, probably with a delay. Is the conventional position that favors the latter policy[22] invariably to be preferred, or does a rational treatment of the merger question require that the allocative efficiency implications of the economies-market power tradeoff be explicitly faced? Put differently, is the admonition to 'make markets operate competitively' too simplistic an approach in light of legitimate efficiency goals?

Joe Bain is one of the few economists who has expressed concern that prevailing enforcement procedures lack rationality. As Bain has commented:

18. 15 U.S.C. § 18 (1970).
19. J. Cable, *Economies as an Antitrust Defense: Does the First Best Matter?* (1975).
20. *Id.* 13.
21. For a somewhat more sympathetic view of price controls – which, however, is very cautious on the merits – see Lanzillotti, 'Industrial Structure and Price/Wage Controls: The U.S. Experience,' in *Markets, Corporate Behavior and the State* 324 (A. Jacquemin & H. de Jong eds. 1976).
22. See, e.g., Harberger, *supra* note 15.

[A] standard of reasonableness, or definition of the grounds on which otherwise offending mergers could be found legal, is clearly needed and should be set forth in Section 7. The one simple rule that is obviously needed is that a merger which may substantially lessen competition should be allowed if the merging firms can demonstrate that the merger would substantially increase real efficiency in production and distribution ... This sort of amendment would strengthen a very significant piece of legislation, and tend to assure that its enforcement would be in accord with accepted principles of economic rationality.[23]

I believe that, at the very least, a parametric analysis of some of the simple cases is needed to reveal the implicit costs of a strict market power rule. The issue should not be avoided merely because tradeoff analysis cannot be implemented immediately. Discouraging irrational argumentation and administratively suppressing bad cases are surely goals that justify an analysis of the economies defense.

2.2. The naive tradeoff model[24]

For purposes of developing the tradeoff model, assume that the merging firms in question are duopolists[25] of either a local or national sort, that the product is homogeneous, and that the degree of price increase is 'margin restricted' by the prospect that geographically remote rivals will ship into the region or that potential entry will be activated locally.[26] It will simplify the argument to further

23. J. Bain, *Industrial Organization* 658 (2d ed. 1968).

24. The model in this subsection relies on that in Williamson, *supra* note 1, as corrected in Williamson, 'Economies as an Antitrust Defense,' in *Readings in Industrial Economics* (C. Rowley ed. 1972).

25. 'Duopoly' refers to the situation in which there are only two *sellers* in the relevant market.

26. Implicitly, this is an entry barriers analysis. Entry barrier analysis with emphasis on potential competition is scarcely novel. Numbered among its early expositors are Alfred Marshall, 'Some Aspects of Competition,' in *Memorials of Alfred Marshall* 256, 269–80 (A. Pigou ed. 1956), and J. B. Clark, *The Context of Trusts* 25–30 (1914). More recent contributors include Tibor Scitovsky, *Welfare and Competition* 22–23 (1951), Paulo Sylos Labini, *Oligopoly and Technical Progress* (1962), and Franco Modigliani, 'New Developments on the Oligopoly Front,' 66 *J. Pol. Econ.* 215 (1958). Scitovsky expresses it as follows:

> The individual price maker has to meet two forms of competition: the actual competition of his established rivals and the threat of competition from newcomers to his market ... Of the two ... the threat from newcomers and restraints on their entry to the market are by far the more important from the price maker's point of view.

T. Scitovsky, *supra*, at 22–23. Although perhaps this should be qualified, in that the significance of potential competition is vastly greater if the number of established rivals is small, it nevertheless imparts the spirit of entry barrier analysis.

Entry barrier analysis of potential competition is not, however, without its critics. George Stigler argues that it is tantamount to solving the oligopoly problem 'by murder.' G. Stigler, *The Organization of Industry* 21 (1968). Jagdish Bhagwati, by contrast, regards the entry barrier focus on potential competition as *the* 'really fundamental innovation in oligopoly theory.' Bhagwati, 'Oligopoly Theory, Entry-Prevention, and Growth,' in 22 *Oxford Economic Papers* 297, 298 (1970).

assume that only competitive returns were being realized before the merger. The effects on resource allocation of a merger that yields both economies and post-merger market power can then be investigated in a partial equilibrium context with the help of Figure 1. The horizontal line labeled AC_1 represents the level of average costs of the two firms before combination, while AC_2 shows the level of average costs after the merger. The price before the merger is given by P_1 and is equal to AC_1. The price after the merger is given by P_2 and is assumed to exceed P_1; since if it were less than P_1 the immediate economic effects of the merger would be strictly positive.[27]

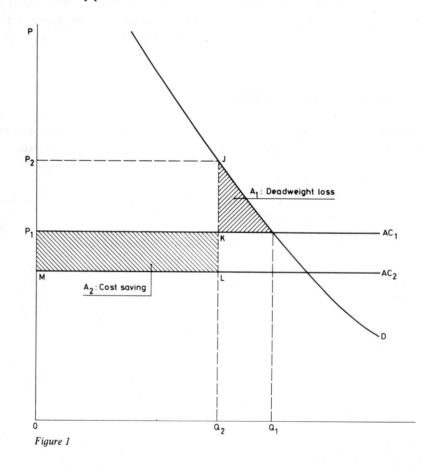

Figure 1

27. This is a simple but basic point. It reveals that market power is only a necessary and not a sufficient condition for undesirable price effects to exist. It would be wholly irrational to regard an increase in the price to average cost ratio (i.e., $P_2/AC_2 > P_1/AC_1$) as grounds for opposing a merger if, at the same time, the post-merger price was less than the pre-merger level (i.e., $P_2 < P_1$) and the qualifications discussed below are insubstantial.

The net welfare effects of the merger are represented by the two shaded areas in the Figure.[28] The area designated A_1 is the familiar deadweight loss that would result if price were increased from P_1 to P_2, assuming that costs remain constant.[29] But since average costs are actually reduced by the merger, the area designated A_2, which represents cost savings, must also be taken into account. Geometrically, the net allocative efficiency effect of the combined price increase and cost reduction resulting from the merger (judged in naive terms) will be positive if the area represented by A_2 is greater than the area represented by A_1. Conversely, if A_1 is greater than A_2, the effect will be negative. If A_1 and A_2 are equal, the merger has neutral effects.

The two welfare effects also can be expressed algebraically as follows:

$$A_1 = \tfrac{1}{2}(P_2 - P_1)(Q_1 - Q_2) = \tfrac{1}{2}(\Delta P)(\Delta Q)$$

$$A_2 = (AC_1 - AC_2)Q_2 = [\Delta(AC)]Q_2$$

The net allocative efficiency effect is then given by $A_2 - A_1$. This will be positive if the following inequality holds:

$$\{\Delta(AC)]Q_2 - \tfrac{1}{2}(\Delta P)(\Delta Q) > 0$$

Dividing through by P_1Q_1, substituting for $\Delta Q/Q_1$ the expression $\eta(\Delta P/P_1)$, where η is the elasticity of demand, and recognizing that $P_1 = AC_1$, we obtain

$$\frac{\Delta(AC)}{AC_1} - \tfrac{1}{2}\eta \frac{Q_1}{Q_2}\left(\frac{\Delta P}{P_1}\right)^2 > 0$$

If this inequality holds, the net allocative effect of the merger is positive. If the difference is equal to zero, the merger has neutral effects. If the inequality is

28. The conventional partial equilibrium welfare function is given by $W = (TR + S) - (TC - R)$, where, under appropriate restrictions, the terms in the first set of parentheses reflect social benefits (total revenue plus consumers' surplus) and those in the second reflect social costs (total pecuniary costs less intramarginal rents). It will be convenient here and throughout the argument to assume that R is negligible.

29. My use of dead-weight loss is somewhat restrictive. Inefficiency is also a dead-weight loss. For convenience of exposition, however, I refer to the Marshallian triangle as the dead-weight loss and compare this to the cost saving aspects of a merger. Estimating the value of consumers' suplus by the Marshallian triangle follows the common and broadly defensible practice of suppressing the income effects associated with a price change. The net social benefit associated with a particular cost-price configuration is defined as total revenue plus consumers' surplus less social cost, when social and private costs are assumed to be identical and externalities and producers' surplus are both assumed to be zero.

reversed, the proposed merger would have negative allocative consequences. In other words, this inequality says that if the decimal fraction reduction in average costs exceeds the square of the decimal fraction increase in price premultiplied by one-half times the elasticity of demand times the ratio of the initial to final outputs, the allocative effect of the merger (judged in naive terms) is positive.

The cost reductions necessary to offset price increases for various values of the elasticity of demand are shown in Table 1.[30] Inspection of Table 1 discloses that a relatively modest cost reduction is sufficient to offset relatively large price increases even if the elasticity of demand is as high as 2, which for most commodities is probably a reasonable upper bound.[31] Because firms whose prices are margin restricted by the threat of entry can increase prices only modestly above minimum average costs – normally by less than a ten percent premium[32] – the naive model suggests that a merger that promises nontrivial economies – say greater than two per cent – will generally yield a net allocative efficiency gain. This conclusion may be altered, however, by consideration of the qualifications to the naive model that follow.

Table 1. Percentage cost reduction $[(\Delta(AC)/AC) \times 100]$ sufficient to offset percentage price increases $[(\Delta P/P) \times 100]$ for selected values of η.

$(\Delta P/P \times 100)$	η 3	2	1	1/2
5	.44	.27	.13	.06
10	2.00	1.21	.55	.26
20	10.38	5.76	2.40	1.10

30. The computations assume that demand is isoelastic in the relevant range.
31. Werner Hirsch's survey of price elasticities in the 1950's suggested an upper bound price elasticity of three. Hirsch, 'A Survey of Price Elasticities,' 19 *Rev. Econ. Studies* (1950–51). More recent work by Hendrick Houthakker and Lester Taylor suggests somewhat lower upper-bound elasticities. H. Houthakker & L. Taylor, *Consumer Demand in the United States, 1929–7* (1966).
32. In a sample of eighty-eight food manufacturing firms in the United Kingdom during the period 1965–1969, Keith Cowling, et al. found only four cases where the price to cost ratio exceeded 1.10 and none where it exceeded 1.20. K. Cowling, J. Cable, M. P. Kelly & A. J. McGuinness, *Advertising and Economic Behavior* (1975).

2.3. Qualifications

I have previously discussed a number of qualifications to the naive model,[33] including matters of timing and incipiency. Timing refers to the fact that significant economies can often be realized through internal expansion, especially in a growing market, if the merger option is blocked. Whether the delayed realization of economies is more than offset by the rivalry gains from prohibiting the merger requires an examination of the time stream of benefits and costs associated with the merger versus nonmerger options.

Incipiency is concerned with market power effects of a merger that are not adequately displayed by considering each merger in isolation. That is, instead of a single merger, suppose that a series of mergers is contemplated, each of which realizes identical economies and, by itself, has negligible effects on market power. Cumulatively, however, the market power effects may be substantial. Merger assessments in such circumstances cannot proceed in a simple pairwise fashion, although net benefits analysis of the same generic kind can nevertheless be employed.

A common objection to the partial equilibrium welfare economics model is that it makes insufficient allowance for income distribution effects. This can take alternative (though related) forms. One of these is that demand curves may not accurately reflect social benefits: 'if the distribution of wealth ... is unjust, there is no reason to pay heed to the tastes of those who have benefited from the injustice.'[34] A second is that purchaser interests and supplier interest ought not to be weighted equally, which is at variance with Harberger's third postulate.

I interpret the first to imply that the distribution of wealth is not merely incorrect but is egregiously unjust. This in turn implies, I believe, a serious breakdown in the political process. Where this has occurred, evaluating policy alternatives in conventional partial equilibrium welfare economics terms amounts to tinkering and is apt to be unrewarding, because a massive reshaping of the system is really needed.

Lest arguments of this kind be invoked uncritically, however, those who take such positions should presumably advance arguments and evidence which, when displayed, will elicit widespread popular support. Otherwise a presumption that such defects as exist are less than egregious seems warranted. Where this latter obtains, it is surely too strong to claim that, in general, no heed be paid to existing tastes (as disclosed by demand curves). To the contrary, where only modest income redistribution is indicated and is being effected by conventional measures

---

33. Williamson, 'Economies as an Antitrust Defense,' in *Readings in Industrial Economics* (C. Rowley ed. 1972).
34. Feldman, *supra* note 17, at 519.

(which normally involves taxes and transfers of a general rather than commodity-specific kind), the contention that social valuations are poorly reflected by a particular demand curve ought to be considered the exception rather than the rule and should be accompanied by supporting evidence.

The second objection, that purchaser and supplier interests ought not to be weighted equally, is a variant on the above which essentially reduces to a dispute over how the region P_2JKP_1 in Figure 1 should be treated. Note in this connection that the area between the demand curve and the price at which a final product is purchased is a rough measure of consumers' surplus. In the pre-merger period, this area included the region P_2JKP_1. In the post-merger period, the price increases from P_1 to P_2, whence this region is 'monetized' and shows up as profit. This transformation of benefits from one form (consumers' surplus) to another (profit) is treated as a wash under the conventional welfare economics model.

It may, however, be that for some products the interests of users warrant greater weight in relation to sellers; for other products (e.g., products that are sold to the very rich which are produced by disadvantaged minorities), a reversal might be indicated. But a general case that user interests greatly outweigh seller interests is not easy to make and probably reflects a failure to understand how profits ramify through the system (as taxes, dividends, retained earnings, etc.) in ways which greatly attentuate the notion that monolithic 'producer interests' exist and are favored. In any event, a product-specific claim that user and producer interests should be weighted unequally as they relate to the region P_2JKP_1 does not vitiate the partial equilibrium model. It merely requires that the appropriate weights be specified. To the extent that purchaser interests are given greater weight than supplier interests, the economies burden is increased, *ceteris paribus*.

Additional or related qualifications to the naive model include the following:

(1) second best considerations: the possibility that price increases compensate for or compound distortions in other sectors should be recognized. The effects, however, can go either way and, in any event, are rarely estimable;

(2) pre-existing market power: where the merging firms enjoyed pre-merger market power, somewhat greater economies are needed to offset the welfare losses of a post-merger price increase. The model is easily augmented to make allowance for this;

(3) dispersion: while the economies that a merger produces are usually limited to the combining firms, the price increase may be spread across a wider class of firms. On the other hand, it may be true that although the economies of the merger are limited, the market power effects are even more restricted. Thus the merging firms may realize production economies on all transactions but

enjoy monopoly power in only some of their markets.[35] Dispersion effects can thus go either way, depending on the particular circumstances;

(4) technological progress: though the naive model is easily extended to make allowance for such effects, the direction of the effects will vary and is apt to be difficult to ascertain in particular cases;

(5) politics: a rule limiting acquisitions by giant-sized firms may be warranted on populist, political grounds.

A further qualification that to my knowledge has not been treated, but deserves consideration, is the possibility that additional real costs in the form of induced transportation expense will be incurred as a result of the merger. Implicit to the naive model is an assumption that customers will reduce their purchases in response to price increases but will not deflect their purchases of the same commodity to buy from more remote suppliers. Some customers, however, may find it attractive to shift their purchases to more remote suppliers. This alternative will be advantageous to those buyers for whom the delivered price by an adjacent supplier is less than the delivered post-merger price of the combining duopolists, assuming that there is no price discrimination so that f.o.b. pricing prevails for all duopoly customers. Although the *effective* price to these mobile customers is less than the post-merger duopoly price, the *real cost* of supplying this group of customers is increased by the incremental transportation expense.

A simple spatial model to illustrate and assess these transportation expense effects is developed in the Appendix. The model reveals that if customers are widely distributed, the induced transportation expense may be considerable. Since individual purchasing decisions are made on a pecuniary rather than a real cost basis, the allocative efficiency consequences of a pecuniary price distortion may differ greatly from the results predicted by the naive model.

3. Monopoly rent transformation

3.1. General

Rent transformation refers to any of several processes whereby either the prospect or the realization of supernormal profits induces expenditures to be

---

35. The alleged monopoly effects in *Brown Shoe* were clearly of this variety, Brown Shoe Co. v. United States, 370 U.S. 294 (1962), and the Pabst-Blatz merger also appears to have been of this type, United States v. Pabst Brewing Co., 384 U.S. 546 (1966).

incurred in partially or fully offsetting amounts. These expenditures can be of an *ex ante* or *ex post* kind. In the former case, the anticipation of winning the prize (a monopolistic income stream) elicits pre-award rivalry; aspirants incur real costs designed to better qualify them for the award. Although only one or a few will be declared winners, the aggregate expenses of such rivalry may be substantial. Rent transformation will be exhaustive if the aggregate pre-award expenses equal the expected, discounted gain.

Ex post rent transformation also involves rivalry. Given that prices exceed competitive levels, rivals incur expenses designed to improve their respective market shares. Again, rent transformation is exhaustive if the resulting expenses drive average costs up to the supernormal price level.

An early statement of the *ex ante* rent transformation argument was made by Arnold Plant in the context of his discussion of patents.[36] Plant argued that the prospect of securing a patent would induce *ex ante* resources to be expended until the expected return to inventive activities was reduced to competitive levels. Anne Krueger's discussion of *ex ante* rent transformation in the context of bribing public officials is particularly intriguing.[37] Assuming that the benefits of favors, once conferred by public officials, are not undone by *ex post* rivalry and that bribes to secure favors are pecuniary transfers, *ex ante* real costs will be incurred by those who aspire to receive bribes: 'Competition takes place through attaining the appropriate credentials for entry into government service and through accepting unemployment while making efforts to obtain appointments. Efforts to influence those in charge of making appointments, of course, just carry the argument one step further back.'[38]

The regulation of the price of, and entry into, commercial airline service is an illustration of *ex post* rent transformation. Assuming that the regulated price exceeds the cost of supplying service and that entry to new firms is barred, existing firms engage in competition of a service-related kind, with the result that profits are reduced to competitive levels.[39] Unlike normal competitive processes, wherein the influx of additional resources has supply augmenting effects, whence prices fall towards competitive cost levels, here costs rise to the level of the regulated price.

---

36. Plant, 'The Economic Theory Concerning Patents,' 1 *Economica* 30 (1934).
37. Krueger, 'The Political Economy of the Rent-Seeking Society,' 64 *Am. Econ. Rev.* 291 (1974).
38. *Id.* 293. Bribes and contributions offered by those seeking political favors strike me as trivial in relation to the expected benefits that are conferred. Research on this, including an examination of the factors responsible for the gap between payment and realizations, would be useful.
39. Douglas and Miller, 'The CAB's Domestic Passenger Fare Investigation,' 5 *Bell J. Econ. and Mngmnt. Sci.* 204 (1974).

3.2. Application to mergers

Posner contends that the apparent benefits of an economies defense are vitiated by the prospect of rent transformation. His argument runs as follows:

> Oliver Williamson ... has argued that the refusal of the courts to recognize a defense of economies of scale in merger cases under the Clayton Act is questionable because, under plausible assumptions concerning the elasticity of demand, only a small reduction in the merging firms' costs is necessary to offset any deadweight loss created by the price increase that the merger enables the firms to make ...
>
> This analysis is incomplete, however. The expected profits of the merger ... will generate *an equivalent amount* of costs as the firms vie to make such mergers or, after they are made, to engross the profits generated by the higher post-merger price through service competition or whatever.[40]

My responses to this are several, the first of which is that the naive model, to which Posner evidently refers, is subject to a number of qualifications, most of which have been set out above.[41] Whether or not only a small cost reduction is needed turns on a specific assessment of these qualifications. Suppose, however, that none of these are quantitatively significant and that the merger gives rise to profits in the amount $P_2 JLM$ in Figure 1.

The issue then is whether *ex ante* or *ex post* costs will be incurred, if an economies defense is admitted, such that this profit region will be exhausted. Note in this connection that we are not dealing with a regulated industry, whence prices are not fixed at P_2 but will fall in response to new entry.[42] Reference to 'service competition or whatever,' which is relevant in the regulatory context, thus appears to be inapposite. Rather, *ex post* rivalry responses to the monopolistic price P_2 will be of a normal, procompetitive kind and are not to be confused with rent transformation. Assume, furthermore (for reasons that are developed more fully in Section V), that the costs of litigating an economies defense are not great. Posner's argument evidently turns, therefore, on *ex ante* rent transformation. Assessing this entails an examination of *process*. Posner is silent on this issue.

---

40. Posner, 'The Social Costs of Monopoly and Regulation,' 83 *J. Pol. Econ.* 807, 821 (1975) (emphasis supplied).
41. See text accompanying notes 33–36 *supra*.
42. This assumes that existing firms maintain or expand output in response to entry. If existing firms adopt instead a conciliatory policy and withdraw supplies, thereby to make a place for entrants, price can be maintained at the P_2 level. Umbrella pricing does invite entry by high cost firms and hence can result in rent transformation. Posner does not, however, indicate that he relies on umbrella pricing.

3.3. 'Ex ante' adaptation – the N-firm case

Assume that there are N equally qualified firms, where N is a large number, any one of which when joined with firm $N + 1$ can realize the economies in question. Assume further that the N firms engage in a *pecuniary bidding* competition such that the amount offered to firm $N + 1$ is equal to the discounted expected profits of the merger. The stockholders or managers of firm $N + 1$ will then appropriate the entire profitability gain if noncollusive pecuniary bids are solicited. In the first instance at least, this is not a real cost transfer and hence is not to be regarded as a welfare loss in assessing the real cost consequences of the merger.

Might, however, the prospect of being the beneficiary of the pecuniary offer induce prior investments of a strategic positioning kind? At least with respect to the stockholders, this seems doubtful. Outsiders who perceive that a profit enhancing merger can be arranged may buy in and bid up the stock of firm $N + 1$ in advance of the merger bid. But this is an entirely pecuniary undertaking.

Consider, therefore, the managers of the firm and assume that (1) managers are in a position to appropriate the full value of any profitability increment that accrues from the merger and (2) legal prohibitions against malfeasance are without effect. The first of these assumptions requires that managers enjoy an unusual degree of insularity from stockholder control. Indeed, the market for corporate control must not merely be weak, it must have collapsed altogether. This assumption is at variance with a good deal of opinion and some evidence to the contrary[43] and thus will be rejected. Moreover, merely establishing that managers enjoy some degree of insularity does not imply that they are in a position to accept bribes. In advanced Western economies, legal and moral sanctions with respect to personal aggrandizement surely restrain behavior of this kind. It is thus extremely doubtful that bribes will be forthcoming in an amount that accounts for even a significant fraction, much less the full value, of the merger.

For purposes of completing the argument, however, assume that managers can and do accept bribes in the amount of the full profitability gain associated with the merger. A credentializing process presumably will then be set in motion with the result that executives will be overqualified for their jobs. Educational and other expenses will be incurred by a large number of would-be executives in order to improve their prospects for being awarded a strategic management post from which they will be in a position to demand and receive pecuniary bribes. Rents are transformed into real cost in this way.

---

43. Manne, 'Mergers and the Market for Corporate Control,' 73 *J. Pol. Econ.* 110, 112 (1965). See generally P. O. Steiner, *Mergers: Motives, Effects, Policies* (1965).

For the argument to reach this far, the management insularity assumptions noted above must be met. As indicated, I regard these as implausible. But even if these were to be granted, incurring credentializing costs for what surely must be regarded as a low probability event would require considerable foresight. Recent experimental studies of insurance purchases disclose that human agents respond less to low probability events than expected utility theory would predict.[44] Unless a threshold probability level is reached, low probability, high consequence events are treated *as though* the probability of occurrence were zero.

To be sure, these experimental findings relate to insurance behavior and have uncertain ramifications for strategic investments made in the quest of low probability, high yield managerial gains. For one thing, although most subjects in the experiments had relatively high probability thresholds, some of the subjects responded to very low probability hazards. Conceivably, rent transformation of a strategic positioning kind will occur with only modest participation, though this remains to be shown. Also, individuals may behave differently when faced with low probability opportunities than with low probability hazards. Both of these factors may support a more optimistic assessment of rent transformation than an initial reading of the experiments would suggest.

There are offsetting considerations, however, which I find very troublesome for the rent transformation hypothesis. The insurance experiments involved well defined hazards, and interdependencies among the subjects were absent. By contrast, the rewards of winning managerial games are vaguely defined and the underlying strategic investments involve many interdependencies. Vaguely defined rewards involving complex educational and career path games among unidentified players do not seem to me to be stuff upon which claims of exhaustive rent transformation are securely based.

A related consideration, although of secondary importance, is that the credentializing outlays that must be incurred in advance are presumably less than the expected value of the uncertain reward if, as seems reasonable, diminishing marginal utility of money obtains. Before refinements of this kind are even relevant, however, proponents of the rent transformation theory must show that the probability thresholds of potential managers are reached and, if they are, that the gaming interdependencies referred to above do not render efforts to project net returns on strategic credentializing expenses nugatory.

Plausibility standards plainly vary. Those who are easily persuaded that managers enjoy extensive insularity, that managers *fully* credentialize on the basis of low probability events, and that the marginal utility of money is fairly

---

44. Kunreuther, et al., Limited Knowledge and Insurance Protection, June 1976 (research report), Chap. 7.

constant will conclude that exhaustive *ex ante* rent transformation occurs in the merger context, as required by Posner's theory. On the other hand, those who are skeptical of any of these assumptions will conclude that rent transformation will be incomplete. As for myself, I believe that the insularity assumption is most doubtful. Absent this assumption, the entire argument collapses.

3.4. 'Ex ante' adaptation – the bilateral case

Posner's argument on *ex ante* expenditures is not saved by introducing heterogeneity among bidding firms. Suppose that instead of parity among all N bidding rivals, one firm among the N, firm K, enjoys an advantage in relation to the other firms with regard to the magnitude of the acquisition gain. Firm K will thus presumably win the bidding competition by offering an epsilon more than the other $N - 1$ bidders. To be sure, firm $N + 1$ may ask that firm K pay the full value of the capitalized monopoly gain that will be realized by joining firms K and $N + 1$. But all that can be established in bilateral monopoly cases of this kind is that the pecuniary bid that firm K will tender is bounded from below by what other less well situated firms will offer and from above by the full value of the capitalized gain. Within this bargaining range, the actual terms under which an agreement is struck are indeterminate – being largely dependent on bargaining skills.[45]

In circumstances in which bids fail to reflect full valuations, there is even more reason to be skeptical that real cost credentializing processes will occur which exhaust the rents in question. Complex games with indeterminate results simply do not form the basis upon which confident claims of rent transformation easily rest.

Even if pecuniary bidding does not elicit human capital expenses in amounts sufficient to accomplish exhaustive rent transformation, direct investments in physical capital might be made which do effect such a result. It will be instructive, for purposes of examining this possibility, to consider a specific example – which is also a useful strategy for purposes of evaluating rent transformation arguments in other contexts as well. Because exhaustive rent transformation relies on frictionlessness at some stage of the process, the relevant issue is whether the necessary *process linkages* can be forged to yield a plausible rent transformation result. To the extent that a microanalytic examination of process discloses that

---

45. See generally W. Fellner, *Competition Among the Few* (1949). I conjecture that Prince Bernhard, who plainly enjoyed a unique advantage in relation to other administrators in the Dutch government, failed to extract the full value of the favors he dispensed in his dealings with aircraft suppliers.

nontrivial frictions are being assumed away, exhaustive rent transformation arguments are suspect.

Consider, therefore, the following example: Products A and B are initially produced by firms X and Y. Firm X has a plant at location I from which it produces both A and B, using a partly common but not identical technology; firm Y has a similar plant producing A and B at location II. The costs of shipping A and B between locations I and II are considerable, but X and Y nevertheless compete rather vigorously for sales at the boundary of regions I and II. Further assume that A and B are manufactured under conditions of increasing returns and that economies of scale for neither A nor B are exhausted at either plant. Suppose that an exogenous transportation innovation is now made that has diffuse effects, including a reduction in the costs of shipping items A and B between locations I and II. In particular, assume that although transportation costs initially precluded plant specialization, such specialization now becomes economical, in that more efficient final supply will result if a single product is produced at each plant, thereby more fully exhausting economies of scale in manufacturing. Low cost shipment – to both near and distant users – from each of the specialized plants would then result.

The question now becomes how to arrange for such specialization to occur. Independent decisions to specialize is one possibility, but there is a malcoordination risk that both will choose the same product. If, as would be expected, there are higher net returns from specialization in one product rather than the other, the likelihood of malcoordination is especially great. To avoid this, agreement between the parties might be attempted; but problems of interfirm pooling would then have to be faced. For reasons given elsewhere, at least one of the parties is likely to find profit pooling unattractive,[46] even if it were lawful. Because of such problems, the firms are likely to favor a merger. Not only are recurrent profit pooling disputes avoided in this way, but merger also facilitates a more cooperative general attitude, perhaps including the exchange of personnel that are specialized in the production of products A and B.

Market power effects may nevertheless appear. Not only does boundary competition between firms X and Y vanish when specialization occurs, but threats of potential competition out of the specialized product into the other product are also sacrificed if the firms merge. Both cost reductions and price increases may result.

Assuming that the profits resulting from merger economies are not dissipated *ex post*, is it reasonable to argue that *ex ante* costs will be incurred in offsetting amounts? Two possibilities suggest themselves. First, assuming that users have

46. W. Fellner, *supra* note 45, at 129–36; O. Williamson, *supra* note 10 at 234–47.

access to exogenous innovations on nondiscriminatory terms, investors as a group, in anticipation of innovations of this kind, can incur *ex ante* expenses of a strategic positioning kind. Being strategically situated then permits them to reap the gains of such innovations when they occur. Alternatively, assume that inventors are able to extract the full value of an invention from all users, however remote. This alternative relies on price discrimination being feasible and lawful. The information requirements for price discrimination are frequently prohibitive, however, and it is commonly unlawful. I will accordingly restrict my attention to the first alternative, which depends on the proposition that the world generates no 'surprises.' All prospective gains must be anticipated in advance and real resources must be allocated in such a way that parties are strategically situated to take advantage of them.

To be sure, this does not imply that all investments must have assured deterministic outcomes. Many involve investment in the face of uncertainty. As a class, however, each type of stochastic reward must induce resources to be invested such that marginal costs equal expected returns. Projects which prospectively generate monopoly rents naturally induce larger strategic investments than those which promise only competitive returns. Although there may be only a single winner for projects of this kind, and *his* return will vastly exceed *his* expenditures, aggregate investments made in the hope of acquiring the monopoly position must fully exhaust the discounted net returns if the rent transformation theory is correct.

In circumstances, however, where agents are myopic and only a fraction of the possible near-period outcomes are perceived, these assumptions are not valid. 'Surprises' will occur, because investors in firms such as X and Y usually will have no idea how to preposition themselves to take advantage of these possibilities, even in a stochastic sense. Investors such as these – who may reap nonappropriable second- or third-order benefits from events originating elsewhere – are more accurately described in windfall-gain than in strategic-positioning terms.

Whether the full transformation or incomplete transformation scenario is the more accurate depends in the final analysis on the computational powers of economic agents in relation to the degree of complexity and uncertainty with which they are expected to contend. The issues here are akin to those examined by Roy Radner in his treatment of incomplete contingent claims contracting[47] and which I have previously treated in the context of markets and hierarchies.[48] I submit that for many problems, of which the above example is an illustration, the world is relatively complex in relation to the powers of human agents and that the

47. R. Radner, 'Problems in the Theory of Markets under Uncertainty,' 60 *Amer. Econ. Rev.* 454 (1970).
48. O. Williamson, *supra* note 10, at 21–26, 253–58.

myopic, incomplete anticipation hypothesis is transactionally the more accurate one.[49] If I am correct, Posner's general rent transformation theorem, at least with respect to the merger policy implications that he associates with it, must be qualified.

3.5. Systems considerations – the invisible hand

An alternative adjustment process in response to profits resulting from efficiency gains to Posner's rent transformation theory is that the appearance of unanticipated supernormal profits signals investment opportunities, in response to which resources are reallocated from lower to higher yield uses with beneficial social results. This is the conventional resource allocation response to differential returns among sectors. Groups and individuals seeking to promote their own interests effect a reallocation of resources such that risks adjusted among sectors are equalized.[50]

Consider, for example, two sectors, say manufacturing and commercial real estate, for which returns are initially equalized, and assume that higher returns have now become available in manufacturing. Assume, in particular, that the manufacturing sector is relieved of prior restrictions (e.g., excessively severe product testing restrictions are relaxed) with the result that real cost savings, which show up initially as profitability gains, are realized.

The appearance of higher profits in manufacturing signals changed investment opportunities. Additional resources will presumably be drawn into manufacturing until marginal returns are equalized. Absent reasons to believe otherwise, this reassignment of resources to higher yield uses is the 'invisible hand' operating in the public interest, rather than pernicious rent transformation of a socially wasteful kind.

The usual presumption that profit opportunities give rise to resource reallocations of a socially beneficial kind can, of course, be rebutted by a showing

---

49. The arguments here have been nicely expressed by J. E. Stiglitz as follows:

> The fact that the outcome of 'fundamental research' cannot be predicted throws serious doubt on the applicability of that fundamental construct of the modern attempt to extend conventional analysis to inter-temporal and risk situations: the Arrow-Debreu or contingent-claim securities. For how can there be securities for classes of events before those events are conceived of? How, to take an absurd case, could there have been an Arrow-Debreu security for 'an atomic disaster' before the possibility of an atomic bomb was conceived of?

Stiglitz, 'Information and Economic Analysis,' in *Current Economic Problems* 27, 44 (Parkin and Nobay eds. 1975).

50. See Hayek, 'The Use of Knowledge in Society,' 35 *Am. Econ. Rev.* 519, 524–28 (1945), for a discussion of invisible hand responses to changing economic opportunities.

that the adjustment process is instead of a wasteful kind. But those who make such claims bear the burden of describing the process defects in sufficient detail to permit these claims to be evaluated. As Laurence Sullivan has correctly noted, Posner's work on antitrust is typically silent in process respects.[51] This observation applies with special force to his treatment of mergers encouraged by economies.[52]

To be sure, partial equilibrium welfare economics sometimes misses system responses of a significant kind. Posner's general rent transformation position – 'competition to obtain a monopoly results in the transformation of expected monopoly profits into social costs'[53] – is designed to capture system effects that had hitherto been neglected. I submit, however, that rent transformation occurs only under carefully delimited conditions which are not present in the mergers for economies context. To the contrary, if the threshold effects of changing conditions of the kind discussed in the manufacturing/commercial real estate hypothetical are sufficient to give rise to a system-wide response, invisible hand resource allocation processes of the usual kind seem likely to govern.

4. Transactional efficiencies

Discussions of possible economies attributable to merger usually treat these economies in production function terms. I submit, however, that the cost savings attributable to mergers frequently are not of a production function kind but instead have transactional origins.

A complete discussion of the transaction cost approach is a major undertaking. Some flavor of the approach is imparted, however, by the following statement:

[T]he transaction cost approach attempts to identify a set of market or *transactional factors* which together with a related set of *human factors* explain the circumstances under which complex contracts involving contingent claims will be costly to write, execute, and enforce. Faced with such difficulties, and considering the risks that simple, and therefore incomplete, contingent claims contracts pose, the firm may decide to bypass the market and resort to hierarchical modes of organization. Transactions that might otherwise be handled in the market would then be performed internally and governed by administrative processes.[54]

51. Sullivan, Book Review, 75 *Colum. L. Rev.* 1214 (1975).
52. Arguments favoring franchise bidding for natural monopolies also illustrate the basic point: process arguments require self-conscious attention to transactional detail. Williamson, 'Franchise Bidding for Natural Monopolies – in general and with respect to CATV,' 7 *Bell J. Econ.* 73 (1976).
53. Posner, *supra* note 40, at 807.
54. Williamson, 'The Economics of Antitrust: Transaction Cost Considerations,' 122 *U. Pa. L. Rev.* 1439, 1443 (1974) (footnotes omitted).

It is my contention that mergers for conventional scale economy reasons are much less common than mergers for transactional economy reasons. In situations in which autonomous market contracting actually or prospectively incurs nontrivial transaction costs, nonmarket or market assisted modes warrant active consideration. Put another way, administrative modes of organization – firms – and autonomous contracting modes of organization – markets – are *alternative* ways of executing transactions. Unfortunately, this proposition, which is both familiar and acceptable as an abstract matter, has had only a limited impact on economic analysis of the firm[55] and even less of an impact on antitrust enforcement. This is especially true with respect to merger policy. Mergers, I submit, should be regarded affirmatively when internal organization yields transactional economies which bring about a desired contractual result, provided that the resulting combination does not give rise, directly or indirectly, to market power effects which outweigh the transactional benefits.

Returning to the example in section 3.2 above, recall that the realization of economies of specialization required the two firms to move coordinately. If both specialized in the same product, the full benefits of specialization would be incompletely achieved. In principle, the firms could have arranged for coordination and profit pooling by contract, assuming that such arrangements are lawful. But the expense of writing and negotiating a comprehensive contract that both effectuates specialization and provides for effective adaptation to changing circumstances when added to the expense of policing such agreements, often makes merger a more attractive alternative. Thus transactional economies occur in the context of horizontal mergers when the joining of two otherwise rivalrous firms facilitates efficient adaptations that would otherwise be incompletely realized.

Horizontal mergers, however, are less apt to be the source of transactional economies than are vertical or conglomerate mergers. Furthermore, although vertical and conglomerate mergers can have market power effects,[56] such effects are usually much more serious when horizontal mergers are at issue. It is therefore especially instructive to consider vertical and conglomerate mergers in transaction cost terms.

Consistent with the production function bias noted above, vertical integration is usually regarded either in technological terms[57] or as a device which facilitates the anticompetitive purpose of foreclosing markets. If the costs of operating

55. Coase, 'Industrial Organization: A Proposal for Research,' in *Policy Issues and Research Opportunities in Industrial Organization* 59, 63 (V. R. Fuchs ed. 1972).
56. O. Williamson, *supra* note 10, at 109–15, 163–70.
57. E.g., J. Bain, *supra* note 23, at 381.

competitive markets are zero, 'as is usually assumed in our theoretical analysis,'[58] why else would a firm integrate?

Reformulating the vertical integration question in transaction cost terms calls attention to the difficulties sometimes encountered in market contracting for intermediate products. The analysis, which is somewhat involved and has been set out in detail elsewhere,[59] turns on the following proposition: the conditions under which intermediate product will be available from a large number of equally qualified suppliers frequently fail to be satisfied. To be sure, large numbers of well qualified rivals may be available at the outset. If, however, experience acquired by a winning bidder greatly reduces the number of qualified suppliers (presumably because learning by doing is important and human capital thus acquired is imperfectly transferable), and if occasions to adapt to changing market circumstances are many, autonomous market contracting can easily give rise to costly and fractious bargaining. Inasmuch as social gains are realized whenever there are real cost savings, regardless of whether they are technological or transactional in nature, reorganizational changes which reduce bargaining and maladaptation costs – as vertical integration predictably does under the circumstances described above – warrant affirmative antitrust standing.

Whereas vertical integration is usefully examined in the context of substituting internal organization for imperfect competition in intermediate product markets, conglomerate organization of the appropriate kind[60] is usefully regarded as an internal organizational response to imperfections in the capital market. Again, the issues are rather involved and have been set out elsewhere.[61] In brief, the conglomerate firm can, and sometimes does, act as a miniature capital market by transferring resources from lower to higher yield employment more efficaciously than the market. Such shifts typically yield social gains, and acquisitions which promote this process thus warrant affirmative antitrust standing.

More generally the argument is this: economizing on bounded rationality and attenuating opportunism are central to an understanding of economic organization. To neglect these in favor of a strictly technological approach to the study of firm and market organization is at the very least incomplete. But it is worse than that; it is apt to be misleading. The misadventures of antitrust enforcement

---

58. Joint Economic Committee, 91st Cong., 1st Sess., *An Analysis and Evaluation of Public Expenditures: the PPB System* 47, 48 (Comm. Print 1969).
59. O. Williamson, *supra* note 10, at 82–105.
60. This qualification is essential. For an elaboration, see O. Williamson, *supra* note 10, at 156–58.
61. *Id.* chapters 8–9; Williamson, *supra* note 54, at 1480–91.

with respect to both vertical integration[62] and conglomerate organization[63] are fundamentally attributable to such neglect.

5. Public policy

Determining the public policy impact of the economies defense dialogue during the past eight years is rather difficult. I tend to think that there has been a genuine transformation, but the evidence is fragmentary. Causality, moreover, is not implied by establishing that a transformation in attitudes about economies has occurred; some or all of the change might have taken place in the absence of the tradeoff analysis and transaction cost arguments that are set out above. Be that as it may, it is of interest to examine some of the shifts that have been observed and suggest areas in which attention to the economies issue would be particularly useful.

5.1. Academic argument

Whether one disputes my tradeoff analysis on theoretical or operational grounds, the fact remains that tradeoffs sometimes exist; yet the early literature frequently attempted to suppress the issues. The Bork and Bowman v. Blake and Jones exchange,[64] which took up almost the entire March, 1965 issue of the *Columbia Law Review*, is illustrative. Lacking a tradeoff relation, Bork is forced to assert that

[E]conomic analysis does away with the need to measure efficiencies directly. It is enough to know in what sorts of transactions efficiencies are likely to be present and in what sorts anticompetitive effects are likely to be present. The law can then develop objective criteria, such as market shares, to divide transactions [into those predominately one type or the other].[65]

62. The Vertical Merger Guidelines of the Department of Justice give no affirmative standing whatsoever to transaction cost considerations. [1975] 1 *Trade Reg. Rep.* (CCH) 6 4510. A reformulation of these guidelines in transaction cost terms would, I believe, result in a more discriminating set of criteria. O. Williamson, *supra* note 10, at 258–59.
63. The intervention of the Justice Department in the effort by Northwest Industries to take over B.F. Goodrich is an example of ill-conceived, protectionist antitrust enforcement in which competition in the capital market considerations were given no apparent standing. See O. Williamson, *Corporate Control and Business Behavior* 100–103 (1970).
64. Bork, Bowman, Blake and Jones, 'The Goals of Anti-Trust: A Dialogue on Policy,' 65 *Colum. L. Rev.* 363 (1965).
65. *Id.* 411.

But this obviously leaves the mixed cases, which are the hard ones, unresolved. Indeed, unless one has some rough sense of the relative magnitudes of the efficiency and market power effects, it is easy to understand how Professors Blake and Jones reach the conclusion that 'claims of economic efficiency will not justify a course of conduct conferring excessive market power. The objective of maintaining a system of self-policing markets requires that all such claims be rejected.'[66] But what are the standards for 'excessive' market power and 'self-policing' markets? Are these standards really absolute or do they reflect an implicit tradeoff calculation? If the latter is correct, shouldn't an attempt be made to make this tradeoff explicit?

More recently, the denial of tradeoffs that appeared in some of the earlier literature seems to have vanished and academic discussions of the economies defense issue are more sensitive to tradeoff and transaction cost considerations.[67] To be sure, academic dialogue does not control policy. But the antitrust enforcement agencies do monitor the antitrust literature with interest and concern. Thus, although academic developments rarely occasion an explicit and abrupt reversal of policy,gradual and subtle effects are common. The evidence examined below suggests that such effects have occurred – at least in the limited sense that the affirmative merits of economies are now clearly valued.[68]

5.2. Uses of the economies defense

Although my knowledge of economies defense arguments in litigation, at the administrative level, and in pending legislation is incomplete, those aspects of the record with which I am familiar do suggest that there is a growing sensitivity to the economies issue. As I indicated in Section I, I do not think it feasible or rewarding for the courts explicitly to entertain an economies defense involving a full-blown tradeoff assessment. The courts may nevertheless find it instructive to permit arguments pertaining to technological and transactional economies to be brought before them. For one thing, permitting these kinds of affirmative arguments assures that economies will not be perversely regarded as anticompetitive. Additionally, an economies defense may help put the relevant issues in perspective. If the Government argues that a merger has anticompetitive purpose

66. *Id.* 427 (footnotes omitted).
67. This paper is based on my introductory address to the Third Annual Conference on Economics of Industrial Structure sponsored by the European Industrial Economics Organization and held in Brussels in September, 1976. The conference theme was 'Antitrust and Economic Efficiency.' All of the papers dealt with efficiency and many with tradeoff considerations.
68. This was not always so. See, for example, the quotation from the FTC's opinion in *In re* Foremost Dairies, Inc., 60 F.T.C. 944, 1084 (1962), at text accompanying note 18 *supra*.

or effect, when, in fact, the evidence of either is extremely thin and speculative, permitting the defense to demonstrate that nontrivial economies exist will presumably make the court more reluctant to accept the Government's contentions. On the other hand, when affirmative economies cannot be shown or appear to be negligible, courts will perceive little social loss in holding for the Government.

The recent decision by the Federal Trade Commission to vacate the administrative law judge's order and dismiss the complaint in the *Budd Co.* case[69] is illustrative. There the economies arguments introduced by the defendant appear to have been given careful consideration. FTC lawyers had relied almost entirely on concentration ratio statistics for narrowly defined product markets; for example, open top vans were said to constitute a line of commerce economically distinct from closed top vans. The complaint stressed Budd's importance as a potential entrant and claimed that benefits conferred by Budd disadvantaged small rivals.

The defendant responded that all van trailers constituted the relevant market and that Budd was never perceived to be and was not a *de novo* potential entrant. The defendant also presented an affirmative case for the economies resulting from the acquisition. The Commission agreed with the defendant's definition of the relevant market and regarded the acquisition as pro-competitive, stressing that the acquired firm had labored under various handicaps that Budd's efforts helped overcome. One commentator has observed that the 'importance of *Budd* ... [resides] in its economically realistic application of complex antitrust concepts.'[70]

The Supreme Court has recently made clear its views that 'competition based on efficiency is a positive value that the antitrust laws strive to protect.'[71] Although the case in question was not a merger case, the Court's opinion has since been cited favorably in entering judgment for the defendant in *Purex Corp. v. Proctor and Gamble.*[72] This latter case involved, among other things, a claim by the plaintiff that the acquisition of Clorox by Proctor and Gamble yielded real economies which gave Clorox an unfair advantage. An expert witness for Purex testified at one point that 'efficiencies ... from whatever source are a double-

---

69. The Budd Co., [1973–1976 Transfer Binder] *Trade Reg. Rep.* (CCH) 6 20.998.

70. 89 *Harv. L. Rev.* 800, 802 (1976). Note that the complaint in *Budd* relied heavily on Brown Shoe Co. v. United States, 370 U.S. 270 (1962) (discussed at text accompanying notes 5–6 *supra*), which is notable for its absence of careful economic reasoning. Hopefully, reliance on this aspect of *Brown Shoe* will decrease in the future.

71. Connell Construction Co. v. Plumbers and Steamfitters Local Union No. 100, 421 U.S. 616 at 623 (1975).

72. 419 F. Supp. 931 at 936 (1976).

edged sword.'[73] But the district court was not persuaded that a return to *Foremost Dairies* standards[74] was warranted. Indeed, although misconceptions of economies are difficult to put to rest, Turner's characterization of the Commission's views in *Foremost Dairies* as bad law and bad economics[75] seems to be gaining ascendency.

The courtroom, however, is not the only place where an affirmative attitude towards economies can manifest itself. As Carl Kaysen has pointed out, 'policy change comes about, in large part, by the way in which the enforcing agencies select cases and frame issues for courts and commissions to decide.'[76] Thus, in the preliminary discussions that commonly take place before an antimerger suit is filed, the antitrust enforcement agencies could explore possible economies with defense counsel, company officials, and economists. Cases in which anticompetitive effects are of a highly speculative nature, but for which a reasonably plausible showing of real economies can be made, then might be suppressed administratively.

One indication that the economies defense has had a policy impact at the administrative level is furnished by two internal 'policy protocols' prepared during the past year by Wesley J. Liebeler, recent Director of the Office of Policy Planning and Evaluation of the Federal Trade Commission. One of these deals with vertical integration and relies extensively on my transaction cost approach to the issue. The other is concerned with 'industry-wide matters,' including horizontal mergers, and urges caution in bringing horizontal merger cases, partly for the tradeoff reasons developed in Section 2. Although both are merely discussion papers, it is relevant to note that a sensitivity to economies that expressly relies on transaction cost and tradeoff considerations of the types discussed above is making inroads into the policy making process.

The Merger Guidelines that were issued on the last day of Donald Turner's term as head of the Antitrust Division are mainly cautious with respect to an economies defense.[77] While the Guidelines do not regard economies negatively,

73. Trial Transcript, p. 2386.
74. See the text, note 3 *supra*.
75. Turner, 'Conglomerate Mergers,' note 7 *supra*, at 1324.
76. Kaysen, 'Models and Decision Makers: Economists and the Policy Process,' 1968 *Pub. Int.* 80, 85. These were sent to me (and others) by FTC but are not published documents.
77. The Merger Guidelines treat horizontal economies as follows:

Unless there are exceptional circumstances, the Department will not accept as a justification for an acquisition normally subject to challenge under its horizontal merger standards the claim that the merger will produce economies (i.e., improvements in efficiency) because, among other reasons, (i) the Department's adherence to the standards will usually result in no challenge being made to mergers of the kind most likely to involve companies operating significantly below the size necessary to achieve significant economies of scale; (ii) where substantial economies are potentially available to a firm, they can normally be realized through internal expansion; and (iii) there usually

they do state that an economies defense is normally beyond the courts' competence to adjudicate. In light of the administrative opportunities to consider the economies issue prior to filing a merger suit and the admitted difficulties of burdening the courts with a *quantitative* assessment of an economies defense in all merger cases, this seems to be a reasonable balance of theoretical merit with practice, although courts should be sensitive to qualitative economic arguments and consider *gross* effects of economies whenever the significance of the anticompetitive effects of a proposed merger is a close question. Moreover, since the Merger Guidelines reflect the prevailing technological bias on the sources of economies which existed at the time they were prepared, whence transaction cost economies were neglected, an effort to reshape the Guidelines at this time would seem to be warranted. In particular, the Vertical Merger Guidelines, which advise that acquisitions will be subject to challenge when a ten per cent firm at one stage of an industry acquires a six per cent firm at another stage, appear to be unnecessarily restrictive.

5.3. The dominant firm context

The Monopolization Reform Act of 1976, which Senator Hart introduced on May 13, 1976 as an amendment to the Sherman Act, expressly provides for an economies defense.[78] The bill is designed to deal with dominant firm industries.

are severe difficulties in accurately establishing the existence and magnitude of economies cited for a merger.

1 *Trade Reg. Rep.* (CCH) *6* 4510.

A similar statement applies to vertical merger economies:

[T]he Department will not accept as a justification for an acquisition normally subject to challenge under its vertical merger standards the claim that the merger will produce economies, because, among other reasons, (i) where substantial economies of vertical integration are potentially available to a firm, they can normally be realized through internal expansion into the supplying or purchasing market, and (ii) where barriers prevent entry into the supplying or purchasing market by internal expansion, the Department's adherence to the vertical merger standards will in any event usually result in no challenge being made to the acquisition of a firm or firms of sufficient size to overcome or adequately minimize the barriers to entry.

Id. The conglomerate economies reservation is even stronger:

Unless there are exceptional circumstances, the Department will not accept as a justification for a merger inconsistent with the standards of this paragraph ... the claim that the merger will produce economies, because, among other reasons, the Department believes that equivalent economies can be normally achieved either through internal expansion or through a small firm acquisition or other acquisition not inconsistent with the standards herein.

Id.
78. S. 3429, 94th Cong., 2d Sess. § 3 (1976).

As the law is currently interpreted, dominance does not costitute a section 2 violation if the structure of the industry is attributable to 'a superior product, business acumen, or historic accident.'[79] But as Professor Turner has pointed out, 'There is no apparent reason why any firm should have a right to enjoy indefinitely, or even for seventeen years, the fruits of monopoly from sources other than original unexpired patents or economies of scale.'[80] Since standards for superiority are typically relative rather than absolute, dominance that has its origins in 'default failure' or 'chance event failure' does not obviously warrant antitrust insularity.[81] Rather than bring dominant firm cases on what often appears to be contrived conduct grounds,[82] I urge that structural cases be brought whenever a persistent dominant firm condition is observed that is unlikely to be upset by unassisted market forces. The dominant firm charged with such a violation should be permitted, however, 'to rebut the presumption of unlawful monopolization by demonstrating that its dominance was the result of economies of scale leading to a natural monopoly, of the exercise of an unexpired patent, or of a continuing indivisible, absolute management superiority.'[83]

Senator Hart's argument in support of the Monopolization Reform Act runs along similar lines. In discussing the bill in the Senate, he observed that a principal impediment to a section 2 monopoly case under existing law is

the disproportionate amount of time ... spent on questions of intent and superior performance. Government attorneys cull through the defendant's records in hopes of finding the hot document from which predation might be inferred ... Meanwhile, little or no attention is given to what ought to be the principal question: Does the defendant firm have a degree of economic power which should no longer be accepted in a competitive economy?[84]

Regarding the economies issue, the bill stipulates that a 'defendant shall not be required to divest itself of such monopoly power if it can show that such monopoly power is due solely to valid patents lawfully acquired and lawfully used, or that such a divestiture would result in the loss of substantial economies of scale.'[85] This now raises a new issue: if a full-blown economies defense should not

79. United States v. Grinnell Corp., 384 U.S. 563, 571 (1966).
80. Turner, 'The Scope of Antitrust and Other Economic Regulatory Policies,' 82 *Harv. L. Rev.* 1207, 1220 (1969).
81. Williamson, 'Dominant Firms and the Monopoly Problem: Market Failure Considerations,' 85 *Harv. L. Rev.* 1512 (1972).
82. O. Williamson, *supra* note 10, at 226–27.
83. *Id.* 221 (footnotes omitted).
84. 122 *Cong. Rec.* S. 7153 (daily ed. May 13, 1976) (remarks of Senator Hart).
85. S. 3429, 94th Cong., 2d Sess. § 3 (1976). The White House Task Force on Antitrust Policy also offered an economies defense in connection with its proposed decentralization policy, but the Task Force doubted that such a defense can be successfully argued. *White House Task Force Report on Antitrust Policy* 12–14 (Spec. Supp., Part II, 1969).

be permitted in a merger proceding, why litigate economies in the context of a dominant firm case? I submit that there are significant differences between merger and dominant firm cases which justify the distinctions: (1) Mergers are already relatively numerous, and if an economies defense was permitted, the number of proposed mergers in which market power effects arguably obtain might increase greatly. By contrast, dominant firms[86] are a pre-existing condition, and their numbers are relatively small.[87] Thus allowing an economies defense would neither alter the number of dominant firms nor would it arise in a large number of cases. (2) Ordering dissolution is a much more serious economic undertaking than ordering divestiture. In the latter case, the acquired assets are reasonably well-defined and the prospect of serious loss of economies is limited by the prior 'natural' division of functions that existed between the previously autonomous firms. A badly conceived dissolution order, however, could give rise to severe diseconomies, since natural dividing lines may not be apparent without an inquiry into economies.

To be sure, an economies defense still poses serious economic and legal difficulties in the context of a dominant firm case. Unless, however, one dismisses or condones chance event and default failures – which appears to be Posner's position[88] (he disregards the first and condones the second in the context of a superior skill defense) – there are no easy choices. In circumstances in which unassisted market forces have little prospect in the short run of upsetting dominance of either chance conferred or default failure kinds, an acquiescence to outcomes understandably lead to charges that antitrust enforcement is a charade.[89] This has demoralizing consequences and encourages countervailing power arguments and actions of dubious merit. A bill such as Senator Hart's Monopolization Reform Act should help to avoid these outcomes. Attaching an economies defense to such a bill should serve to deter antitrust enforcement of a counterproductive kind.

86. Dominant firm industries are those in which the output of a single firm has persistently exceeded sixty per cent of the relevant market, and entry barriers are great.
87. In national markets there are less than a dozen, although they are by no means insignificant in terms of aggregate volume of business. W. Shepherd, *Market Power and Economic Welfare*, 153–56 (1970).
88. Posner disregards chance events and condones default failure in the context of a superior skill defense. Posner, 'Oligopoly and Antitrust Laws: A Suggested Approach,' 21 *Stan. L. Rev.* 1562, 1597 (1969).
89. Galbraith, 'Control of Prices and People,' *The Listener* 793, 794 (1966).

6. Conclusions

Specialization among the social sciences has some of the same advantages as does advocacy in legal argument: faced with events of considerable complexity, an understanding of core issues may be achieved only if particular – even partisan – points of view are pressed vigorously. The specialist role assigned to economists is that of examining issues in a 'rational spirit.' Kenneth Arrow expresses it as follows: 'An economist by training thinks of himself as the guardian of rationality, the ascriber of rationality to others, and the prescriber of rationality to the social world.'[90] Such a rational spirit orientation is, I think, useful to antitrust enforcement. Even to raise the possibility that economies might be affirmatively regarded as a defense to an otherwise unlawful merger suggests that enforcement of section 7 of the Clayton Act may be amenable to rational design. This was not always so.

It should be understood that reference to rationality does not imply that allocative efficiency is all that matters. Allocative efficiency is, however, a valued social goal. Moreover, as between alternative public policy instruments – which include taxes, government spending, transfer payments, the enforcement of civil rights laws, and the like – antitrust is unusually well suited to promote efficiency goals. Since a matching of goals with instruments generally promotes effectiveness, in both public and private sectors, allocative efficiency ought presumably to be featured prominently in the formulation of antitrust policy and its enforcement. At the very least, the implied sacrifices in efficiency which the pursuit of other valued social goals entails ought, whenever possible, to be expressly set out.

The 'naive' tradeoff model and the amendments thereto that are described in this paper contribute to such a purpose. They supply a framework within which sociopolitical and other economic objectives thought to be relevant to merger policy can be examined in relation to an allocative efficiency goal. Tradeoffs are faced more directly rather than suppressed. The misuse of antitrust on behalf of protectionist interests is less easy to justify as a result.

Although severe operational problems would be posed if the courts were to entertain a full-blown economies defense in connection with mergers, whence I do not recommend such an effort, the benefits of tradeoff analysis do not vanish on this account. Merely to display efficiency consequences in qualitative or crude quantitative terms should help to create and sustain an enforcement atmosphere in which economies are socially valued. Allowing economies to be introduced informally into pre-trial discussions with the antitrust enforcement agencies and affirmatively represented to the courts should further contribute to this simple, but basic and worthwhile, purpose.

90. Arrow, *The Limits of Organization* 16 (1974).

APPENDIX

To the extent that price increases by the merging firms induce adjacent producers to ship into the region, so that additional transportation expense is incurred, the welfare assessment needs to be corrected accordingly. A simple spatial competition model will serve to illustrate the argument.

Suppose the market is a loop market of length L with N sellers located at intervals L/N along the loop. Assume that customers are uniformly distributed and that each has a completely inelastic demand.[1] Competitive conditions prevail initially, so that entry takes place until f.o.b. price is reduced to AC_1. Delivered price thus is given by $AC_1 + td$, where t is the transportation expense per unit of travel and d is the distance of the customer from the nearest producer. Each supplier then will sell to the customers located $\frac{1}{2}(L/N)$ on each side of his plant and delivered price to the most remote customer will be $AC_1 + \frac{1}{2}(L/N)t$.

Suppose now that two adjacent firms merge and, for reasons unique to their situation, realize a reduction in average costs in amount δ. At the same time f.o.b. price is increased to P_2. In the new equilibrium, the 'duopolists' will serve the entire region between their two plants and will serve customers on each side to a distance D, where $0 < D < \frac{1}{2}(L/N)$. The delivered price at D is given by

$$P_2 + tD = P_1 + t(L/N - D), \tag{A-1}$$

where $P_1 = AC_1$.

Profits by the duopolists are given by

$$\pi = P_2 Q_2 - AC_2 Q_2 \tag{A-2}$$

where P_2 is as given above, $Q_2 = L/N + 2D$, and $AC_2 = AC_1 - \delta$. Substituting these relations into (A-2) and differentiating the resulting expression with respect to D, the optimal value of D is

$$D^* = \frac{\delta}{4t}, \tag{A-3}$$

---

1. The inelastic demand assumption is unrealistic but greatly simplifies the exposition. This precludes customers from adapting by reducing their consumption of the commodity in question as its price is increased (which is the usual source of monopoly dead-weight losses); instead, customers adjust by buying from more remote suppliers.

and the resulting value of P_2^* is

$$P_2^* = AC_1 + t(L/N) - \tfrac{1}{2}\delta \tag{A-4}$$

Whether the price is raised the full amount or somewhat less than this, the welfare effects can be assessed by considering the shaded regions of figure 1-A.

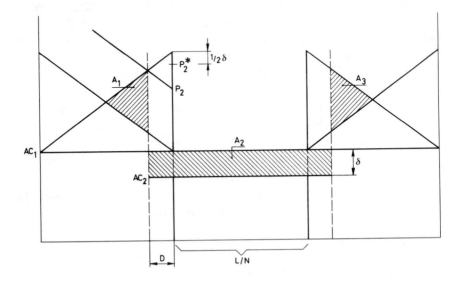

The area A_2 is the cost savings resulting from economies of production and is given by $\delta(L/N + 2D)$. A_1 and A_3 are the incremental transportation expenses of supplying customers from more distant locations. The two triangles are equal and their area is given by one half the base times the height of each, where $B = t(L/N - 2D)$ and $H = \tfrac{1}{2}(L/N) - D$. The welfare gain is given by $A_2 - (A_1 + A_3)$. The critical test relation thus is

$$\Delta W = \delta(L/N + 2D) - \tfrac{1}{2}t(L/N - 2D)^2 \tag{A-5}$$

If P_2 is set at the profit maximizing value given by (A-4) and D is given by (A-3), a welfare gain will obtain if δ exceeds $0.31(L/N)t$. Plainly, if transportation expense to remote customers had been a nontrivial fraction of the delivered price total, the production economies needed to realize a welfare gain are correspondingly great.

The situation is improved, of course, if the duopolists are subject to a threat of entry whenever f.o.b. price exceeds AC_1 or if adjacent firms can also merge and realize the production economies in question. Net welfare gains from the merger (and similar mergers) assessed in terms of the trade-off between production economies and the induced transportation expense, then become much more likely.

To be sure, the model is overly simple, and the argument is only illustrative. Nonetheless, the model demonstrates that differential transportation expense is a real cost that needs to be recognized in circumstances in which a price increase by the merging firms predictably results in local customers shifting their purchases to more remote suppliers.

XIII. ECONOMIES OF SCALE, INDUSTRIAL STRUCTURE AND EFFICIENCY: THE BREWING INDUSTRY IN NINE NATIONS*

Anthony Cockerill

1. Introduction

There is now a considerable body of evidence to show that economies of scale exist across a wide range of manufacturing industries (Bain 1956, Haldi and Whitcomb 1969, Pratten and Dean 1965, Pratten 1971, Silberston 1972, Scherer 1975). Yet the average sizes of plants and firms within a given industry frequently vary substantially between countries and the variation of sizes around the mean is often considerable (Bain 1966, Cockerill 1974, Scherer 1975). This suggests that nations differ in the degree to which scale economies are taken up. Further, in most industrialized nations scale economies frequently extend to output levels which are a substantial fraction of overall domestic demand. To obtain the full benefits of scale requires only a limited number of suppliers. But this may cause a serious decline in the level of competition. At what point are the savings from increased scale offset by the reduction in competition?[1] A difficult problem is thus

* This article has its origins in a paper presented at the Second Conference on Economics of Industrial Structure, held at Nijenrode, The Netherlands, April 1–3, 1975. This appeared under the title 'Market Structure, Economies of Scale and Technical Efficiency: International Perspectives on the Brewing Industry' in International Institute of Management, *Seminar Proceedings, Second Conference on Economics of Industrial Structure*, (Berlin: mimeo.), 1975, pre-print I/75–45, 2 vols., and was published as 'Strutture di mercato, economia di scala ed efficienza tecnica: prospettive internazionali dell'industria della birra,' *Rivista di Economia e Politica Industriale*, November 1975. Subsequently the material of the original paper has been extensively reworked and the text almost entirely rewritten. To avoid confusion it seemed desirable, therefore, to publish the revision under a different title.

The present analysis owes much to the perceptive comments of H. W. de Jong and Winfried Seeringer. Financial support from the Social Science Research Council is gratefully acknowledged. Thanks are also due to R. J. Tetley and L. F. Roberts of Allied Breweries (UK) Ltd. for advice on the preparation of the cost models and to Marion Hughes and Frank Wilkinson of the Department of Applied Economics, Cambridge University, for help with data processing. The sole responsibility for errors of fact or interpretation rests with the author. The research is part of a wider study covering in addition the steel and man-made fibres industries, in collaboration with Aubrey Silberston of Nuffield College, Oxford. The first fruits of this work are reported in Cockerill (1974a, 1974c).
1. One of the first and most important contributions in this area is Williamson (1968).

posed for the formulation of public policy towards industry. The dilemma, it should be noted, is typically more severe among the fragmented industries of Western Europe than in the integrated markets of the USA.[2]

The brewing industry offers the hope of some rich insights into the interactions between market structure, economies of scale, efficiency levels and competition. In many countries, a few very large firms coexist with a number of smaller entities. Amongst the leading producers, sales promotion activity is important. The control of distribution channels appears to be an important factor in the continued existence of large and small producers alike in several countries. Consumers taste preferences are often alleged to be a significant element in the evolution of market structures. In recent years several West European countries, as well as the USA, have instigated enquiries into certain aspects of competitive activity in the industry. But the overall effect of any liberalizing policy depends crucially on the importance or otherwise of economies of scale, and until recently there has been very little evidence on this.[3]

In this paper, therefore, the structure of the brewing industry is described and compared in the founder members of the European Economic Community (EEC), the UK, the USA, Canada and Japan. New estimates are presented on the sources and extent of economies of scale. In turn these are used to assess the level of technical efficiency in each industry. The reasons for the continuous existence of sub-optimal capacity are reviewed, and finally the effects on competition of policies to raise the technical efficiency levels are considered.

2. Structure comparisons

In 1972 the nine countries covered in this survey brewed 418 million hectolitres of beer, or about 54 per cent of total world production. Table 1 gives details of output, consumption and foreign trade for each nation. In terms of output, the industry is largest in the United States (166 million hl.), followed by West Germany (91 million hl.) and the UK (58 million hl.), with Italy the smallest producer (6.6 million hl.). With three exceptions, the growth of output during the period 1960 to 1972 was moderate, at less than five per cent annually (France having the slowest growth of 1.6 per cent). Production grew at the fastest rate in the Netherlands (10.4 per cent) and Japan (9.9 per cent), with Italy registering a 7.5 per cent expansion. As may be expected for a relatively low-priced product for

2. Scherer (1970) pp. 93–5 notes the strong emphasis placed on scale economies by European industrial economists in comparison with their American colleagues.
3. To the best of my knowledge, my unpublished dissertation (Cockerill 1971) was the first such inquiry. There are now also two papers by Seeringer (1975a, 1975b).

Table 1. Beer: production, foreign trade and apparent consumption, 1972; output growth 1960–72, by country.

(1) Country	(2) Production	(3) Annual growth 1960–72	(4) Exports[1]	(5) Imports	(6) Apparent consumption	(7) Export share of production (col. 4/col. 2)	(8) Import share of consumption (col. 5/col. 6)
	'000 hl.	% compound	'000 hl.	'000 hl.	'000 hl.	%	%
Belgium-Luxembourg	14,117	2.55	1,395	888	13,610	9.9	6.5
France	19,816	1.55	363	1,472	20,925	1.8	7.0
Germany, FR	91,044	4.23	1,585	500	89,959	1.7	0.6
Italy	6,550	7.45	52	361	6,859	0.8	5.3
Netherlands	9,875	10.38	1,387	268	8,756	14.0	3.1
UK	57,721	2.35	705	3,365[2]	60,381	1.2	5.6
USA	165,763	3.74	77[3]	1,113	166,799	—	0.7
Canada	17,941	3.96	165	53	17,829	0.9	0.3
Japan	35,114	9.89	100[4]	1,842[4]	36,856	—	5.0

Notes
— less than 0.1 per cent.
1. excluding ships' stores, except Netherlands.
2. including re-exports, mainly of beer received from Irish Republic.
3. excluding shipments to armed forces overseas.
4. estimated.

Sources
EEC '6' plus UK: CBMC (1973) and Sociéf d'Edition de la Brasserie et de la Malterie Française (1972).
USA: USBA (1973).
Canada: Research Company of America (1974).
Japan: United Nations (1973).

immediate consumption, the expansion paths for output during the period have been generally smooth. They are plotted in Figure 1, taking production in 1960 as 100. France is notable for the virtual standstill in production between 1966 and 1969.

The bulk of the growth in output in each country has come from similar increases in consumption. The proportion of output going for export is typically negligible (less than 2 per cent). The exceptions are the Netherlands (14.0 per cent), where the United States is the most important country of shipment, and Belgium-Luxembourg, where over one-half of exports are moved to France. At the same time, in most of the countries, imports are increasing in importance having the largest market share in France (7.7 per cent). Imports are insignificant in West Germany (where strict regulation of the type and quality of brewing materials debars the majority of foreign produced beers), North America, and Japan.

There are considerable variations between the countries in the *per capita* consumption of beer; the details for 1972 are set out in Table 2. Consumption is heaviest in the more northern countries of Europe – West Germany, Belgium-Luxembourg and the UK. The predominantly wine-drinking countries of Italy and France have the lowest consumption rates. In North America, consumption levels lie between the European extremes. Beer consumption in Japan has risen sharply in recent years, paralleling the increased demand for wines and spirits.

Table 2. Beer consumption per capita, by country, 1972.

Country	Consumption per capita (litres)
Belgium-Luxembourg	133.5
France	40.3
Germany, FR	145.3
Italy	12.5
Netherlands	65.7
UK	107.5
USA	73.4
Canada	82.6
Japan	30.0[1]

Notes
1. 1971.

Sources
EEC '6' plus UK: CBMC (1973).
USA: USBA (1973).
Canada: Research Company of America (1974) and United Nations (1974).
Japan: United Nations (1974).

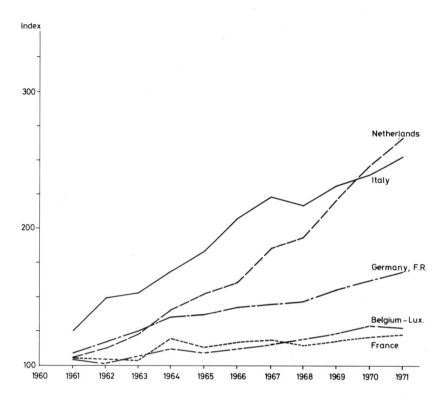

With the exception of the UK, the majority of beer consumed in each country is of the light Pilsner type, brewed by bottom fermentation.[4] By contrast, ale-type beers, brewed by top-fermentation methods,[5] account for about 60 per cent of consumption in the UK, although the demand for Pilsner-type larger beers has shown the fastest rate of growth in recent years (Cockerill 1974b). The greatest variety of qualities of beer offered for sale are in West Germany and the UK, in both of which traditional and regional factors are apparent in demand. Efforts have been made by UK producers to reduce the range of beers offered: between 1967 and 1974 the number of brands of beer brewed fell from 3,000 to about 1,500 (Monopolies Commission 1969 and Financial Times 1974). Beer strength, in terms of its alcoholic content, is highest in West Germany and the Netherlands,

---

4. In the 'bottom fermentation' process a type of yeast is added to the unfermented beer which eventually settles out at the bottom of the vessel. The process is characteristic of the production of Pilsner-type beers.
5. Ale-type beers are fermented with a strain of yeast which rises to the top of the beer towards the end of the process.

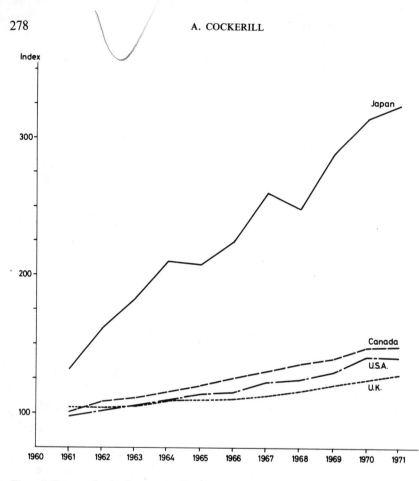

Figure 1. Beer production by country 1960–1971 (1960 = 100).

(a) EEC '6'

(b) UK, North America, Japan

Sources
Société d'Edition de la Brasserie Française (1972); CBMC (1973); USBA (1973); United Nations
(1973).

and lowest in the UK (CBMC 1973 and George Hutchinson and Co. 1974).
Typically, beer is purchased in a pre-packaged form (in bottle or cans) and
consumed at home. Again, the exception is the UK: 73 per cent of beer produced
is draught (supplied in casks or kegs), for consumption at the point of sale
(generally public houses). Elsewhere, pre-packaged beer accounts for 65 per cent
or more of total production (CBMC 1973).

The long-term trend in the structure of production in all countries save Japan has been towards fewer firms and plants. Table 3 shows the changes in the relatively short period between 1967 and 1973. The greatest decline in the numbers of firms and plants was in West Germany but which still remains a country of many breweries. The survival of so many producers, which are typically very small by international standards is due to the preference of consumers for locally-brewed beers (especially in Bavaria), the low rates of taxation paid by small firms, and the loose financial linkages between many firms which have prevented their acquisition. Table 3 also makes clear that the number of firms has typically fallen at a faster rate than the number of plants, leading to an increase in the degree of multi-plant operation (columns 10 and 11). Among those countries for which complete data are available, the UK is the exception. The plant-firm ratio declined as the major brewing groups concentrated their production.

The contraction in the number of firms has been due in part to mergers and in part to liquidations. Mergers have been most important in the UK, where all the retiring firms have left in this manner, as a consequence of the premium attached to their retail outlets (see below). In the other European countries most of the leading firms have also achieved a substantial part of their growth through merger. By contrast in the USA mergers involving the leading producers have been of much less significance, due both to the absence of retail outlet ownership and the application of the anti-trust laws. Horowitz and Horowitz (1968) found that less than one-quarter of the growth of the market shares of the leading 'premium' brewers between 1947 and 1964 was attributable to merger. This form of expansion was, however, much more important for the 'popular-price' brewers, and some fairly sizeable consolidations were permitted (see A. and I. Horowitz 1969).

Set against the slow overall growth of demand in most countries, the reduction in the number of suppliers has led to steady increases in the level of market concentration. Table 4 shows the estimated domestic market concentration ratios at the one to four firm levels. It is clear that with the exception of West Germany concentration is generally high. The four largest firms account for more than 50 per cent of the market in eight of the countries, and this criterion is met at the three-firm level in seven countries and at the two-firm level in five. The concentration levels vary inversely with the size of the domestic market, the coefficient of correlation ranging between -0.71 and -0.63 depending on the number of firms selected. Thus, on average, the domestic sales of the leading suppliers vary less than proportionately with the size of the market, and concentration levels tend to decline as the market expands. Column 7 of Table 4 shows the output-based concentration ratios for the four leading producers in each country, and it is apparent that these correspond closely with the domestic

Table 3. Trends in number of brewing firms and plants in operation, by country, 1967 to 1973 (1972).

Country	Firms				Plants				Plants per firm	
	1967 No.	1973 No.	Change No.	1967–73 %	1967 No.	1973 No.	Change No.	1967–73 %	1967 No.	1973 No.
Belgium-Luxembourg	246	152	−94	38.2	269	197	−72	26.8	1.09	1.30
France	111	61	−50	55.0	144	90	−54	37.5	1.30	1.48
Germany, FR	1,900	1,550	−350	18.4	1,963	1,667	−296	15.1	1.03	1.08
Italy	29	15	−14	48.3	39	37	−2	5.1	1.34	2.47
Netherlands	23	15	−8	65.2	31	23	−8	25.8	1.35	1.53
UK	117	88	−29	24.8	243	162	−81	33.3	2.08	1.84
USA	107	64	−43	40.2	176	108	−68	38.6	1.64	1.69
Canada	n.a.	8	n.a.	n.a.	n.a.	45	n.a.	n.a.	n.a.	5.63
Japan	3	4	+1	33.3	n.a.	27[1]	n.a.	n.a.	n.a.	6.75

Notes
1. Estimated.

Sources
EEC '6' plus UK: CBMC (1967) (1973).
USA: USBA (1973) and Research Company of America (1973).
Canada: Research Company of America (1973).
Japan: Verlag für Internationale Wirtschaftsliteratur (1971).

Table 4. Domestic market and output/capacity concentration ratios for the four largest brewing firms, by country, 1973 (or 1972 or 1970).

Country	Cumulative market shares (%) of largest:				Year of estimate	Output share (%) of largest 4	Year of estimate
	1	2	3	4			
Belgium-Luxembourg	35	43–45	49–51	53–56	1973	50	1967
France	45	53	57	61	1973	58	1970
Germany, FR:							
(a) Firms	10	14	17	20	1973	9	1967
(b) Financial groups	20	30	40(?)	42(?)	1972	40	1973
Italy	33+	53+	64+	75+	1973	66	1970
Netherlands	55	75	85	87	1973	98	1970
UK	18–20	34–38	47–53	57–65	1972	56	1972
USA	21	37	46	53	1973	51	1972
Canada	35	66	92	95	1973	93	1970
Japan	54	78	95	100	1970	100	1970

Sources
(a) Market shares:
EEC '6' plus U.K. – George Hutchinson & Co. (1974).
USA and Canada – Research Company of America (1974).
Japan – *Verlag für Internationale Wirtschaftsliteratur* (1971).
(b) Production shares:
Deutschen Brauer-Bundes eV. (1971).
Verlag für Internationale Wirtschaftsliteratur (1971).
Business Statistics Office (1975).
Research Company of America (1974).

sales ratios. The chief exception is the Netherlands, where the large volume of direct exports shipped by HeinekenAmstel raises the output share of the leading producers above their domestic market share.

The reduction in the number of firms and plants has been associated with increases in the average size of units. Larger firms have expanded at the expense of smaller ones, small breweries have been closed and output concentrated on larger plants, many of which have subsequently been expanded. In some cases new plants with large annual capacities have been built. Some impression of cross-country variations in unit size can be obtained through a comparison of simple averages. But this is likely to distort the impression gained of relative differences in the scale of operations, which is a major concern of this paper. The main drawback is variations between countries in the size frequency distribution. In some countries there may be many small units which form a significant proportion of the total population, but which contribute a relatively small share of total output. The inclusion of these will depress the simple average in comparison with a country in which the 'tail' of small units is less important. Our interest is in the larger units in which the bulk of the scale economies may be expected to operate.

To deal with this, J. S. Bain (1966) in his pioneering study of up to 34 industries in nine nations compared the size of the largest twenty plants and firms, on the basis of their average employment levels. The problems with this are two-fold. First, the choice of a specified number of units distorts the comparison because the number of units and their size distribution varies between countries. Thus, in the smaller producing nations (here Italy, the Netherlands, Canada and Japan), the 'largest twenty' units include some very small fry indeed. Second, a comparison of employment size is misleading because of cross-country variations in labour productivity. Thus although Bain found median plant size in the UK to be 78 per cent of that in the USA, the generally higher productivity levels of the USA widens the gap substantially when output rates are considered.

In an earlier study of the steel industry (Cockerill 1974a, 1974c), these difficulties were tackled by measuring plant and firm size on a physical output (or capacity) basis, and calculating averages for the largest units supplying a specified percentage of the total industry output (or capacity). The approach has been applied to the analysis of size data for the brewing industry, and the results are presented in Table 5. The average annual outputs of the largest plants and firms contributing 50 per cent of output in each country are given, and are compared with the averages for the USA. The 50 per cent threshold is arbitrary: but it is reasonable to suppose that these ratios describe the typical size of unit in each industry in which the economies of scale (if they exist) will primarily operate. This intuition is given some statistical support: the plant and firm averages at the

Table 5. Average annual output (thou.hl.) of the largest brewing plants and firms contributing 50% of industry output, by country.

Country	Date of estimate	Plants '000 hl	Plants % of US	Firms '000 hl	Firms % of US
Belgium-Luxembourg	1967	612	13	1,786	9
France	1970	723	15	3,374	17
Germany, FR	Plants: 1970	622	13	733	4
	Firms: 1967			(1,054)[1]	(5)[1]
Italy	1970	359	8	1,117	6
Netherlands	1970	5,082	108	7,295	37
UK	1972	2,063	44	8,101	41
USA	1972	4,728	100	19,891	100
Canada	1970	1,633	35	4,712	24
Japan	1970	2,038	43	17,500	88

Note
1. Taking account of financial groupings.

Sources
Belgium-Luxembourg (plants), France and Germany, FR (plants) – *Deutschen Brauer-Bundes e.V.* (1971).
Belgium-Luxembourg (firms) – industry estimates.
Germany, FR (firms and financial groups), Italy, Japan, Netherlands – *Verlag für Internationale Wirtschaftsliteratur* (1971).
UK (plants) – Business Statistics Office (1975), (firms) – industry estimates.

50 per cent level correlate very highly (+0.8969 and above) with averages at the 25, 33.3, 66.67 and 75 per cent thresholds.

The results for plants show that with the exception of the Netherlands, the average size of unit is typically small in relation to that of the USA. Italy has the smallest plants, with average output a mere 8 per cent of that in the USA. The very high ratio for the Netherlands (108 per cent) results from the presence of the Heineken brewery with an annual output in excess of 5 million hectolitres, and accounting for 55 per cent of total Dutch beer output.[6]

When average firm sizes are compared, the results are more dispersed in relation to the average for the USA than is the case for plants. Japan comes closest to US firm sizes, with a ratio of 88 per cent, but the remaining nations do not reach one-half of the US level. For each country, the average size of firm is substantially greater than the average size of plant. In five cases, average firm size is at least three times as great as average plant size, reflecting the extent of multi-plant operation, to which reference was made above.

6. There is a positive connection between average plant size and the 1972 output level of each industry. The correlation coefficient is +0.4115, but this is not significant at the five per cent level.

The industries of this enquiry also differ in another dimension – the extent of forward vertical integration. This has developed to the greatest degree in the UK, where almost every brewing firm owns retail outlets and undertakes the distribution of beer and other beverages (alcoholic and soft) together with the provision of catering and entertainment and leisure facilities.[7] In 1967 about sixty per cent of the capital employed of brewing firms were, on average, represented by retail outlets (Monopolies Commission, para. 270, p. 75). This pattern is a consequence, since 1869, of a continuous policy of severe restriction of the total number of outlets licensed for the sale of liquor. This encouraged brewers to purchase retail outlets in order to obtain access to the market (Vaizey, 1960) and, in conditions of declining or slowly growing demand, led to mergers as the only feasible method of significant increases in market share. By 1974, brewing companies owned 42 per cent of the 146,000 retail outlets for alcoholic beverages (Financial Times 1974), but their share of the number of 'full on-licences' (overwhelmingly public houses) was much higher, exceeding three-quarters of the total (Monopolies Commission 1969, Table 17). As a result of this ownership, brewers are able to specify the brands of beer – and to a great extent of other products also – which are sold through their outlets. This power is strengthened through the system of low-interested development loans which they provide to independently controlled outlets. A condition of these is that the outlets purchase specified proportions of their requirements (often 100 per cent) from the brewer providing the finance.

Such 'tying' loans are also a feature of the industry in continental Europe and are currently the subject of an enquiry by the Commission of the European Communities to examine whether the existence of 'tying' loans distorts competition in trade between member states.[8] Outright ownership of outlets, however, has developed to an appreciable degree only in West Germany (George Hutchinson & Co. 1974). To distribute their products, European brewers typically use a combination of independent and franchized wholesalers and direct shipments to retailers. In North America, exclusive dealing arrangements, whether through outlet ownership or contractual agreements, are generally prohibited by anti-trust legislation. Wholesalers may be given areas of 'primary responsibility' for a brewer's brands (Cockerill 1971, Chap. 6). Taking ownership and loans together, the degree of supplier control over distribution is most extensively developed in the UK.

7. For example, amongst the larger firms, hotels, restaurants, dance halls, casinos and betting shops.
8. The starting point of this inquiry was a judgement by the European Court of Justice on an exclusive-dealing contract between Brasserie de Haecht of Belgium and a retailer. The Court reached the conclusion that such contracts do not of themselves violate the objects of Article 85, paragraph 1 of the Rome Treaty, but that taken together with other constraints they may reduce inter-state trade and impair the level of competition. See *Cour de Justice des Communautés Européennes (1967)*.

3. Economies of scale

a. General

Economies of scale are reductions in the real unit costs of production associated with an increase in the scale of operations. Scale is a multi-dimensional concept relating not only to the rate of output of a single product, but also to such aspects as the number of products manufactured, the composition of total output, the total output of a particular product (irrespective of time), the number of integrated processes, the number of manufacturing plants and the number and size of firms.[9] During the past fifteen years, considerable additions have been made to the stock of knowledge about the sources and extent of scale economies (for example, Haldi, 1960, Haldi and Whitcomb, 1967, Pratten and Dean, 1965, Pratten, 1971, Cockerill, 1971, 1974c). A number of techniques are available for the measurement of economies of scale. The most suitable for assessment of benefits from primarily technical sources – in which we are chiefly interested here – is the cost-engineering approach.[10] This consists of building cost models of hypothetical manufacturing facilities with specified characteristics. The advantage of the method is that all influences on costs save that of scale can be held constant (something which is impossible using actual cost data), however the results cannot be verified against actual experience.

Estimates of the economies of scale in the brewing industry have been presented in earlier studies (Cockerill 1971, Cockerill and Rainnie, 1975). However, the present research has enabled this material to be updated and expanded, and with the assistance of some leading European brewing companies, a comprehensive model of production costs has been constructed.[11] In summarizing this, four classes of costs are considered: capital, labour, materials and a residual encompassing all other expenses.

The brewing proces consists of three main stages: (i) the brewing process proper, in which a sweet liquid is produced from cereals (chiefly malt)[12] and water, (ii) fermentation and storage, in which first yeast breaks down the sugars to produce alcohol and carbon dioxide gas, and then the beer is allowed to stabilize and (iii) packaging (using casks, bottles and cans).

9. A thorough analysis of the dimensions of scale and of the sources of economies is given in Silberston (1972).
10. In addition to the engineering technique, the other main methods of analysis are based on cost or accounting data, census of production evidence, or the changing structures of industries (the 'survivor' technique). See Pratten and Dean (1965) and Pratten (1971).
11. The specification and behaviour of the cost model will be set out in detail in an international study of the industry which is in preparation.
12. Malt is barley which has been artificially germinated and then cooked in a kiln.

b. Capital costs

For some time process engineers and others have observed that increases in the design capacity of process plants does not generally cause total capital costs to rise in direct proportion. The form of the cost-capacity relationship can be represented as $C = aX^b$ where C is total capital cost. X is designed capacity, a is a constant and b is an exponent whose expected value is less than unity. Empirical observations suggest that the typical value of the exponent is approximately 0.6 (Chilton 1960, Haldi and Whitcomb 1967). This 'rule' operates mainly because the cost of vessels, tanks, pipes, etc. depends more upon their surface area than upon their capacity. Additionally, many items of equipment have fixed output rates which are frequently large in relation to total plant output, and therefore their cost can be spread over greater outputs as scale increased.

In brewing, fermenting and storage, it is the ability to increase the capacity of individual items of equipment – most of which are custom-built for each brewery – which releases the bulk of the capital scale economies. Modern brewhouses show unit capital cost reductions to at least 2.5 million hectolitres (Cockerill and Rainnie, 1975). At the packaging stage, where equipment tends to be offered in 'lumpy' units of capacity, the chief scale-related savings come from improved 'balancing' of equipment and processes to eliminate bottlenecks and minimize excess capacity. The greatest scope for scale economies operates with canning, where modern equipment can fill 2,000 cans a minute and above, implying an annual output rate approaching two million hectolitres. Cost reduction opportunities are least in filling traditional metal or wooden casks. Plants using more than one type on to higher output levels than indicated as the optimal output rates for each packaging operation are 'balanced' together. Virtually no scale economies are apparent when warehousing operations (including the cost of delivery trucks) are considered. These costs (including building) can account for as much as 50 per cent of the total capital costs of a new brewery, and they reduce the impact of savings at the production and packaging on total unit costs.

Table 6 shows unit capital cost indices for plants with annual outputs ranging from 1 million to 7 million hectolitres, and specializing on the production of keg, traditional cask (draught), bottled and canned beers. In all series, the scale economies are exhausted by 5 million hectolitres, with the rate of reduction fastest for the canned beer series and broadly comparable as between the others. In terms of absolute cost levels, the detailed model indicates that unit production costs are highest for bottled beer production, followed by keg, draught and lastly canned beer, which is cheapest primarily because of the ease of handling at the warehouse stage. The data show cost exponentials of between 0.85 and 0.89, indicating that scale economies are less than would be anticipated from the '0.6 rule'.

Table 6. Indices of total unit capital costs by type of product and designed plant capacity (7m hl = 100).

Capacity (m. hl.)	Product			
	Keg	Draught	Bottled	Canned
1.0	125	127	123	134
2.0	109	110	111	122
3.0	104	104	104	104
4.0	101	101	101	102
5.0	100	100	100	101
6.0	100	100	100	100
7.0	100	100	100	100

c. Labour costs

Labour force requirements in this industry depend overwhelmingly on the number and size of items of capital equipment. Paralleling the 0.6 rule for capital costs, an 0.2 rule for labour expenses has been suggested (*The Economist* 1970) although this has not been subject to such extensive verification. Index series of unit labour costs for breweries producing each of the major classes of product are shown in Table 7. Here, savings with increased scale are most pronounced for the kegdraught series, and in all cases reductions continue to at least 7 million hectolitres. In terms of absolute costs, bottled beer production is most labour intensive (because of the number of stages in the process rather than as a result of any lack of sophistication in equipment), and kegdraught packaging the least. The actual cost exponentials range between 0.52 and 0.76.

Table 7. Indices of unit labour costs by type of product and designed plant capacity (7m hl = 100)

Capacity (m.hl.)	Product		
	Keg/Draught	Bottled	Canned
1.0	255	158	185
2.0	199	135	151
3.0	156	118	127
4.0	133	110	115
5.0	112	102	103
6.0	104	101	101
7.0	100	100	100

d. Materials

The quantity of cereals required to produce one hectolitre of beer depends principally on the specific gravity (s.g.) of the beer before fermentation which it is intended to brew. For a beer of given s.g., therefore, the total cost of brewing materials varies in direct proportion with the quantity of beer produced – in other words, unit materials cost remains constant. However, discounts on bulk purchases are available from suppliers. On the basis of trade information, it appears that these are generally maximized at a rate of final beer output of about 2.5 million hectolitres annually, and at this level represent a reduction of about 9 per cent as compared with prices at one million hectolitres annual output. Similar reductions are available for packaging materials, and in the overall cost estimates given below, it is assumed that total unit materials costs fall linearly to an annual output of 2.5 million hectolitres, thereafter remaining constant.

e. Other production costs

Excise taxes apart (which are considered later) other production costs in the brewery include payments for fuel, water, local property taxes, lighting, repairs and maintenance. Taken together, our evidence is that these items do not show substantial economies of scale, and their unit cost is assumed to remain constant as output varies (Cockerill and Rainnie, 1975).

f. Total production costs

In order to assess the effect of the scale economies identified upon total unit production costs, each of the classes of costs must be weighted according to its approximate share of total costs. Naturally, these percentages vary – often considerably – between the countries of the enquiry. Table 8 gives the proportionate breakdown of items forming the total costs of production of forty UK brewing plants, averaged for the financial years ended 1964–5, as obtained by the National Board for Prices and Incomes (1966). To avoid overestimating the importance of economies of scale, these data have been applied to the cost indices for the production of bottled beer, which show the smallest scale effect, and the outcome is given in column 2 of Table 9. The high weight given to the scale-insensitive 'other costs' eradicates much of the percentage savings from capital and labour, and the series falls by less than 20 per cent over the scale range from 1 to 7 million hectolitres. Indeed, scale economies are completely extinguished by

Table 8. Percentage composition of brewing costs, UK 1964–65.

Item	Percentages
Brewing materials	23.1
Bottling materials	3.9
Production labour	19.1
Depreciation	7.7
Interest on fixed capital	15.4
Other costs	30.8
Total costs	100.0

Source
National Board for Prices and Incomes (1966).

Table 9. Index of total unit costs of beer production a. exclusive, b. inclusive of specific excise taxes, UK (7m.hl = 100).

Capacity (m.hl)	Excluding taxes	Including taxes
1.0	119	107
2.0	110	104
3.0	104	102
4.0	102	101
5.0	100	100
6.0	100	100
7.0	100	100

an annual output of 5 million hectolitres. This output rate, at which unit costs first attain their minimum, may be termed *minimum efficient scale* (m.e.s.) (Bain, 1956, Pratten, 1971).

Such a method of identification of m.e.s. is appropriate where the scale-cost relationship can be estimated with great certainty. But engineering estimates are of necessity highly tentative. In indicating unit cost levels in the range 5 to 7 million hl. annually, European respondents were typically considering plant sizes in excess of those for which any sustained operating experience had been obtained. Consequently, the extent of the scale economies may be alternatively more or less extensive than indicated.

Caution is a wise counsel in such circumstances; a more modest evaluation of m.e.s. will be sought. This is reinforced when the rate of increase in unit costs as scale is reduced below 5 million hl. is considered. A plant of 3 million hl. annual capacity suffers cost increases of only 4 per cent as compared with a plant of 5 million hl. When consideration is given to inter-plant variations in production and demand conditions and to differences in internal efficiency levels which are not related to scale, this cost penalty is very slight.

To take account of these qualifications, m.e.s. can be redefined as a scale of output at which unit costs first achieve a pre-specified rate of decrease. A level at which total unit costs first fall by five per cent or less when scale is doubled is an immediately attractive 'round figure' criterion. Applying it to the present data indicates a plant m.e.s. approaching 3 million hl. and we employ this in the following analysis. It may be noted that cross-national variations in relative factor prices may effect the sensitivity of total unit production costs to movements in those cost component which are influenced by scale economies. As a consequence the slope of the scale curve, and hence the location of the m.e.s. as defined may also vary. In the present state of development of the detailed cost model, it is not possible to indicate how significant a factor this may be.

g. Excise taxes

It is vital at this point to consider the effect of excise taxes. The method of levy differs between the countries, but in all cases, the tax payable on a beer of a given s.g. varies in direct proportion with output – i.e. unit excise taxes are constant. The magnitude of specific excise taxes varies considerably between the countries. In 1974, the average dollar-equivalent tax on a beer of 12.5' Plato[13] in seven of the nations was as follows:[14]

UK	$ 30.46
Netherlands	$ 7.66
Italy	$ 8.41
France	$ 1.31
Belgium-Luxembourg	$ 5.91
Germany, FR	$ 4.40
USA	$ 7.76

These are supplemented by *ad valorem* and local taxes, and of course their importance in final price will depend upon the magnitude of other cost and profit components. However, it is clear that taxes are relatively high in the UK, and

13. Equal to a specific gravity of about 1.051.
14. Data for the USA are from United States Brewers Association (1973); all other data are from CBMC (1973).
15. 15. See Cockerill and Rainnie (1975) for the method of estimation of interest charges.

considering the effect of these on scale economies will give a 'maximum' indication of the diluting influence of excise taxes. In their analysis for 1964–65 the National Board for Prices and Incomes (1966) found excise duty to form 62.3 per cent of total costs (including an allowance for interest on fixed capital).[15] Reweighting the scale economies estimates to allow for taxes gives the result in column 3 of Table 9. The entire scale effect is very severely reduced, with the m.e.s. (by the criterion adopted) occurring at about 2 million hectolitres. This compares with the estimate obtained in our earlier studies of 1.6 million hl., using different data, and indicates that our results are fairly robust (Cockerill 1971, Cockerill and Rainnie 1975).

h. Transport costs

The choice of plant size however, does not depend upon production costs alone. Transportation costs of the final product to customers are also relevant.[16] Typically, as the planned size of a plant at a given location is increased, the market area will expand. As deliveries are made to customers ever more remote from the point of production, transport costs per unit of output (u.t.c.) will rise with plant size. The appropriate plant size will occur where total unit costs, obtained by the summation of unit production costs and u.t.c. at each output level, are minimized. This occurs when the slopes of the unit production cost curve and the u.t.c. curve are equal (i.e. where an increase in plant scale increases u.t.c. by the same absolute amount that unit production costs are increased).

It is not possible, however, to indicate a unique relationship between transport cost and plant size, since transport costs are also affected by the characteristics of product demand and the distribution system. Particularly relevant are the location, size and area density of consumption points, and the nature of the transport network, which influences cost per unit-mile. Assuming a circular market of radius r miles, homogeneous demand density of D units per square mile, a uniform cost T of shipping one unit of output one radial mile and a market share of S, Scherer (1975, pp. 21–4) has shown that the u.t.c. of a plant supplying Q units is given by:

$$\text{t.u.c.} = \frac{2T\sqrt{Q}}{3\sqrt{SD\pi}}$$

16. The inward transportation costs of raw materials are also relevant in the plant size decision, particularly where – as in the steel industry – they form a significant proportion of total transport costs. In brewing they are an insignificant element.

Table 10. Representative production and transport costs for brewing plants, UK 1966.

Annual capacity m.hl.	Production cost/hl.[1] £	Transport cost/hl.[2] £	Total cost/hl. £
1.0	6.24	0.67	6.91
2.0	5.76	0.95	6.71
3.0	5.45	1.16	6.61
4.0	5.34	1.34	6.68
5.0	5.24	1.49	6.73

Notes
1. Obtained by applying the production cost index (exclusive of excise taxes) of Table 9, col. 2 to an estimated 1966 production cost per hl. of £ 6.24 for a plant capacity of 1 m.hl. The latter figure is estimated from accounting data supplied by a large UK brewing firm.
2. For the estimating equation

$$\text{u.t.c.} = \frac{2T\sqrt{Q}}{3\sqrt{S \cdot D \cdot \pi}}$$

T, the 1966 cost of shipping one hectolitre of beer one radial mile, equals £ 0.05, on the basis of interview evidence obtained from one leading UK brewing firm;
Q, the annual volume shipped, equals from 1.0 to 5.0 m.hl.;
S, the market share of the plant, is assumed to equal 1.0 (i.e. the plant is the sole supplier);
D, the density of demand per square mile, equals 791.73 hl. Beer consumption per capita in 1966 was 92.6 litres (calculated from Central Statistical Office 1973). The population per square mile is taken as 855 inhabitants, an adjusted figure derived by deleting areas of sparse population. For details see Scherer (1975), p. 91.

$\pi = 3.1416$.

Employing data for the UK for the mid-1960's,[17] and assuming market share equal to unity, u.t.c. for alternative plant scales can be estimated, as shown in column 2 of Table 10. Column 3 of the table shows estimated unit production costs (exclusive of duty). The total unit costs series (column 4) is minimized at an annual plant output of 3 million hectolitres. The optimum plant size remains the same if excise taxes are included with production costs.

When related to the L-shaped unit production cost (scale) curve, the rising u.t.c. curve will always cause total unit costs to be minimized at a scale below that at which least unit production costs are first attained. (In the present case unit

17. Supplied by a leading UK brewing firm. The date reconciles with that for the production cost data.

production costs continue to fall to 5 million hectolitres). Correspondingly if m.e.s. is calculated at the five per cent cost reduction threshold as in Section (b), this will also be reduced when total unit costs are considered. In this case it falls to about 1 million hl.

It would be unwise, however, to assess the importance of economies of scale in each country on this basis. The position and slope of the u.t.c. function is sensitive to the areal density of total demand, the share of the market and the transport cost per unit mile. Increases in demand density and market share and decreases in transport cost per unit mile will each lower the u.t.c. function and lessen its slope, thus raising the optimum scale of plant and allowing more of the production scale economies to be reaped. The values assigned to these variables will differ between the countries and according as whether urban or rural areas are considered or whether efficient road networks exist. In the absence of any generally applicable assumptions, the m.e.s. of 3 million hectolitres estimated on production costs alone must serve as a proxy for the optimal scale of plant in each country.

i. Multi-plant economies

Despite the transport cost constraint, it is apparent from Table 5 that the size of the largest brewing firms in each nation is well in excess of that required to operate a single plant of efficient scale. These firms typically operate a number of plants. Apart from the increased security provided by size *per se*, firms can achieve additional scale economies by expanding above the scale of the single efficient plant. These economies may be *real* or *pecuniary*.[18]

Multi-plant operation allows the production of certain types of beers to be concentrated on specific plants, thereby releasing some benefits from longer production runs, and – generally of more importance – allowing either the use of specialized equipment in place of more flexible plant, or the fuller utilization of equipment. Larger brewing in the UK is a case in point. Some of the leading firms have constructed purposebuilt breweries for lager, whilst their smaller competitors have to compete (if at all) by producing lager (together with other beers) in plants designed for brewing ale.[19]

18. Real economies reduce the input of productive factors for a given output rate. Pecuniary economies reduce the price of inputs as a result of market imperfection without any true factor saving, e.g. purchase discounts granted to a powerful buyer. See Bain (1956, p. 57).

19. In addition it is argued that lager brewed in custom-built plants is of a higher quality, and that customers are able to perceive this. However, the high promotional expenditure on the premium brands in the UK should be borne in mind. An alternative strategy for the smaller brewer is to purchase lager from another brewer.

In similar vein, multi-plant operation can help to reconcile the various optimum scales for different processes. The most important example is canning, where the minimum efficient scale is high in relation to the brewing process itself. In some cases, therefore, beer is brewed in one plant and transported to a large-scale canning plant which also receives supplies from other brewing plants.[20] Firms with a number of plants are also more flexible in meeting changes in demand. Seasonal variations can be accommodated by maintaining steady production in the larger, more modern units, and allowing smaller plants to bear the brunt of the fluctuations. Over a longer period shifts in consumers' demand (e.g. towards 'real' beer or popular-priced brands) can be tackled better if a number of plants offering a variety of brewing techniques are available. Finally the fear of prolonged shutdowns through strikes or technical difficulties, leading to largely irrecoverable loss of markets, deters many managers from concentrating production on a small number of very large units.

On top of this, one of the most important benefits leading firms to expand beyond the scale of the single efficient plant is sales promotion advantages flowing from national market representation. In 1967 advertising expenditure was about 3.7 per cent of the total cost (net of excise taxes) of a hectolitre of beer brewed in the UK (Monopolies Commission 1969, pp. 178–9). In 1969 a comparable figure for the USA – where sales promotion activity is generally higher – was 10.7 per cent (USBA 1973, Table 29). These averages, however, relate to the entire industry and the ratios for the leading firms are typically higher.[21] Such firms, through catering to the entire market, can frequently secure a price premium over their smaller regional or local competitors on some or all of their brands. For the USA, this 'image' advantage of the national brewers has been put at a margin of between 8 and 40 per cent on the wholesale price (Scherer 1975, Table 7.1, p. 241). The range in the UK appears wider, from 8 to 60 per cent or more.[22] It is also possible for the large firm to capture additional sales by providing a full selection of the types and qualities of beer demanded in each market. On the cost side, once a size sufficient to justify the use of national advertising media has been reached, advertising expenditure per unit of sales may fall with rising demand as a result of media rate discounts and the spreading of

20. This feature is most pronounced in the UK. For example, Allied Breweries produce lager in a purpose-built plant in North Wales and ship it some 90 miles to Burton-on-Trent for packaging. The additional transport cost is more than offset by the savings from the centrally-located high-speed packaging lines.
21. For example, in 1967 in the UK, the seven leading brewers accounted for 82.9 per cent of the total industry estimated expenditure on press and television advertising but contributed 72.7 per cent of production (Cockerill 1971).
22. Estimated from Monopolies Commission (1969, Appendix 6, pp. 132–48).

fixed costs of advertising campaigns.[23] Such benefits, it may be noted, are more a function of domestic market size than of absolute firm size.

In addition to these benefits, there is little doubt that larger firms can raise finance more cheaply and in greater quantities than smaller concerns, and perhaps are able to apply and control it more efficiently. There are also advantages from possessing a large and specialized management team.

It is hard to gauge the significance of these multi-plant economies. Those relating specifically to production appear modest enough, and a firm operating a single efficient plant does not seem unduly disadvantaged. But sales promotion advantages may be substantial and run on to the size of the largest US brewers (25 to 30 million hl. annually). On this basis, given a plant m.e.s. of 3 million hl., firms would need to operate up to 10 plants to secure all the economies of scale. However, the importance of sales promotion varies between the nations of the enquiry, and in addition firms without aspirations to national representation can simply avoid many of the marketing costs. Their market shares will then depend, *inter alia*, upon the success of the leading producers in increasing the demand for premium products. In sum, the efficient scale of firm lies somewhere above that for the single plant, the precise location depending upon the importance of sales promotion. Apart from the special case of the USA, with its geographically extensive market, the further savings to be obtained through operating more than (say) three plants of m.e.s. may be negligible.

4. Scale economies and technical efficiency

Under conditions of economies of scale, technical efficiency requires that production be carried out in units of at least minimum efficient scale, all else equal. Column 2 of Table 11 gives a preliminary view of the extent to which this is achieved by each brewing industry in the sample. The average size of the largest plants supplying one-half of industry capacity is expressed as a percentage of the minimum efficient plant scale of 3 million hl. The ratios of the table are little affected if the 25 or $33\frac{1}{3}$ per cent thresholds for gauging plant size are adopted. There is considerable variation between the countries in the extent to which scale economies are taken up. Three distinct groups can be discerned. First, the Netherlands and the USA are average plant sizes greater than the plant m.e.s., *a priori* evidence of a high degree of technical efficiency. Second, Canada, Japan and the UK[24] fall within the range 50 to 70 per cent of m.e.s., and can be rated as

23. Some evidence of this is found in Cockerill (1971).
24. The UK has increased its efficiency rating sharply in recent years. In 1967 the ratio was 24 per cent.

Table 11. Estimates of technical efficiency levels of brewing plants and firms, by country.

	Average size of largest plants[1] as a percentage of m.e.s.	Average size of largest firms[1] as a percentage of m.e.s.
Belgium-Luxembourg	20.4	59.5
France	24.1	112.5
Germany, FR	20.7	24.4 (35.1)[2]
Italy	12.0	37.2
Netherlands	169.4	243.2
UK	68.8	270.0
USA	157.6	663.0
Canada	54.4	157.1
Japan	67.9	583.3

Source Table 5.
Notes
1. Largest units supplying 50% of total output.
2. Taking account of financial groupings.

fairly efficient. The third category, Italy, Belgium-Luxembourg, West Germany and France have low ratios of between 12 and 24 per cent and must – subject to later qualification – be classed as inefficient from a technical point of view.

These results should, of course, be treated with caution. One important qualification is that the typical age and layout of plants varies between the industries, and this influences operating efficiencies independently of size. Nations with modern facilities will have higher efficiency levels than others with plants equally as large or larger. but which incorporate older equipment. Another vital caveat is that the existence of sub-optimal units of capacity can be quite compatible with overall *economic* efficiency if consumers value product differentiation. Given these qualifications, what factors account for the diversity of observed efficiency levels?

One is the size of the market. From Table 1, only in the Netherlands and Italy is the total consumption level insufficient to support more than two or three plants of minimum efficient scale. Yet this is not an insuperable barrier to efficiency: the Netherlands has the bulk of its beer production concentrated in a single plant, and as a result has the highest efficiency ratio of all the nations. By contrast, production in Italy is fragmented and the ratio is the lowest of the sample.

A second factor is the size of the controlling firms. If average firm size is low, the construction of efficient-sized plants will be impossible without some form of corporate reorganization. Column 3 of Table 11 sheds light on this. Here the average size of the largest firms (at the 50 per cent threshold) are expressed as a percentage of the single plant m.e.s. In six of the nations, average firm size is greater than plant m.e.s. suggesting that corporate structure does not restrict the evolution of efficient plants. In Italy, Belgium-Luxembourg and West Germany, average firm size lies below plant m.e.s. and the technical efficiency ratios (column 2) are also low; in these cases consolidation of production on a reduced number of firms would be necessary to release more of the economies of scale.

Third, the minimum efficient scale of plant may vary across the nations. This can occur if there are differences in the technical conditions of production or in the composition of total costs. In the first case, for example, breweries in the US typically brew a very limited range of beers, a high proportion of which are packaged in cans. Both factors yield economies of scale level than in the more diverse European industries. In the second, countries in which scale-insensitive costs are a high proportion of the total will have more shallow scale curves – and accordingly a lower m.e.s. by the criterion adopted here.

The fourth case of plant size variations is closely associated with the third. The importance of transport costs in total expenses and their variation with plant scale will differ between the countries. Thus, the restriction of rising unit shipping costs on plant size will occur at different scales of operation.

Fifth, sub-optimal plants may represent capacity which is in the process of being retired as a result of rationalization mergers, or which it is not economic to replace at the present. The 'gestation period' after a merger has taken place and before the full efficiency benefits are realized is well known.[25] In addition, where a firm acquires a competitor primarily for the goodwill attached to its brands or its distribution channels, the purchase price may exceed the value of the physical assets taken over. In such conditions the marginal cost of additional brewing capacity can be very low, and will not be replaced until its operating cost equals or exceeds the total cost (including capital charges) of a new plant (Salter 1969). Since in this industry the economies of scale are modest above 2 million hl. annually and technical progress has not been substantial, the effect is probably of some significance.

Finally the differentiated market for beer explains the existence of many small, single plant firms. Consumers may express a preference – as in West Germany and in the UK, for example – for local beers with particular taste characteristics. Small firms can gain additional protection through the possession of their own distribution networks. They are able to survive by avoiding many of the costs (particularly advertising) which the major producers bear, or by charging a slight premium for their 'quality' products or by taking a lower rate of profit – a possible option if the firm is family controlled.

25. See for example Kitching (1967) and Newbould (1970).

Because of these differences in market structure and in cost conditions it is
difficult to measure and compare technical efficiency in each country. On the
basis of the summary ratio, however, there is scope for raising efficiency through
expanding plant size in most of the countries, with the need most pressing in four.

5. Scale economies and competition

The achievement of maximum technical efficiency through the concentration of
all beer production in plants of at least m.e.s. has clear implications for market
structure and hence competition. The fundamental relationship determining the
number of producers and the level of concentration is the ratio of market size to
plant m.e.s. Where this has a low value (i.e. domestic markets are small), the
number of producers compatible with technical efficiency will be small and the
level of concentration will be high.

Column 2 of Table 12 sets out the number of plants of m.e.s. which the 1972

Table 12. Number of suppliers and concentration level a. assuming single-plant firms of
m.e.s.; b. actually prevailing.

	Plants of m.e.s.[1]	Firms in operation 1973	Four-firm concentration ratios	
			with plants of m.e.s. 1972	actual 1970/72/73
	(No.)	(No.)	(%)	(%)
Belgium-Luxembourg	4.5	152	88.2	53–56
France	7.0	61	57.3	61
Germany, FR	30.0	1,550	13.3	20(42)[2]
Italy	2.3	15	100.0[3]	75+
Netherlands	2.9	15	100.0[3]	87
UK	20.1	88	19.9	57–65
USA	55.6	64	7.2	53
Canada	5.9	8	67.3	95

Notes
1. m.e.s. = 3 million hl.; 1972 consumption levels.
2. taking account of financial groupings.
3. 3 firms only.
Sources
cols. 2 and 4 – derived from Table 1.
col. 3 – Table 3.
col. 5 – Table 4.

consumption levels would support in each country, and column 3 shows the actual number of firms in operation in 1973. It is clear that concentrating production solely on efficient plants would reduce the number of suppliers in each country – in some cases, for example West Germany, dramatically. The development of multi-plant firms would reduce the number of suppliers even more. If the distribution network in each country were strictly rational, designed to minimize total unit costs, each plant would serve its own unique hinterland and most consumers would be restricted to a single supplier.

In all except the largest markets of the USA, West Germany, and the UK, the reduced number of suppliers would yield high levels of concentration at the four-firm level, as column 4 of Table 12 shows. These ratios may be compared with the actual four-firm domestic sales ratios for 1972–73 given in column 5. In six of the cases, actual concentration levels have gone beyond that justifiable strictly on the grounds of technical economies of scale, and the divergence is particularly marked in the cases of the USA, and UK and Japan, where a limited number of very large firms have come to dominate the market.

It is clear that in each country – and particularly those with small markets – a direct trade-off is involved between the realization of economies of scale and the diversity of supply. The greater the number of suppliers, the smaller is the average sustainable plant size and the higher are the average unit production costs, *ceteris paribus*. Sub-optimal production structures will be justifiable to the point at which the increased costs just offset the increase in consumers' utility from diversity. There is intuitive evidence that some consumers value variety in the brewing industry[26] and some level of sub-optimal operation is therefore appropriate (but exactly what that level is, it is impossible to say).

The problem becomes more difficult when multi-plant firms are considered. These serve to raise market concentration at any given level of plant technical efficiency. One reason for their development, we have suggested, is to probe more deeply into the advantages of large-scale sales promotion. These benefits are likely to be chiefly of a private nature, internal to the firm, and reflected in higher prices, or more managerial discretion. The cost is a reduction in the consumer surplus. As a counterweight to this it is possible to argue that consumers gain utility from heavily-promoted 'image' products – but economists traditionally are sceptical.

The balance between the requirements of scale and an adequate number of suppliers is most difficult to achieve in the fragmented markets of Western Europe. An appealing solution is to encourage cross-frontier trade in beer, allowing more concentration of production in each country, but an expanded range of choice through imports. But the barriers to trade are formidable and the

26. For example, the small breweries of Bavaria and the 'real ale' movement in the UK.

level of trade is low. Transport costs of a bulky, low-value product are an immediate constraint, but they are reinforced by domestic brewers' control over distribution channels and by various forms of sales promotion. It is encouraging that the European Commission is investigating vertical linkages in the brewing industry.

More generally across the nations of the sample, there is the problem of the large firm. Legislation has a role to play in ensuring that such firms do achieve the real resource savings which they claim exist as a consequence of their size, and that these benefits are passed on to the consumer in the form of lower prices or improved quality of product or service. Monitoring mergers, pricing and sales promotion activity are clearly the main strands of effective policy. It is also encouraging to note, however, that small firms are often able to compete effectively alongside larger organizations through their ability to avoid many of the overheads and to move swiftly in their relationships with customers. The supply of 'own brand' beers for sale through supermarkets is a case in point; the growth of 'real' beer sales another. Finally, increased trade liberalization would raise the competitive pressures on large firms as their domestic markets were opened up to imports.

6. Summary

The nations of the enquiry show considerable diversity in the level and growth of beer production and in the composition of final demand. There has been a general tendency for the number of plants and firms to contract and for production to be concentrated on larger units. Despite this, substantial variation in the number and size of plants and firms persists. Control of distribution channels is a marked feature of the industry in the UK and also – though to a lesser extent – in West Germany.

Economies of scale are present, flowing chiefly from capital and labour as the scale of brewing plant is increased. They are particularly marked in certain packaging operations. Total unit production costs decline with increases in plant scale to an annual output of at least 5 million hl. The minimum efficient scale of plant is 3 million hl., taking m.e.s. to be that output at which unit costs first decline by five per cent or less when output is doubled. Rising unit transport costs limit the expansion of the plant, the effect varying according to the characteristics of the distribution network. Multi-plant operation confers further scale-related benefits on firms, primarily through sales promotion advantages.

Technical efficiency is measured by the ratio of the average size of the largest plants contributing one-half of total industry output to the estimated plant m.e.s.

Efficiency levels are generally fairly high, the exceptions being (in descending order) France, West Germany, Belgium-Luxembourg and Italy. The assessment of technical efficiency must be qualified in several respects, including the size of the market, the size of the controlling firms, the appropriate plant m.e.s., the differential effect of transport costs, the delay before obsolete assets are replaced and the scope for segmenting the market for beer.

The full pursuit of scale economies generally requires a limited number of producers and a fairly high degree of market concentration. Sub-optimal operation can be justified if consumers value diversity of supply at least as much as the extra costs incurred. The public benefits flowing from the few large firms which dominate most markets are uncertain. Liberalizing trade policies offer scope for the simultaneous achievement of scale economies and maintenance of competition, particularly in Western Europe. Regulatory powers to control large firms and reduce barriers to competition also appear necessary.

References

Bain, J. S., *Barriers to New Competition*, Cambridge, Mass., Harvard University Press, 1956.
Bain, J. S., *International Differences in Industrial Structure*, New York, Yale University Press, 1966.
Business Statistics Office, *Business Monitor 1972*, London, HMSO, 1975.
Central Statisticial Office, *Annual Abstract of Statistics 1973*, London, HMSO, 1973.
Chilton, C. H. (ed.), *Cost Engineering in the Process Industries*, New York, McGraw-Hill, 1960.
CBMC, Communauté de Travail des Brasseurs du Marché Commun EFTA Brewing Industry Council, *Combined Statistics*, 1966, 1972.
Cockerill, A., *Economies of Scale in the Brewing Industry: A Comparative Study of the United Kingdom and the United States of America*, unpublished dissertation for the degree of M. Phil., University of Leeds, 1971.
Cockerill, A., 'Economies of Scale and the Structure of the Steel Industry', *The Business Economist*, Vol. 6, No. 1, Spring, 1974a.
Cockerill, A., 'Mergers and Rationalisation in the Brewing Industry', *The Brewer*, Vol. 60, No. 717, July, 1974b.
Cockerill, A. (1974c), *The Steel Industry: International Comparisons of Industrial Structure and Performance* in collaboration with A. Silberston, University of Cambridge Department of Applied Economics Occasional Paper 42, Cambridge, Cambridge University Press, 1974c.
Cockerill, A. and G. F. Rainnie, *Concentration and Economies of Scale in the Brewing Industry* (mimeo.), 1975.
Cour de Justice des Communautés Européennes, *Recueil de la Jurisprudence de la Cour*, Vol. 13–5 (Luxembourg), Affaire 23–67.
Deutschen Brauer-Bundes e.V., *10 Statistischer Bericht 1971* Bonn-Bad Godesberg, 1971.
Economist, The, Supplement, 30 October, p. xiv, 1970.
Financial Times, 24 April, 1974.
Haldi, J., *Economies of Scale in Economic Development*, Stanford Project for Quantitative Research in Economic Development, Memorandum No. 3–7, Department of Economics, Stanford University (mimeo.), November, 1960.
Haldi, J. and D. Whitcomb, 'Economies of Scale in Industrial Plants,' *Journal of Political Economy*, Vol. 75, August, 1967.

Horowitz, A. and I. Horowitz, 'Entropy, Markov Processes and Competition in the Brewing Industry,' *Journal of Industrial Economics*, Vol. XVI, No. 3, July, 1968.

Horowitz, A., 'Concentration, Competition and Mergers in Brewing' in Weston, J. F. and S. Peltzman (eds.), *Public Policy Toward Merger*, Pacific Palisades, Calif.: Goodyear, 1969.

Hutchinson, George & Co., *Brewing in the Common Market*, privately circulated, August, 1974.

Kitching, J., 'Why do Mergers Miscarry?' *Harvard Business Review* November/December, 1967.

Monopolies Commission, *A Report on the Supply of Beer*, London HMSO, 1969.

National Board for Prices and Incomes, *Costs, Prices and Profits in the Brewing Industry*, London, HMSO, Cmnd. 1965.

Newbould, G. D., *Management and Merger Activity*, Liverpool, Guthstead, 1970.

Pratten, C. and R. M. Dean, *Economies of Large-Scale Production in British Industry*, University of Cambridge Department of Applied Economics Occasional Paper 3, Cambridge, Cambridge University Press, 1965.

Pratten, C. F., *Economies of Scale in Manufacturing Industry*, University of Cambridge·Department of Applied Economics Occasional Paper 28, Cambridge, Cambridge University Press, 1971.

Research Company of America, *Brewing Industry Survey 1973, 1974*, New York.

Salter, W. E. G., *Productivity and Technical Change*, University of Cambridge Department of Applied Economics Monograph 6, 2nd. edition with an addendum by W. B. Reddaway, Cambridge, Cambridge University Press, 1969.

Scherer, F. M. (1970), *Industrial Market Structure and Economic Performance*, Chicago, Rand McNally, 1970.

Scherer, F. M., *The Economics of Multi-Plant Operation: An International Comparisons Study*, with A. Beckenstein, E. Kaufer and R. D. Murphy, Cambridge, Mass., Harvard University Press, 1975.

Seeringer, Winfried, *Ein Modell zur Optimalen Betriebsgrosse und Standortplanung am Beispiel der Brauindustrie in der Bundesrepublik Deutschland*, International Institute of Management Report Series IV/75–1, Berlin, mimeo. January, 1975a.

Seeringer, Winfried, *Investitions- und Standortplanung am Beispiel der suddeutschen Brauindustrie*, International Institute of Management Preprint Series I/75–10, Berlin, mimeo., March, 1975b.

Silberston, A., 'Economies of Scale in Theory and Practice,' *Economic Journal*, supplement, March, 1972.

Société d'Edition de la Brasserie Française, *Bios: Statistiques Professionnelles*, Nancy, 1972.

United Nations, *Statistical Yearbook 1973, 1974*, New York, N.Y.

USBA (United States Brewers Association), *Brewers Almanac 1973*, Washington, D.C., 1973.

Vaizey, J., *The Brewing Industry 1886–1951*, London, Pitman, 1960.

Verlag für Internationale Wirtschaftsliteratur, *International Brewers' Directory 1971*.

Williamson, O. E., 'Economies as an Antitrust Defense: The Welfare Tradeoffs,' *American Economic Review*, 58, March, 1968.

XIV. ECONOMIES OF SCALE AND TECHNOLOGICAL CHANGE: AN INTERNATIONAL COMPARISON OF BLAST FURNACE TECHNOLOGY*

Bo Carlsson

1. Introduction

The iron and steel industry is often cited as an example of an industry with significant economies of scale. Yet it is obvious even to a causal observer that iron and steel works of very different sizes continue in operation in various parts of the world. In fact, investments continue to be made in plants far below the average size today. If firms can be assumed to behave rationally and therefore to invest in the most practical or 'best practice' technology (i.e., the 'least-cost' technology available with given relative factor prices) this would indicate either that best practice technology is not particularly strongly related to scale, or that the cost advantages of best practice (large scale) technology are not large enough to ouweigh other considerations.

This paper reports some early results of a study of the users of the best practice technology in the iron and steel industry in five countries (currently being carried out at the Industrial Institute for Economic and Social Research). The study focuses on the blast furnace sector and uses data for individual plants and furnaces in Sweden, the United Kingdom, West Germany, the United States, and Japan. However, this paper deals only with aggregate data for the blast furnace sector in each of the five countries, i.e. only 'average practice' is being examined. But the results should be indicative of what the study of 'best practice' technology in each country and over time might yield.

The purpose of the paper is to examine international differences in scale and in the extent of diffusion of new technologies observable at the macro level. The

* A preliminary version of this paper was presented at the Second IIM Conference on Economics of Industrial Structure at Nijenrode, the Netherlands, April 1–3, 1975. The author would like to thank the discussants at the Conference, representatives of the British Steel Corporation and Oxelösunds Järnverk, and John Hause, Bertil Lindström, Lennart Ohlsson, and Nathan Rosenberg for helpful comments on earlier versions of this paper.

associated differences in operating procedures and input requirements are then analyzed, using Swedish factor prices. Japanese operating costs are found to be the lowest, while of the US are the highest. An investigation into whether the operating cost differences between the small, old Swedish blast furnaces and the large, new Japanese ones are large enough to warrant scrapping the Swedish equipment and investing in Japanese technology yields a negative answer. Another major conclusion is that pure scale economies are not so great that they can not be compensated for by introducing new technologies into old blast furnaces and making the appropriate changes in input mix and rate of operating the furnaces. Given that scale economies in blast furnaces are not overwhelming, the scale of newly built furnaces depends very much on the environment into which they are introduced: the size and structure of the steelmaking facilities in an integrated steel mill, the market outlook for the finished products, etc.

It must be stated at the outset, however, that no attempt is made in this paper to explain the changes and differences in scale and technology reported here. Rather, the object is to structure the pertinent information in such a way that an analysis of the forces behind these developments can be made in the continuing work at the micro level.

There are several reasons for choosing the blast furnace process as the object of study. The output of blast furnaces is relatively homogeneous and its quality has remained largely unaffected by technological change. This means that it is possible to confine the study of the effects of innovations to the input side. The blast furnace process is placed at the beginning of the production process in steelworks, and its interaction with later stages in the production process is relatively simple. The possibility of studying this process separately from others is further enhanced by the fact that blast furnace operations often constitute separate economic units within steelworks and have been studied very carefully within the steel industry. This means that detailed data are often available, sometimes covering very long periods.

In Section 2, a brief description of the blast furnace process is given. In Section 3, a comparison is made of the development of 'average practice' from 1950 and onwards in the five countries investigated. The differences in raw material input requirements in 1973 are evaluated in terms of Swedish factor prices in Section 4. A similarly hypothetical total cost analysis is made in Section 5. In Section 6, the implication of the results are reviewed in the light of linkages to other processes in integral steel works.

2. The blast furnace process

A blast furnace is essentially a hearth (which may be over 40 ft. (12 m.) in diameter) at the bottom of a large column or stack which may be over 100 ft. (30 m.) tall. The stack is filled from the top with iron raw materials, coke, limestone, and small amounts of other materials, in alternating layers. Combustion is obtained by forcing a current of air and pressure into the furnace just above the bottom of the hearth.

Blast furnaces are usually made of a steel shell with a firebrick lining on the inside. This lining has to be replaced about every three to five years. Since the continuous operation of the blast furnace is essential for avoiding stoppages in subsequent production steps in fully integrated steelworks, the replacement operation (which takes approximately 2 to 3 months) has to be carefully planned. At the same time as the lining is replaced, however, it is possible to introduce new technology. The mere size of the capital invested in a blast furnace, combined with this periodic updating, accounts for the very long average life of blast furnaces. Another important factor, of course, is the rate of change of best practice technology; if this rate is high, old furnaces will have to be scrapped sooner than otherwise.

3. An international comparison of the development of average practice in blast furnaces 1950–1973

3.1. The development of blast furnace size

In order to compare the average size of blast furnaces in various countries one would ideally like to have data on the total number of existing blast furnaces and their total *capacity*. Unfortunately, data on both of these variables are difficult to obtain; they are available for some countries but not for others. Therefore, in order to obtain comparability, Table 1 presents data on annual *production* and the number of blast furnaces actually in blast on a given date.[1] It is obvious that the latter number may be considerably smaller than the number of existing furnaces. But since production differs from capacity in the same manner, average output per blast furnace should be a reasonably satisfactory measure of average capacity.

Given this assumption, and recognizing the difficulties that always arise in

---

1. Except in the case of Sweden, where the number of funaces refers to the number used at all during the year.

Table 1. Number of blast furnaces in blast, annual production, and average output per blast furnace in five countries 1950–1974.

Year	Sweden			United Kingdom			West Germany			United States[b]			Japan		
	Number of blast furnaces[a]	Annual production 1,000 tons	Average output per blast furnace 1,000 tons	Number of blast furnaces	Annual production 1,000 tons	Average output per blast furnace 1,000 tons	Number of blast furnaces	Annual production 1,000 tons	Average output per blast furnace 1,000 tons	Number of blast furnaces	Annual production 1,000 tons	Average output per blast furnace 1,000 tons	Number of blast furnaces[c]	Annual production 1,000 tons	Average output per blast furnace 1,000 tons
	1	2	3	1	2	3	1	2	3	1	2	3	1	2	3
1950	11	446	40,5	100	9633	96,3	72	9473	131,6	221	58593	265.1	37	5558	150,2
1955	13	965	74,2	99	12470	126,0	106	16482	155,5	198	69726	352.1	33	7715	233,8
1960	13	1237	95,2	85	16016	188,4	129	25739	199,5	218	60312	276.7	25	6813	272,5
1965	14	2079	148,5	66	17740	268,8	104	26990	259,5	184	80001	434.8	48	25534	532,0
1970	13	2522	194,0	56	17672	315,6	80	33627	420,3	167	82950	496.7	64	76050	1188,3
1973	14	2530	180,7	45	16838	374,2	76	36828	484,6	141	91479	648.8	63[d]	92690[d]	1471,3[d]

Notes:
(a) Only coke-operated non-electrical blast furnaces which were in use at all during the year.
(b) Only coke-operated blast furnaces and excluding ferro-alloys.
(c) Total number; data on furnaces in blast not available.
(d) Refers to 1972.

Sources:
Sweden: SOS Bergshantering.
United Kingdom: Iron and Steel Industry, Annual Statistics for the United Kingdom.
West Germany: Statistisches Jahrbuch für die Eisen- und Stahlindustrie.
United States: American Iron and Steel Institute, Annual Statistical Report.
Japan: 1950–65:   Japanese Iron and Steel Federation, Statistical Yearbook.
                       Data on output 1968–72 are obtained from Ministry of International Trade and Industry, Statistics on Japanese Industries 1973.
                       Data on the number of blast furnaces after 1967 are obtained from various issues of JISF, The Steel Industry of Japan.

comparing data from different sources, we observe that average blast furnace size has increased manifold since 1950 in all five countries studied. It has more than doubled in the USA and increased tenfold in Japan. In 1950, an average blast furnace in the USA produced about 265,000 tons per year, which was nearly twice the output of an average Japanese blast furnace and almost seven times that of a Swedish one. In 1973, an average US blast furnace produced 650,000 tons, but this was then less than half of the output of an average Japanese blast furnace. An average Swedish blast furnace still produced less than $\frac{1}{7}$th (180,000 tons) of the output in an average furnace in the country with the largest furnaces.[2]

As one would expect, the average size has grown fastest in the countries with the highest rate of growth of output (Japan and Sweden) and most slowly in the country with the lowest rate of growth of output (the United States).

3.1.1. *Increased physical size of blast furnaces.* The increase in output per blast furnace can be decomposed into two components, namely an increase in physical size and an increase in driving rates, i.e. the rates at which blast furnaces are operated. Increases in average blast furnace size, in turn, may be attributable to construction of new, larger furnaces, scrapping of old, small furnaces, and enlargement of existing furnaces in connection with relinings. No detailed data are available on the relative importance of these sub-components. But since there were very few new blast furnaces built in Sweden, the UK, and the USA during the 1960's, the shrinking number of blast furnaces in the latter two countries would indicate that physical furnace size must have increased there mainly due to scrapping of old furnaces. In Sweden, on the other hand, whatever increase there may have been in physical blast furnace size must be attributable to enlarged existing furnaces, since the number of furnaces has been constant. In West Germany, where there have been at least 45 new blast furnaces built since 1960,[3] increasing physical size must be attributed to both scrapping and new construction. In Japan it would appear that increasing physical size is due mostly to construction of new furnaces.[4]

3.1.2. *Increased driving rates.* Increasing driving rates have also contributed to increased output and capacity per blast furnace. Japanese data indicate that the

2. The reason that average output per blast furnace decreased in Sweden between 1970 and 1973 is that a large new blast furnace was started up in 1973 without affecting output in that year.
3. Verein Deutscher Eisenhüttenleute, *Stahleisen-Kalender 1975* (Düsseldorf: Verlag Stahleisen 1974), pp. 100–103 (figure computed by the author).
4. According to the Japanese Iron and Steel Federation, *The Steel Industry of Japan 1965*, p. 23, there were 34 blast furnaces with a physical volume of 1,500 m^3 or less in that year in Japan. According to the same publication for 1974, p. 18, there were 25 blast furnaces of that size at the end of 1973. The total number of furnaces increased from 15 in 1965 to 69 in 1973.

average daily output per cubic meter of working volume increased from .835 tons
in 1958 to 2.04 tons in 1973.[5] Similarly, an unweighted average for Swedish blast
furnaces increased from 1.22 tons in 1956 to 1.86 tons in 1966.[6] However, it is
difficult to compare figures of this sort, since the definitions of working volume
may differ, and since the assumed number of blast furnace days per year may
differ. Nevertheless, in Table 2 an attempt is made to carry out such a
comparison, eliminating the latter difficulty but not the former. However, it is not
believed that the definitions of working volume differ so much as to seriously
affect the figures. The table shows that Japanese blast furnaces are not only twice
the size of American and West German ones; they are also operated at a 75 per

Table 2. Average blast furnace output, working volume, and driving rate in Sweden, the
UK, West Germany, the USA, and Japan.

	Sweden (1973)	UK (1970)	West Germany (1973)	USA (1973)	Japan (1972)
Number of blast furnaces in blast	13	56	76	141	n.a.
Total number of blast furnaces	13[(a)]	56	88	212	63
Average output per furnace in blast, 1000 tons	195	316	485	649	n.a.
Average output per existing furnace, 1000 tons	195	316	419	432	1471
Average working volume, m^3	345[(b)]	900	1007	1100[(b)]	2120[(b)]
Output per m^3 per day, tons	1.55	0.96	1.14	1.08	1.90

Notes
(a) The new blast furnace in Luleå was started up in May 1973 but did not significantly affect total
output in 1973. It has therefore been omitted in this table.
(b) Because of the way in which the underlying individual furnace data were obtained, it is uncertain
to what extent these figures are inflated due to reported but not completed investments in new or
expanded furnaces.

Sources:
Lines 1 and 3: Table 1.
Line 2:   Same as in Table 1 except the UK (source: British Steel Corporation).
Line 4:   Obtained by dividing output in Table 1 by line 2 here.
Line 5:   Sweden, USA, and Japan: Raymond Cordero and Richard Serjeantson (editors), *Iron and
          Steel Works of the World*, 6th edition, 1974 (London: Metal Bulletin Books Limited, 1974).
          UK: British Steel Corporation.
          West Germany: Verein Deutscher Eisenhüttenleute, *Stahleisen-Kalender 1975* (Düsseldorf:
          Verlag Stahleisen m.b.H. (1974).
Line 6:   Obtained by dividing line 4 by line 5 and dividing by 365.

5. JISF, *The Steel Industry of Japan*, various issues.
6. Soläng and Lindgren, *Svenska Masugnars Resultat*, Figure 2.

cent higher rate and at twice the rate of British blast furnaces. Perhaps somewhat surprisingly, Swedish blast furnaces seem to be operated at significantly higher rates than those of competing nations with the exception of Japan.

Care must be taken in interpreting these figures: as indicated in the notes to the table, the comparison is based upon total output figures divided by the total number of furnaces, not just those in operation. The resulting figures therefore reflect not only technical factors but also under-utilization of capacity due to unfavorable business conditions. To the extent that the countries compared were in different business cycle phases, the comparison may be somewhat misleading as far as technical aspects are concerned. Ideally, one would have wanted data for a year with full capacity utilization everywhere, such as 1974.

Nevertheless, the figures probably do roughly indicate the order of magnitude of the differences among countries in driving rates. It is interesting, therefore, to try to find out what the underlying technological differences are. Thus, in the next section an attempt will be made to outline the technological change in blast furnaces which has taken place in the last twenty years. Due to both practical and theoretical considerations it has not been possible to integrate all these changes in a single model or production function. However, in Section 4 an attempt is made to bring the analysis together by calculating the cost implications of the technological choices made in each country.

3.2. Changing input requirements

The two most important inputs in blast furnaces are iron raw materials and coke. The pure iron (Fe) content of iron raw materials varies, but there seems to have been little change in the efficiency with which this is converted into pig iron. As shown in Table 3, however, there has been a considerable reduction in the iron raw material consumption per ton of pig iron (called *the burden rate*) in all the countries except Sweden and Japan. This is due primarily to an increase in the iron content per ton of iron raw materials. Part of this increase has to do with the use of richer ores, part of it with an increased use of agglomerates (sinter and pellets). It was the depletion of the relatively rich iron ores in the Mesabi field in the USA in the 1950's which necessitated the form of iron ore enrichment known as pelletization.[7] The main difference between pellets and sinter is that pellets are uniform in size and shape. Because of this, they increase the permeability of the blast furnace charge, thereby allowing the blast furnace gas to rise more quickly

7. William Peirce, *Technological Change and Investment Planning: A Case Study of Ore Pelletization*, working paper No. 39A, Research Program in Industrial Economics, Case Western Reserve University.

B. CARLSSON

Table 3. Iron raw materials consumption (in tons) per ton of pig iron in five countries 1950–1973.

	1950	1955	1960	1965	1970	1973
Sweden						
Total	1.66	1.71	1.69	1.67	1.67	1.65
% Sinter	89	91	94	92	79	74
% Pellets	–	–	–	3	12	18
United Kingdom						
Total	2.17	2.15	1.98	1.80	1.71	1.64
% Sinter[a]	16	29	47	68	69	65
West Germany						
Total	n.a.	1.91	1.92	1.69	1.64	1.63
% Sinter[b]	n.a.	34	46	63	63	65
United States						
Total	1.90	1.86	1.71	1.64	1.67	1.68
% Sinter	16	17	42	37	30	27
% Pellets	0	2	10	24	40	45
Japan						
Total	1.69	1.63	1.62	1.61	1.59	1.61[c]
% Sinter	31	43	42	58	66	71[c]
% Pellets	–	0	3	6	15	13[c]

Notes:
(a) Data on pellets not available.
(b) From 1960 onwards, the figures for sinter include pellets.
(c) Refers to 1971.

Sources: See Table 1.

through the charge, increasing the rate of combustion and therefore increasing the capacity of the blast furnace while deducing coke consumption per ton of pig iron (see below).

Since both sinter and pellets usually have a higher iron content per ton than natural ore, they reduce the burden rate. This is shown in Table 3. In Sweden, where sinter has been the predominant iron-bearing input since the 1930's, the burden rate was as low as 1.66 already in 1950 and has remained constant since then while the share of agglomerates has also remained constant. In Japan the burden rate has decreased somewhat since 1950 from an already low level. In this case, the burden rate reduction has been very small even though the agglomerate share has increased very substantially. A possible explanation for this is that the iron content of the natural ores replaced by agglomerates may have been very high. Since Japan has to import virtually all iron raw materials, transport cost considerations would seem to favor imports of ores with relatively high iron content. In the United Kingdom, West Germany, and the United States there seems to be a clear relationship between falling burden rates and increasing agglomerate shares. While there was a considerable spread in the burden rate among the five countries in 1950, they all seem to be converging to a burden rate of 1.6 in the 1970's.

Another sign of technological change in blast furnaces is a *reduction in coke consumption per ton of pig iron*, shown in Figure 1. In all five countries the coke

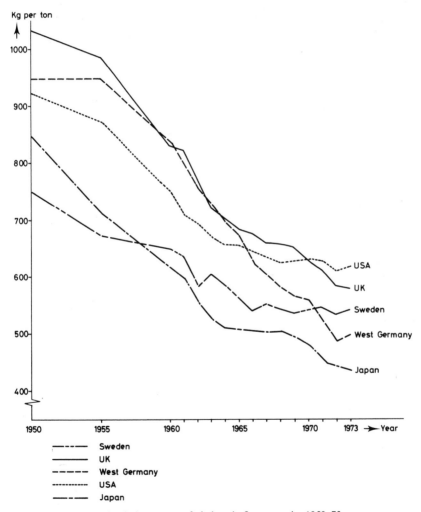

Figure 1. Coke consumption in kg per ton of pig iron in five countries 1950–73.

consumption has decreased considerably. Sweden started out with the lowest coke consumption in 1950 but was passed by Japan in 1960 and also by West Germany in 1971. The Japanese coke rate was down to 434 kg per ton of pig iron in 1973, while the US rate was 617 kg, the highest of the countries studied.

There are several explanations for the reduction in coke rates. The falling burden rates have already been mentioned: with less inputs per ton of output, there is a smaller amount of material to be heated in the blast furnace. The fuel economy improvements associated with the increasing agglomerate shares go beyond the lower burden rates, however; this has to do with the fact that it has been possible to add limestone to the agglomerates in the sintering and pelletization processes, thus reducing the need for limestone in the blast furnace.[8] The reason lime is added to sinter is that it prevents calcination in the furnace, which reduces the coke rate and therefore increases capacity. Even though the same amount of limestone has to be added no matter whether it is done in the sintering process or directly in the blast furnace, it is more economical to do it in the sintering process, since cheaper fuels can be used: coke breeze and fuel oil rather than coke.

Another reason for the reduction in coke rates is the introduction of *auxiliary fuels in the air blast*. By adding fuel oil, coke-oven gas, and even tar from coke ovens, it is possible to reduce the consumption of coke while also increasing capacity. As shown in Table 4, the specific fuel oil consumption has increased from virtually zero in 1960 to over 70 kg/ton in West Germany in 1973. Data for Japan are not available for later years, but it seems reasonable to assume that the fuel oil consumption is even higher in Japan. The figures for the USA seem rather low; a possible explanation is that other fuels are used instead of fuel oil, such as coke-oven gas or natural gas. On the other hand, the relatively high coke rate in

Table 4. Specific fuel oil consumption in blast furnaces in five countries 1960–73, kg/ton.

	1960	1965	1970	1973
Sweden	2.0	11.1	21.2	36.9
United Kingdom	0	9.4	19.6	n.a.
West Germany	0	8.1	50.3	70.9
United States	n.a.	2.3	6.0	14.7
Japan	0	37.9	n.a.	n.a.

Sources: See Table 1.

8. Limestone is put into the furnace primarily in order to form a slag which can absorb the impurities in the iron. The basic limestone combines with acidic materials. It is important to regulate the ratio of basic to acidic materials, since this ratio affects both the quality of the iron and the operation of the furnace.

the USA may indicate a fairly limited extent of substitution of other fuels for coke in that country.

In order to take account of both coke and fuel oil inputs, both of these should be converted to the same base (e.g. Mcal) and added. The results of such a calculation are shown in Table 5. In this comparison, Japan turns out to have the lowest combined energy inputs in the early 1960's. If Japan is assumed to have used the same amount of fuel oil per ton of pig iron as West Germany in 1973, the Japanese combined energy figure for that year would have been approximately 3,740 Mcal, or by far the lowest of all the countries in the comparison. It is noteworthy that total energy inputs in Sweden have actually increased since 1965 due to a larger addition of fuel oil than is compensated by a coke reduction. Still, the Swedish figures for 1970 and 1973 are the lowest in the comparison, excepting Japan.

Table 5. Combined coke and fuel oil inputs per ton of pig iron in five countries 1960–1973, in Mcal.

	1960	1965	1970	1973
Sweden	4563	4029	4009	4126
United Kingdom	5775	4853	4568	. .
West Germany	5845	4784	4401	4163
United States	5243	4615	4469	4464
Japan	4319	3922	. .	. .

Note: The conversion rates used are 7,000 Mcal per ton of coke and 9,850 Mcal per ton of fuel oil.

Sources: Figure 1 and Table 4.

Improved process control has had beneficial effects upon the coke rate and other aspects of performance. One component in improved process control is more accurate measurement of coke moisture content. In its natural condition, coke holds a certain moisture content which varies with the climate. In order to ensure large enough coke inputs in the charge, a certain allowance for variation in moisture content has to be made. By measuring the actual moisture content of the coke more accurately before inserting it into the blast furnace, it is possible to reduce coke inputs and increase capacity.

Another aspect of improved process control is the introduction of screening and grading of inputs. In order to operate efficiently, a blast furnace is dependent upon the charge (consisting mainly of iron raw material and coke) being made up of blocks small and uniform enough to melt but also large enough to allow the gas formed during the process to pass through the charge. By screening and grading inputs, it is possible to increase the permeability of the charge and thus decrease the amount of time required in the blast furnace, thereby increasing production capacity and reducing fuel consumption. The Japanese seem to have been the first to introduce this technology in the 1950's.[9]

The introduction of new bell arrangements in blast furnace tops has also improved process control. Since the charge is put into the blast furnace from the top, the design of the cones through which the charge passes into the furnace is important because it determines the distribution of the charge in the furnace. The normal procedure is to alternate iron raw material layers and coke layers, where each layer has a certain desired composition in terms of size of particles. The sequence of layers varies from one type of blast furnace top to another and depends also on what kinds of inputs are used (e.g. whether pellets are used instead of natural ore or sinter, whether limestone has to be added, whether inputs of both coke and iron raw materials are screened and graded, etc.). With a changing composition of inputs (due e.g. to increased use of agglomerates) the desired distribution of the charge in the blast furnace also changes in order to ensure efficient operation of the furnace and to avoid stoppages. One way to alter the distribution of the charge is to introduce flexible steel armor plates along the inside walls of the top of the blast furnace (so-called flexible throat), so that the charge can be distributed more to the sides or to the middle of the furnace as desired.

As we have seen, a number of measures have been taken to shorten the duration of the blast furnace process. Another step in this direction is the introduction of *pressurized blast furnace tops* which raise the combustion rate by permitting higher pressure. The problem is that of keeping from 'blowing out' the charge when the air blast pressure is increasing. Since a blast furnace operates continuously, the top having to be opened at intervals for putting in more raw materials and coke, pressurized tops require a sluicing arrangement in order to prevent the pressure from leaking out.

Also, with higher speeds of operation, the wear on the bell increases. In order to reduce the wear, the Japanese have introduced 3-bell systems, while the Germans have experimented with a bell-less (continuous charging) system.

A pressurized top has been installed (in 1973) on a new blast furnace in Sweden. This is the only such installation in Sweden as yet. The exact extent to which this innovation has been introduced in other countries is not known at present but will be investigated in the continued research. However, it is well known that virtually all new Japanese blast furnaces operate at high pressure.

The relationship between the coke and the pressure in the blast furnace

9. Sven Soläng and P. O. Lindgren: 'Svenska masugnars resultat,' *Jernkontorets Forskning*, Series C, No. 312, 1967, p. 11.

provides an example of the interrelatedness between various innovations mentioned here. As shown in Figure 2, the coke rate falls with the air blast flow in

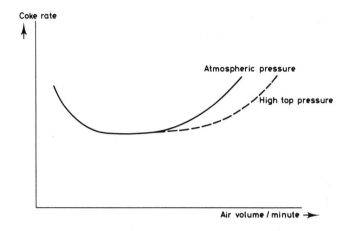

Figure 2.

a certain range, is constant in a certain range, and increases when the flow gets very large. By introducing high top pressure, the range in which coke consumption is constant increases. Thus, increasing air pressure and air volume per minute at the same time tends to both reduce the coke rate and increase capacity – within the limits imposed by the given furnace equipment.

Another measure which has had beneficial effects on both the coke rate and the capacity of the furnace is *increasing the temperature of the air blast*. Figure 3 indicates that considerable improvement has taken place in Sweden in the 1960's in this respect. But at the same time the blast temperatures are considerably lower in Swedish blast furnaces than in West German and Japanese ones.

It is interesting to note in Figure 3 that while there was a considerable spread among plants with respect to the blast furnace temperature in the 1950's, this spread has narrowed considerably in the 1960's. An examination of similar data for other aspects of blast furnace performance (e.g. slag volume per ton of raw iron, silicon content of the raw iron, coke consumption per ton, and limestone inputs per ton) shows a similar pattern of a narrowing spread among plants. It would be interesting to find out in our further work.

a. whether such tendencies are observable also in other countries, and

b. whether such tendencies reflect increasing market pressure.

Beginning in the early 1960's *oxygen has been added to the air blast*. This has had the effect of increasing capacity, but the way in which this capacity increase

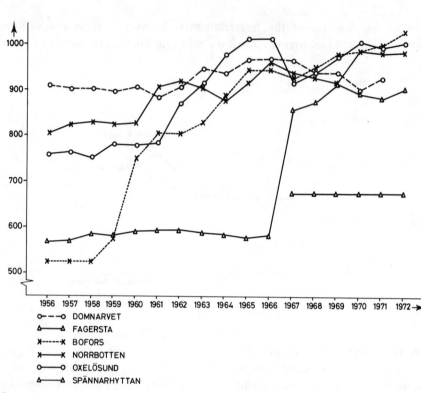

Source:
1956–1966: Soläng and P. O. Lindgren, 'Svenska Masugnars Resultat,' *Jernkontorets Forskning,* Series C, No. 312.
1967–1972: Soläng and Lindgren, 'Nordiska Masugnars Driftsresultat,' *Jernkontorets Annaler* 157 (1973).

Figure 3. The development of blast temperatures in Swedish blast furnaces 1956–1972.

has been obtained is another example of the interrelatedness of technological change in blast furnaces.

Suppose that we start with a certain combination of coke rate, blast temperature, and blast volume per minute. If we replace some of the air in the blast with pure oxygen, several things happen. The nitrogen content in the blast is reduced. The nitrogen in the air blast has no function in the blast furnace other than that of giving off its heat content to the charge: it enters the furnace at, say, 1,000°C and goes out via the blast furnace gas at, say, 200°C. Thus, substituting oxygen for preheated nitrogen increases the coke rate, because the coke will now supply the required heat.

Secondly, the use of oxygen raises the flame temperature. If unabated, this

Table 6. Oxygen consumption per ton of pig iron in four countries.

| Year | 1960–73, Nm³/ton | | | |
	Sweden	UK[a]	West Germany	USA[b]
1960	–	0.4	n.a.	1.9
1965	n.a.	6.5	1.7	3.1
1970	15.1	2.0	4.8	4.2
1973	29.6	n.a.	12.1	4.4

Notes:

(a) The original British figures are given in cubic feet at 60°F and 30″ mercury. The temperature difference between 60°F and 0°C is ignored in the conversion.
(b) Million cubic feet in gaseous form converted to Nm³, assuming the temperature is 0°C and the pressure 760 mm mercury.

Sources: See Table 1.

could cause the blast furnace to blow up, because the iron in the lower part of the furnace would melt too fast while the iron higher up in the furnace would not melt fast enough. Therefore, to control flame temperature, steam or fuel oil (cold) is required in the air blast. By adding fuel oil, of course, it is possible also to decrease the coke inputs.

Thirdly, however, the higher oxygen content also means that the rate of combustion increases, and the whole process is speeded up, thus increasing blast furnace capacity.

The final impact on the coke rate and on furnace capacity therefore depends very much on the particular circumstances. It appears to be the case that the lower the blast temperature, the larger the increase in output when oxygen is added. The impact on the coke rate appears much smaller and less predictable.[10]

As indicated in Table 6, oxygen was added to the blast fairly early in the USA. Sweden was a latecomer but now appears to have the highest rate of oxygen consumption, with the probable exception of Japan. The UK has the highest rate of oxygen consumption in 1965 but seems to have reduced it considerably in later years.

So far, oxygen seems to have been used in blast furnaces mainly in cases of excess capacity (i.e. when the oxygen is not needed in oxygen converters for steelmaking). However, an oxygen plant solely for blast furnaces was installed in the UK in 1965, and August Thyssen-Hütte is reported to be working on such a

10. Soläng and Lindgren, 'Svenska masugnars resultat,' op. cit., Figure 13.

plant. Since the oxygen used in steel converters is required to meet much higher standards (in terms of purity and pressure) than that used in blast furnaces, there are economic incentives for building oxygen plants separately for blast furnaces. However, it appears that very large blast furnace operations are required to make such investments profitable.

Due to the introduction of screened and graded inputs, higher blast temperatures, etc., the iron content of the charge has been raised and the duration of the process has been shortened. This means, in turn, that for each ton of raw iron, less inputs are needed, lowering the required level of the charge in the furnace. When the permeability is increased the process of melting the iron is speeded up. In order to make full use of these advantages, *new design (profiles) of the blast furnace* are called for.

Old blast furnaces were designed for a much less permeable charge and for a slower melting process and are therefore considerably higher and narrower than modern blast furnaces. Whereas other innovations mentioned up to now can be introduced in existing blast furnaces, at least in principle (it may be cheaper, all things considered, to scrap an old furnace and build a new one than to introduce major changes in an old one), a lower blast furnace profile can be obtained only in connection with construction of new blast furnaces. The diffusion of lower furnace profiles is therefore heavily dependent on the rate of growth of the market and the age structure of existing capital equipment.

4. Cost implications of differences in raw material input requirements

The impression one gets from an examination of the comparative data presented above is that if there are economies of scale in the use of raw materials in blast furnaces, they are by no means overwhelming. In order to get a clearer picture of what *cost* advantages there are, let us make the following hypothetical calculation. Using Swedish factor prices in 1973, let us calculate what it would have cost to produce a ton of pig iron with the raw material input requirements of the other countries in that year and then compare those costs with the price of pig iron in Sweden. The results of such a calculation are shown in Table 7.

The table shows that the 'total' raw material costs vary between $ 45.00 with average Japanese technology and $ 54.00 with average US technology. The costs with Britain and Swedish technology are about equal at $ 50.00, while West German technology would have resulted in somewhat lower costs, namely about $ 48.00.

The conclusion we may draw is that on the basis of the material inputs for which

Table 7. Hypothetical costs of pig iron production in five countries, 1973, using Swedish factor prices.

	Price $/ton	Input costs per ton of pig iron in US $				
		Sweden	UK	West Germany	USA	Japan
Iron ore	14	1.80	5.75[a]	8.00	6.60	3.65[b]
Sinter	15	18.30	16.00	13.45[a]	6.80	17.15[b]
Pellets	18	5.35	2.95[a]	2.95[a]	13.60	3.80[b]
Total iron raw materials		25.45	24.70	24.40	27.00	24.60
Coke	43	23.20	24.80	21.30	26.55	18.65
Fuel oil	29	1.05	.60[c]	2.05	.45	2.05[d]
Total energy inputs		24.25	25.40	23.35	27.00	20.70
Total raw material cost		49.70	50.10	47.75	54.00	45.30

Notes:
(a) Assuming that pellets make up 10% of the burden.
(b) 1971 coefficients used.
(c) 1970 coefficient used.
(d) Assuming 70 kg fuel oil per ton.

data have been presented in Section 3, the small blast furnaces in Sweden do not seem to suffer any decisive disadvantage in comparison with the much larger blast furnaces in other countries, excepting Japan. The 'pure scale effect' on cost seems to be small, if indeed it exists at all: the USA with the second largest average blast furnace size has the highest raw material costs. Of course, part of this may be due to the assumed relative factor prices, which might be particularly unfavorable to the US input mix. But the UK and West Germany, with relative factor prices probably more similar to the Swedish ones but with almost as large average blast furnace size as the USA, have almost the same raw material costs as Sweden. Therefore, it does not seem likely that the pure scale effect is very large. Indeed, the difference in raw material costs among these three countries with roughly similar blast furnace size point to the importance of differing degrees of diffusion of the new technologies discussed above.

5. Calculation of total cost differences

Since Japan is widely regarded as the technological leader in iron and steel making today, it is not surprising that Japan turns out in Table 7 to have the lowest raw material costs. The cost difference between Sweden and Japan, for example, is about $ 4.50. Thus, if a decision were to be made to scrap the old Swedish furnaces and replace them with new ones built to Japanese standards, there would be a saving on raw materials of $ 4.50.

Now the question arises as to whether this difference in raw material costs is compensated for by other factors. What we would like to know is whether other components of operating costs alter the differential, and what the difference in capital cost is. If the difference in total operating cost is smaller than the capital cost of new equipment, it will be profitable to continue operating the relatively small Swedish blast furnaces; otherwise they should be scrapped and replaced by Japanese technology – if it is still considered desirable to have pig iron production in Sweden at all. An obvious third alternative, that of continuing to invest in updating the Swedish blast furnaces, is not considered here due to lack of data.

Table 8 presents a hypothetical comparison of total cost per ton of pig iron in Sweden and Japan for 1973. The calculation is based on Table 7 supplemented by additional information and assumption which are specified in Appendix A. The comparison yields a total operating cost difference of $ 3.35.[11] This difference turns out to be much smaller than the 'gross profits' figures obtained by subtracting the total operating cost form the assumed market price for pig iron. The 'gross profits' include depreciation, interest, omitted cost items, and profits. If this crude calculation is at least roughly correct, it would indicate that Swedish blast furnaces of average size should not be scrapped: they yield 'gross profits' three or four times larger than the difference in operating cost with the alternative technology.

Of course, it is extremely difficult to compare capital costs between countries. Even though the same technology may be available to all countries at the same cost to the supplier, the equipment is often delivered in components or has to be constructed entirely on location. Therefore, differences in the efficiency of the construction industry in local markets, wage and transportation cost differences, environmental differences, etc., influence the capital cost. It is also difficult to know what auxiliary equipment is included in the few cost figures available in the literature. But being aware of these difficulties, let us consider some recent German cost figures.[12] Two alternatives are considered: one 14-metre blast furnace or two 10-metre furnaces. In the first case the investment cost per ton of annual capacity is $ 50–60 (in 1975 prices and exchange rates); in the latter the same cost ranges between $ 55 and $ 65. Assuming 10 per cent interest and 10-year depreciation period, these investment costs would imply capital costs per

11. The primary reason for the discrepancy between this figure and the figure of $ 4.50 obtained in Table 7 is the inclusion of oxygen and blast furnace gas in the comparison.
12. W. D. Roepke, 'An Answer to Giants,' *Metal Bulletin Monthly*, April 1975, p. 36.

ton of pig iron ranging from $ 7.50 to $ 10.00. If we assume 20 per cent interest and 15 years' depreciation instead, the range is from $ 8.25 to $ 11.00 per ton of pig iron.

Thus, even if the assumed market price for pig iron of $ 63.00 per ton should be too high and the 'gross profit' margin calculated in Table 8 be too high, the conclusion would still hold: a capital cost of $ 7.50 per ton is still about twice the difference in operating cost.

6. Some conclusions

It must be stressed again that the figures in Tables 7 and 8 are to a large extent hypothetical. They say nothing about the competitiveness of the countries involved, since this would obviously depend on the factor prices prevailing in each country, and upon transport costs, etc. Also, if another country's factor

Table 8. Hypothetical total cost comparison between Swedish and Japanese pig iron production, 1973.

Input	Unit	Price per unit, $	Cost per ton of pig iron	
			Sweden	Japan
Iron ore	ton	14	1.80	3.65
Sinter	ton	15	18.30	17.15
Pellets	ton	18	5.35	3.80
Limestone	ton	10	.15	.20
Total non-energy raw materials			25.60	24.80
Coke	ton	43	23.20	18.65
Fuel oil	ton	29	1.05	2.05
Oxygen	1000 m^3	10	.30	1.20
Blast furnace gas, credit	1000 m^3	4.40	−3.05	−2.75
Total energy inputs			21.50	19.15
Labor	hour	4	1.20	1.00
Relining			1.50	1.50
Total operating cost			49.80	46.45
Capital cost, profits, etc.			13.20	16.55
Price per ton of liquid raw iron			63.00	63.00

prices had been used instead of the Swedish ones, the ranking of the countries in terms of costs might have been different.

The main conclusions which may be drawn from the present study are that many improvements have occurred in blast furnace technology during the last 25 years, that these seem to have been of a step-by-step rather than revolutionary kind, that they have been adopted to varying degrees in various countries, and that these improvements seem to have had a much greater impact on input requirements and costs than increases in scale *per se*. Thus, given the necessity of periodically rebuilding existing blast furnaces, it appears to have been cheaper to install new technologies in old furnaces than to scrap them and build new ones incorporating both new technologies and scale economies.

The results reported here largely confirm those obtained earlier by Leckie who found, using data for individual furnaces, that 'although there is little doubt that large furnaces should be used for new plants or plant extensions, it is not automatically rewarding to scrap serviceable small units and replace them with a smaller number of large ones.'[13]

In comparing two 20 ft 9 in furnaces with one 32 ft furnace producing the same tonnage, he found the difference in operating cost to be 4 shillings (approximately $ .50) per ton in 1966.

Buth the cost of building a new 32 ft furnace would be around £ 5 m., on the rather optimistic assumption that certain ancillary equipment, e.g. boilers and generating plant, gasholders and cooling towers, etc., could serve the new furnace without replacement. That is, the return on the investment, before depreciation, would be just over $3\frac{1}{2}$ per cent. It is easy to understand why so many modernized works are retaining relatively small blast furnaces which are in good operating condition, and we can see that many of these furnaces are likely to be with us well into 'tomorrow.' Few furnaces in the UK are yet working at high [driving rates] and it may be better to spend capital on equipment to allow these to increase their [driving rates] than to replace good small furnaces with big ones.[14]

Leckie also shows that operating a plant at a high proportion of its rated capacity is just as important as plant size:

The biggest sizes of blast furnace and ancillaries give the most economic production over only about half the range of output up to about $2\frac{1}{2}$ m. tons a year, but do so over the whole of the top 25 per cent of the range. Although it is safe to design on the basis of large furnaces (30 ft plus) when planning a new ironworks, provided they will be kept operating at a high rate of capacity, the actual size

13. A. H. Leckie, 'Technical and Economic Considerations Affecting the Optimum Size of Plant' in The Iron and Steel Institute, *Ironmaking, Tomorrow*, Publication 102, 1967, p. 17.
14. *Ibid.*, p. 18.

should always be selected after a careful analysis of the probable range of output over which the plant will operate.[15]

Of course, the rate of capacity utilization depends on a number of factors: the size and rate of growth of the market for the finished products, the capacity of the steelworks with which the ironmaking plant is integrated, whether it is an entirely new plant or a supplementary investment in an old one, etc. The fact that newly built West German blast furnaces in 1972–73 vary between 234 and 4,085 m^3 illustrates the point and confirms the results obtained here.[16] At the same time, the explanation for the huge size of Japanese blast furnaces built in recent years appears to be the combination of scale economies, a high rate of capacity utilization due to demand expanding rapidly enough to warrant construction of entirely new facilities, and constraints on the amount of land available.

Appendix A

The purpose of this appendix is to explain how the figures in Table 8 in the text have been obtained. Whereas Table 7 summarizes the information concerning input requirements in Section 3 of the text for all five countries in the study, weighted by Swedish factor prices, Table 8 tries to get a little closer to the conventional definition of operating cost by including some additional information which is not available for all five countries.

On the non-energy raw material input side, the only major item omitted from Table 7 is limestone. Data on fluxing materials are available only for Sweden and the USA. In Sweden the input of limestone and similar materials amounted to 14 kg per ton of pig iron in 1973,[17] while the corresponding rate for the USA was 143 kg/ton.[18] This has to do with the larger share of agglomerates in Sweden – flux is added to these in the sintering and pelletizing stages. With a cost of approximately $ 10 per ton of flux, the cost per ton of pig iron would be $ .15. Considering the agglomerate share of the burden in Japan, inputs of fluxing materials are probably slightly larger there than in Sweden. A cost of $ .20 per ton of pig iron has been assumed.

As far as energy inputs are concerned, two items have been added to those in Table 7, namely oxygen and blast furnace gas. Unfortunately, no data are available for Japan on oxygen consumption, but it is assumed that the oxygen

15. *Ibid.*, p. 17.
16. Verein Deutscher Eisenhüttenleute, *Stahleisen-Kalender 1975* (Düsseldorf: Verlag Stahleisen m.b.H., 1974), pp. 100–103.
17. SOS *Bergshantering 1973*, Table 37.
18. American Iron and Steel Institute, *Annual Statistical Report 1973*.

consumption per ton of pig iron was about four times as high as in Sweden in 1973. The assumed price of $ 10 per 1,000 m³ refers only to the marginal (energy) cost of producing of the quality required for oxygen converters for steelmaking.[19] This oxygen has higher pressure and a higher degree of purity than that required for blast furnaces, but since there existed no oxygen plant in Sweden purely designed for producing blast furnace oxygen, the assumption seems justified. It could be, however, that oxygen consumption at the Japanese rate could not have been obtained on the basis of excess capacity in existing oxygen plants (for converters). In that case, further investments would have been required, and we would have to consider not marginal cost (which would probably be lower) but *average* cost (which would probably be higher). But this possibility is ignored in Table 8.

Part of the blast furnace gas generated in pig iron production is used outside the blast furnace (in steelmaking operations, for electricity generation, etc.) and should therefore be credited to the blast furnace. The volume of gas to be credited depends on the amount and mix of fuel inputs into the furnace and on the extent to which the blast furnace gas is actually utilized. In Sweden the volume of blast furnace gas actually utilized outside blast furnaces in 1970 was about 690 nm³ per ton of pig iron.[20] Since the fuel inputs per ton of pig iron are about 10 per cent lower in Japan than in Sweden, the credit would be 10 per cent smaller in Japan, assuming the same utilization rates. The price assumed is $\frac{2}{3}$ of the price per calorie of town gas delivered to large industrial customers.

Labour inputs are difficult to determine. According to Boylan[21] the labour costs for a ton of pig iron in the USA in 1963 varied between $ 4.68 in a blast furnace with a 20-foot hearth diameter and a natural ore burden to $ 1.03 in a 35-foot furnace with a pellet burden. Ribrant estimates labour costs in Sweden in 1966 to $ 2.50 per ton of pig iron with a natural ore burden and $ 1.00 per ton with a pellet burden.[22] According to Soläng & Lindgren, labour inputs per ton of pig iron remained constant at .3 manhours in Sweden and Finland between 1967 and 1971.[23] With wage costs running at $ 4.00 per hour in the Swedish iron and steel industry in 1971, this would mean an average labour cost of $ 1.20 per ton of pig iron.[24]

19. Obtained by multiplying electricity consumption of approximately 0.9 kWh/nm³ and a price of $ .01 per kWh.
20. According to information obtained from Jernkontoret.
21. Myles, G. Boylan, *The Economics of Changes in the Scale of Production in the US Iron and Steel Industry from 1900 to 1970*, unpubl. doctoral dissertation, Case Western Reserve University, 1973, p. 304.
22. Gunnar Ribrant, *Stordriftsfördelar inom industriproduktionen*, SOU 1970:30, Stockholm, 1970, p. 165.
23. Soläng and Lindgren, 'Nordiska masugnars driftsresultat,' op. cit., p. 3.
24. Swedish Employers' Confederation, *Direct and Total Wage Costs for Workers*, International Survey 1961–1971, p. 67.

According to Gold, the labour costs in Japanese blast furnaces in the early 1970's are less than 1 per cent of total costs per ton of pig iron.[25] With Japanese wages approximately half of Swedish ones, this would also indicate labour costs with Japanese technology but with Swedish factor prices in the neighborhood of $ 1.00.

Relining costs of approximately $ 1.50 have been assumed for both Sweden and Japan.

Finally, a few remarks concerning the assumed price of pig iron. Since most pig iron is produced in integrated steelworks, the market for pig iron is very limited and it is therefore difficult to determine the market price. For lack of better information, let us assume that the price paid in 1973 for pig iron sold in inter-plant trade represented a fair market price. This price was $ 72.00.[26]

But since raw iron delivered from one plant to another is usually cast into cold pig and there are costs associated with this operation, this price is probably too high. It can be compared to a price of $ 69.60 per ton of (cold) pig iron used in open hearth furnaces in the UK in 1971, whereas the price of liquid raw iron delivered to steel furnaces was $ 62.40.[27] Applying the same ratio between hot and cold metal prices to our present data yields a price of approximately $ 63.00 per ton. This is the price used for the comparison in Table 8.

25. Bela Gold, 'Evaluating Scale Economies: The Case of Japanese Blast Furnaces,' *Journal of Industrial Economics*, XXIII, No. 1 (September 1974), p. 8.

26. Calculated from SOS *Bergshantering 1973* (Stockholm: National Central Bureau of Statistics, 1974) table 37.

27. A. Cockerill, with A. Silberston, *The Steel Industry: International Comparisons of Industrial Structure and Performance*, University of Cambridge Department of Applied Economics, Occasional Paper 42 (Cambridge: Cambridge University Press, 1973), p. 23.

PART FIVE

INDUSTRIAL POLICIES

XV. AN INVESTIGATION INTO THE EFFECTIVENESS OF A CAPITAL MARKET SANCTION ON POOR PERFORMANCE*

J. R. Davies and D. A. Kuehn

1. Introduction

It has become part of the economist's conventional wisdom to recognize that competitive forces in the product market are insufficiently strong to ensure the non-survival of those firms failing to attempt to vigorously and effectively maximize their profits. It has been suggested that the strength of the pressures generated by competition and the minimal threat of bankruptcy has failed to provide effective sanction on either the inefficient companies or those pursuing non-profit goals. It must be remembered, however, that the infrequent occurrence of the ultimate sanction of bankruptcy should not necessarily be taken as an accurate indication of the inadequacy of competitive forces in the product market. The infrequency of bankruptcy may simply be a result of the fact that capital market discipline through takeover is serving to eliminate inefficient management at an earlier stage. As Baumol has pointed out 'The role of guardian of efficiency is one which is natural to expect to be assigned to the Stock Market.'[1] It is the purpose of this paper firstly, to provide an analysis of the character of the capital market's role in disciplining the poor performing company, secondly, to provide the empirical assessment of its capability and effectiveness in fulfilling this role, and thirdly, to discuss some of the more general theoretical implications of these findings.

2. Capital market discipline

It is almost traditional to concentrate empirical investigation on the surviving efficient firms. Research into their successes would hopefully offer guidance to other management wishing to emulate the efficient firm's performance whilst

---

* The authors wish to both acknowledge and thank the Institute of Finance and Investment, University of Stirling, for the provision of research assistance for this project.
1. W. J. Baumol (1965), p. 74.

investigations of company 'deaths' whether from bankruptcy or takeover, have encountered substantial problems of data collection. Recently, however, more attention has been focused on this phenomenon as a result of the wave of UK takeovers which eliminated 47 per cent of all public quoted companies existing between 1957–70.[2] As an extension of some of this work, we will concentrate our attention on the asserted ability of the capital market to exercise some discipline on companies which perform poorly.

Capital market discipline may be exercized in two ways. First, it directly influences firms by 'meting out rewards and punishments in the form of cheaper or more expensive capital funds,'[3] and at the extreme, by the denial of such funds at any price. In general, this potential disciplinary influence has not been too onerous as the majority of firms rely largely on internal finance.[4] It might, however, retain some relevance for the low performance firm unable to generate sufficient capital internally but requiring funds to finance a recovery. The second way by which the capital market may exercize its discipline has already been discussed. Through takeover, a means is provided for the transfer of control from less efficient management to management who can utilize the assets more effectively.

Not all takeovers, however, reflect the exercise of capital market discipline. The motives behind takeovers can be extremely varied and complex. Some takeovers involve the acquisition of efficient and profitable firms, as occurs when a takeover is a means of getting control of an enterprising and efficient management team that has demonstrated its worth in a smaller company. Other takeovers, such as the acquisition of an aggressive and troublesome rival, are designed to reduce competition and increase monopoly power.

Takeovers which could provide the basis of the capital market's disciplinary powers are of a different character. They arise from the exploitation of the opportunities presented by the lower market value of the poorly managed firm. Inefficient management implies the firm's earnings will be depressed. As earnings are a major determinant of the value of the firm, the market value will therefore be depressed. A sufficiently inefficient management can lower the market value of the firm below the value of the firm's assets to some other company.[5] This is when a takeover bid will appear to be a profitable proposition. Inefficient managers

2. See D. A. Kuehn (1975). For a detailed analysis of UK takeovers covering the earlier period 1948–60, see A. Singh (1971).
3. W. J. Baumol (1965), p. 76.
4. See A. J. Merrett, M. Howe and G. D. Newbould (1967).
5. This is compatible with the theory of takeovers postulated by R. L. Marris (1964), although his analysis was primarily directed towards firms which had sacrificed profitability in favour of growth.

fear such bids, since, following a raid, they are liable to be dismissed.[6] The existence of a well-developed capital market makes possible the takeover process and fear of becoming a victim of this process could provide a potentially substantial incentive to the efficient utilization of assets.

The relatively rare occurrence of bankruptcy may be explained by the disappearance through takeover of poorly managed firms before they reach the state of insolvency. It is in this sense that Dewey has described the takeover of inefficient firms as 'a civilized alternative to bankruptcy or voluntary liquidation that transfers assets from falling to rising firms.'[7] Indeed, if bankruptcies were a commonly observed phenomenon in industries that were not contracting rapidly, it would suggest that a product market sanction was operational and the capital market was not playing the major role as a disciplinary force. As this is not the case, we are forced to rely on the takeover mechanism to ensure that no inefficient managers maintain their positions and their control of firms.

If the preceding analysis is found to have a strong empirical foundation then it would imply that capital market discipline is severe, and no managerial inefficiency or the pursuit of non-profit maximizing goals will be tolerated in the longer term. Alternatively, if it emerges that a large number of firms are able to survive a capital market sanction exercized in the form of a takeover despite continued and prolonged poor performance, the weight of the evidence would suggest the opposite conclusion.

3. Data and method of assessment

In order to examine the strength and effectiveness of any direct threat to survival, a census of all public companies quoted at any of the UK Stock Exchanges was obtained.[8] We extracted both the average annual rate of return on net assets before tax (pre-tax profits) and the average annual valuation ratio (defined as the annual mean price of the ordinary voting shares divided by the net assets per share or equivalently as the annual mean market value of the company over the book value) for all 2,015 companies surviving the entire period 1957–62. These companies were then grouped by each of these performance indices and further examined up to December 1969 to discover whether they had been taken over,

---

6. In a separate study we have found that approximately 70 per cent of the board of directors of unprofitable companies which are taken over fail to be hired by the acquiring company while only 30 per cent of the board of directors of profitable companies which are taken over end up losing their positions.
7. D. Dewey (1961), p. 257.
8. This data comes from D. A. Kuehn (1975).

Table 1. 1963–69 survival probabilities of firms existing 1957–62 by grouped pre-tax profit rate.

Group	Takeover %		Bankruptcy %		Survival %		Total %	
−0.50 to 0.06	90	39.6	17	7.5	120	52.9	227	100.0
0.06 to 0.10	112	39.7	14	5.0	156	55.3	282	100.0
0.10 to 0.13	108	37.2	6	2.1	176	60.7	290	100.0
0.13 to 0.17	132	33.5	7	1.8	255	64.7	394	100.0
0.17 to 0.20	82	36.8	3	1.3	138	61.9	223	100.0
0.20 to 0.25	85	29.6	3	1.0	199	69.3	287	99.9*
0.25 to 0.30	44	28.4	1	0.6	110	71.0	155	100.0
0.30 to 0.40	35	30.7	1	0.9	78	68.4	114	100.0
0.40 to 1.00	12	27.9	1	2.3	30	69.8	43	100.0
Total	700	34.7	53	2.6	1262	62.6	2015	99.9*

Table 2. 1963–69 survival probabilities of firms existing 1957–62 by grouped valuation ratio.

Group	Takeover %		Bankruptcy %		Survival %		Total %	
0.0 to 0.5	95	45.5	6	2.9	108	51.7	209	100.1*
0.5 to 0.8	188	38.2	14	2.8	290	58.9	492	99.9*
0.8 to 1.1	145	30.3	10	2.1	323	67.6	478	100.0
1.1 to 1.5	124	32.2	8	2.1	253	65.7	385	100.0
1.5 to 2.0	87	33.7	8	3.1	163	63.2	258	100.0
2.0 to 4.0	55	35.5	6	3.9	94	60.6	155	100.0
4.0 and over	6	15.8	1	2.6	31	81.6	38	100.0
Total	700	34.7	53	2.6	1262	62.6	2015	99.9*

* values differing from 100.0% are due to rounding errors.

gone bankrupt, or continued to survive. The results of this are shown in Tables 1 and 2.

It is clear from these tables there is a consistent tendency for poor performance in the period 1957–62, both in terms of profitability and market standing, to negatively influence the likelihood of surviving in the subsequent time period 1963–69. In the case of the pre-tax profit rate criterion of performance, the chance of takeover during the subsequent seven years is just under 40 per cent in the lowest group and declines to just under 28 per cent in the highest profit grouping. There also emerges a strong tendency for the bankruptcies to fall in the lowest profit grouping, the chance dropping virtually monotonically from $7\frac{1}{2}$ per cent to less than 1 per cent[9] (with the exception of the one bankruptcy in the highest profit group whose proportion is enhanced by the small number of observations of survivors and takeovers). The chance of survival improves with profit performance from just under 53 per cent to nearly 70 per cent. A similar pattern emerges with the valuation ratio in Table 2 although some differences exist. The risk of takeover seems, if anything, more strongly influenced by a low market valuation relative to net assets while the chance of bankruptcy appears almost entirely unrelated to the valuation ratio. The chance of survival improves from just under 52 per cent to nearly 82 per cent. Thus there appears a consistent tendency for survival to be related to performance; and in particular, for low profitability and low market valuation to place a company at a higher risk of death through takeover, or more rarely, bankruptcy.

These two tables, however, raise more questions than they answer regarding the nature of a capital market sanction:

1. Does the evidence so far presented provide a sufficiently strong basis for believing that the capital market can encourage firms to seek efficiency and greater profitability?
2. Are there any financial factors or characteristics that distinguish the survivors from the non-survivors in the low performance groups of firms; and if so, do such differences offer an explanation of how survival was achieved by some poor performing firms and not by others? That is, does any capital market sanction appear to be selecting some low performance firms for survival on the basis of aspects of their behaviour or characteristics, other than profitability or market standing, while at the same time encouraging non-survival through takeover or bankruptcy for others?
3. Among the non-survivors, are there any significant differences between the acquired firms and the bankruptcies that would indicate whether the transfer of assets intact to another set of management by takeover was indicated in preference to the breaking up of the assets through bankruptcy, on the basis of aspects of their behaviour or characteristics other than profitability or market standing?

The answers to these questions have clear implications for the assessment of the capital market's ability to act as a 'guardian of efficiency.' Furthermore, they have a direct bearing on the formulation of the Government's industrial policies: the

---

9. The performance, it will be remembered, is taken in a previous time period which has the effect of introducing considerable 'noise' to the probabilities in the sense that neither takeovers nor bankruptcies are being examined just prior to the event. This nevertheless prevents the analysis of bankruptcy from being tautological.

identification of companies lacking survival potential would allow remedial action to be taken far earlier, and possibly lead to the avoidance or mitigation of some of the consequences of their disappearance. The implications for the individual businessman and the investor are obvious and need not be discussed here.

4. Profitability and survival ability of firms

To examine the first of these questions, we focussed our attention on the lowest profit rate and valuation ratio grouping in Tables 1 and 2; the 227 firms which earned an average annual pre-tax profit rate of less than 6 per cent and the 209 firms whose average annual mean valuation ratio was less than 0.5. Of the low profitability firms, nearly 53 per cent survived the subsequent period 1963–69, just under 40 per cent were taken over and $7\frac{1}{2}$ per cent went bankrupt. It would appear from this evidence that any capital market constraint that serves to transfer assets away from poor performing firms is at best weak. The majority of firms able to survive for a six year period with a very low and in some cases negative rate of return on net assets, are also able to survive for a least another seven years, the majority of which continue to earn very low profits. An analogous conclusion may be drawn for the 209 firms in the lowest valuation ratio grouping where again the most likely occurrence in the second period is survival.

The initial stage in the consideration of the second question posed above, i.e. whether the low performance firms that survive in the longer term are different in any identifiable way from those that are eliminated by takeover or bankruptcy, is to examine those characteristics and policy variables of firms that may be associated with survival potential. Some of the propositions and hypotheses concerning survival potential are impossible to test on an empirical basis. In this paper attention is focused on those characteristics and policy variables of firms that can be measured and for which data could be collected.

One of the most widely held propositions is that survival ability is dependent on size.[10] Large firms have various advantages over their small rivals – for example they can pool their risks to reduce the impact of failure and are generally better fitted to cope with adverse changes in their operating environment. And while there is no evidence to suggest that large firms are any more profitable than small firms there is evidence to suggest that their earnings record is more stable.[11]

10. See J. Steindl (1945); T. M. Whitin and M. H. Peston (1954); O. E. Williamson (1963); and W. H. Starbuck (1965).
11. A. Singh and G. Whittington (1968).

Size would also offer insulation from the threat of takeover in so far as the larger a firm becomes, the fewer larger firms there are who could take it over. The UK evidence on this, however, indicates that if there is any size effect it only serves to insulate a few very large companies. For the vast majority of companies, size has been found to be unrelated to the probability of takeover.[12]

It has also been widely asserted that the probability of survival is positively related to the age of the firm.[13] It is believed that young firms will tend to have relatively inexperienced management and consequently will find survival more difficult, all else being equal, than the older firm endowed with a more experienced and mature management team. Contrary to the expectations based on this hypothesis, an examination of all takeovers in the UK between 1957–69 has shown that age is positively related to the probability of takeover. The chance of being taken over during this period ranged from just over 20 per cent for companies that were between $4\frac{1}{2}$–10 years old to over 50 per cent for companies that were more than 60 years old.[14]

The liquidity variables (the cash flow and the liquidity ratio) are expected to be positively related to survival ability at a given level of profitability. Of course, the liquidity of the firm could be increased at the expense of profitability and this might increase the probability of a takeover. However, when poorly performing firms are being considered, the liquidity variables would be expected to be positively associated with survival ability. A healthy liquidity position will help a firm to stave off the possibility of bankruptcy and could provide the basis for the finance of a recovery through diversification into a different line of business. Moreover, the problems associated with the short-term debt – measured in our tests as a component of the liquidity ratio – may be an immediate cause of insolvency.

Growth may be positively or negatively related to survival ability depending on the circumstances of the particular firm. For instance, it might be the case that the 120 survivors among the firms earning less than 6 per cent pre-tax profits were predominantly of the type of firm Marris expects to characterize 'managerial capitalism.' Such firms would be sacrificing profits for fast growth and as such are more likely to survive than firms displaying both mediocre profits and slow growth. If this turned out to be the case it might be that it was the healthy growth rate of the survivors that led to the market preferring such firms for survival. Unlike the inefficient low growth firms these firms would be in a position to lower their growth target and improve their earnings and valuation if their survival was threatened by a takeover.

12. D. A. Kuehn (1975).
13. For example W. L. Crum (1953), E. Mansfield (1962) and W. H. Starbuck (1965).
14. D. A. Kuehn (1975).

Again in the case of the firm's dividend policy it is not possible to make any simple predictions about the relationship between payout policy and general survival potential. If the firm has no investment opportunities on which it expects to secure a reasonable rate of return, then the higher the payout ratio, the greater will be the valuation ratio and consequently, the lower will be the probability of being taken over. Alternatively, a high payout policy may be disastrous for a firm on the verge of bankruptcy with major liquidity problems.

5. Difficulty of recognizing survival potential in low performance firms

The next step was to employ these variables to discover whether, in a group of low performance firms, those firms that managed to survive in the longer term differed in any significant and systematic manner from those that failed to survive. Regressions of the linear probability type, i.e. those employing a dummy dependent variable, which in this case reflected the occurrence or non-occurrence of survival, were run in an attempt to identify the potential survivors. The independent variables were measured over the period 1957–62 with the dependent variable reflecting the 1963–69 outcome. Two performance criteria – an average valuation ratio of less than 0.5 and an average profit rate of less than 6 per cent – were employed to identify two groups of low performance firms, and a separate set of regressions was run for each group.

The results of these tests were negative: on the basis of these particular tests and variables it did not prove possible for the data on the low performance firms during the period 1957–62 to indicate whether or not any specific firm would be likely to survive the period 1963–69. None of the variables employed in the regression equations was statistically significant. These results suggest that among low performance firms, those with the potential to survive have no readily identifiable characteristics that allow them to be differentiated from firms with no survival potential. This finding has direct implications for our understanding of the effectiveness of the capital market's discipline. The more difficult it is to recognize survival potential the more difficult it is to believe that the capital market can effectively fulfil its assigned role as a 'guardian of efficiency.'

6. Examining propositions on takeover and bankruptcy

Turning to the third and final question concerning the empirical nature of any effective capital market sanction on poorly performing companies, we repeated the linear probability regressions in an attempt to discover whether any differences emerged between the firms whose assets were transferred to different management intact through takeover and the firms forced into liquidation. As bankruptcy is an even more final condemnation of a firm's potential than a takeover, it might be expected that a bankrupt firm would have the more dismal performance record. Moreover, the extreme nature of bankruptcy is likely to be the culmination of a prolonged deterioration in performance that dissipates the reserves of the firm. Among the low performance firms the records of those taken over would be expected to indicate significantly higher profitability, faster growth, and a more liquid position than the records of bankrupt firms. The better performance of firms eventually taken over would also suggest that their capital market standing reflected in the valuation ratio would be higher than those of firms that end in bankruptcy. All else being equal it could be argued that the valuation ratio of bankrupt firms might in some cases be higher than that of taken over firms – the high valuation ratio being a bar to a takeover that could have saved the firm from bankruptcy. Generally, the *ceteris paribus* clause would not be expected to be fulfilled and the valuation ratio would be expected to be lower for a firm heading for bankruptcy than for a firm destined to be taken over.

We attempted to examine these propositions in the same way as before and again found that none of the firm characteristics or financial variables previously listed, except the alternative measures of profitability, served to distinguish between those firms which were taken over and those which were eventually declared bankrupt for both the 107 firms in the lowest profit grouping from Table 1 or the 101 firms in the lowest valuation ratio grouping in Table 2. Moreover, profitability itself provides only a rough means of distinguishing between takeovers and bankruptcies. Only through the cash flow variable do bankrupts emerge as displaying significantly lower profits among the 107 low profit non-survivors but the explanatory power as indicated by the corrected R^2 is less than 0.1. Slightly better results emerged from the examination of the 101 non-survivors in the lowest valuation ratio group. All three alternative measures of profitability, pre-tax, post-tax, and cash flow proved to be significant; but again the explanatory power remained unimpressive, the corrected R^2 ranging from 0.077 for the equation containing cash flow to 0.208 for the equation employing post-tax profits.

It was decided not to report directly all the regression equations estimated because of their indecisive nature. We have, however, presented in Table 3 the means and standard deviations of the regression variables for each category of second period outcome, survival, takeover, and bankruptcy for both the firms selected as satisfying the low profit criterion and firms satisfying the low valuation criterion. This has the advantage of not only demonstrating the homogeneous character of the poor performing firms, but also indicating the average levels of each variable considered.

The final results concerning the bankrupt firms are of some interest as a number of attempts to use financial ratios to predict the failure of firms have been reported in recent years. Possibly the most widely discussed of these is that of Altman (1968). Although the discriminant functions he generates to distinguish between bankrupts and survivors have been criticized as being tautological – the financial characteristics attributed to bankrupt firms defining the state of bankruptcy[15] – the results for profitability reported here, where performance is measured in a time period distinct from the actual event of bankruptcy, provide some limited support for Altman's contention that bankrupt firms can be identified before bankruptcy takes place. Nevertheless, on the basis of the variables used in this analysis one cannot determine, with any acceptable degree of confidence, the particular firms which will survive or die in the subsequent time period. (See Table 3.)

7. First conclusions

The analysis up to this stage has attempted to empirically examine the relevance of the capital market as a source of discipline on poor performance. By examining characteristics and financial records of low performance firms, we attempted to indicate the possibilities for the identification of firms with the potential to survive. We have also attempted to indicate the possibilities for the identification of takeovers as opposed to bankruptcies on the basis of earlier performance. We have found little scope for such identification and hence no basis on which to believe that the capital market can effectively serve to transfer the control of assets to where they can be used more efficiently.

Furthermore, the continued survival of inefficient firms, whose potential value under efficient management would appear to be much greater than their current market value, suggests that the takeover mechanism is inefficient and consequently the threat is ineffectual.[16] Bankruptcy, the other threat to survival, has been shown to only occur in extreme cases. Even in depressed industries, firms seem to be able to generate sufficient cash either from their business or through bank lending to cover their commitments for quite some time despite low or even negative profitability. Thus not only is the threat of bankruptcy small, it appears to operate only as the product market's ultimate and final sanction.

15. C. R. Johnson (1970).
16. Debate has continued concerning the implications of similar results on the appropriate theory of the firm. For differing views see A. Singh (1971), B. Hindley (1972), and D. A. Kuehn (1975).

Table 3. Mean and standard deviation of regression variables for survivors, takeovers, and bankrupts satisfying the low profit rate and low valuation ratio criteria.

Variable	Pre-tax profit rate all companies less than 6% 1957–62			Valuation ratio all companies less than 0.5% 1957–62		
	Survivors	Takeovers	Bankrupts	Survivors	Takeovers	Bankrupts
Age (years from (1970))	44.7433 (24.7258)	45.5784 (23.1442)	40.7178 (15.9585)	47.6714 (26.0896)	50.3930 (24.0280)	46.2386 (16.6741)
Size (net assets) £ m	8.0819 (29.0353)	4.0039 (8.6597)	0.9782 (1.2990)	6.5064 (2.4124)	3.8587 (6.9687)	1.5717 (1.7528)
Pre-tax profit rate	0.0160 (0.0452)	0.0286 (0.0302)	0.0046 (0.0414)	0.0612 (0.0482)	0.0647 (0.0416)	0.0067 (0.0594)
Post-tax profit rate	-0.0029 (0.0431)	0.0066 (0.0272)	-0.0195 (0.0506)	0.0264 (0.0282)	0.0286 (0.0238)	-0.0156 (0.0510)
Cash flow	0.0281 (0.0443)	0.0369 (0.0239)	-0.0159 (0.1072)	0.0589 (0.0360)	0.0587 (0.0311)	0.0208 (0.0410)
Valuation ratio	0.9156 (1.4831)	0.6275 (0.4298)	0.7745 (0.4177)	0.4387 (0.2937)	0.4049 (0.0675)	0.4386 (0.1533)
Growth rate	0.0474 (0.1365)	0.0377 (0.1308)	0.0152 (0.0663)	0.0475 (0.1035)	0.0350 (0.0675)	0.0169 (0.0787)
Liquidity ratio	-0.0721 (0.2649)	-0.0706 (0.2012)	-0.0946 (0.2489)	-0.0456 (0.2071)	-0.0338 (0.1977)	-0.0584 (0.1858)
Dividend/size	0.0041 (0.1018)	0.0149 (0.0072)	0.0145 (0.0093)	0.0173 (0.0100)	0.0187 (0.0079)	0.0148 (0.0069)
Number of Cos	120	90	17	108	95	6

8. Implications of ownership and of firms in declining industries

There remain conceptually only two possibilities that could serve to explain the high incidence of long-run survival of poor performing companies. It might be that a large proportion of these survivors are insulated from the threat of takeover in some way which is not indicated by their financial policies or circumstances. An obvious situation in which such insulation would occur arises when a substantial proportion of the voting control of the company is in the hands of the directors. That such firms could survive the takeover threat is hardly surprising since any raider would find it difficult, if not impossible, to acquire the assets of the company against the will of the owner-managers.

Secondly, there might exist a pervasive downward bias in our measures of performance, profit rates and valuation ratio, for some surviving firms. This might occur where these survivors were in overtly declining industries such that the book value of the assets (in the dominator of both measures of performance) are likely to exaggerate their economic value, thereby lowering the profit rate and valuation ratio and giving a false impression of the incumbent management's operating efficiency. In the UK the textile manufacturing and shipbuilding and repairing industries are recognized as being in this category.[17]

In order to examine whether either circumstance existed to any marked degree within the group of long-run poor performing survivors, we chose to identify all firms which maintained an average valuation ratio of less than 0.5 and all firms with an average return on net assets before tax of less than 6 per cent during the *entire* period 1957–69. It was not possible to repeat the earlier regressions taking into account the ownership characteristics of the poor performing firms since this data has only become readily available since 1968. There were 57 UK firms with a long-term poor market valuation as defined above and 117 UK firms that satisfied the low profit requirement. Of the 57 firms with low valuation ratios, 2 went bankrupt over the next three years up to the end of 1972, one became Government controlled, and 14 were taken over,[18] leaving 40 out of the 57 as poor performing survivors apparently able to withstand the Stock Market's supposed disciplining effect. When share ownership by the board was examined, however, a majority of these 40 surviving companies emerged as predominantly owner controlled: in 11 companies the board directly controlled over 50 per cent of the voting equity and in a further 15 companies the directors possessed greater

17. See C. Miles (1968) and R. M. Geddes (1966).
18. The majority of these acquired firms were managerially controlled. In 8 out of the 14 acquired poor performers the board controlled less than 20 per cent of the voting shares.

than 20 per cent of the voting control.[19] Where the owner control is substantial but less than absolute, effective insulation may still be provided since any takeover becomes not only difficult but also costly. If the offer does not receive the blessing of the incumbent board of directors, the bid premium necessary to obtain a majority of the shares is likely to rise, and this reduces the potential rewards of the raid.

Of the remaining 14 companies where voting control in the hands of directors was less than 20 per cent, 9 were in overtly declining industries – textiles and shipbuilding and repairing – where not only are the opportunities for more profitable use of assets severely limited, but also, the excess capacity, if carried on the books, would lead to an exaggeration of their economic value and hence a downward bias in the measures of performance employed in this study. Any such firms may be earning a satisfactory return on assets employed but nevertheless a very low return on assets on the books. Thus the picture that emerges from the examination of the 57 long-term survivors with an average market valuation of less than 50 per cent of their book value is that for non-owner controlled firms outside the textile and shipbuilding and repairing industries facing a potential takeover raid, survival is indeed difficult. Only 5 such firms out of the 57 companies selected for their poor market valuation between 1957–69, or 8.8 per cent, managed to survive despite their poor performance.

The picture that emerges with regard to the 117 firms earning pre-tax profits of less than 6 per cent is largely similar to those satisfying the low valuation ratio criterion. Eleven of these firms went into bankruptcy up to the end of 1972, one became Government controlled and 32 were taken over,[20] leaving 73 out of the 117 as apparently able to survive the threat of takeover and bankruptcy in the long term. Again one finds that a majority of these remaining firms are to varying degrees owner controlled. In 24 of these companies, the board directly controlled over 50 per cent of the voting shares while in a total of 47 companies the board controlled more than 20 per cent of the votes. Of the remaining 26 surviving companies whose directors controlled less than 20 per cent of the voting equity, 13 belonged to either the textile or shipbuilding and repairing industries. Thus only 13 non-owner controlled firms outside the shipbuilding and repairing and textile industries out of the 117 companies selected for their poor profitability between 1957–69, or 11.1 per cent, managed to survive despite their poor performance.

19. The figure of 20 per cent, while arbitrary, was chosen to be compatible with other studies of owner-controlled firms. Nevertheless, it must be remembered that the figure employed is the proportion controlled by the board and as such will tend to understate the concentration of share ownership as this is the minimum figure of closely held voting shares.

20. The majority of these acquired firms were managerially controlled. The board controlled less than 20 per cent of the voting shares in 20 of the 32 taken over firms.

These results regarding the ownership of long-term poor performing survivors suggest that the discipline exercized by the capital market is rather more severe than implied by the survival probabilities for poor performers contained in Tables 1 and 2. While the takeover mechanism may work slowly it appears to prove a major threat to non-owner controlled firms which are inefficiently managed.

This, of course, is not to say that the capital market threat is such that any inefficiency or the pursual of non-profit goals will be immediately and finally penalized by the takeover of the offending firm. There are numerous market imperfections that impede the full functioning of the takeover mechanism. One of the most important impediments is the limited supply of raiders and their limited capacity to digest acquisitions. This ensures that only a minority of potential raids will be completed during each period of time.

A factor that reduces the profitability of takeovers, and thereby probably reduces the number that occur (and consequently the magnitude of the threat of takeover), is the apparent necessity for the bidder to share some of the anticipated gains with the stockholders of the victim company.[21] Newbould found that 'the final bid prices in uncontested mergers were on average 33.4 per cent higher than the prices a few weeks before the first bid; the mean increases for the contested bids were much higher, 77 per cent in the case of those contested by directors and 73.9 per cent where third parties were involved.'[22] Of course, it could be argued that bids much in excess of current prices were a reflection of the anticipated gains and do not necessarily provide an indication of the inefficiency that can be maintained without attracting a bid. But, such is the range of defensive tactics that could be employed by the incumbent management, a raider has to anticipate paying a substantial premium to complete a bid if they meet opposition.

9. Implications of this examination of poorly performing firms

Our investigation has suggested that the continued survival of poorly performing firms in the face of a capital market constraint is rather more precarious than is generally appreciated. Unless firms are artificially insulated from capital market forces their long-term survival probability is low. The capital market does seem to encourage firms to regard profits as of some relevance; it brings to bear a real sanction in the form of a threat to survival for managerial firms failing to earn at least a satisfactory rate of return on assets. No theory of the firm will be complete

21. The average bid premium for all UK takeovers, 1957–69, was 64.9%. See D. A. Kuehn (1975).
22. G. D. Newbould (1970), p. 56.

without a recognition of the need to satisfy the ultimate requirements of the capital market. Even the analysis of firms in the context of the pursual of the 'easy-life,' part of which must entail some desire for survival, must take explicit account of the external sanctioning power of the capital market on their performance.

The emphasis on the threat of takeover might suggest that the appropriate model of firm behaviour is of the type developed by Marris. This model involves the explicit recognition of the threat to security imposed via the Stock Market, and the consequential impact this threat has on the managerial objective function which firms are seen to maximize.[23] But as we have seen, the firms, considered here are not well-managed companies who have sacrificed profits in the attempt to maximize their rate of growth. Rather, these firms are inefficiently run and/or 'easy-lifers' and are possibly more appropriately interpreted within the context of the behavioural theory of the firm of the type proposed by Cyert and March. Given the apparent effectiveness of the takeover threat, it might prove fruitful to specify the satisfying level of profits with regard to the externally imposed capital market requirements. After all, the determination of a satisfactory rate of return must incorporate survival potential.

References

Altman, E., Financial Ratios, Discriminant Analysis, and the Prediction of Corporate Bankruptcy, *Journal of Finance*, September 1968.

Baumol, W. J., *The Stock Market and Economic Efficiency*, Fordham University Press, 1965.

Crum, W. L., *The Age Structure of Corporate System*, University of California, 1953.

Cyert, R. M. and J. G. March, *A Behavioural Theory of the Firm*, Prentice-Hall, 1963.

Dewey, D., Mergers and Cartels: Some Reservations About Policy, *American Economic Review*, May 1961.

Geddes, R. M. (Chairman), *Shipbuilding Inquiry Committee, 1965–66 Report*, Cmnd. 2937, HMSO, London, 1966.

Hindley, B., Recent Theory and Evidence on Corporate Merger, in K. G. Cowling (ed.), *Market Structure and Corporate Behaviour: Theory and Empirical Analysis*, Grey Mills, 1972.

Johnson, C. G., Ratio Analysis and the Prediction of Financial Failure, *Journal of Finance*, December 1970.

Kuehn, D. A., Takeover Raiders and the Growth Maximisation Hypothesis, in K. G. Cowling (ed.), *Market Structure and Corporate Behaviour: Theory and Empirical Analysis*, Grey Mills, 1972.

Kuehn, D. A., *Takeovers and the Theory of the Firm: An Empirical Analysis for the U.K. 1957–69*, Macmillan, 1975.

Mansfield, E., Entry, Gibrat's Law, Innovation and the Growth of Firms, *American Economic Review*, 1962.

Marris, R. L., *The Economic Theory of Managerial Capitalism*, Macmillan, 1964.

23. See D. A. Kuehn (1972) for a development of the Marris model with respect to the active UK takeover raiders.

Merrett, A. D., M. Howe and G. D. Newbould, *Equity Issues and the London Capital Market*, Longmans, 1967.

Miles, C., *Lancashire Textiles: A Case Study of Industrial Change*, Cambridge University Press, 1968.

Newbould, G. D., *Management and Merger Activity*, Guthstead, 1970.

Singh, A., *Takeovers*, Cambridge University Press, 1971.

Singh, A. and G. Whittington, *Growth, Profitability and Valuation*, Cambridge University Press, 1968.

Starbuck, W. H., Organizational Growth and Development, in J. G. March (ed.), *Handbook of Organizations*, Chicago, 1965.

Steindl, J., *Small and Big Business*, Blackwell, 1945.

Whitin, T. M. and M. H. Peston, Random Variations, Risk, and Returns to Scale, *Quarterly Journal of Economics*, 1954.

Williamson, O. E., *A Model of Rational Behaviour*, in Cyert and March, 1963.

XVI. THE ABOLITION OF CARTELS AND STRUCTURAL CHANGE IN THE UNITED KINGDOM *

D. C. Elliott and J. D. Gribbin

In 1943 and 1944 two studies on cartels were carried out in the Board of Trade as part of the thinking about post-war reconstruction. The first, on British firms' participation in international cartels (1) was prompted by discussions with the United States on post-war policies on international trade and payments as these cartels were regarded as a major impediment to trade liberalization, and also the question of restrictive practices had become an important issue of internal reconstruction policy. The second, on internal cartels (2) was a continuation of the first and was intended to collect information on monopoly and restrictive practices to provide a factual basis for legislation and its subsequent implementation. As both reports were assembled mostly from confidential data in the hands of Government Departments they were classified as 'secret' and so have not been generally known, but they have now been declassified under the 'thirty-year' rule and placed in the Public Records Office in London and are available for use.

As the reports have only recently been released it is not possible to make a full assessment of their connections with subsequent policy developments, but it seems reasonably clear from a preliminary examination that they provided the background for the Coalition Government's commitment in 1944 to introduce competition legislation (3) and were influential in determining its form and implementation. The studies on which the reports were based were carried out with limited resources so they did not cover all the known restrictive arrangements, but an attempt was made to be as comprehensive as possible for the international cartels. The report on internal cartels was deliberately restricted to areas of particular interest since it was regarded as being a first instalment, but the reports taken together provide the most comprehensive material available on restrictive arrangements affecting UK industry in the immediate pre-war period and as such are an invaluable bench-mark.

* Our thanks are due to Mrs K. Atkins and J. Sonke for their patient and careful work in preparation of this paper.

The international cartel report examined 125 products and seems to cover all the principal pre-war international arrangements. For example, there is a substantial section on the International Steel Cartel (*Entente Internationale de l'Acier*) which contained almost all the European producers as well as the members of the Steel Export Association of the USA. There are also well-documented sections on engineering, shipbuilding, electrical machinery and engineering, radio and telecommunications, non-ferrous metals and chemicals. The internal cartel study covered about sixty products, including iron and steel, building materials, electrical goods and a general section embracing textiles, bread and milling, linoleum, metal boxes etc.

Besides being a valuable source of information on individual industries and cartels the reports also permit an estimate to be made of the proportion of output from manufacturing industries subject to restrictive arrangements. The international study estimated about 30 per cent of exports were regulated in 1938 and 16 per cent of total gross output (in value) of UK factory trades in 1935.

Although the internal cartel study is not comprehensive we have estimated an additional 10 per cent of total gross output in 1935 was in these products. This suggests about 25 per cent of manufacturing output was in industries of restricted competition in the immediate pre-war period, but such figures are only approximate because it is now impossible to obtain breakdowns of 'Census trades' at the same level of aggregation as in the cartel studies. On the other hand it is known from evidence which became available later that the domestic cartels in the internal study were only a small proportion of those which existed, so the 25 per cent is an underestimate of the true position (4).

Many, if not most, of the cartels arose as a response to the depressed economic conditions of the late 1920's and 1930's and were attempts to limit home and import competition and get rid of excess capacity. During the Second World War the Government used their organizations to regulate production, and it can be seen from Monopolies Commission enquiries not only were existing cartels strengthened but new ones were brought into existence as instruments of wartime economic planning. This no doubt led to the suggestion by G. C. Allen (5) that by the end of the 1940's monopoly and restrictive practices were more extensive than before the war and the latter had become 'characteristic of a large part, perhaps the greater part of British industry.'

1. The post-war legislation

The Coalition Government's 1944 commitment was honoured by the first post-war Labour Government with the Monopolies and Restrictive Practices

(Inquiry and Control) Act 1948. Because of their history, the experience of the war and the continuance of Government regulation in the late 1940's the law did not presume monopoly and cartels to be *per se* illegal. The Government took a neutral stance and established an administrative body, the Monopolies and Restrictive Practices Commission, to investigate 'references' made to it by the Board of Trade and decide whether the behaviour and performance of the firms investigated were against the 'public interest.'

The criteria for reference covered both monopoly and cartels and were flexible in the definition of the latter permitting informal arrangements to be investigated. Monopoly was defined as one firm or a group of financially interconnected firms controlling at least a one-third share of the market, and cartels were caught if with the same market share criteria 'two or more persons who, whether voluntarily or not, and whether by agreement or arrangement or not, so conduct their respective affairs as in any way to prevent or restrict competition ...' Reference could cover only the supply of goods in the UK, or include exports. Services were excluded from the legislation.

The 'public interest' test was carefully worded and permitted the Commission to take into account any relevant circumstances. It drew particular attention to the need to achieve the efficient production and distribution of goods, increasing efficiency, encouragement of new enterprise, technical progressiveness and an efficient regional distribution of employment and resources. There was no presumption that competition was the most effective means of securing these desirable policy objectives, it was open to the Commission to find that some monopoly or types of cartels produced the economic performance which best met the public interest.

2. Implementation 1948–1956

During this period the Commission investigated twenty industries and made a 'general' enquiry into the effects of similar practices which restricted competition in a larger number, the report on 'Collective Discrimination.' The twenty enquiries are listed in Table 1, showing the number of producers, type of enquiry i.e. whether a cartel or a single dominant firm and market shares.

The main direction of investigation was into cartel arrangements; these divided into nine containing a dominant firm, seven without and two local cartels, and all except one were concerned with prices. The most frequent practice was collectively agreeing to fix common minimum prices and these were often supported or enforced by market sharing, aggregated and loyalty rebates, exclusive dealing, collective boycotts, import restrictions and in six industries

Table 1. Monopolies Commission Reports 1948–1956.

Report	Number of suppliers in Reference	Market share of dominant	
		cartel	firm
1. Dental goods	70	90	50
2. Cast iron rainwater goods	51	90	36
3. Electric lamps	8	73	–
4. Insulated wires and cables	29	77	–
5. Insulin	3	100	33
6. Matches, matchmaking machinery	1	–	87
7. Imported timber	67, 82, 110	90	–
8. Calico printing	36	98	50
9. London building industry	250	65	–
10. Semi-manufactures of copper, alloys	70	76	–
11. Pneumatic tyres	11	90	48
12. Sand and gravel, Central Scotland	5	50	–
13. Hard fibre cordage	19	88	–
14. Linoleum	6	80	–
15. Rubber footwear	6	66	33
16. Industrial gases	1	–	98
17. Electrical allied plant and machinery	3–17	70–79	39
18. Electric valves, cathode ray tubes	10	92	51–67
19. Supply of tea	–	55	–
20. Metal windows	38	90	40

collective or individual enforcement of retail prices. Collusive tendering also occurred relatively frequently and was investigated in the *Supply of Buildings in the Greater London Area.*

The cartel investigations were the first to be made into the Commission's post-war operation and because the Commission's conclusions determined subsequent legislative developments a brief review of them is given here. It is mainly concerned with the thirteen cartels which involved fixing common minimum prices and where the Commission was required to consider the public interest consequences. These cartels represented the majority known to exist. They are listed in Table 2, and it can be seen eight were judged to be against the public interest, four not and in insulated cables the arrangements in some sub-markets were against and in others not. The Commission was required to decide if the arrangements currently operated against the 'public interest' or were likely to do so in the future, and the test applied was how the cartels contributed to achieving the desirable economic performance contained in that definition.

Table 2. Common price systems and the 'public interest.'

Profit measured on	Cost data used	Profits average %	Profit range % points	Range/ average	Common prices
CAPITAL:					
Calico printing	NO	26.3	–	–	A
Pneumatic tyres	YES	10.8 (a)	17.7	1.64	A
Sand & gravel, Scotland	NO	30.0	36.9	1.23	A
Hard fibre cordage	YES	17.5	–	–	A
AVERAGE		21.2	–	1.44	
Electric lamps	NO	7.7	33.0	4.26	NA
Metal windows	YES	12.4	30.7	2.48	NA
AVERAGE		10.1	–	3.37	
SALES:					
Cast iron rainwater goods	NO	6.5	16.0	2.46	A
Rubber footwear	NO	4.1	17.3	4.22	A
AVERAGE		5.3	–	3.34	
Insulin	NO	15.6	7.5	0.47	NA
Linoleum	YES	10.6 (b)	7.6	0.72	NA
AVERAGE		13.1	–	0.60	
COSTS:					
Semi-manufacture, copper	YES	–	19.7 (d)	–	A
Electrical plant, machinery	YES	15.2 (c)	24.0	1.58	A
CAPITAL:					
Insulated cables	YES	14.9	38.6	2.57	A, NA

Notes:
A   = Against public interest.
NA = Not against public interest.
–   = Not available.
(a) = Five largest manufacturers.
(b) = Four largest manufacturers.
(c) = Equivalent to 22% return on capital.
(d) = Equivalent to range of – 3.2% to 69.7% on capital.

The Commission first considered the strength of any independent competition from other producers or products, and also if buyers had countervailing power. To apply the economic performance test it examined the methods used to determine prices, the average levels of profits and the range of costs and profits of the individual producers. The Commission's purpose was to decide if prices, costs and profits were excessive, and if there was a wide spread of efficiency between the cartel members.

Table 2 contains some of the more important information used in the performance test. It is grouped by the profit measure used, i.e. return on capital or sales or costs, whether common prices were against the public interest, and it shows if cost data was used for price determination.

Although the Commission collected cost information it is not comprehensive so we have used variability of individual profit rates as a proxy for variations in cost and efficiency. While in any individual case this might be incorrect, the Commission regarded them as being broadly correlated and of course the information is of interest in its own right.

As the figures show, there was individual variability of profits, and therefore costs and efficiency in the thirteen industries, however, it was not necessarily considered detrimental even where substantial as in *Electric lamps* and *Metal windows* because there are many reasons why they should vary between firms in the same industry. The Commission was concerned to establish two things: first, whether an effective internal transfer mechanism operated so that efficient firms grew at the expense of the less. Such a mechanism would eliminate the high-cost firms, reduce variability, and by favouring the efficient continuously reduce the average level of costs in the industry. Second, the Commission wished to know if efficiency gains were shared with consumers in lower prices, improved products and a widened range of choice.

Although the Act contained no presumption that price competition (the theoretically ideal mechanism) would perform these functions better than any other the Commission quickly reached the conclusion that it would. It noted in the eight industries condemned a lack of effective competition outside the cartels, an absence of countervailing buying power, and that the common prices were supported or enforced with other collective restrictions on individual initiative which resulted in undue structural rigidity.

The Commission was also critical of the methods of collective price determination, noting in half the cases no cost information was available when prices were fixed, and were sceptical of its quality and comprehensiveness in the industries which attempted to use it for that purpose. Indeed this aspect of the enquiries revealed one of the more important failures of the cartels. Because decisions were collective there was an absence of information on costs, efficiency, prices, profit and investment opportunities which would normally be available to an efficient firm. This meant many participants made no attempt to improve their internal efficiency, often not being aware it was low because there was no comparative data. The absence of competitive pressure meant there was no means of extinguishing high-cost capacity, so on average costs were higher than they need have been, efficiency lower and their variability greater. Absence of competition also weakened the desire to innovate and in some industries desirable cost-reduction methods and more efficient plant were introduced only because of wartime pressures. However, the Commission did not consider, on average, that profits were excessive, but it did conclude that prices were too high because they were set to meet the costs of the inefficient, and the higher profits of the efficient would often have permitted price reductions.

The exceptions to these adverse conclusions were *Electric lamps, Metal windows, Insulin* and *Linoleum;* but it was only the effectiveness of Government price control which saved the latter from condemnation. The Commission thought, however, when control was abolished the arrangements would be likely to operate against the public interest, and would only agree to their continuance if substantial modifications were made. In the other cartels there was either a transfer mechanism operating effectively, as in *Metal windows,* or restricted competition permitted an exchange of technical information between suppliers which had been demonstrated to result in increased efficiency and lower prices to consumers, as in *Electric lamps* and *Insulin.* In addition, there were safeguards against abuse, from a substantial and growing competitor in *Electric lamps,* and the Government as the principal purchaser of insulin. Countervailing buying power from the Post Office and the Central Electricity Generating Board also saved part of the *Insulated cable* arrangements from condemnation.

In addition to the price cartels the Commission judged the public interest consequences of four others. *Dental goods* was condemned because of collective enforcement of the price fixed by individual suppliers, *Imported timber* was condemned for exclusive dealing restricting entry, the *London building industry* condemned for collusive tendering, and the *London tea auction* cleared because of inter-Governmental agreements supporting prices.

3. Conclusions on cartel investigations

Taking the results as a whole a clear impression emerges that the Commission considered cartels to have fared badly in terms of performance. Of seventeen only three emerged without some condemnation and one (*Tea*) because of Government involvement. The remaining thirteen either had to abandon their collective price fixing and other arrangements or modify them very substantially because they were judged to operate against the public interest.

Although these cartels were only a small sample there are no strong reasons for believing they were not representative of the larger number which regulated prices and output in more than a quarter of UK manufacturing industry in the immediate pre-war period. In fact there was a deliberate attempt by the Board of Trade to choose a representative sample of cartels for reference, it initially made four references and these were among the 185 (approx) described in the wartime reports. The Board stated: those references were chosen to cover a wide range of different types of allegedly restrictive practices so that the Commission's first reports should enable a considerable section of industry to look at its trading practices in the light of authoritative judgements (6), and over the period nine of the eighteen investigated were from the 185. For the remainder there was considerable information in Government departments, so it seems reasonable to think this objective was achieved.

If this is accepted it is also reasonable to suggest that the Commission's investigations led to the inescapable conclusion that cartels, whatever their value before and during the war, were serving the UK economy badly through poor economic performance. In addition they were major obstacles in the way of achieving the increased efficiency so clearly needed if the UK was to respond to a very different environment and the expectations of the post-war generation. It was clear, therefore, that cartels had to be disbanded, and this was accepted by the new Conservative Government which introduced legislation into Parliament.

4. The Restrictive Trade Practices Act, 1956

The legislation dealing with cartels is contained in this Act which made three important changes. First, agreements between competitors became issues to be judged in the new Restrictive Practices Court. Next, it presumed agreements to

Table 3. Agreements registered under 1956 Act.

Period ending	Cumulative total		%
	Registered	Action taken on	
December 1959	2,240	723	32
June 1961	2,350	1,203	51
June 1963	2,430	1,610	66
June 1966	2,550	2,110	82
June 1969	2,660	2,370	89
June 1972	2,875	2,620	94

Source
Reports of the Registrar of Restrictive Trading Agreements, at the above dates.

be against the 'public interest,' but permitted the participants to rebut by convincing the Court that one or more of the economic benefits known as 'gateways' more than offset all the detriments from the restrictions on competition. Finally, it created a new post, the Registrar of Restrictive Trading Agreements, whose function was to compile a public register of agreements and take them to the Court unless they were minor or of no economic significance.

The public register revealed for the first time the full extent of cartel regulation in the UK, and Table 3 shows the numbers registered. Although agreements existed in almost all sectors of industry not every one had the same economic significance. Many were local in character, and in complex trades there were multiple agreements so numbers are misleading as to the degree of control exercized. Others regulated distribution and retailing, for example wholesalers were party to about 350 and retailers to about 400. Types of restrictions also varied, about 60 per cent governed prices and 50 per cent terms and conditions.

The Registrar said in his first report that 970 agreements were of nationwide

Table 4. Registered restrictive agreements in manufacturing industry 1958.

SIC order	Description	Number of agreements		% Sales covered by agreements
		Total	Price	
I	Agriculture	4	3	NA
II	Mining and quarrying	6	5	3.1
III	Food, drink and tobacco	52	43	67.6
IV	Coal and petroleum products	11	8	48.5
V	Chemical and allied industries	36	26	26.4
VI	Metal manufacture	79	65	76.2
VII	Mechanical engineering	59	48	29.6
VIII	Instrument engineering	10	10	25.8
IX	Electrical engineering	70	55	77.6
X XI	Shipbuilding and marine engineering Vehicles	10	6	49.2
XII	Metal goods nes	114	106	43.6
XIII	Textiles	61	54	60.4
XIV	Leather, leather goods, fur	5	3	3.2
XV	Clothing and footwear	10	5	10.4
XVI	Bricks, pottery, glass, cement, etc.	47	39	80.7
XVII	Timber, furniture, etc.	7	6	60.1
XVIII	Paper, printing and publishing	62	52	70.3
XIX	Other manufacturing nes	18	17	59.6
	Total	661	551	54.1

applicability and importance, and 730 of them were price agreements between manufacturers. We have reviewed them and removed a number not relevant for our purpose, and allocated the remainder to the main headings of the Standard Industrial Classification for 1958. The results are in Table 4 and, as can be seen, there were no sections of industry free from agreements. However, this does not . mean every Census 'trade' or 'product' was regulated by cartels; so to obtain an indication of their importance and a comparison with the estimates for 1935 we have matched the price agreements with the 'principal products' of the 1958 Census of Production. On the assumptions that the agreements affected the greater part of the market of the 'principal product,' and those registered by 1959 were in operation in 1958, we estimate that in 1958 50–60 per cent of output in UK manufacturing industry was subject to cartel regulation. This compares with the estimate for 1935 of 26 per cent.

While our figure should be treated as an estimate subject to amendment after further verification it has a reasonably secure empirical base, and provides support for G. C. Allen's view that by the end of the 1940's the greater part of manufacturing industry was characterized by restrictive practices, and their incidence had increased substantially over the immediate pre-war period. If the cartels investigated by the Monopolies Commission were representative of those registered by 1959 it would seem the UK was paying a high price in the 1950's for the absence of competition in many important industries.

5. Action on agreements

There is some evidence that even before the 1956 Act became law agreements were abandoned in the expection that they would not get through the Court (7) but substantial abolition only began in 1959. This took a number of forms; agreements were amended to remove restrictions or terminated and the Registrar notified the parties to 490 of this intention to start Court proceedings. 320 were terminated quickly but the major movement to abandon began only after the Court decision in the *Yarn spinners* case in January 1959. The agreement was the second to be contested but the first involving prices, and notwithstanding the claim, conceded by the Court, that its abolition might lead to further serious unemployment in an area of the UK already with an above-average rate, the agreement was 'struck down.' It is believed this decision was crucial and began the process of wholesale abandonment.

Further registration and Court proceedings did take place, and their summary history is that up to the end of 1972 only 37 agreements were contested, 11 being approved; in 321 undefended proceedings the Court made Orders prohibiting the parties from making other agreements 'to the like effect,' and 225 were declared to be of minor or no economic significance. However, the most substantial action was voluntary termination and well over 2,000 of those registered, the overwhelming majority, were abandoned by the parties by about the end of 1966. By then cartels in manufacturing industry, many of which had been in operation for 30 to 40 years, ceased to have legal existence.

6. The effects of abandonment

There are two previous substantial studies on the consequences of the termination of agreements. The first, by J. B. Heath (8) examined, through questionnaire and interview in 1960, a sample of 159 and was concerned with the short-term consequences. Because of buoyant demand in the economy Heath found the effects to be relatively small; less than one-third of the participants thought competition had increased, but a high proportion of these thought that prices were lower as a consequence. There were some favourable effects on efficiency in a small number of firms but Heath noted that information agreements came into existence in about half of the sample and mergers and concentration, though at that time on a small scale, also influenced the degree of competition.

The second study, by Swann, O'Brien, Maunder and Howe (9), examined the short- and long-term consequences. Their sample was 40 industries, of which 36 had the agreements terminated by the parties or the Court. In the short-term they found generally the same results as Heath. Competition in prices and discounts emerged in about half the industries, in some cases it was substantial with falls up to 25 per cent but often this did not persist. In electric cables, for example, prices recovered within six months, and within a year for sanitary ware, however lower prices lasted for three years in wire ropes and six years for electric motors. Initially increased competition came from existing suppliers, and excess capacity appeared to be an important cause, but the study also found in about half of the sample information agreements were the most important short-term response to termination.

In the long-term other developments in the economy and in competition law have had beneficial effects by consolidating the newly emerging competition. For example, the Resale Prices Act of 1964 banned resale price maintenance, successful Court action was taken by the Registrar against two information agreements, and the 1968 Act effectively outlawed them. Innovation appears to have been important in about one-third of the industries as new products resulted in substantial re-alignments of demand and supply, and trade liberalization increased import competition. Possibly the most important development was the growing concentration of the economy which had important effects on cartels even before 1956, particularly the major merger wave which is now known to have been an important causal factor. The inter-relationship between the ending of cartels and mergers has not yet been satisfactorily studied but this study, and others, show mergers in many industries after termination were probably the major cause of increased concentration.

Although the authors point out that the increased concentration which followed the abolition of cartels has resulted in price leadership and price parallelism, in some industries they have replaced cartel pricing (10), and some firms have devised new means of colluding, they concluded that in the majority of the industries studied the ending of cartels had resulted in improved efficiency and resource allocation, and therefore the 1956 Act was beneficial to the UK economy.

7. The present study

Our investigation into the effects of the 1956 Act has been undertaken because we wished to have more understanding of the structural changes which have taken place since the end of the war. While these would have happened if the 1948 and 1956 Acts had never been passed, there is evidence from the study of Swann et al. and elsewhere, to show that competition laws have interacted with the changes and substantially influenced their impact in many industries. This appears to be particularly true about the growth of concentration, the most notable feature of structural change, and the one which poses difficult problems for the development of competition policies.

The reports of the Monopolies Commission between 1948 and 1956 were conclusive in the adverse judgements on cartels, but the Commission's judgements about the successor to cartels, higher concentration, does not lead to such a clear presumption about its economic consequences. This is because the abolition of cartels which followed the Act provided increased opportunities for firms to grow internally and externally and in many cases this has resulted in the real efficiency gains it was hoped would follow. Indeed Governments deliberately promoted both forms of growth for that purpose. On the other hand, higher concentration brought about by merger was frequently the means by which newly emerging or potential competition was brought under control, so concentration may have increased without bringing any efficiency gains. Our study was not designed to answer the question of whether increased concentration has been beneficial or not, this requires more detailed analysis than we have done, but we examined certain data for a wider range of industries than is possible in case studies in our attempt to investigate possible relationships between the impact of the competition laws and the growth of concentration.

'Our data has been derived from the agreements registered up to 1959 and subsequently terminated, the Census' of Production for 1954, 1958, 1963 and 1968, and the Business Statistics Office has kindly provided information on the number of enterprises which had not previously been available for the level of aggregation at which we have worked. The starting point is an examination of changes in concentration between 1958 and 1968 obtained from the Census' data on five-firm concentration ratios. These are the share of product sales of the five largest firms at either a four-digit or lower level of aggregation in the Standard Industrial Classification, and to those with comparable ratios in each of the years we have allocated the terminated agreements used for compiling Table 4. There have, of course, been changes in Census definitions, data revision and in later years considerable additions, so the number of ratios on which comparisons are based varies accordingly; however, we think changes in definition etc. had only a marginal effect, if any, on the comparisons.

Table 5 contains the results of the allocation and shows the initial levels of concentration and subsequent changes for the products formerly regulated by agreements and those not. The data permit two comparisons of changes: that for the longer period being based on fewer observations. However, although this may affect the precision of any estimate, both sets are consistent. As can be seen, while the initial levels of concentration on the groups were almost identical, over the ten-year period there was a clear divergence between them, the products with terminated agreements showed a significantly greater rise. The lack of a significant difference between the changes in the groups from 1958 to 1963 is of interest and seems to be explained by the findings of Heath and Swann *et al.* that

Table 5. Changes in product level concentration 1958–1968 (percentage points).

	Initial level 1958	1958–63		1958–68		1963–68	
		Change	No.	Change	No.	Change	No.
Products with terminated agreements	56.3	3.18	90	10.0	90	7.04	142
Products not subject to agreements	56.8	2.53	64	6.73	64	3.22	127
Difference	0.5	0.65	–	3.27	–	3.82	–
't' value	NS	NS		1.8		2.0	

the initial effects of abolition were small and structural change slow to develop. But a differential effect did occur between 1963 and 1968 and the group with terminated agreements ended the period with a significantly higher level of concentration: its increase was almost twice that for the other group.

This conclusion raises an interesting question about the relative importance of the causes of the increased concentration in the groups. Hart, Utton and Walshe (11) estimated from a random sample of thirty products that one-third of the net increase in concentration between 1958 and 1963 was due to mergers, and in the industries in their sample which increased in concentration, internal growth and mergers were of equal causal importance. But it is not possible to decide from their results whether mergers had a greater effect in the industries with agreements compared with those which did not.

A major difficulty in investigating the relationship between mergers and concentration is that although there are reasonably comprehensive official merger statistics they have only been classified to two-digit Census industries and this is too high a level of aggregation for detailed analysis. Nevertheless, it is possible to obtain indications of a possible relationship from that data and other sources. The first is given by relating the final column of Table 4, the percentage of two-digit industry sales estimated to have been affected by cartels in 1958, to the estimates of the average proportion of company funds spent on the acquisition of subsidiaries between 1964 and 1968 as a percentage of those spent on fixed assets. This ratio is used as a measure of external growth compared to internal growth. Since both are crude estimates we have done only a rank correlation between them, but this gives a positive coefficient of 0.46, significant at the 10 per cent level. Although not conclusive it provides support for the hypothesis that merger activity in the 1960's was related in some degree to the abolition of cartels. No evidence was found relating changes in merger activity over the period 1958–68 to the degree of cartelization.

For a further insight into the relationship we have examined all proposed horizontal mergers between 1963 and 1968 of manufacturing enterprises for which the gross assets to be acquired exceeded £ 5-million. The results are set out in Table 6. It is apparent from these figures that mergers were occurring at a significant rate in previously cartelized industries reaching a peak in 1966 when some 45 per cent of total assets acquired in the largest horizontal mergers involved those previously parties to a common restrictive agreement.

Another indication is given in Table 7, derived from the additional data provided by the Business Statistics Office. It shows the average number of enterprises supplying each product within the groups in 1963, and the average reduction in their number which occurred by 1968. We have not investigated the reasons for these changes; no doubt at least two common factors were the

Table 6. Proposed horizontal mergers involving registered agreements.

	1965 (part)	1966	1967	1968
Total proposed horizontal mergers where gross assets > £ 5-million	11	27	32	48
Mergers where acquired and acquiring companies were parties to same agreement (a):				
by number	1	8	8	8
by % gross assets	2.7	45.8	30.6	27.0
Mergers where acquired company was party to an agreement excluding (a):				
by number	2	2	10	13
by % gross assets	17.9	5.9	56.5	47.9
Mergers where acquiring company was party to an agreement excluding (a):				
by number	2	6	12	6
by % gross assets	13.5	19.6	58.3	12.6
Number of companies involved	22	54	64	96
Number of companies with agreements	6	24	38	35

Table 7. Change in the number of enterprises between 1963 and 1968 – average per product group.

	Average number 1963	Change in average 1963–68
Products with terminated agreements	100.8	− 11.8
Products not subject to agreements	71.6	− 5.2
Difference	29.2	6.6

'natural' disappearance of small enterprises kept in existence by the war, but which were ceasing to be viable in a different environment (see S. J. Prais (12)), and merger activity which affected all sections of manufacturing industry. However, there was a significantly greater fall (5 per cent level) in the number for the group with terminated agreements which requires additional explanation. Two possibilities suggest themselves; first, the greater degree of competition following the abolition of cartels might have resulted in a higher rate of 'natural' disappearances; alternatively enterprises might have ceased to exist because of a differentially higher rate of merger activity. There is not sufficient data to assess the relative importance of these but it may be questioned whether competition would have had such a powerful effect in a relatively short time-period. Our view is that probably a higher rate of merger activity was the more important reason and this is lent some support by the figures above.

8. Regression results

Because the existing UK merger statistics are less precise, and at a higher level of aggregation than the concentration and cartel data, we are unable to make a direct test of the hypothesis that mergers were the principal cause of the greater change in concentration in the previously cartelized industries, and the results given above, although in support, do not demonstrate it with assurance. One way to proceed would be to allocate the merger data to the product groups with concentration ratios, but while this might be adequate for the smaller and more numerous mergers it would result in severe problems with the larger mergers which often involved a number of separate products. Another way would be to conduct many more case studies following on Hart *et al.* and Swann *et al.*, but these take time and resources not currently available therefore we could not go in this direction.

Given this background we have attempted a regression analysis of the change in concentration between 1963 and 1968 in the hope that it would provide stronger, though still indirect, evidence of the hypothesis. Its form was suggested, in part, by theory and, in part, by results from other analyses of concentration. We included as explanatory variables the initial level of concentration in 1963, the growth of product sales, and the change in average size of enterprise, and distinguished their effects in the two groups by partitioning the variables.

Although the available data confines the analysis to 1963–68 we believe the results of the case studies and Table 5 suggest that it was not until after 1963 did the changes in structure begin to show themselves, therefore this time-period is suitable for our purpose.

A number of formulations were estimated, and we experimented by comparing groups with agreements with those without, and also price cartels with a group with either no restrictions or only affecting non-price matters. A typical result is as follows:

$$\Delta C = -3.89\,(P) + 4.59\,(NP) + 0.356\,(CP) + 0.120\,(CNP)$$
$$\quad\;\;(1)\qquad\quad(1.1)\qquad\quad(2.6)\qquad\quad(0.8)$$
$$\qquad\quad - 0.0036\,(CP)^2 - 0.0019\,(CNP)^2$$
$$\qquad\qquad\;\;(3.1)\qquad\qquad(1.6)$$
$$\qquad\quad - 10.78\,\%\Delta SP - 4.95\,\%\Delta SNP$$
$$\qquad\qquad\;(4.3)\qquad\qquad(4.3)$$
$$\qquad\quad + 10.87\,\%\Delta SOEP + 4.27\,\%\Delta SOENP \qquad\qquad (1)$$
$$\qquad\qquad\;\;(7.1)\qquad\qquad\;(2.5)$$
$$R^2 = .368 \qquad SE = 6.59 \qquad t \text{ values in parenthesis}$$

where,

ΔC = change in concentration 1963–8.
P = a zero-one dummy variable for the price agreements group.
NP = the corresponding for the non-price and no agreement group.
CP = initial level of concentration in 1963 – price agreement products, similarly CNP for all other products.
$\%\Delta SP$ = percentage change in sales value – price agreement products, similarly $\%\Delta SNP$ for all other products.
$\%\Delta SOEP$ = percentage increase in size of enterprise (measured by sales value) for price agreement products. Similarly $\%\Delta SOENP$ for all other products.

The general conclusions to emerge from the different formulations are that the change in concentration is related to a quadratic function of the initial level, negatively to the growth in sales and positively to the growth in the size of enterprise.

Each of these findings, while not unexpected, is of interest. The significant quadratic term though small in effect means that the less-concentrated products tended to have a slightly greater increase in concentration and the more-highly concentrated products to have slightly less. The de-concentrating effect of sales growth is quite marked and in accordance with theoretical prediction, as is the concentrating effect of growth in the size of enterprise.

When differential effects are considered it appears the growth of sales and change in size of enterprise are significantly different in their operation in each group, the 't' statistic for differences in the coefficients being 2.1 and 2.9 respectively. This means that in the group of products previously subject to price agreements growth of total sales had a greater de-concentrating effect but increases in the average size of enterprise produced more concentration. To help the interpretation of these results the growth experience for three periods spanning fourteen years is given in Table 8, and an additional analysis of the change in size of enterprise is reported below.

Table 8. Growth of sales 1954–68, percentage change in each period.

	1954–58		1958–63		1963–68	
	Growth	No.	Growth	No.	Growth	No.
Products with terminated price agreements	18.3	82	28.1	127	32.9	127
Products not subject to price agreements	28.8	63	47.0	112	45.6	112
Difference in growth	10.5	–	18.9	–	12.7	–
't' value	1.8	–	3.4	–	3.6	–

Growth in Table 8 is measured as the percentage change in sales value and is undeflated for price movements, but there is no reason to believe that this biases comparisons. Perhaps the most interesting feature is the significantly lower growth for the cartelized group. We have not investigated the reasons for this difference, and no doubt it is in part due to the relative ease with which cartels were established in the industries in long-term decline: but this is not a full explanation since many were also a response to the depression of the 1930's which affected fast and slow growing industries alike. Whatever the original reason for their formation the difference in growth rates shown in the table is supporting evidence for the Monopolies Commission's conclusion of poor economic performance. Most of the cartels were formed for defensive reasons and the participants wished to keep them in existence post-war in case the conditions of the 1930's returned, so no doubt this attitude had considerable effects on the willingness to invest and seek growth.

The additional analysis on the size of enterprise was done not only because this is an important variable in its own right for explaining changes in concentration but also because the results might provide further insight into the differential effect of changes in size and possibly on merger activity. Ideally we would have liked data on the size distribution of firms, but as this is not available because of disclosure we have examined the influence of changes in size of the five largest firms and in the remainder, and changes in the number of the latter. A typical result is:

$$\%\Delta C = 0.290\,\%\Delta FP + 0.152\,\%\Delta FNP - 0.123\,\%\Delta SP$$
$$\quad\quad\quad (10.6) \quad\quad\quad (6.9) \quad\quad\quad (4.3)$$
$$- 0.060\,\%\Delta SNP - 0.180\,\%\Delta E\dot{P}$$
$$(3.8) \quad\quad\quad (3.9)$$
$$- 0.07\,\%\Delta ENP \quad\quad\quad\quad\quad\quad (2)$$
$$(2.9)$$
$$R^2 = 0.37 \quad\quad n = 235$$

where,

$\%\Delta C$ = percentage change in concentration between 1963 and 1968.

$\%\Delta FP$ = percentage change in average size of the 5 largest enterprises between 1963 and 1968 in the group with price agreements and $\%\Delta FNP$ for the non-price and no-agreement group.

$\%\Delta SP$ = percentage change in average size of the remaining enterprises between 1963 and 1968 in the group with price agreements, and $\%\Delta SNP$ for the non-price and no-agreement group.

$\%\Delta EP$ = percentage change in the number of enterprises excluding the largest five, in the group with price agreements and $\%\Delta ENP$ for the non-price and no-agreement group.

As well as significant effects for each of the independent variables they each had differential effects in the two groups. The growth of the five largest firms and the fall in the number of the remainder resulted in more concentration in the previously cartelized group, while the growth of the remaining firms outside the five largest had a proportionately greater de-concentrating effect.

Following previous studies we included overall sales growth as an explanatory variable in our first equation, and in the second we have attempted to distinguish its two possible effects on the average size of firm, first as it impinges on the largest five and increases concentration as measured, and second as it affects the remaining firms and reduces concentration. The theoretical view is that sales growth is de-concentrating through its effects on the size and number of firms outside the top five, and these results show that although the numbers fell the average growth of the smaller firms did have a significant de-concentrating effect.

The average size of both sets of firms in the groups and its change between 1963 and 1968 are shown in Table 9, and these figures raise a further question about the relative influence of internal and external growth on size. The average size of the five largest and the other firms in the markets not cartelized changed at about the same rate, and the earlier evidence suggests these had less intensive merger activity so it is possible that an expanding overall market caused both groups to grow at about the same rate. However, the same is not true for the cartelized group, since the smaller firms in it had a significantly lower growth rate than the five largest. If growth of the total market does favour both without a bias towards size a possible explanation for the significantly higher rate of growth of the five largest would be a higher rate of merger activity, and this is in accord with the previous indirect evidence on merger activity.

Table 9. Average size of firm and its percentage change 1963–68.

	Products with price agreements	Products without price agreements
Change in average size of top five	43.4	52.8
Change in average size of firms outside top five	27.5	54.9
Average size of all firms in 1963 £-million	1.15	1.95

9. Conclusion

The explanations we have offered here for our findings do not provide the conclusive evidence which would be desirable for resolving such an important issue and we are conscious that our analysis of changing concentration has widened the range of questions rather than provided a firm empirical base for policy recommendations. At present this is inevitable and reflects the relative lack of research results, but we hope this will be remedied in the future. Until then our view is that probably the greater growth of concentration in previously cartelized industries was mainly owing to a relatively higher rate of merger activity and this poses a dilemma.

Looking back to the early 1950's when between 50 and 60 per cent of manufacturing output was regulated by cartels, and the authoritative judgements of the Monopolies Commission began to reveal their adverse consequences there was little doubt that the judgements had to be abolished. When this happened there were growth opportunities for efficient firms and many took these opportunities through mergers as well as by growing internally, so it seems inevitable that concentration should have increased as a consequence. However, in a number of industries the opportunity for growth was used to acquire competitors by merger thus substituting a structural change for a former cartel without altering the degree of competition. Although we do not, at present, have a substantial amount of evidence on the effects of mergers, there are growing indications from industry and academic research that their success rate is not high and long time-periods are needed before real economies are realized in those which originally had that potential.

It is possible that mergers, while being an important instrument of rapid structural change in the cartelized industries may, on balance, have not brought about the efficiency gains which ought to have followed abolition. If this is so, there would be a good case for developing monopoly and merger policy in the UK in the direction of giving greater scrutiny to high concentration caused by merger in the previously cartelized industries.

References

1. *Survey of International Cartels*, Board of Trade, 1944.
2. *Survey of Internal Cartels*, Board of Trade, 1944.
3. *Employment Policy*, Government White Paper, CMD 6527, 1944.
4. *Register of Restrictive Trading Agreements*, Report for the period 7 August 1956 to 31 December 1959, CMND 1273, HMSO.
5. *The Structure of Industry in Britain*, G. C. Allen, Longmans, 1961, pages 80 and 81.
6. *Annual Report of Board of Trade on the operation of the Monopolies and Restrictive Practices Act, 1948*, for the period ending 31 December 1949, para 14, HMSO.
7. *Competition in British Industry*, Swann, O'Brien, Maunder and Howe, Allen and Unwin Ltd, 1974, pages 153–4.
8. *Restrictive Practices and After*, J. B. Heath, Manchester School of Economic and Social Studies, Vol. 29, May 1961.
9. Ibid.
10. *Parallel Pricing, The Monopolies Commission*, 1973, CMND 5330, HMSO.
11. *Mergers and Concentration in British Industry*, Hart, Utton and Walshe, Cambridge University Press, 1973.
12. *A New Look at Concentration*, S. J. Prais, Oxford Economic Papers, July 1974.

XVII. THE REGULATION AND CONTROL OF PUBLIC UTILITY PRICES: BRITISH EXPERIENCE 1960–1975

R. W. Daniels

In 1973 the total number of public corporations in Britain numbered thirty-four. The list includes all the fuel industries with the exception of oil, the railways, a major portion of the bus service and road transport, the national airline, and the BBC. The most significant acts of nationalization occurred in the 1946–9 period. The steel industry was nationalized for a second time in 1967. The supply of water has been under public control for many years and recently reorganization has established very large Regional Water Authorities.

In terms of their size public corporations are of major significance for the British economy. They employ together 8 per cent of the total labour force. The National Coal Board, British Railways and the Post Office are the three largest employers of labour in the world outside the USA. In 1971 the total investment of the nationalized industries amounted to £ 1,587 million, 35 per cent of all public sector investment, and 16 per cent of the total investment in the British economy. The net assets of the Electricity Authorities are $2\frac{1}{2}$ times those of ICT. The industries contribute 7–8 per cent of the total Gross Domestic Product of Britain.

Given the influence the industries exert over the use of national resources and the disposition of wealth, the determination of their prices is of the utmost importance. It is essential that both the principle and practice of their pricing policy are based on sound criteria and conductive to the achievement of the national good. This paper is concerned with the British approach to pricing in the nationalized industries and developments within the last fifteen years. It falls into three main sections. The first section considers briefly the developments and criticisms of price theory which have appeared in the English language literature. The second section places the pricing decision within the broader context of British economic policy towards the nationalized industries and concentrates on principles. It points to some weaknesses in that policy. The third section outlines briefly the inflationary situation in Britain since 1960 and it considers the use made of the nationalized industries by the Government in their attempts to regulate the economy. This section considers the short-term adjustments made to their investment programmes in the interests of deflation. It also discusses the history of price regulation by the Government in the fifteen years and the recent severity with which it has been imposed. The final concluding section discusses the costs to the industries of price regulation and questions whether the policy as outlined in the second section of the paper or the price restraint policy discussed in the third section should be considered the normal state of things in the nationalized industries.

1. Developments in normative price theory

The economics of Pigou and Pareto provided the initial framework in this field. Their models provided the basic criteria for the determination of 'ideal output' and optimum resource allocation. The details are well documented and need not be pursued here (2). The applicability of this model to the pricing decisions of the public utility was discussed through the 1930's. On the one hand it was established that a perfect competition model fulfilled the conditions necessary to ensure the attainment of maximum social welfare. On the other hand it was concluded especially in an article by Hotelling (4) that for public utilities the Paretian theory dictated that price must equal marginal costs as a necessary condition for the attainment of an optimum. An incisive contribution and evaluation of the debate is to be found in Ruggles (15).

We discuss later the pricing policy of the British nationalized industries. Note however that by the later 1940's, theory had concluded in favour of the marginal cost pricing rule. The moment of such a conclusion had little noticeable impact on the practice of the British industries. For a decade at least industry was more concerned with postwar reconstruction and physical scarcity. However leaving aside the behaviour of the industries the theoretical issues were themselves far from resolved. The Paretian model is itself a theoretical construct of great power and elegance. However the extrapolation of its conclusions from theory to practice should not have been self-evident. The restrictive assumptions of the model in terms of convexity and differentiability of functions, decreasing returns, etc. should have prescribed caution. In the years that followed a debate took place. The applicability of the Paretian pricing model was questioned. The actual conditions in the industries did not meet the requirements of the model.

In practice the assumption of perfect knowledge seems dubious. The National Board for Prices and Incomes reporting on the Post Office in 1968 criticized the industry for lack of knowledge regarding their costs of service. In 1960 the Select Committee on Nationalised Industries reporting on the Railways noted the difficulties inherent in costing rail services. With some irritation and amazement the Committee noted that the ministry was unable to determine which services were actually making financial losses.

Supply functions may contain 'lumpiness' and discontinuities. Again the railways provide examples in passenger transport. Short-run marginal costs will have the form of a step function such that the practical difficulties involved in publishing and administering a tariff make the theoretical requirements unworkable.

The industries do not supply a single homogeneous product nor operate one production plant. Joint-costs occur as can be well illustrated in transport. This gives rise to the inherently difficult costing problems. Multiplant operation utilizing different vintages of technology (e.g. electricity generating capacity) or the exploiting of differing potential (e.g. coal-fields) provide alternative marginal costs. As a result the industries' marginal costs will be based on an averaging of plant costs. This was fully illustrated in 1971 by a report published on coal prices. Inevitably this practice leads to the cross-subsidation of consumers. Shepherd (15) has argued that the effects of cross-subsidation are to be weighed by their empirical significance rather than by *a priori* theoretical reasoning. In discussing the related problem of a complex versus a uniform tariff structure for supplies having differing costs, Turvey (16) shows that if a complex tariff raises administrative costs above those for a uniform price then the latter could be preferable for welfare. The optimum uniform price is shown to be a weighted average of the differing marginal costs with the weights being the slope coefficients of the consumers' inverse demand functions. The uniform price resulting implies that cross-subsidation takes place.

Externalities also need consideration. The Paretian model discusses resource allocation for the maximization of social welfare. Any price rule therefore given to a public utility must be stated in terms of social costs which in the presence of externalities will diverge from private costs. Economic and accounting costs might in any case diverge a requirement to fix prices in relation to social costs and might conflict further with 'commercial' criteria. Alternatively it raises the issue of a tax or subsidy policy. In terms of the Paretian model the presence of externalities seriously undermines the price system as a basis for decentralized decision-making in a market economy (9).

The problem of taxes and subsidies also arises in the case of a decreasing cost industry, for example Gas or Electricity. There are two points here. Firstly this situation is incompatible with the attainment of a Paretian social welfare optimum. A second point is that on the basis of the standard marginalist analysis the increasing returns implies falling marginal costs. Setting price equal to marginal cost carries the inevitable consequence that financial losses will be incurred. This requires the Government to provide subsidies to the extent of the deficit. The resulting taxation affects society's distribution of income which as Little (6) has pointed out is of vital importance in assessing a welfare improvement.

A further point of criticism concerns the time-scale over which the optimization takes place. This is not a question of intertemporal optimization. It is that the definition of marginal cost is sensitive to the time horizon chosen. As has been pointed out (17) in the long-run all factor inputs are variable, in the short-run some inputs may be fixed in amount. In consequence marginal cost will differ according to the time period chosen. Short and long-run optimization may conflict. If short-run excess capacity exists price may be set below long-run marginal cost to utilize fully the available capacity. If a scarcity existed, price may be set above cost to achieve an optimum rationing between consumers.

In principle one of the most destructive attacks on the marginal cost pricing rule has been the theory of second-best highlighted by Lipsey and Lancaster in 1956. In the context of public utility pricing the nub of the second-best argument was to show that unless the equation of price with marginal cost held for all sectors in the economy the application of such a rule in the public sector alone did not result necessarily in an improved social welfare. Although the analysis leading to this conclusion was developed in terms of a traditional production and exchange model and did not consider the points we have raised above, the attack struck fundamentally at the relevance for public utility pricing of the Paretian' theory. Attempts have been made at salvage, for example by Mishan (8). Rees in an interesting article (13) analyzed the importance of intersectoral interdependence in establishing second-best conditions and showed the informational requirement of such models to be enormous. In the light of this second-best debate there has been retreat from the earlier wholehearted reliance on a general equilibrium welfare model of the Pareto type. At best normative propositions are now put forward on the basis of a partial equilibrium analysis. In many discussions pragmatic dogma has taken over.

A relatively recent development in the derivation of decision rules for public utilities has come via activity analysis. Attention has been devoted to the application to the pricing problem of the Kuhn-Tucker theorems of non-linear programming. The mathematical analysis can be found for example in Hadley (3) while Naylor and Vernon (10) show its general applicability to the price output-factor use decisions of the firm under an assumption of profit maximization. Their analysis expresses the constraints on factor use (i.e. the production function) and maximum capacity in terms of weak inequalities and they derive results consistent with neo-classical theory. However the analysis goes further in that the solution to the dual programme giving the shadow prices to be associated with the capacity constraints that any surplus capacity has attached to it a zero shadow price or value. These shadow prices equal the multipliers of the constrained function to be optimized.

More specific applications of the programming approach to public utilities can be found in the work by Littlechild on the pricing of the telephone in the USA (7). An article by Pressman (12) in the same journal analyzes the peak-load pricing problem. It is interesting that both these examples are based on welfare maximization analysis. Unlike the Paretian approach however the welfare function used implies a partial optimization model. The welfare function is expressed in terms of the consumers net benefit. The approach has historic antecedents with Dupuit in 1844 who argued that the measure of satisfaction for a bridge or canal was not the profit yield as this failed, in the absence of perfect discrimination, to measure the total satisfaction of consumers. A measure of the total satisfaction needs to take account of the consumers' maximum willingness to pay. On this basis the criteria for the determination of the optimum is given by:

$$\text{Max (consumers' surplus + total revenue} - \text{total cost)}$$

which is equivalent to:

$$\text{Max (gross benefit} - \text{total cost)} = \text{Max (Net Benefit)}$$

Using this objective function both the Littlechild and Pressman models show that a necessary condition for optimization is either one of the following:

1. When no surplus capacity exists, public utility price should be set equal to long-run marginal cost (including an element to cover the user costs associated with capital).
2. When surplus capacity is available price should be set equal to short-run marginal cost.

Although the programming analysis provides a rigorous derivation of these results the marginal cost pricing rule can be derived more informally as shown by Nath (9).

In Figure 1 is represented a case of monopoly. Under profit maximization, output would be at F, price P_1 and profit would be CP_1EB. From the definition given above Net Benefit equals AP_1EB. If however output were increased to G at which $P_2 = MC$ then net benefit is AP_2B. Since $AP_2B > AP_1EB$ net benefit has increased with the increased output. Furthermore it is maximized at G where price equals marginal cost.

It is interesting to note the reversal of the programming analysis to a partial

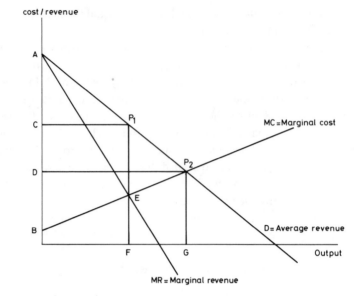

Figure 1. A case of monopoly.

approach aimed at the maximization of consumers net benefit rather that the more general social welfare function. In so doing it avoids the difficulties posed by the second-best problem. It makes prescriptions only for its own industry. As such it takes no account of externalities. Littlechild's analysis is short-run and explicitly avoids the long/short-run dilemma. If one despaired with regard to the general equilibrium analysis of Pareto then the programming approach provides an alternative. It provides insights and reasserts the marginal cost pricing principle.

In attempting to assess the state of the art in public utility pricing theory one might quote Nath's views arising out of his work on theoretical welfare economics: 'The conclusion . . . , then, is that economists cannot recommend that the price of a public enterprise must equal its marginal costs or that it must equal its average cost.' This conclusion he derives from his analysis of a general welfare model. Another writer, Nove (11), sees the major barrier as uncertainty. He quotes Hitch as saying: '. . . most of our relations are so unpredictable that we do well to get the right sign and order of magnitude of the first differential.' Nove agrees and suggests leaving optima to the textbooks. He doubts whether in practice optima are identifiable let alone attainable. A similar point is made by Turvey. On the basis of his experience at the National Board for Prices and Incomes 1967–71 and latterly its Deputy Chairman he provides himself with a working hypothesis based on the maximization of Net Benefit. He gives the public enterprise no responsibility for the distribution of income. He generally ignores externalities unless specified. He assumes that 'what is not known should be ignored.' He concludes: '... very often certain important parameters are unknown and can be estimated only very roughly. In such cases it is just not workmanlike to set up an elaborate model which requires that they be accurately known. It is surely better to succeed in moving in the right direction than to fail in an attempt to locate unknowable optimum' (16).

Whilst normative theory might provide a framework for the discussion of public utility pricing we should not expect it to be fertile in qualitative prediction nor a complete guide to pricing practice.

2. Policy framework for the nationalized industries in Britain

A. Aspects of economic and political control

The nationalized industries being public corporations are subject to government control. The majority party in Parliament forms a Government under the leadership of the Prime Minister who appoints his team of ministers. The ministers are responsible to Parliament for departments staffed by permanent civil servants. The organization has varied. At present the nationalized industries are under two departments. Transport is under the Department of the Environment and the remainder are under the Department of Trade and Industry. The Treasury has responsibility for the public exchequer as well as economic forecasting and the management of the economy.

The nationalized industries are organized on corporate lines with a managing Board under an executive Chairman, none of which are political appointments. Members of the Boards, some of which are part-time, are appointed on fixed-term contracts on the basis of their experience in industry, finance, or the universities. The Board is responsible for the management of their corporation and are initiators of policy. Their powers are subject to limitations under the statutes which for example might on the one hand provide them with a total monopoly of the industry and on the other lay on them certain obligations to supply all consumers requesting service. The staff are public sector employees but not civil servants.

The political control exercized over the industries is an aspect of importance. In theory (but perhaps not in practice) the industry's management is responsible for operations, they also initiate policy proposals but are subject to coordination and supervision by the minister and his departmental staff. Matters of finance and top-level economic policy are settled between the industry's department and the Treasury.

Some aspects of control are statutory and formal. The minister is broadly responsible for the industries in Parliament and is called on to answer questions on matters of policy. The industries present their annual reports and accounts to Parliament and these can be debated. Legislation is passed regulating their affairs. The parliamentary process gives rise to discussion. A system of parliamentary Select Committee of the House of Commons, with membership drawn from the political parties, subjects particular industries to broad review. Their reports are published.

The minister has powers to appoint the membership of the Boards. He can issue specific directives requiring certain things to be done although this power has been used only twice. The investment programmes are subject to ministerial review and approval. This power over investment provides the minister with leverage over a wide range of the industries' policies.

A great deal of ministerial influence stems from informal powers. Since 1956 investment capital not provided from profit surpluses of the industries can only be obtained from the Exchequer. The capital (with one exception) is always fixed-interest debt capital repayable over a fixed number of years.

Industries operating in deficit are subject to greater ministerial control than others. Particular examples have been coal and rail. Deficits can be covered either by cash grants voted in the supply estimates to the minister in the annual budget. Alternatively the interest on debt unpaid to the Government due to the deficit can be carried forward in the industry's accounts as further borrowing. In either case the dependence of the industry on ministerial goodwill is increased.

Price changes are initiated by the industries but invariably the minister is consulted. The minister has responsibility for coordinating the policies of the industries in the same sector as well as representing to them the wider issues of the public interest. Practice has differed with the varying personalities of ministers and industry chairmen. In recent years the demarcation has been made clearer with ministers being involved in the broader issues rather than the detail of management.

B. Financial and economic obligations of the industries

A major question concerns the appropriate balance between public and private sectors in a mixed economy. A policy system requires some basis for comparing the allocation of resources between sectors and judging economic performance. A number of changes have taken place in Britain regarding the selection of policy instruments for these purposes. The three sections below refer briefly to the pre-1960 situation, the changes of 1961, and finally the post-1967 situation.

1. *Pre-1960.* The base reference up to 1960 was from the statutes which established the nationalized industries in the postwar period. Essentially this was a cost of service approach with the industries being expected to pay their way over an average of good and bad years. Revenues were to cover interest, depreciation, redemption of debt capital, and reserves. In practice this was interpreted as breaking-even. The statutes provide little guidance on depreciation procedures, financial reserve criteria or the amount of self finance. In consequence their return on capital was low. In 1954–9 their return on net assets (inclusive of interest and profit) was in most cases less than 5 per cent while private sector manufacturing was in the same period 15–17 per cent. In consequence the Exchequer had to provide approximately 60 per cent of the finance capital for the industries. Prices emphasized levels and were based on average costs and what the market would bear. There was a confusion between financial and non-commercial, social criteria. Investment was not adequately evaluated in economic terms as evidenced by subsequent severe criticism made of a modernization programme for the railways costing £ 1,240 million undertaken in the 1950's.

2. *1961 Managerial and financial approach.* In 1961 a new policy was stated in a White Paper (20) published on behalf of the Government. This was not statutory but established guidelines for future practice. Its adoption resulted from the informal ministerial influence mentioned in section A above.

The document provided for the nationalized industries what it termed 'a new financial framework.' It made no change in the original financial and economic principles of the statutes. It represented a re-interpretation of the financial objectives.

In future the minimum expectation was that the Revenue Account should balance in the medium term over a five-year period. The surplus in addition to covering all operating expenses was to be sufficient to cover depreciation, interest, reserves against obsolescence, and the excess of the replacement costs of capital over historic costs, plus make a contribution to the capital development of the industry.

Each industry was also to be provided with a financial target tailored to fit their individual circumstances. Under this policy the initial targets were set for a five-year term running 1962–7. Many factors were to be reflected in the target: its past performance, its growth, its capital needs. Deficit industries were generally required to achieve break-even while others were set a target rate of return on net assets including interest, depreciation, and surplus. The first target for electricity was set at 12.4 per cent, while that for gas was 10.2 per cent.

On capital account a new system of investment review was established based on a five-year rolling programme reviewed annually. The review was to be made from approximately February until August for the five-year period commencing the following April. The programme on approval by the Treasury, would show the final programme for year one in aggregate and with major projects distinguished involving matters of policy. For year two similar detail would be provided although approval would be given for only up to 95 per cent of the capital expenditure. For the remaining three years an outline programme diminishing in detail would be given largely for ministerial information. A capital budget accompanied the proposals showing the financial requirements and external borrowing required. The initial programme might be the subject of considerable discussion and amendment before being approved.

The procedure of the 1961 policy represented a major step forward in the control of the nationalized industries. It implied greater reliance on strategic as opposed to tactical control and clarified some aspects of the industries' objectives. An adequacy of the policy was its emphasis on ends while it provided little guidance on the means to be adopted.

A major emphasis was also comparability between public and private sectors as an objective. The level of business saving required was to correspond with the average achieved in the private sector. Profit requirements would be incorporated in the financial targets adopted. One factor taken into account in setting targets would be sector comparability.

The scheme of the 1961 policy appeared to contain two strands. One was the emphasis it placed on finance and financial objectives. In this respect the Government adopted a 'merchant banker's' view of their financial operations. The other was concerned with management policy and objectives. It codified the investment review and capital budgeting procedures. It established a uniform scheme for investment programming and capital development. It encouraged the industries in forward planning and provided some confidence in the amount of capital spending over a two-year horizon.

The financial targets were a management incentive scheme reminiscent of management by objectives. They were not statutory (one cannot legislate for success) but they provided some measure of a Board's attainment and potential performance. The theory of targets has foundations in management science. In practice they were welcomed by the industries and up to 1968 the majority were achieved. Their simplicity may have obscured their limitations and the exercise of judgment required. In essence they reflect aspiration levels of a behavioural type. Later analysis of the first targets demonstrated some confusions and inconsistant rationale. For the airlines the target reflected what was attainable, for London Transport it expressed the requirement to break-even although this was unattainable, for electricity and the Post Office facing inelastic demand the implied surpluses gave more guidance for pricing than a spur for managerial efficiency. Despite the ambiguity of the criteria, targets became a major control instrument of the system after 1961 and are still in use today.

The 1961 White Paper made explicit reference to both prices and costs. Industries were exhorted to minimize costs and achieve efficiency. Prices are subordinate to the financial target. The price level has to be consistent with the required rate of return. Ministerial influence also want prices to reflect the requirements of macro-economic policy. The dual role of prices as instruments for the achievement of the industries financial targets and also to support the wider aims of government economic policy has been symptomatic of the British experience.

A proposal to review prices upwards is only made by the industry when their target is not being achieved. This pricing model can be represented schematically as in Figure 2 below.

Financial targets play a central role in this model. Given an initial price and

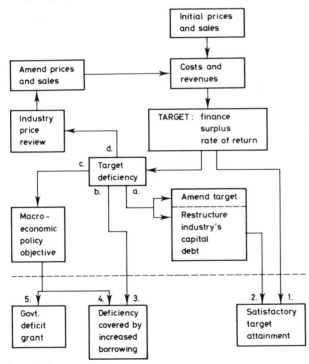

Figure 2. Pricing model.

sales level the resultant of the target represents success or failure. If the latter, the diagram passes to outcome 1 'satisfactory target attainment' and there are no further consequences.

If the outcome is a failure the 'target deficiency' presents four alternatives a, b, c and d. Three provide an outcome without changing price:

a. Erroneous judgement may have fixed the target too high. Officialdom never admits to errors but due to for example price restraint in 1967 the planned target for Electricity in 1967–8 was changed and held at a previous, lower level to thereby alleviate a failure.
Alternatively a solution adopted for industries with endemic deficits has been a restructuring of the book-value of their debts to the Government. This might be rationalized by the writing-off of obsolete assets or to relieve the industry of past errors of investment. Unlike private business a public corporation cannot be bankrupt and a capital write-off may be preferable psychology to the accounts showing persistent losses. Such a policy was adopted for Rail (= £1,262 million in 1968), London Transport (= £270 million in 1965), Airlines (= £135 million in 1965–8), Coal (= £415 million in 1965). A write-off transforms the industry's accounts by removing the interest burden. They may provide deceptive impressions of improved efficiency. The Exchequer is still burdened with servicing the debt and the foregone interest represents a continuing hidden subsidy to the industry. In the diagram both possibilities lead to outcome number 2.
b. Acceptance of the target deficiency will lead to increased borrowing from the Exchequer. A failure to achieve the target means profit has been lower than planned. Profit, depreciation, and reserves make up internal finance for investment which must be less. Given a level of capital expenditure there must therefore be a greater dependence on borrowing from the Exchequer: outcome number 3.
c. An overriding constraint preventing a price rise might be a 'macro-economic policy objective.' A prices and incomes policy has been operative in Britain since 1966 (discussed below in section 3). This policy can restrain prices despite a target deficiency and perhaps the industry in consequence is in deficit. Two alternatives are possible. The deficiency may reflect itself in increased borrowing as in the previous case resulting in outcome 4. Alternatively the Government may provide a deficit grant and shift the financial burden from the industry to the Exchequer giving outcome number 5. This was the case with London Transport where grants in excess of £16 million were made between 1966–8 to cover losses due to price restraint. This type of situation in the 1970's is discussed in section 3.

d. The final alternative involves a price increase, a change in sales, but the increase in net revenue leads to a successful attainment of the target. Prior to 1967 this was a common situation. In some instances, such as Electricity and Gas in 1965, ministers suggested a price increase to ensure the attainment of the target.

As a model of price determination the 1961 policy showed weakness. Monopoly power could make the target a determinant of prices rather than a spur to managerial efficiency as intended. Prices become a residual and their level adjusted to ensure the attainment of the target. The model provided no criteria for price structures, nor the target rate of return any guidance for the selection or evaluation of marginal investment. As a control system it left the need for external checks on efficiency by ministers. It failed to account for productive efficiency and price increases could always circumvent the target making cost minimization less essential.

3. *The economic approach post-1967.* The following years saw further development in thinking on the part of the Treasury. A system of strategic control was required which established procedures and criteria but within that policy framework the industries ought to have freedom to manage. In this respect the 1961 policy was inadequate. It focused on the return on capital. Sir Alec Cairncross pointed out in evidence to the 1968 Select Committee (18) the approach made prices and investment secondary matters, subservient to the achievement of the financial objective. Preferably these roles ought to be reversed with the financial outcome simply reflecting optimal pricing and investment policies.

In the period following 1961 official thinking became heavily influenced by the economic resource allocation model discussed in the first section of this paper. That model as we saw concentrated on pricing and resource allocation at the margin. Allocative efficiency criteria received the official imprimatur in 1967 with the publication of a new White Paper prepared by the Treasury.

Some elements central to the 1961 policy continued. For example the annual review of the industries' rolling investment programme was unchanged. The system of targets remained but on a more uniform basis for the different industries after 1967. Comparing the first targets and those for the second five-year period, Coal was unchanged, Electricity was reduced from 8 to 7 per cent and Gas was raised from 6.2 to 7 per cent when comparisons are made before interest payments in both periods. Rail failed to reach its first target, but both Electricity and Gas achieved theirs.

Although the amount of self-finance required from the industries was increased under the 1961 policy this aspect of the target was later informally abandoned (41, Treasury Evidence). Subsequently it was said that the actual source of capital finance was of less significance than that of ensuring investment projects were evaluated on sound criteria. A view was expressed both by the Treasury and Select Committees (41, 43) that the proportion of self-finance increased significantly after 1961. However analysis of the figures show no discernible change in the 1960's. During the 1950's the proportion for the fuel and power industries had generally been 62–63 per cent and in 1966–7 was 62.5 per cent. In practice the emphasis on the amount of self-finance was never enforced.

The 1967 White Paper devoted its attention firstly to the question of investment evaluation and criteria for capital expenditure. Its proposals did not represent necessarily new practice but a formal adoption of a procedure which had been increasingly encouraged by the Treasury since 1962. In some industries (e.g. electricity generation but not transmission) it was accepted and used wherever possible. In others it was positively resisted, for example in the coal industry (18, Evidence). The 1967 policy required the evaluation of all new investment by discounted cash flow techniques as standard practice throughout the nationalized industries. A uniform test discount rate was to be adopted for equivalent risk proposals in all the industries. The appropriate discount rate was to be fixed again on the basis of the comparable rate of return from marginal investment in the private sector. Due regard being given to differing public-private sector risks, investment allowances, and tax liabilities, the Treasury concluded the appropriate rate was 8 per cent in 1967. This was raised to 10 per cent in 1967 and has remained at this rate since. Normal practice required the net present value (= NPV) of marginal low risk investment to be not less than zero. Investment of higher risk would be discounted at a higher rate but the White Paper offers little specific guidance as to the level of these rates. During the annual investment review procedure the Treasury and the ministry would require all investment proposals to be supported by a DCF evaluation. The adoption of these techniques has taken probably until 1972–3 for their wide-spread acceptance. (19, Evidence of Coal Board).

Two points are worthy of note in the 1967 policy on investment evaluation. There is the technique itself which ensures an adequate appraisal of investment alternatives. In this regard the policy adopted sound management practice and should have improved the quality of decision-making. On the other hand the emphasis has shifted from consideration of the average rates of return on assets to that of the marginal analysis of new investment. This follows from an adoption of the marginal resource allocation model. Provided the test discount rate (= TDR) adequately reflects the cost of capital for the whole economy, the procedure ensures an optimal allocation of capital between both public and private sectors. While this was an objective of the 1961 policy its methods failed to achieve just that because it lacked a criteria for the margin. A further point in favour of the 1967 policy is its emphasis on criteria rather than actual investment projects. Establishment of criteria to be used by the industries will ensure the problem of goal congruence between the decision-makers at the industry level and Government will be minimized. There should be a reduction in the need for interference in the management of the industries. Investment should be self-regulating.

The 1967 policy in applying the resource allocation model to achieve sectoral balance is specific and unambiguous. Practice depends in a crucial way both on the test discount rate and managerial judgement. Judgement is exercized in terms of management's knowledge of their industry and the bringing forward particular proposals for evaluation. The data input for the evaluation is important and raises the question of forecasting. No amount of refinement of technique eliminates the management problem or is likely to compensate for data inadequacies.

The White Paper highlights pricing as being equal to investment in importance. To ensure optimal allocation of current resources and provide a sound basis for the evaluation of investment the White Paper concludes that prices should be equated with long-run marginal costs. However its position was anything but dogmatic and considerably qualified. For this they were criticized as ambivalent by the Select Committee in 1968. The pricing criteria of the resource allocation model clearly formed the basis of the White Paper's position. It was picked up and developed as a catch-phrase by some who knew little of the theory and by others who failed to take account of the assumptions of that theory in pressing for its adoption. The caution of the White Paper was well founded.

The discussion of the resource allocation model in section 1 of this paper raised many of the points noted in the White Paper of 1967. For example the question of criteria when a short-run surplus or scarcity of capacity exists, distinctions between private and social costs. The practical definition and concept of 'long-run' raises difficulties in itself (16).

The White Paper fully noted that the covering of total costs and marginal cost pricing might be incompatible where costs are falling. It could not resolve the difficulty but emphasized the need for the industries to cover their full costs. It was the possibility of financial losses arising from the straight application of marginal cost pricing which brought sharp reaction from the industries. The conflict reflects a difference between the economic and a management view. The Ministry of Power (18, Evidence of Posner) fully acknowledged the force of the allocative efficiency argument implied in the marginal cost pricing rule but pointed out that the taxpayer expected financial probity. In the Railways case a good deal of pricing was done to meet competition. Marginal cost pricing would mean increased prices, a smaller system, failure to meet statutory obligations of service, and losses. The industry view has with time moved to the acceptance of long-run marginal cost as a principle but subject to qualification in practice. By and large it hinges on whether pricing policy is reducible to a cost formula. Whether pricing is an art or a science.[1] Pricing in practice seems to contain a good deal of judgement concerning uncertainties, competition, technology, politics, etc.

Despite its lack of firmness regarding the pricing rule the White Paper of 1967 did improve on the 1961 policy. It established in the forefront the criteria of optimal resource allocation based on economic analysis. In terms of pricing the rule was subject to qualification and less clear. It was to be applied wherever possible and provided a norm. The Select Committee in 1968 considered the 1967 policy in detail and, while welcoming the advance in thinking over 1961, felt that a more forceful application was required. They accepted the orthodoxy of the economic resource allocation model with its pricing and investment rules. As new converts they tended perhaps to greater extremism in this view than the evidence presented to them supported.[2]

The Select Committee's approach picked up the importance of price and investment criteria for economic allocative efficiency and recognized the potential conflict if financial targets were set independently. A good deal of questioning in the evidence pursued the interrelationships between targets, pricing and investment criteria. The Committee's model for these three variables was essentially akin to a mathematical simultaneous equation system. With a system of $n = 3$ variables one had at most $(n - 1) = 2$ degrees of freedom. A choice of two variables from either prices, investment or the rate of return on assets would determine the value of the third. A choice of prices and the level of investment would determine the rate of return. In consequence setting financial targets independently was a meaningless exercise in the view of the Committee. One needed only to select criteria for two of the variables and the third was also determined as a residual. The Committee on this analysis concluded that a potential inconsistency existed between economic resource allocation criteria and financial targetry. This dilemma they resolved by adhereing to the orthodox model. They urged the primacy of pricing equated with long-run marginal cost and investment determined by DCF and a test rate of discount reflecting the cost of capital in the economy. Targetry, while acknowledged to have useful managerial significance, was relegated to be of secondary importance.

A weakness of this approach was its heavy reliance on a deterministic model.

1. See the case study on General Motors (5).
2. For example by Posner, Cairncross, Wiseman, Munby, Sargent.

This view was adopted despite testimony from Sir Alec Cairncross (Head of the Government Economic Service) who while recognizing the relevance of the three elements urged that the analysis was not perhaps as precise as the Committee would want to put it. This view the Committee rejected.

A further criticism of the over-emphasis on the resource allocation model is that when the latter is discussed in the institutional setting of the British system, the likelihood of an optimal allocation of resources between the private and public sectors is open to serious doubt. It is unlikely on the evidence of the nationalized industries' investment behaviour that price could be equated with long-run marginal cost. Government rationing of investment funds makes this equation perhaps even less likely. To demonstrate these conclusions we develop an investment model for the nationalized industries relating the supply and demand of investment with its internal rate of return.

In Figure 3 an I_s schedule is drawn relating the internal rate of return ($= i$) to the quantity of investment undertaken by the industry. The function is affected also by price: shifting to the right with an increase and vice versa. Ignoring the I_d schedule for the moment, assume the authorities fix the test discount rate ($= 10\%$) at r. This rate in conjunction with the I_s schedule determines the amount of investment the industry would be willing to undertake. At the cut-off rate ($= r$) it follows that with $i = r$ the NPV of marginal investment would equal zero. Given price, if investment equals I_1 in the figure (where $r = i$) it follows that the price must equal long-run marginal cost of production.

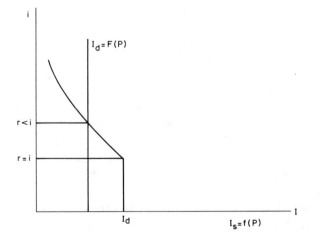

Figure 3

The I_s function reflects only the supply side of capacity. We now consider the demand side. Evidence from the industries (18) shows that, for example, in the case of electricity the growth of demand is the prime determinant of the level of investment required. 'Experience shows that fluctuations in the annual growth rates of industrial production and consumers' expenditure. ... If, ..., demand for electricity is increasing, it is the duty of the Boards to keep pace and maintain security of supply.' (18, Appendix 36) Hence anticipated demand for electricity in 5–6 years ahead is estimated and, given technology, this demand is converted to current investment demand. For simplicity it is convenient to assume the demand for investment is sensitive to prices but unaffected by the cost of capital or returns to public sector investment. This is represented by I_d in the figure.

Putting the two parts of this model together we can state as an equilibrium condition that the capacity the industry is willing to supply must equal current investment demand, that is $I_s = I_d$. Furthermore we assume that actual investment undertaken always equals I_d as seems to be suggested by the industries' evidence quoted above.

It would be fortuitous if $I_d = I_s$ at I_1 given in Figure 3. In the figure with actual investment equal to I_d it follows that given the I_s function, $r < i$. If r represents the comparable rate of return on investment funds in the private sector, then public sector investment is too low. Alternatively price must be above long-run marginal cost in the nationalized industry represented in the figure.

It follows from the analysis that a reduction in price would shift the I_d function to the right (by assumption) and from the calculation which lies behind the I_s function this price reduction would cause I_s to shift to the left. With such a price adjustment therefore I_d and I_s could be made equal at an amount less than I_1 but at a rate of return ($= r$). In this way the NPV of marginal investment could be brought equal to zero and price equated with long-run marginal cost. However from the evidence to the Select Committee in 1968 there is no evidence that this price adjustment takes place or investment is actually undertaken until the NPV at the margin is zero. (18, Appendix 14) The DCF procedure adopted in the nationalized industries requires a consideration of the NPV of the investment but not all projects with a positive NPV are undertaken and therefore one must conclude that the marginal rate of return in the industries exceeds that in the private sector. A corollary of that conclusion is that price must exceed long-run marginal cost.

The investment review procedure can also be introduced and let us assume that investment capital is restricted as happens (18, Appendix 4; 19, Q.933). Assume as shown in Figure 4 below that with prices at P_1 the investment schedule is given by I_{s1} and correspondingly we have I_{d1}. For purposes of exposition the figure shows $I_{s1} = I_{d1}$ at $r = i$ so that the NPV at the margin equals zero and P_1 equals long-

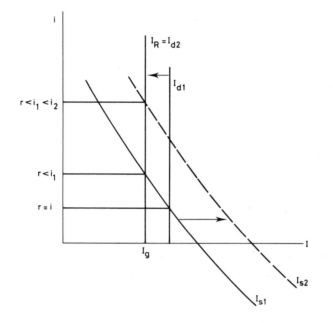

Figure 4

run marginal costs. Equilibrium exists in the demand for and the supply of investment. However assume that due to a restrictive investment review, permitted investment by the Government $(= I_g)$ is less than I_d as shown in the figure. Actual investment will of course equal I_g and not I_d. Consequently given I_{s1} and I_g, $r < i$ and a sectoral misallocation of investment takes place. Notice that in this case no price adjustment can establish $r = i$ or price equal to long-run marginal cost. For example, a price increase shifts I_s to the right and I_d to the left. At some price, I_d would fall to I_g, that is to the permitted level of investment by the Government, but this increases the deviation of r and i even further.

On the basis of this analysis one must conclude that the Select Committee not only placed too great a reliance on the theoretical resource allocation model, but within the context of their own discussion too readily assumed that their price and investment criteria were sufficient to ensure an optimal allocation of resources between the public and private sectors.

The theoretical and institutional weakness of the resource allocation model can be taken further. The evidence of the industries' memoranda shows that investment is determined by future demand. In turn prices affect that demand Hence prices influence investment. On the other hand investment determines the industries' debts to the Exchequer and the interest charges which have to be covered. Price has to cover operating expenses and interest charges. Therefore investment in turn via the interest charges affects the industry's price. A simultaneous equation problem relating price and investment through the demand for capacity and the debt charges. For purposes of argument the formality need not concern us. The interrelationships are illustrated in Figure 5.

Figure 5

Such a model bears some resemblance to reality. Its implications are significant. The cost of capital on exchequer borrowing for the industry is fixed at the National Loan Fund (= NLF) rate which is the rate at which the Exchequer is borrowing rounded to the nearest $\frac{1}{8}$ per cent. In the 1960's the NLF rate was around 5 per cent and at present it is of the order of 9 per cent. If the industries borrow at the NLF rate (= 5–9 per cent) and use a TDR of 10 per cent does this have significance for their investment criteria, prices, and resource allocation?

The interest charges and debt cost in Figure 5 are based on the NLF rate which is the actual cost of capital. Given outstanding indebtedness to the Exchequer, the interest charges are a cost to be deducted from the profit and loss account in deriving the final surplus. As a requirement to cover costs is to be met by the industries under the 1961 and the 1967 policies, increases in the interest charges reduces profits. A fall in profit places pressure on prices which will tend to rise. It seems therefore likely that an increase in the NLF rate will tend to raise prices.

By using a TDR determined independently of the actual cost of capital to the industries' debt charges and therefore the NLF rate do not enter directly into the DCF calculation. (19, Treasury memorandum). However there is likely to be an indirect effect on investment of a change in the NLF rate due to the pressure on prices. Reference to Figure 3 shows that as prices rise the demand for investment will fall and thus actual investment will be reduced. A further consequence will be that the price rise shifts the investment function (I_s) to the right and thereby raises the return on investment. The excess of the rate of return on marginal investment (= i) over the TDR (= r) increases. In this indirect way therefore the effectiveness of the TDR in determining the rate of return on marginal investment is even less than supposed. While the DCF calculation and therefore the I_s schedule is not directly affected by changes in the NLF rate the amount of investment is likely to change nevertheless. Thus it appears that the TDR may not have much direct effect on the level of long-term investment. Control of investment by the NLF rate might be more effective. However according to the optimal resource allocation model used, the key control instrument is the TDR and the NLF rate is assumed to have no effect.

The theoretical resource allocation model is therefore acceptable only in part. The weakness is not in the theory but stems from its application without regard to real world constraints and organization. The Select Committee emphasized resource allocation criteria but did not pay enough attention to practice. Furthermore they discounted too heavily public expectations and perceptions. Despite the attitude of the Select Committee the public expect financial probity. The political economy of the situation therefore requires this to be taken into account. Despite the views of the Treasury given in evidence history since 1960 shows that the rationing of investment capital to the public sector has been not infrequent.

Any model of the nationalized industries needs to incorporate the relevant economic analysis and have due regard to institutional reality. The strong point of the resource allocation model is its emphasis on price structures and problems associated with cross-subsidization between consumers. If society's view is that the industries must cover costs or management are more effective when working to financial targets then they must be taken into account. In Britain a pressing contemporary problem is the rising rate of public expenditure. It is likely that the ability of the industries to raise a large part of their investment capital internally will be of growing concern in the future. If these things are not reflected in the theory then it does not warrant treating the world as an aberration.

Elementary economic analysis emphasizes the role of the price mechanism as a signaling system between producers and consumers. In the case of the nationalized industries there are time lags in adjusting both consumption patterns and the installation of productive plant. This is well illustrated by the recent fuel crisis. Pricing and investment are closely interrelated as our analysis has illustrated. Regarding the appropriate signals to transmit one approach in the case of the nationalized industries is to believe the matter can be settled on the basis of an arithmetic calculation. Derive the right formula and turn the handle for the results. This seems a mistaken view and a fallacy coming from the straightforward application of the resource allocation model. Given the scale and complexity of the industries and the economic environment, problems cannot be simplified to such a degree. Pricing involves policy and is a specific function of management. Theory, analysis, and technique provide the information structure within which management exercises its discretion. Judgement is involved in the weighing of competing objectives and imponderables. Decision-making with regard to pricing and investment seem very much to involve these things.

Although the economic framework embodied in the 1967 policy is still reflected in contemporary British thinking it is more in term of the circumspect view of the White Paper than the formalism of the Select Committee. All the variables still figure in the discussion and the DCF technique and a 10 per cent test discount rate are standard practice. Marginal cost pricing is recognized as an important variable in the attainment of allocative efficiency which other things being equal is a worthy objective. However other aspects weigh heavily in addition: inflation, balance of payments, finance, productive efficiency to name but a few. Government is requiring more long-term thinking on the part of the nationalized industries. Since 1972 corporate plants are produced and submitted to the minister for approval. This is in addition to their five-year investment programmes submitted annually. It shows a new emphasis on the development of longer-term stategies against which a pricing proposal or an investment project can be set. The exercise is a useful discipline but, as the discussion in the final section shows, coping with short-term crises undermines any longer-run thinking. In this present section we have considered principles and we now turn to Government regulation in practice.

3. Management of the economy via the nationalized industries

A. Counter-inflationary policy since 1960

The practice in regard to pricing and investment has in part only followed from principle due to overriding macro considerations. Wider issues concerned with the management of the economy and the control of inflation have been to the forefront to a greater or lesser degree throughout the period since 1960. The impact of economic crises on the nationalized industries and the consequent 'temporary' modification of policy norms is now considered.

Space does not permit a full account of the macro-economic history of Britain since 1960. However in order to provide a perspective to the discussion it is necessary to outline briefly some of the more major developments.

For the purpose of our discussions the period has been dominated by attempts to devise an effective prices and incomes policy to combat inflation and alleviate balance-of-payments difficulties. In general the policies have rested on voluntary restraint with the exception of 1966–7 and the post-1972 statutory standstill. Since the latter, policy has moved towards greater administrative control and a lesser reliance on moral persuasion. Towards the beginning of the period policy was aimed specifically at directly influencing wages. Profits and dividends were subjected to exhortation and no more. By the mid-1960's the policy measures were aimed at both prices and wages. Before the end of the decade profits and dividends were also included. The earlier basis of policy took the root cause of inflation as rising costs due directly to wages. Initial solutions, aimed directly at this source, alienated the labour unions and a more cooperative approach did not develop until after the election in 1964. As a generalization therefore the nationalized industries did not begin to feel serious strain in terms of their prices until after 1965. From then onwards they became both a real and a symbolic part of the British Prices and Incomes Policy. In like manner their capital investment programmes were utilized as part of the 'stop-go' control of public expenditure.

The summer of 1961 brought a balance-of-payments crisis and a package of monetary and fiscal measures. A 'pay-pause' was introduced bringing a temporary halt to pay increases in the public sector and the nationalized industries. Private industry was *asked* to follow suit and companies to restrain dividends. The pause lasted nine months and its discriminatory effect on the public sector caused considerable unrest. It was followed by a 'guiding light' principle giving a voluntary norm of $2-2\frac{1}{2}$ per cent rate of increase for pay in 1962. In 1963 it was raised to $3-3\frac{1}{2}$ per cent. The policy seems to have had little effect.

In 1964 a Labour Government was elected and secured a move towards greater cooperation between unions, management, and Government with the tripartite signing of a 'statement of intent'. This had no legal force but was a common accord on prices, incomes, and economic growth. In April 1965 the National Board for Prices and Incomes was set up to report on proposed price and wage increases. In support of this procedure in November 1965 an 'early warning system' was instituted. Enterprises and employers were asked to notify the Government of intended price or wage increases. They were expected to withhold increases until the Government gave its view or the Prices Board reported.

While the machinery worked well, the norms were exceeded. Prices rose 7 per cent in the period 1964–66. The balance of payments remained in deficit and another sterling crisis occured in 1966. In mid-1966 a six-month standstill of wages, salaries, dividends and prices was brought in followed by a further six months of 'severe restraint'. At first the system was voluntary but when this proved to be insufficient it was made statutory in October 1966. The legislation expired in July 1967 and Britain reverted to a voluntary scheme which remained until the 1970's. The norms varied from zero in 1967–8 to $4\frac{1}{2}$ per cent after 1969. The Government had powers to delay increases in wages, prices and dividends. In November 1967 a growing crisis forced devaluation. In 1968 there were two deflationary budgets. Pressure on prices continued. Wage settlements despite the policy were in excess of the norms.

By the time of the election in 1970 the inflationary situation was worse with prices rising at 8 per cent and wage rates $13\frac{1}{2}$ per cent. The new Government's policy was to exert its influence on both public and private sectors to make them resist inflation pay claims.

In 1971 the Confederation of British Industry (CBI) took on and asked its members to limit price increases to 5 per cent for 12 months. This move was widely accepted. The Government imposed the same limit on the nationalized industries. In July 1972 the Government opened tripartite talks with the unions and employers on the question of a voluntary prices and incomes policy. In November 1972 these talks broke down and a Counter Inflation Act was passed on November 30. This legislation was very specific and not based on a voluntary principle. There have now been four stages. Stage 1 provided for a complete standstill (without exception) on all prices, pay, dividends, and rents.

Stage 2 commenced in April 1973. Under this legislation the Government took powers for three years to regulate prices, dividends, and rents. It established a new body in a Price Commission. A 'Code' requires all larger firms to give 28-days prior notice to the Commission of its intention to raise prices. Within this period the Commission may disallow or modify the proposal but if no action is taken the price increase may be made. Fresh foods, imports and exported goods are exempt but about two-thirds of consumers expenditure on goods and services are covered by the Commission.

The criteria for a price rise are provided in detail. It permits the covering of unavoidable 'allowable' cost increases first incurred after 30 September 1972. Allowable costs cover raw materials, fuel and power, rent, interest, transport and insurance, etc. Initially only half and then later four-fifths the increased labour costs are allowed. The difference is to be absorbed by increased labour productivity. In addition the increase in price must not raise net profit margins above the average level in the best two of the previous five years. Some leniency could be exercized in the case of loss-making companies.

Under this system which still operates, administrative control of prices is exercized by the Commission with the backing of statutory powers of enforcement. The present Price Commission shows both contrasts and similarity to the National Board for Prices and Incomes (NBIP) of 1965–71. Both were given powers of investigation and were non-political agents of Government. The latter however had references made to it and its reports were advisory. It had no powers of enforcement but nevertheless it carried great weight and was effective. The Commission needs no reference, notification is mandatory. It has statutory powers and its decisions must be accepted. The pricing of the nationalized industries has been subject to control by both these bodies. Both were established in a time of crisis. The NBPI was particularly important for the nationalized industries after 1967. The Commission was set up in 1973 and still operates. They both represent significant attempts by Government to control inflation.

British counter-inflationary policy has made significant use of the nationalized industries. Their investment programmes have been modified and their prices subject to restraint. The period of the statutory standstill in 1967 and in 1973 with the operation of the current legislation provide some contrasts. We firstly consider the control exercized over investment and then the regulation of their prices. Both aspect of regulation are superimposed on the 1961 and 1967 policies discussed in section 2.

B. Regulation via investment

Control of the macro economy by demand management using monetary and fiscal policy is an accepted function of Government. Deflationary measures can be aimed at reducing private sector consumption and investment. However in terms of speed and directness, influence only over the private sector is insufficient. Government stabilization measures also act directly on the public sector and especially the investment programmes of the nationalized industries.

According to the industries' investment evaluation procedures under the 1967 policy the quantity of investment could in principle be changed by the Government through the regulation of the TDR. This possibility is officially rejected for a number of reasons: investment may be insensitive to short-run variations in the TDR, resource mis-allocation between the public and private sectors may result, a variation in the TDR may shift the labour/capital intensity of investment against the long-run trend of factor prices, etc. While our discussion in section 2 casts doubt on the theoretical validity of the implied assumptions, nevertheless using the TDR as a control instrument for investment in the nationalized industries is rejected by the Treasury in favour of the direct manipulation of total capital expenditure.

This manipulation has not always been in the form of cuts. At the time of the election in 1970 the Conservative Party stated their intention to use the nationalized industries openly and explicitly in the control of the economy. In 1972 the industries were asked to bring forward investment projects to sustain employment. In 1963, as another example, the Government provided £ 7 million to the nationalized industries to increase spending in areas of high unemployment.

In making these adjustments the view of the Treasury is that reductions do not represent 'cuts' but 'rephasing'. They consider adjustments of up to 5 per cent on an annual programme to be 'marginal' and ones which the industries should accommodate without undue burden (19.Q.1006). Public announcements in Parliament of cuts suggest that they are a given percentage 'off the top' across all the industries but this is denied. They are emphasized as selective and result from ministerial discussions as to feasibility. The notion of rephasing is a euphemism for a cut. They can be expensive in terms of abandoned programmes and are not liked by the industries. They provide opportunities for ministerial interference in industrial management. Some ministerial cuts and initiatives however can be beneficial. In 1965–6 the demand forecasts for electricity use by the industry were too optimistic. Treasury intervention revised these downwards by 5.5 and 9.5 per cent reducing proposed capital expenditure by £ 88 million in two years (18, Appendix).

In discussing investment cuts it is not our intention to review the whole period but contrast two significant cuts made in the programmes for 1966–7 and 1973. Two aspects need consideration. Economic growth forecasts are adjusted and therefore current invest-requirements are amended. This is more routine and continually happening. It is the purpose of the Investment Review to make these adjustments in the rolling investment plan. Officially the adjustments are termed 'estimating Cuts'. In addition there are emergency cuts in government expenditure due to economic crisis that are superimposed on other adjustments. These are termed 'Policy Cuts'. The contrast we wish to make is primarily between the latter made in July 1966 at the time of the Statutory Policy on Prices and Incomes, those in November 1967 at devaluation, those in April 1973 upon the introduction of Stage 2, and those in December 1973 at the time of the energy crisis and the balance-of-payments troubles.

The emergency Policy Cuts in July 1966 amounted to £ 95 million in the capital expenditure of the nationalized industries and equalled 6 per cent of their 1967–8 programme. These cuts were announced while the 1966 Investment Review was in progress and were thus taken into account in a total cut-back (viz Policy and Estimating) of 6.5 per cent in their agreed programme. In fact the final out-turn shows that little if any cut-back occured from the industries' original submission in their Investment Review. No explanation for these discrepancies can be found and one concludes therefore that the proposed cuts did not materialize.

Turning to the other three Policy cuts, Table 1 shows both the monetary and percentage cuts in the capital expenditure involved. The date of the announced cut and the programme year affected is shown. In May 1973 this covered two years and the December 1973 were additional. The table itemises the Policy and Estimating Cuts separately.

Table 1 shows that the magnitude of the cuts both in 1967 and 1973 either in monetary or percentage terms was significant. In the case of the November and December cuts these were to programmes agreed 2 to 3 months earlier and were

Table 1. Cuts in capital expenditure 1967 and 1973. *Unit: £'s million*

Date	Nov. 1967	May 1973		Dec. 1973
Programme year affected	'68–9	'73–4	'74–5	'74–5
Policy Cut Estimating	− 70 (− 4)[+]	− 46 (− 2.5)	− 144 (− 7.0)	n.a.
Cut	− 104 (− 6)*	− 261 (− 14.4)	− 110 (− 5.3)	n.a.
Total:	− 174 (− 10)	− 307 (− 16.9)	− 254 (− 12.3)	− 264 (− 17.3)

Notes: [+] percentages
    * estimated

Sources: (18), Public Expenditure Cmnd 5519
    Midland Bank Review.
    M.D.S. May 1970

to take effect within 4 to 5 months of the announcement. Inevitably the industries affected could scarcely have had much warning and to a greater or lesser extent all were affected. The time scales involved gave rise to feelings of frustration on the part of the industries, wasted planning effort, and created additional work. The figures suggest that the size of the cuts increased between the 1960's and the 1970's. In the 1960's two Policy Cuts were made within the space of 17 months. In 1973 there were two cuts in the same year within 8 months of each other. The 1974–5 programme was cut twice.

In the 1970's a good proportion of the cuts were Estimation Cuts and resulted from reduced forecasts of national growth. Latterly the cuts are increasingly due to policy changes in attempts by Government to reduce the growth in public expenditure. However it should be noted that the cuts in capital expenditure for 1973–4 and 1974–5 are in part offset by additional government subsidies of £ 175 million per annum on revenue account. The 1973 cuts in capital expenditure affected government sectors other than the nationalized industries for example, Health and Roads. However the nationalized industries bore a heavy burden of the total reductions. In the May cuts of 1973 43 per cent of the total government cuts in 1973–4 and 28 per cent in 1974–5 was borne by the capital programmes of these industries. In the December cuts of 1973 their burden reduced slightly but not much.

Overall, these figures show the extent to which the expenditure programmes of the industries are used as economic regulators and the sizeable proportion of the total burden they are required to carry.

C. Regulation via prices

The National Board for Prices and Incomes was set up under Mr. Aubrey Jones as Chairman in 1965 and operated until disbanded by a new Government in 1971. (1) After 1967 all proposals for price increases by the nationalized industries were referred to the Board who within 3 to 5 months on average provided a report in the form of an advisory document to the Government. Some commentators have suggested the Board was a scapegoat either preventing unpopular price rises or shielding the Government from blame if they were to be allowed. In some respects this judgement is unjust as the Board presented a more positive stance and became a powerful force to be reckoned with by both Government and industry.

In the period up to 1971 there were 170 reports published, just under half of these covered price increases and the remainder wages and salaries. Twenty-five percent (19 reports)[3] covered the nationalized industries. The terms of reference of the Board explicitly required consideration of the industries' cost control and thus provided an opportunity for the consideration of efficiency, forecasting and managerial decision-making. The Board took a broad view of its functions and eight of the nineteen reports were concerned with questions of managerial efficiency and proposed methods for reducing costs. On the question of prices the Board advocated the resource allocation model expounded by the Treasury and the 1967 policy. Prices were to be based on long-run marginal cost and reports insisted that an industry's price structure moved in that direction. If costing were inadequate for the identification of long-run marginal costs, price proposals were roundly condemned. It was intended that the Boards would operate within the 1961 policy and accept the industry's financial target as datum and scrutinize the price level accordingly. In some cases the Board refused to do this, emphasizing allocative efficiency and price structure more than the price level where there was a conflict with the financial target set by the Minister.

Thus the Board played a prominent role in the price control system of the nationalized industries in the 1960's. Its establishment arose from a growing concern about inflation. It was flexible in its approach and in no way became a purely negative body preventing price change. It took every opportunity to comment on both the productive and allocative efficiency of industry. It became for the nationalized industries an enforcement agency for marginal cost pricing. It made the raising of prices considerably more difficult. The industries saw it as a source of delay and interference in their internal affairs. It was a source of irritation. On the demise of the Board in 1971 the entire responsibility for vetoing price proposals reverted to the ministries as in the pre-1965 situation.[4]

3. Viz: Rail 3 Reports, Coal 5, Gas 4, London Transport 3, GPO 2, Others 2.
4. Since 1970 some responsibility also rests with the Monopolies Commission.

From 1970–1 there existed no administrative tribunal to which a price proposal could be referred and a number of price increases were granted to the nationalized industries. As we have seen, from 1971 to 1972 there was the CBI initiative and this was imposed on the public sector by the Government. It effectively stopped any further price rise for the nationalized industries until in early 1972 a number were permitted an increase of 5 per cent which was considered inadequate to forestall deficits. From November 1972 until April 1973 all price increases were prevented by law. After April 1973 the Price Code is operative, again severely limiting the price increases the nationalized industries have been permitted to make.

The control of inflation under the Price Code represents a solution by administrative methods on a large scale. This rests on statutory powers making reference to the Commission by large firms mandatory and decisions binding. The process is one of a routine administrative system. Unlike the Board, the Commission is less concerned with principles and norms but more with pragmatic control. Its powers and duties are specific. Its deliberations must in some measure depend on judgement but appear more matters of calculation on the basis of the accounting data presented by companies. By and large prices are now regulated by an accounting control system. Judgement is speedy and effectively given within 28 days of submission. It represents a rigidity of economic control more usually found in war than in peacetime Britain. It operates on a large-scale receiving a total of 4,171 applications from large companies in the first twenty months. In three months up to November 1974 it handled 21,166 price complaints from the public covering all industries. The Commission's function is not to cure inflation since that will depend on the success of Government policy. It is rather aimed at containing the rate of price increase to the increase in 'allowable costs' and subject to restrictions on permitted company profit levels.

The Price Code also applies to the nationalized industries and they are required to submit their proposals to the Commission for scrutiny. Unlike the earlier reports of the Board very little information is published concerning submissions apart from the name of the industry, the proposed percentage increase and the increased turnover that would result. For the industries process is restrictive, emphasizing price levels and bearing little reference to the criteria of the 1967 policy. The Code pays lip service to efficiency but the submissions being based essentially on accounting data will provide little opportunity for checking such factors.

The nationalized industries, as other industries in the private sectors, went from the CBI initiative in 1972, into the standstill in 1972–3, and then into regulation under the Price Commission. However while private sector profitability was buoyant in 1972 the nationalized industries were already suffering the effects of a price restraint policy by the Government in 1971. By 1972 the majority were in deficit, owing to rising costs. Their situation deteriorated further owing to the standstill in 1973. There is some evidence to support the view that the Commission dealt particularly harshly with their price submissions. Figure 6 shows the timing of price submissions and the increased turnover permitted by the Commission's decisions. For the nationalized industries it shows a rise in applications around August 1973 which for many industries would be approximately 18 months after their previous price rise. There is also an increase in submissions 9 to 10 months later.

The approach of the Commission to the nationalized industries can be illustrated by two references submitted for an increase in electricity tariffs. One occurs in the first period identified in the Figure 6 and the second in the later period. In September–October 1973 the Electricity Council submitted proposals to the Commission on behalf of 12 Area Boards in England and Wales. These were aimed at restoring profitability and were rejected by the Commission as increases above allowable costs. The proposals were allowed in a modified form

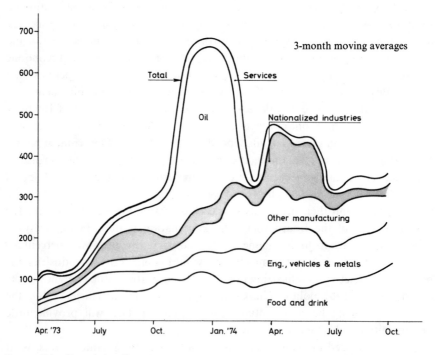

Source: Price Commission Report

Figure 6. Notification to Price Commission: amount of price increase resulting (£ million per annum)

by the Commission on the grounds that the industries were making losses. A second submission was made in June–July 1974 and allowed in full.

Taking all the Area Boards together the average submission for the industry in 1973 equalled 7.3 per cent increase and the Commission permitted 4.4 per cent. All the submissions of private sector companies averaged 8.0 per cent and the average allowed was 6.0 per cent at that time. Given losses in Electricity the reduction in their proposal seems more severe. The submission in 1974 was for an average of 4.7 per cent and not disputed. At the same time the average for all submissions in this second period was 8.6 per cent and the average allowed was 7.4 per cent. The Commissions' own index for the annual rate of price increase for large firms under the Commission's scrutiny was $9\frac{1}{2}$ per cent. In 1974 the price increase allowed in Electricity therefore was less than the going rate being permitted overall. The industry was no happier in 1974 at the workings of price restraint but their moderation was part of a Government drive in July 1974 to reduce the rate of increase in the cost of living and forestall wage increases automatically linked to it. A further reason was that since May 1974 domestic prices had a fuel adjustment factor added along the lines common for the industrial user. The Government had also begun paying subsidies to the nationalized industries to compensate them for the effects of the price restraint policy. In 1972 British Railways negotiated a payment from the Government of £ 27 million from the Government as compensation for lost revenues during 1971–2 (Industry's Annual Report 1971–2). The Treasury estimate for the costs of price restraint on all the nationalized industries together in 1972–3 was £ 150 million (19). They accepted the principle that compensation was both justified and needed. In 1973/4 and 1974/5 total subsidies paid to the industries in compensation was £ 175 million in each year.

4. Conclusions

The effects of the price restraint policy can be summarized under three headings. The first is the direct, short-run, financial cost. As measured by the industry's shortfall on their financial target the electricity industry had a reduced revenue of £ 172 million in 1971, £ 98 million in 1972, and an accumulated shortfall in the first three years of their quinquennial target of £ 269 million. The gas industry similarly suffered by £ 23 million in 1970. A further dimension is provided by the delays caused by a Prices and Incomes Board investigation. The gas industry estimates that the holding-up of their increases accepted in the end by the Board in 1965 cost the industry £ $2\frac{3}{4}$ million. A report by the same body in 1970 delayed the increase in prices by 12 months at a cost to the industry of £ 15 million in lost revenues that could not in retrospect be recouped. Financial costs are also increased due to the lower financial surpluses earned and increased debt. The electricity industry estimates the reduced self-finance between 1969–71 raised the interest charges to the industry in 1971 by £9 million. The financial burdens placed on the Exchequer are increased either by the need to fund additional investment capital or the payment of special subsidies as in 1973–5.

A further longer-term misallocation occurs through the effect price constraint has on investment. This is primarily of an economic nature through the distortion abnormally low prices introduce into investment criteria. On the one hand low prices depress the NPV of investment in the DCF calculation. On the other as discussed above, investment is in the view of the industries the result of their statutory obligations to meet forecasted demand. Low prices stimulate demand, increase the need for future capacity and therefore the need for current investment. The industry either accepts the actual prices and plans accordingly or they take a long-term view and invest on the basis of what prices ought to be rather than what they are. This reflects the classic dilemma of the nationalized industries in the last 2–3 years (19, Evidence). The electricity industry has estimated that as a result of price restraint in the last six years, extra investment in the region of £400–500 million is required.

The third effect of price restraint refers to the financial targets of the industries and their managerial effect. The rationale was discussed above but as a result of price restraint and rapidly rising cost in the seventies the five-year targets set in 1968 have become meaningless. Indeed that of the Post Office expired in 1972–3 and no action was taken to renew it. Generally speaking the system of financial targets has perforce been abandoned since 1972 as unattainable. The Treasury admits that in current conditions it does not know what their levels ought to be.[19] In consequence management incentive is diminished and morale is low. The electricity industry reports with some bitterness that owing to price control they went into deficit in 1971 for the first time in their history.

Increasing concern over inflation and the performance of the British economy has brought a change in attitude from the Government. Despite efforts public expenditure has been increasing rapidly and determined efforts are in hand to reverse this trend. Until 1974 the cause of inflation was attributed to rapid rises in fuel costs and world commodities in the first instance and then general pressure of demand. Since mid 1974 the pressure has come from inflationary wage awards and the approach of the Chancellor recently has been to cease cushioning the economy from the full effects of inflation by subsidies. He is deflating the economy and allowing unemployment to rise. This change of policy has had major repercussions on the nationalized industries. In the Budget of November 1974 it was announced that the price subsidies (i.e. £175 million), especially those for energy, would be phased out as soon as possible and prices allowed to rise. In December 1974 Stage 4 of the Price Code came into force. Besides expanding the definition of 'allowable cost', it specifically relaxed the profit constraint applied to the nationalized industries. Under Stage 3 price increases had been permitted, not to allow attainment of the industries' financial targets (which had had either lapsed or were being disregarded) but only to offset deficits. The new provision effectively reinstates the targets by allowing the nationalized industries to secure either 2 per cent on turnover or 10 per cent on net assets. Actual pricing up to these limits is subject to ministerial discretion but the Code itself is considerably more liberal. As a result of the new policy electricity prices for domestic consumers were permitted to rise by 28.5 per cent in April 1975. The application to the Price Commission had been for 31 per cent and was reduced by only 2.5 per cent. In addition fuel adjustment charges will automatically increase, raising prices an estimated 40 per cent by July 1975. The rise in the basic price for industrial uses is 7.5 per cent.

A recent plea from the industries is to be allowed to return to 'normality' and the 'policy of 1967'. The review of the last fifteen years casts some doubt on the definition of 'normality'. The financial targets were implemented from 1962–3, ineffective due to the crisis in 1967–8, and inoperative since 1972. To date therefore the system has worked for nine years out of fourteen. Marginal cost pricing – we have suggested – was somewhat overemphasized particularly by the Select Committee. Even so, in the eight years since 1967 it can have been a serious consideration in practice until say 1971, since which time the pressure of price restraint has emphasized a preference for average cost and financial viability in place of long-term economic efficiency.

The evidence shows that in terms of the pricing freedom of the industries since 1960, a considerable number of price adjustments took place up to the standstill of 1967. In the remaining eight years to 1975 price restraint has been the normal situation and was becoming increasingly severe until very recently. One must conclude that the price regulation in the 1960's was more of a nuisance and a strain for the nationalized industries. In the 1970's it made their situation impossible.

References

1. Fels, A., *The Prices and Incomes Board*, 1972.
2. Hadar, J., *Mathematical Theory of Economic Behavior*, 1971.
3. Hadley, G., *Non-linear and Dynamic Programming*, 1964.
4. Hotelling, H., The General Welfare in Relation to problems of Taxation and of Railway and Utility Rates. *Econometrica*, 1938.

5. Kaplan, Dirlam, and Lanzillotti, *Pricing in Big Business*, 1958.
6. Little, I. M. D., *A Critique of Welfare Economics*, 1957.
7. Littlechild, S., Pricing Telephone Service *Bell Journal of Economics and Management Science*, Autumn 1970.
8. Mishan, E. J., Second thoughts on Second-best *Oxford Economic Papers*, 1962.
9. Nath, S. K., *A Reappraisal of Welfare Economics*, 1969.
10. Naylor and Vernon, *Micro Economics and Decision Models of the Firm*, 1969.
11. Nove, A., *Efficiency Criteria for Nationalised Industries*, 1973.
12. Pressman, I., Peak Load Pricing *Bell Journal op.cit.*, Autumn 1970.
13. Rees, R., Second Best Rules for Public Enterprise Pricing, *Economica*, 1968.
14. Ruggles, N., Recent Developments in the theory of Marginal Cost Pricing *Review of Economic Studies*, 1949–50.
15. Shepherd, W. G., *Economic Performance under Public Ownership British Fuel & Power*, 1956.
16. Turvey, R., *Economic Analysis and Public Enterprise*, 1971.
17. Wiseman, J., The Theory of Public Utility Price – an empty box. *Oxford Economic Papers*, 1957.
18. *First Report from the Select Committee on Nationalised Industries*, Ministerial Control of the Nationalised Industries (3 volumes), 1968.
19. *First Report from the Select Committee on Nationalised Industries*, Capital Investment Procedures, 1973.
20. *The Financial and Economic Obligations of the Nationalised Industries*, Cmnd 1337, HMSO, 1961.
21. Nationalised, *A Review of Economic and Financial Objectives*. Cmnd 3437, HMSO, 1967.

XVIII. FRENCH ANTITRUST LEGISLATION: AN EXERCISE IN FUTILITY

Frédéric Jenny and André-Paul Weber

The statutes[1] enacted in France in 1953 and modified in 1967 prohibit agreements, express or tacit, which tend towards, or might lead to impair, competition; particularly agreements which might prevent a decrease in production costs or in the market price of products, agreements which encourage an artificial price increase, agreements which prevent technical progress, and to an agreement which prevents free competition by firms not party to the agreement. The statutes also prohibit anticompetitive behaviour by individual firms which have either a monopoly position or an 'obvious power' on the market.

The same statutes exempt from the aforementioned prohibition agreements which result from legislation and those for which producers can show that gains in efficiency or technical progress will be achieved as a by-product.

A Commission[2] serving as an advisory board to the Minister of Finance and Economic Affairs is entrusted with the enforcement of the statutes. The Commission currently has fourteen members: six civil servants, six representatives of the business community and two economists. The Minister of Finance and Economic Affairs must, or any court of law may, ask the Commission for its advice on any particular agreement; the Commission also may act on its own initiative. After debating a case, the commission makes recommendations to the Minister of Finance and Economic Affairs; so far, the Minister has always followed the Commission's recommendations. The Commission's recommendations fall into two categories:

1. From a legal standpoint, the Commission determines whether in its opinion an agreement is of a type prohibited by the statutes, whether there is sufficient cause to exempt it, and if it is a prohibited agreement which cannot be exempted, whether the case should be taken to court.
2. From an economic standpoint, the Commission can make general policy

---

1. Ordonnance n° 45.1483, 30 June 1945.
2. The Commission's full name is: *Commission Technique des Ententes et des Positions Dominantes*. In this paper it will be referred to as: the Commission.

recommendations concerning the structure of the industry, acceptable forms of agreements, the necessity for government surveillance of the firms etc.

The Commission considers these economic recommendations to be an essential part of its role. Accordingly in its 1954 'report to the Minister', the Commission stated that:

'It will, in each case, attempt to show to the firms concerned and if need be to the Government, the path which each one should follow in order to contribute effectively to economic progress and thus benefit both the consumer and the economy at large'.[3]

As French courts of law have little or no understanding of economic matters, they tend to rely on the Commission's judgement of whether or not an agreement is prohibited by the statutes. For this reason, although the Commission is merely an advisory board, it has an indirect judicial power. Thus France fits Corwin Edwards'[4] description of European attitudes towards antitrust: 'Whereas American political institutions were formulated after overthrowing colonial status, under the influence of a philosophy that distrusted concentrated governmental power and in a setting affected by the individualism of the frontier, European political institutions have evolved gradually from origins of monarchy in the state and hierarchy in the church ... The European libertarian movements that expressed distrust of state power and sought to curtail state functions found their program in guarantees of freedom of contract and freedom of association ... But as the market economy developed, free association came to mean that businessmen were free to form cartels, and free contract came to include the right to make agreements by which the parties impaired free trade and free competition. Thus the programs that challenged the power of the state tended to strengthen rather than to challenge the power of cartels. It is understandable that as programs to curb cartels developed they tended to accept and rely upon a broad exercise of the regulatory power of the state as a major instrument of control. '(These) inherited attitudes ... have resulted in cartel laws which characteristically grant broad discretion to public officials to amend cartels in accord with their own view of the public interest'.

To assess the efficiency of the French competition enforcement system, it is necessary to study in detail the Commission's position on key questions. Basically we will argue that the enforcement of competition in France has largely been an exercise in futility for the following reasons:

3. *Rapport de la Commission* n° 1193.1, p. 46.
4. Corwin Edwards *Cartelization in Western Europe*, Washington DC, US Department of State, 1964 pp. 46–47 (quoted in F. M. Scherer *Industrial Market Structure and Economic Performance*, Rand Mc. Nally, Chicago, 1970, p. 442).

1. Poor judgement on the part of the Commission due to its frequently blind acceptance of unproved conventional ideas among public policy makers such as the advantages of large firm size or that competition has to be 'organized'. The Commission has also shown its inability to cope with the problem of monopolies;
2. Lack of interest in the French government for the general problem of enforcement of competition, this lack of interest has had the following effects:
   a. The means (both in terms of finance and men) given to the Commission are extremely limited restricting its ability to appraise correctly the real and potential effects of cartels, and to examine more than a highly limited number of cases each year;
   b. Other Ministries, and particularly the Ministry of Industry, ignore the Commission. There is a basic inconsistency between the actions of many technical Ministries which encourage implicitly or explicitly firms to cartelize their industries and the Commission's work;
3. Chauvinistic attitude on the part of the various French administrations which have always refused to cooperate with the EEC Commission whenever French firms were involved.
4. Finally, the inability of courts (due to their lack of understanding of economic problems) to deal with anticompetitive agreements without first asking the advice of the Commission limits considerably the deterrent effect of judicial action.

This paper is divided into four parts. The first part describes the prohibited agreements, the second part details the conditions of exemptions, then in part 3 the recommendations of the Commission to the Minister of Finance and Economic Affairs are analyzed, finally the policy implications of the analysis are presented.

1. Prohibited agreements

The original 1953 statutes prohibited only 'agreements, express or tacit, which encourage the artificial increase of prices or prevent a decrease in the cost of production'. Thus the price variable was the principal basis for determining which agreements were prohibited and which were not. Because, during its early years of activity, the Commission chose to use a strictly literal interpretation of the statutes, many agreements whose principal aim was to raise barriers to entry or which could not be shown to directly affect the price level were not declared illegal. The statutes were modified in 1967[5] and their scope broadened but, as will be implicitly obvious below, the Commission has not been able to apply the new statutes comprehensively and has to a large extent continued to focus its attention on the price variable.

For an agreement to be declared illegal a direct link has to be established between the agreement and the alleged violation. The violation may be real or potential. The Commission being an administrative body has more freedom than a court regarding standards of proof. Specifically, as early as 1958, in the case of an alleged violation of the statutes by manufacturers of steel railway switches[6] the Commission held that although the firms denied having entered an agreement, there was enough circumstantial evidence to deal with the case as if the agreement had in fact existed. The Commission has consistently held this view ever since. Accordingly in the case of steel wire manufacturers,[7] the Commission held that the monthly publication of orders and deliveries of the individual producers, the stability of the market share of each firm, the publication of a price list by the trade association and the actual identity of individual firms' prices with the price list formed sufficient evidence to prove the existence of a prohibited agreement.

An interesting implication of the Commission's reasoning lies in the fact that regardless of whether parallel pricing behaviour by a set of firms results from implicit agreement or independent decisions, it is likely to be considered illegal. In a case that dealt with the plaster industry,[8] the Commission held that simultaneous increases in price of the same magnitude by the firms involved over a period of time violated the statutes despite the fact that no signs of an explicit agreement could be found and no collusive behaviour was noted as far as market sharing, investing etc., were concerned.

However in 1972,[9] the Commission specified the fact that it would consider parallel pricing a violation of the statutes only in the case of price increases and only if the product concerned was not subject to price control. In the sandstone tile case,[10] the manufacturers argued that if production techniques are similar within the industry and if there is competition among the firms then pricing should be identical. Although the Commission agreed on the theoretical validity of this argument, it did not think that such an argument could be used to assess the competitive nature of an industry characterized by a consistent pattern of

---

5. *Ordonnance* n° 67.835, 28 september 1967.
6. *Rapport de la Commission Technique des Ententes* n° 1193.1, p. 45.
7. *Rapport de la Commission* n° 1193.72, p. 3.
8. *Rapport de la Commission, entente dans l'industrie du platre, 6.12.1972, Journal Officiel* – II January 1974.
9. *Rapport de la Commission Technique des Ententes, Journal Officiel*, n° 2, II January 1974, p. 25.
10. *Idem* n° 66. 19 July 1974, pp. 2614–2617.

simultaneous price increases of the same magnitude. It held that in the real world, in the case of a competitive industry, one could expect short-term differences in cost due to differences in the timing of investments and occasional attempts by individual firms to increase their market share by decreasing their price-cost margins.

The specific practices prohibited

Four types of practices are held illegal: market sharing, price fixing, cartelized volume discounts, and abuse of market power. In each case, after having succinctly described the practices criticized by the Commission, both the Commission's position and the reasoning underlying it are analyzed. The Commission appears to have significantly improved its economic reasoning in the last few years.

1. *Market sharing and production quotas.* This practice, whether implicit or explicit, seems to be extremely widespread. Numerous variants can be observed: production quotas (with or without penalties for firms producing more than their alloted quotas), geographical division of markets among firms, pure market sharing, fixed allocation of customers among the firms with fines levied on firms dealing with customers which were not attributed to them, etc. In most cases, either the trade association or a special association set up for this purpose enforces the agreement. Firms are required to send a duplicate of every invoice to the enforcement association. In a few cases, the association uses inspectors to check the accounts of member firms.

The Commission has always taken a dim view of rigid production quotas and market-sharing agreements. In its first case,[11] the Commission dealt with the problem only indirectly. Indeed it argued that in the industry examined, the fines levied on firms that produced more than their alloted quotas would increase the firm's costs and that therefore the agreement was illegal. It is clear that in this case the Commission used an extremely weak argument since one could argue that firms whose productions were inferior to their quotas received these fines and that their unit costs were decreased. The Commission's position in this case seems to result from an excessively litt~ral interpretation of the statutes.

The Commission changed its reasoning quite rapidly and held, starting in 1955,[12] that market sharing and production quotas are illegal practices because

11. *Rapport de la Commission Technique des Ententes n° 1193.1, entente dans l'industrie des savons de ménage, avis du 23 Avril 1955,* p. 8 (soap industry).
12. *Rapport de la Commission Technique des Ententes n° 1193.1, entente dans l'industrie et le commerce de la levure de panification,* 24 September 1955, p. 9 (Yeast industry).

they are usually designed to protect less efficient firms that would have disappeared or lost a significant market share if competition had prevailed; they contribute to a misallocation of resources which in itself leads to an increase in unit costs and therefore should be prohibited.

Between 1957 and 1963 the Commission qualified its thinking on these problems in a number of ways. First it held that fixed production quotas and market sharing are illegal even if they are not respected in fact. Second if the agreement calls for flexible quotas or market shares but if this flexibility does not occur, the agreement is also held illegal. On the contrary, in the flat glass industry case,[13] the Commission stated that it is not averse to systems of production quotas or market sharing if such arrangements provide for flexibility and if the flexibility is not purely theoretical. Indeed the Commission believes that such flexible market sharing might give the firms sufficient security, at least in the short run, to entice them to develop important investment programs that they would not engage in otherwise. Thus the Commission holds that in industries in which minimum efficient scales of plants are comparatively large and in which there are high capital costs, flexible market sharing and production quotas are not necessarily illegal. The Commission held that the argument does not apply, for example, in the case of the steel wire drawing industry because in this industry which has a simple technology, minimum efficient scales are small and capital costs not important enough.

The Commission's view can be criticized on at least two grounds:

- firm's decisions regarding heavy investments programs are more likely to be geared to long-run prospects rather than short-run ones and it would seem that short-run fixity of market share is therefore quite irrelevant to the investment process (or at least only a minor consideration).
- the Commission basically argues that investment performances will be better (that is that the rate of investment will be higher) in industries in which market shares of individual firms are relatively stable than in industries in which there is a high level of instability in market shares. The empirical validity of such an assertion could only be assessed by an inter-industry comparison of investment performances. To our knowledge neither the Commission nor anyone in France has done such a study.

2. *Price fixing.* Price fixing is probably the most common collective anticompetitive practice in France. Price-fixing methods are similar to those observed elsewhere. In very simple cartels, it may be the only provision of the agreement. It is also quite often associated with market sharing in more sophisticated

13. *Idem, entente dans l'industrie du verre plat,* 23 January 1957, p. 36 (flat glass industry).

agreements. In some cases both price and selling conditions are agreed upon by the manufacturers and/or distributors. Fines can be levied upon firms that try to undercut other cartel members or upon distributors who give unauthorized discounts to customers. Parallel pricing behaviour can also be observed. Finally in a number of cases involving more than one product, elaborate schemes are set up by the manufacturers who have fixed the various prices so that the firms who manufacture the products for which the price cost margin is the smallest can be compensated by firms selling products on which the margin is higher. It is also worth mentioning that frequently in the case of collusive tendering the pre-designated lowest bidder makes his price known to the other members of the cartel to ensure that they will not underbid him.

The Commission has always held that standard price fixing agreements are illegal for two reasons:

- because in the short run they lead to prices that exceed competitive prices and such are a direct violation of the antitrust statutes;
- because in the long run they permit the survival of marginal firms and hamper the reallocation of resources.

In its 1960–1963 report[14] the Commission gave a list of specific practices that it held *per se* illegal.

1. All price-fixing agreements accompanied by compensation schemes whatever their stated motives. Thus in the case of producers of superphosphates[15] who were trying to fix the market price and to compensate those firms which had to pay a higher price for their raw materials, the agreement was considered to be a violation of the statutes. A compensation scheme was again held illegal in the case of producers of road materials[16] who used a system of uniform delivered price so that firms far from the market location would not be at a disadvantage. The Commission rightly considered that such a system would lead to inefficiencies in the transportation of ponderous materials.
2. Posted price list and uniform discounts are illegal if they are associated with a system of fines for firms cutting prices (scythes and sickles industry,[17]

14. *Rapport de la Commission Technique des Ententes, Journal Officiel n° 2*, 7 February 1964.
15. *Rapport de la Commission Technique des Ententes, Journal Officiel n° 2*, 7 February 1964, *entente dans l'industrie du superphosphate*, 21 May 1960, p. 18 (superphosphate industry).
16. *Rapport de la Commission Technique des Ententes, Journal Officiel n° 2*, 7 February 1964, *entente dans le marché des matériaux de viabilité*, 6 November 1960, p. 22 (road material market).
17. *Rapport de la Commission Technique des Ententes, Journal Officiel n° 2*, 7 February 1964, *entente entre fabricants de faux et faucilles*, 17 March 1961, p. 26 (Scythes and sickles).

shippers[18]) or if they are followed in fact (imported lumber,[19] eyeglass lenses[20]).

3. Systematic similarity of prices even without a posted price list is, also illegal as we have seen above (linoleum industry[21]).

Thus identical pricing is held illegal in most cases. But with respect to posted price lists the Commission takes an ambiguous position. In 1960 it recognized the fact that such publications by a trade association may contribute to better information of customers and may also help firms to evaluate their costs when a number of small firms without a sophisticated system of accounting are concerned.[22] For these reasons, the Commission held in 1962 that the publication of price lists by a trade association is not in itself automatically illegal. In the 1967 water meter case,[23] the Commission considered that if a trade association publishes a price list only for information purposes and if it does not recommend that members adhere to the price list, there is no violation of the statutes. But the conditions for the validity of this practice were restricted by the Commission in 1972. Namely, in the plant nursery case[24] the Commission held that trade association price lists would be considered legal only if they reported past transactions. The Commission thought that if the price lists reported anything but past transactions, there would be an implicit incentive for member firms to adhere to the posted prices. Although the Commission did not state explicitly that information on past transactions should not identify the firms who have conducted particular transactions, it seems fair to assume that this is implicit in its 1972 reasoning.

The Commission also devotes a great deal of its time to the question of pricing behaviour regarding tender offers because of the importance of the public sector in France. The Commission feels that local governments and public utilities are particularly vulnerable to market sharing with price fixing because they are responsible for the continuity of public services and because of the special

18. *Rapport de la Commission Technique des Ententes, Journal Officiel n° 2*, 7 February 1964, *entente entre armateurs et transitaires*, 21 April 1961, p. 28 (Shippers).

19. *Rapport de la Commission Technique des Ententes, Journal Officiel n° 2*, 7 February 1964, *entente entre importateurs de Bois du Nord*, 17 December 1960, p. 24 (Lumber importers).

20. *Rapport de la Commission Technique des Ententes, Journal Officiel n° 2*, 7 February 1964, *entente dans l'industrie de verres de lunettes*, 16 June 1961, p. 31 (Eyeglass lenses).

21. Cf. Linoleum industry, 21 october 1961, *Journal Officiel n° 2*, 7 February 1964, p. 33.

22. *Rapport de la Commission Technique des Ententes*, n° 1193-69, *Entente entre fabricants d'échelles en bois*, 19 May 1967, p. 5 (wooden ladder manufacturers).

23. *Rapport de la Commission Technique des Ententes*, n° 1193-67, *entente dans l'industrie des compteurs d'eau*, 18 March 1966, p. 33 (Water meter manufacturers).

24. *Rapport de la Commission Technique des Ententes, Journal Officiel n° 2*, 11 January 1974, *entente entre pépiniéristes*, 21 January 1972, p. 29 (plant nursery industry).

administrative procedures which they are required to follow when contracting with private firms. Two problems are discussed by the Commission in this respect. On the one hand unrealistic bids when made to ensure that the firm predesignated by the cartel to get the contract will be the lowest bidder are held to be illegal.[25] On the other hand, on a purely empirical level, the Commission came to recognize the fact that local governments and public utilities tend to consult only those firms which have submitted bids for previous tender contracts. Therefore a number of firms not interested in a particular contract send a wholly unrealistic bid, not to get the contract, but to make sure that they will be kept informed of future tender offers.

Although deploring such practices, the Commission has no power to change them and in those instances where unrealistic bids are not associated with predetermination of the lowest bidder by an agreement between the potential competitors, the Commission does not hold that the statutes are violated.

Cartelized volume discounts and barriers to entry

In most instances in France, as would be expected, anticompetitive behaviour is associated with high concentration on the sellers' side. But for anticompetitive collusive practices to be successful, firms have to be protected from potential competition. In many instances, there are fairly strong natural barriers to entry; in others collusive behaviour of firms may succeed in preventing potential competition. The most frequent strategies, when natural barriers to entry such as economies of scale, high capital costs, or product differentiation are weak, are either to set up a system of cartelized volume discounts or to prevent firms which are not part of the agreement from having access to a professional card or a seal of quality delivered by the trade association. It is also possible to deny non-member firms access to raw materials when members of a cartel integrate backward and are able to secure a monopoly on the raw materials market. Similarly, member firms can also use their market power at the retail outlet level and share their monopoly profits with retailers to successfully prevent potential competitors from offering goods to consumers. At an international level, market sharing that successfully decreases the pressure of potential foreign competition is also extremely widespread.

Whenever a group of firms attempts to cartelize a particular market by monopolizing a different market or by entering an international market-sharing

25. *Rapport de la Commission Technique des Ententes*, n° 1193-67, *entente entre installateurs de lignes électriques à haute tension*, 19 February 1966, p. 31 (installers of high tension electrical equipment).

agreement, it is highly likely that this attempt will go undetected by the Commission for the following two reasons:

- the Commission restricts its investigation to the narrowly defined market on which the alleged violation has taken place. This occurs both because of bad economic reasoning and because of the Commission's limited means;
- mainly for chauvinistic reasons, in France, there is a traditional lack of cooperation with the EEC Commission whenever French firms are involved in international cartels.

For these reasons, the Commission's performance in detecting systematic behaviour of protection from potential competition has been dismal to say the least. From this point of view, it is particularly significant that the Commission has never tried to analyze why in some instances entry to a particular market has not occurred in several decades. On the whole, the importance of potential competition to ensure competitive performances in individual markets has never been correctly analyzed.

Cartelized volume discounting is the only type of artificial barrier to entry that has been systematically investigated probably both because it is the easiest to detect, and because it most visibly affects pricing.

In 1957, in the agricultural hand tools case,[26] the Commission held that cartelized volume discount practices are prohibited by the statutes only if their aim is to prevent potential competition. If, on the other hand, the possibility of potential competition can be excluded *a priori*, as in the aforementioned case because the industry is declining, these practices are held legal because they may help to prevent inefficient distribution of a product. Indeed in this case the Commission was favourable to the fact that the manufacturers had set up a common selling agency. In this instance the Commission's reasoning can be criticized on two counts:

- The Commission stated further on in its discussion of the industry that the upcoming lowering of tariff barriers due to EEC agreements will by itself prevent any attempt to set prices at non-competitive levels. This would then indicate that in the Commission's own judgement foreign competition could not be discounted *a priori* and that therefore the purpose of the cartelized volume discounts may very well have been to prevent potential competition.
- It is not obvious that a common selling agency will necessarily substantially decrease selling costs. The Commission's underlying reasoning is that there are

26. *Rapport de la Commission Technique des Ententes, n° 1193-1, entente entre fabricants d'outils agricoles à main,* 22 June 1957, p. 34 (manufacturers of agricultural hand tools).

scale economies of distribution. Although this may be the case, further evidence would be needed.

In 1963[27] the Commission took a stronger stand on cartelized volume discounts and held them illegal barring 'exceptional circumstances'. In two instances the Commission held that the circumstances were exceptional and that therefore the cartelized volume discounts concerned were not in violation of the statutes.

In the semi-finished copper products case[28] the Commission held that the discounts were too small to significantly deter potential competitors; in the cotton spinner case[29] the exemption was based on the fact that the cartelized volume discounts had been set by a group of small firms who were competing against much larger firms, the fact that cotton spinning was a declining industry, and finally the fact that the discounts were small.

It is difficult to understand why the Commission does not apply a *per se* prohibition of cartelized volume discounts. One could indeed argue that if the discounts are not of significant magnitude, presumably the competitive situation of the firms will not be affected if such discounts are prohibited or that if they are high enough to deter internal or international competition they are in direct violation of the statutes. What is more from a theoretical point of view there seems to be no economic justification for such a practice.

The Commission has focused its attention on cartelized volume discounts and apparently has held volume discounts by individual firms legal.[30] As many economists have argued, a strong case can be made against individual volume discounts.[31] This would seem to be all the more relevant in France where monopolies are frequent.

In three cases the Commission had to deal with outright attempts to exclude competitors. In the first case (advertising)[32] entry into the industry was made impossible without a professional card delivered by the trade association. The Commission held that such a practice could be legal only if Government

---

27. *Rapport de la Commission Technique des Ententes, Journal Officiel n° 2*, 7 February 1964, p. 13.

28. *Rapport de la Commission Technique des Ententes, n° 1193-67, entente entre fabricants de demi-produits en métaux cuivreux*, 22 March 1963, p. 6 (manufacturers of semi finished copper products).

29. *Rapport de la Commission Technique des Ententes, n° 1193-70, entente dans l'industrie de la filature de coton cardé du Nord et de l'Ouest*, 22 March 1968, p. 6 (Cotton spinning industry).

30. *Rapport de la Commission Technique des Ententes, Journal Officiel n° 66*, 19 July 1974, *situation de la concurrence dans l'industrie du ramassage et de la régénération des huiles usagées*, 28 March 1973, p. 2609 (recycling of used oil).

31. See 'Volume Discounts as Barriers to Entry and Access', Robert C. Brooks Jr., in *Readings in the Regulation of Business*, Scranton Penn., International Textbook Cny, 1968, pp. 78–87.

32. *Rapport de la Commission Technique des Ententes, n° 1193-1, entente professionnelle dans le domaine de la publicité*, 15 January 1958, p. 38 (advertising).

supervision insured its fairness. Similarly in the petroleum tank case[33] the Commission held that a guarantee of product quality given by a trade association would not violate the statutes if the guarantee was given in a fair and impartial way. Finally in the photographic processing laboratories case[34] the three largest firms succeeded in monopolizing contracts for developing army films (with obvious complicity of their customer) although they apparently had not overcharged the army for their services. The Commission held this last practice, intended to prevent free competition, to be a violation of the statutes.

Dominant position and abuse of market power

The 1963 amendments to the statutes[35] extended their scope to individual firms or groups of firms having a monopoly or a dominant position on a market when there is an intent or a possibility to abuse market power. Unfortunately between 1963 and 1973, only six cases were examined by the Commission exclusively under this new provision. One can nevertheless begin to answer two questions pertaining to the abuse of market power:

- How does the Commission define dominant position?
- What constitutes an abuse of market power?

Before tackling those questions, it is worth recalling that in its 1960–1963 report the Commission noted that a dominant position in itself is not considered illegal in France. On this point, the Commission went so far as mentioning that 'not only is it legal to acquire a dominant position on a market, but the prejudice caused to other firms in trying to monopolize a market is not considered an abuse if this power is acquired through legal means.'[36] The Commission's position on this point is consistent with French industrial policy over the last twenty years which has encouraged horizontal mergers on the assumption (or rather the common idea) that the larger the firms, the more efficient and competitive they will be. Although there is some empirical evidence undermining this assumption, both

---

33. *Rapport de la Commission Technique des Ententes, Journal Officiel n° 66*, 19 July 1974, *Situation de la concurrence dans l'industrie des cuves et citernes à hydrocarbures*, 18 May 1973, p. 2612 (manufacturers of petroleum tanks).
34. *Rapport de la Commission Technique des Ententes, n° 2193-72, entente entre laboratoires de développement et tirage de films*, 16 January 1970, p. 5 (photographic processing laboratories).
35. *Loi du 27 juillet 1963.*
36. *Rapport de la Commission Technique des Ententes, n° 1193-72, situation de la concurrence dans le secteur des services funéraires*, 18 June 1971, p. 12 (funeral industry).

for France and at the European level,[37] debate on the advantages (or disadvantages) of firm sizes had been largely limited to academic circles and had not yet permeated the closed world of public policy makers. Even though dominant position is not illegal per se, it is still necessary to define it in order to apply the statutes regarding abuse of market power.

How does the Commission define dominant position? In the case of showing of commercial films on TV[38] the Commission held that presentation of films on TV and in theatres were substitutes and that TV has a dominant position on this market mainly on the basis of the fact that there was strong indication that when films were shown on TV, there was a significant decrease in attendance at movie theaters. This case being somewhat out of the ordinary, the Commission later tried to define dominant position in structural terms. In the funeral industry case,[39] it held that one firm which had more than 50 per cent of the main market (and a monopoly on the particularly small market of funeral homes) had a dominant position. The Commission based its judgement on the fact that the other 50 per cent of the market was shared by a large number of very small firms. Thus the Commission seems to consider that both the absolute market share of the firm under consideration and the distribution of firm size in the industry are relevant criteria for the definition of 'dominant position'. In the 1973 vinyl pipes case,[40] the Commission held that if a firm had less than 25 per cent of a market and if the rest was divided among a limited number of firms, it could not conclude that there was a dominant position. Although the Commission has not expressed itself further on this point, it seems that in the future it will give a more precise structural definition of dominant position.

What constitutes an abuse of power by a firm in a dominant position? Again the limited number of cases examined makes it impossible to have a clear idea on this point. On the one hand, the sheer use of market power to set prices at a monopoly level (cement case)[41] or the exclude potential or real competitors (plastic

---

37. A. P. Jacquemin et M. Cardon de Lichtbuer. Size structure, stability and performance of the largest British and EEC firms, *European Economic Review*, Dec. 1973.

38. *Rapport de la Commission Technique des Ententes, n° 1193-72, Journal Officiel n° 2,* 11 January 1974, *Films cinématographiques à la télévision,* 22 November 1968 (showing of Commercial films on TV).

39. *Rapport de la Commission Technique des Ententes, n° 1193-72, situation de la concurrence dans le secteur des services funéraires,* 18 June 1971, p. 12 (funeral industry).

40. *Rapport de la Commission Technique des Ententes, Journal Officiel n° 66,* 19 July 1974, *entente dans l'industrie des tuyaux en chlorure de polyvinyle,* 17 October 1973, p. 2619 (Vinyl pipes industry).

41. *Rapport de la Commission Technique des Ententes, n° 1193-71, entente dans l'industrie des ciments et liants hydrauliques,* 20 June 1969, p. 9 (Cement industry).

container case)[42] are held to violate the statutes. On the other hand volume discounts by a firm in a dominant position do not seem to be illegal *per se* (recycled oil case)[43] unless they are used to further a more general strategy of exclusion of competitors. Finally in its 1972 report,[44] the Commission expressed the same idea that it had for cartel agreements, that is, there should be a direct causal link between the violation and the firm's dominant position.

The considerations lead us to raise a few questions about the implicit logic of the Commission's system for dealing with the problem of dominant positions. More specifically, if one argues that the setting of price above marginal cost is socially harmful, and if one thinks that a firm without market power will not be able to escape the pressure of competition, then it would seem that antitrust authorities should concern themselves only with the actual performances of firms, irrespective of their market share. On the other hand, one could take the position that continued control of individual firms' performances is not feasible and that therefore the key control variable should be the market share of firms. The underlying assumption of this reasoning is that an excessively high level of concentration (i.e. level of concentration significantly higher than that which is required to benefit from scale economies) on individual markets should be prohibited because it may have socially harmful consequences.

The Commission's rule for controlling firms having a dominant position seems to be neither a strict performance rule nor a simple structural one. Some behaviour (particularly setting price above marginal cost) seems to be considered acceptable if the firm's market share is below a certain level (because it is assumed that it is in a relatively competitive environment) but is deemed illegal once the firm reaches a given relative size on the market. In other words depending on the firm's market share, different standards are applied to decide whether or not its behaviour violates the antitrust statutes. Unfortunately the Commission has not so far made clear which is the critical size level and which behaviour it will focus on to determine abuse of market power by a firm having a dominant position.

All in all the Commission seems to rely more and more on *per se* rules to declare agreements in violation of the statutes. But to appreciate fully the efficiency of the

42. *Rapport de la Commission Technique des Ententes, n° 1193-72, pratiques anti-concurrentielles dans l'industrie des casiers à bouteilles en matière plastique*, 17 March 1971, p. 11 (Plastic container industry).
43. *Rapport de la Commission Technique des Ententes, Journal Officiel n° 66,* 19 July 1974, *situation de la concurrence dans l'industrie du ramassage et de la régénération des huiles usagées,* 28 March 1973, p. 2609 (Recycled oil industry).
44. *Rapport de la Commission Technique des Ententes, Journal Officiel n° 2,* 11 January 1974, p. 26.

French antitrust system, one must examine the conditions under which otherwise illegal agreements can benefit from exemptions.

2. Exemptions

General conditions of exemption

According to the 1953 statutes in order to be exempted from their prohibition, the firms which have entered into an illegal agreement must show that the agreement has the effect of contributing to the growth of the industry or that it contributes to general economic progress through rationalization and specialization of production.

There must be a direct link between the illegal agreement and the alleged positive effects.[45] In addition, the positive results must benefit not only the member firms but also the customers and the economy at large. Thus in the 1972 petroleum industry case,[46] the Commission held that the fact that the agreement enabled the firms to increase their price cost margins making it possible to invest without borrowing, was not sufficient to exempt it from the general prohibition of the antitrust statutes. The Commission also held that the more serious the anticompetitive practices are, the more important must be the alleged favourable effects for the firms to benefit from the exemption.[47] Finally an agreement can be exempted because of its favourable effects only if firms do not pretend that the agreement has never existed. On this point, the Commission's position is that if the firms deny the existence of an agreement that the Commission feels existed, the firms' bad faith should be held against them. Nevertheless, if the Commission feels that an illegal agreement denied by the firms involved has in fact significantly contributed to general economic progress, it will take this latter fact into consideration when it decides what recommendations to make to the Minister of Finance and Economic Affairs.[48,49]

In order to assess the significance of the economic progress due to an agreement the Commission will have to rely on either one of two methods of reasoning: either

45. *Rapport de la Commission Technique des Ententes, Journal Officiel n° 2*, 11 January 1974, p. 26.
46. *Rapport de la Commission Technique des Ententes, Journal Officiel n° 66*, 19 July 1974, p. 2609, *entente dans le commerce et la distribution de produits pétroliers*, 3 March 1972 (Petroleum industry).
47. *Rapport de la Commission Technique des Ententes, Journal Officiel n° 2*, 7 February 1964, p. 13.
48. *Rapport de la Commission Technique des Ententes, Journal Officiel n° 2*, 7 February 1964, p. 14.
49. *Rapport de la Commission Technique des Ententes, n° 1193-61*, p. 5.

- it will try to compare what has happened in fact with what would have happened had competition prevailed on the market considered; or
- it will compare the performance of the industry (or group of firms involved in the agreement) with performances observed abroad in the same industry.[50]

Unfortunately neither method can be considered reliable. Indeed the first method may be criticized when the Commission has to decide what would have been the competitive performances in areas where both theoretical considerations and empirical evidence lead to ambiguous predictions.[51] Similarly the comparison of observed performances with performances of foreign firms or industries, which is most commonly used by the Commission, is dangerous unless one can be sure that competition actually prevails on these foreign markets and that general conditions are otherwise similar.

The Commission's assessment of the favourable effects of an agreement will also be heavily dependent on the notion of economic progress which it adopts. As seen the statutes enacted in 1953 restricted the notion of economic progress to the ideas of rationalization and specialization of production and to growth of the industry. They were, therefore, particularly questionable. Indeed it would not seem that the efforts of the members of a cartelized industry to maintain or develop their share of the domestic market through systematic exclusion of foreign competitors contribute unambiguously to the economic progress of society. Similarly one may wonder what social benefit would accrue from a specialization of production which would ultimately lead to an increase in sellers' concentration in industries for which it is not clear that there are economies of scale.

The modified statutes of 1967 do away with specific references to specialization and rationalization of production and mention only the undefined notion of economic progress as grounds for exemption. Thus, the Commission is no longer restricted by the original 1953 definition with which it might have felt slightly ill at ease but it must find its own concept of economic progress.

The study of the abrasives case[52] shows the difficulty of defining the elusive notion of economic progress and establishing the existence of a link between anticompetitive agreements and economic progress. Indeed in this case, the Commission held that the agreement had contributed significantly to economic progress on the grounds that the industry's output had been significantly increased and that production costs had greatly decreased. Nevertheless, one

50. *Rapport de la Commission Technique des Ententes, n° 1193-1*, p. 6.
51. Such as for example: Rand D. Performances.
52. *Rapport de la Commission Technique des Ententes, n° 1193-1, entente entre fabricants de meules et de produits abrasifs*, 17 December 1955, p. 13 (Abrasive products industry).

must note that the agreement had been enforced over a 28-year period and that, except in rare case, one could expect the output of any industry to increase significantly over such a long period of time. Similarly, the decrease in production costs is in itself meaningless if one does not know by how much they would have diminished had the industry been competitive. On this last point, the Commission mentions elsewhere in its discussion of the case that French exports are still negligible and that the lowering of tariff barriers may in the future put French firms in difficulties. It would then seem that whatever the decrease in unit production costs has been, the industry is not competitive on the international market and one can wonder why this is so. In addition to the two aforementioned reasons for exemption, the Commission seems to consider that systematic exchange of technological information among member firms contributes to economic progress. But one could argue that it is not clear whether such agreements do not actually contribute to decreasing the level of R & D spending by each firm either to create new products or to lower their production costs.

The Commission invokes several elements to exempt agreements from the statute's general prohibitions. Among these are,

a. *Specialization of production.* The underlying idea is that if market sharing or production quotas are accompanied by specialization of production, unit costs or production will decrease. Thus in the pitchfork and pick case[53] the Commission held that the fact that the number of models had been decreased from 82 to 74 and the fact that there were one, two, exceptionally three manufacturers left for each model, were sufficient to exempt the agreement between the four firms in the industry from the prohibition of the statutes. Indeed the Commission thought that under the agreement each firm had been able to better specialize its manpower and its equipment and that therefore the unit costs of productions had decreased. As mentioned before, one would logically expect specialization to contribute to economic progress only in industries in which they are economies of scale. The existence of such economies seems far from obvious in the pitchfork and pick industry which does not require highly sophisticated technology. Furthermore, if there are significant cost advantages to specialization, one wonders whether the pressure associated with a competitive situation will not naturally lead the firms to reduce the number of products they manufacture just as fast or efficiently as a cartel agreement.

53. *Rapport de la Commission Technique des Ententes, n° 1193-1, entente entre fabricants d'outils agricoles à main,* 26 June 1967, p. 34 (Pitchfork and pick industry).

b. *Rationalization of production techniques* which decreases production costs is also frequently held to be a motive for exemption on the grounds of significant contribution to economic progress. Specifically, the Commission takes into account the attempts by firms to increase the efficiency of their distribution systems, to decrease their production costs, and to lower their overhead costs. To be considered a motive for exemption, the decrease in costs must be accompanied by a decrease in prices that benefit the consumer. Nevertheless, in most cases, the Commission (or the firms involved) do not show convincingly that the decrease in cost could not have been achieved without an anticompetitive agreement.

A good example of the Commission's thinking is the cast iron pipe case[54] where the Commission stated:

'Efforts to increase productivity have led to a satisfactory price and cost levels... Given also that cast iron pipes face increasing competition on the domestic gas and water pipe market from steel pipes, cement pipes, and plastic pipes... the agreement should be exempted.'

Unfortunately the Commission did not explain how it established that the price level was 'satisfactory.' It must have been all the more difficult since the cast iron pipe industry is cartelized throughout Europe and consequently international comparison of prices (the method most favoured by the Commission) is in this case of dubious validity. What is more one may argue that if the price and cost level were in fact satisfactory, it was mainly because of 'increasing competition' from substitutes on the market and that the price and cost level would probably had been 'reasonable' whether the agreement had existed or not. Finally the Commission seems to have erred in its assessment of the competitive forces on the market since it seemed to have overlooked the fact that the substitute products were produced by the manufacturers of cast iron pipes.

c. *Mergers.* Until very recently the Commission seems to have shared the view that mergers promoted efficiency unambiguously and thus it exempted a number of restrictive agreements on the grounds that they were 'necessary' to prepare a merger between the firms involved even when it was not obvious that there were scale economies. In addition to the fact that it is not obvious that restrictive agreements are a necessary prerequisite to mergers, there is some evidence that as we have shown elsewhere for France and as others have shown at the European level that efficiency of firms might well decrease with size at least beyond a certain level. One may also argue that had the Commission taken a tougher stand on

54. *Rapport de la Commission Technique des Ententes, Journal Officiel n° 2*, 7 February 1964, *entente dans l'industrie des tuyaux de fonte*, 19 May 1961, p. 29 (cast iron pipe industry).

restrictive agreements, in the long run firms would have had a greater incentive to merge as long as market shares are not prohibited *per se*. Indeed the competitive pressure would have forced firms that are below the minimum efficient scale to merge, grow or disappear. There seems to be little justification for the Commission's indiscriminate acceptance of the virtues of large firms and the policy it followed on the merger question may well have been self defeating in the long run.

In addition, as we have mentioned before the substitution of a cartel by a dominant position or a monopoly may leave the situation in a particular industry substantially unchanged from the standpoint of allocation of resources. For example, the Commission examined the light bulb industry in 1956[55] and in 1966.[56] Between these dates important mergers took place and concentration of the industry which was substantial in 1956 was increased even further (in 1966 only two of the original eight firms were left on the market). The restrictive practices which had been noted by the Commission in 1956 were found to be substantially unchanged in 1966.

d. *Investment*. A coordinated investment policy is also likely to lead to an agreement's exemption from the antitrust prohibition. The Commission's underlying reasoning is that stability of market shares and specialization of productions can be necessary to rationalize investment (i.e. eliminate excess capacity) and that the security provided by the agreement could bring about a higher overall level of investment than would otherwise have existed. The Commission, though, redefined its views on good investment performances in its 1973 report to the Ministry of Finance and Economic Affairs.[57] Normally, it held that an agreement could not be exempted if the policy of the firms which were parties to the agreement had been to restrict the development of investment. In other words, the report stated that the Commission accepted the idea that a certain amount of excess capacity could be the guarantee of workable competition and future economic progress.

There are only two situations in which the Commission feels that excess capacity serves no socially useful purpose: in declining industries or if unit equipment is so large compared to market size that there is a risk of durable disequilibrium between supply and demand (an example of this latter situation would be the flat glass industry). In those situations, the Commission considers

55. *Rapport de la Commission Technique des Ententes, n° 1193-1, entente entre fabricants de lampes électriques*, 26 May 1956, p. 22 (Light bulb manufacturers).

56. *Rapport de la Commission Technique des Ententes, n° 1193-67, entente dans l'industrie des lampes électriques*, 22 April 1966, p. 34 (Light bulb manufacturers).

57. *Rapport de la Commission Technique des Ententes, Journal Officiel, n° 66*, 10 July 1974, p. 2606.

full employment of capacity to be a significant contribution to economic progress. In all other situations the Commission will not consider a reasonable amount of excess capacity to be a sign of poor economic performance. But lack of excess capacity may be held against firms as a sign of Malthusianism. Unfortunately, it is difficult to know on which consideration the Commission will base its judgement of Malthusianism. Indeed if a group of firms sets price at a monopoly level, the quantity demanded at this price will be lower than it would have been in a competitive situation. Thus while the firms may have excess capacity at a given monopolistic price, they may not have sufficient equipment to face up to the quantity which would have been demanded had the price been at a competitive level. In other words, observed excess capacity is not proof that firms have not in fact followed a restrictive investment policy. What is more, a certain amount of excess capacity may be desirable from the cartel's point of view to be able to react to any entry into the industry. Thus it is probably going to be quite difficult for the Commission to use this criterion in any economically meaningful way to assess the real nature of an agreement.

e. *Exports.* Finally export performances of firms which are parties to a restrictive agreement are frequently taken into account to decide whether an exemption from the prohibition of the statutes is justified. When firms have formed an export cartel as well as a domestic one, the Commission sometimes holds that market sharing on the home market is a necessary condition for the firms' success on foreign markets. In instances where there is only a domestic restrictive agreement, the Commission uses the relative volume of individual member firm's exports as an indicator of their general economic performance. In this latter case, though, the Commission implicitly assumes that the amount of imports and exports on the international market can only result from the relative efficiency of firms in the different countries. The Commission seems to ignore that widespread international cartels may effect the current of exchanges among countries and thus one may ask whether the high level of exports noted in industries such as steel tubes, pig iron pipes, electric bulbs, or paper products (industries for which there is some evidence that there is a European cartel) is the result of an international division of markets or whether it reflects in some sense the efficiency of French industry.

All in all most of the economic reasons used by the Commission to exempt restrictive agreements seem questionable both because it is difficult to show that there is in fact a direct link between the alleged advantages and the restrictive agreements and because it seems quite difficult to define the notion of positive effects.

Legal exemptions

As mentioned before, some restrictive agreements are exempted on the grounds that they are the inevitable result of a given law or decree. The Commission has attempted to make a very literal interpretation of the statutes on this point and has refused to exempt, on this ground, a number of restrictive agreements that were openly supported either by the Ministry of Agriculture[58] or by the Ministry of Industry[59] but which did not qualify under this literal interpretation. In some cases, though,[60] the Commission had to recognize that the restrictive agreements were in fact the inevitable result of a given law or decree and therefore should be exempted. The Commission's literal interpretation of the statutes on this point usefully counterbalances the initiatives of technical ministries which seem rarely, if ever, to concern themselves with maintaining an acceptable level of competition on individual markets. The question of the inconsistency between the Commission's efforts to promote competition and the lack of interest of technical ministries for competitive processes will be taken up later on.

3. The Commission's recommendations

The Commission makes two types of recommendations to the Minister of Finance and Economic Affairs. The first type deals with the legal course of action that should be taken. If an agreement is not deemed to violate the statutes, the Commission dismisses the case. If an agreement is deemed illegal but if the Commission feels that the conditions for exemption were met in the past, it may decide not to act immediately but that it will re-examine the case at some later date to determine whether the grounds for exemption still hold. If it is deemed that an agreement is illegal and cannot be exempted from the prohibition, the Commission can recommend two courses of action, either

- it can suggest that the case be taken to court; or
- it can recommend that a delay (usually varying between three months and three years) be given to the firms to abandon their illegal practices.

The second type of recommendation deals with economic courses of action. The

58. *Rapport de la Commission Technique des Ententes, n° 1193-70, entente dans l'industrie de la conserverie de champignons de couche*, 18 October 1968, p. 10 (mushroom canning industry).
59. *Rapport de la Commission Technique des Ententes, Journal Officiel n° 66*, 19 July 1974, *situation de la concurrence dans le secteur de la distribution des produits pétroliers*, 9 February 1973, p. 2607 (distribution of petroleum products).
60. See for example: *Rapport de la Commission Technique des Ententes, n° 1193-67, entente entre fabricants d'explosifs industriels et d'accessoires de mines*, 27 May 1966, p. 37 (manufacturers of industrial explosives).

Commission may make broad policy suggestions on how to alter the structure of the industry or on the ways and means through which the agreement could be exempted in the future.

A. The Commission's general philosophy regarding legal prosecution

During its first fifteen years of existence, the Commission judged that there was not much to be gained from taking cases to court and that a more conciliatory policy of reprimanding firms who had violated the statutes was likely to bring about more positive results. In its 1968 report[61] to the Minister of Finance and Economic Affairs, the Commission noted that the number of restrictive agreements for which the firms involved did not even bother to try to contribute to economic progress continued to be unexpectedly high. So the Commission reluctantly embarked on a tougher course and decided to recommend that firms be taken to court in cases of agreements that it thought presented a particular social danger. Altogether, the Commission examined 105 cases between 1954 and 1973. The Commission first sent a case to court in 1966. Between 1966 and 1973, of the 47 cases it examined, 3 were not proved to violate the statutes, 1 was exempted for legal reasons, 8 were exempted on the ground of positive contribution to economic progress. Out of the remaining 35 cases which involved violation of the statutes, only 8 were taken to court. As is obvious from these figures, this procedure remains fairly exceptional and one may wonder whether this does not explain why, up to now, the deterrent effect of the Commission has been extremely limited. In any case, it is worth examining the way in which the Commission reaches a decision on whether it should send a case to court. Again it will apply a rule of reason by examining possible extenuating or aggravating circumstances.

B. Extenuating and aggravating circumstances

Two elements are taken into consideration: the facts themselves and the behaviour of the firms involved.

---

61. *Rapport de la Commission Technique des Ententes, n° 1193-70*, p. 3.
62. *Rapport de la Commission Technique des Ententes, Journal Officiel n° 2*, 11 January 1974, *entente dans l'industrie du plâtre*, 6 December 1972, p. 32 (plaster industry).

1. The facts

The Commission evaluates the seriousness of the violation, the nature of the market on which the restrictive agreement has existed, the time period during which the illegal practices were followed and the date at which the practices ceased.

a. *The seriousness of the violation.* The seriousness of the violation is assessed by the Commission with respect to a combination of two factors: the intent of the authors of the agreement and the potential social harm due to the restrictive practices noted. The Commission is thus likely to be more lenient if the agreement has been such that the potential effect of the anticompetitive practices was in fact limited[62] or if the firms have not used all the possibilities offered to them by the anticompetitive agreement to hamper competition.[63]

Nevertheless, the Commission feels that if the lack of any socially harmful effect from an agreement comes from circumstances beyond the power of the parties to the agreement (such as the existence of a close substitute or the reaction of a customer) this cannot be considered an extenuating circumstance.[64]

b. *The nature of the market.* In its 1973 report to the Minister of Finance and Economic Affairs,[65] the Commission mentioned that it would treat agreements violating the antitrust statutes more severely when the customers are either local governments, government agencies or public utilities than when they are private firms or citizens. Indeed the Commission feels that local governments, government agencies and public utilities are more vulnerable than private customers to anticompetitive practices on the part of their suppliers because of the strictly delineated conditions under which they can contract and their obligation to provide uninterrupted public services. The Commission therefore seems to feel that price fixing and market sharing on these markets should be prohibited *per se.*[66]

c. *The length of practices and their date of occurrence.* The Commission does not feel that long-abandoned practices which are not likely to reappear or short-lived agreements should be sent to court. It should be noted, however, that on this point the Commission has sometimes left the way open to possible future abuses.

---

63. *Rapport de la Commission Technique des Ententes, Journal Officiel n° 2,* 7 February 1964, *entente dans l'industrie de l'acier moulé,* 22 June 1962, p. 37 (molded steel industry).
64. *Rapport de la Commission Technique des Ententes, n° 1193-72,* p. 4.
65. *Rapport de la Commission Technique des Ententes, Journal Officiel n° 66,* 19 July 1974, p. 2606.
66. *Rapport de la Commission Technique des Ententes, Journal Officiel n° 66,* 19 July 1974, p. 2606.

Thus in 1973, it did not refer an illegal agreement between plaster manufactures[67] to court on the grounds that since the parties to the agreement had merged creating a monopoly in the industry, the collusive behaviour could not reappear. One could argue that had the parties been taken to court, the newly formed firm might have been deterred from its dominant position in the future.

d. *The general state of the industry.* For its final decision, the Commission also takes into consideration the general state of the industry. It is more lenient towards (i.e. will not send to court) the parties to a restrictive agreement in declining industries.[68] It will also take into consideration the market power of the group of firms involved. Thus in the cotton spinning case,[69] it held that because the firms that had entered the agreement were very small and competing with much larger firms, they should not be sent to court.

The Commission also considers the possible disruptive effects of returning to a competitive situation. It is unlikely to take a tough stand in cases where a rapid return to a competitive situation could lead to severe local unemployment problems[70] or to a drastic change in the structure and the habits of the industry considered.[71] On this latter point, the Commission's position seems all the more questionable since the more completely cartelized the industry is, the greater the changes it will undergo if competition on the market is enforced. Thus in order to benefit from the Commission's leniency, it will be in the firms interest to cartelize their industries as completely as possible rather than to set up less complex restrictive agreements.

2. Behaviour of firms, customer, and Ministries

a. *Behaviour of parties to an illegal agreement.* The Commission has consistently held the view that it should be lenient to the point of not referring cases to court when the firms concerned have abandoned their illegal practices as soon as an investigation has started.[72] Such a position is all the more questionable because it offers virtual immunity from prosecution to firms who react promptly to the

67. *Rapport de la Commission Technique des Ententes, Journal Officiel n° 2,* 11 January 1974, *entente dans l'industrie du plâtre,* 6 December 1972, p. 32 (plaster industry).
68. *Rapport de la Commission Technique des Ententes, n° 1193-70,* p. 3.
69. *Rapport de la Commission Technique des Ententes, n° 1193-70, entente dans l'industrie de la filature de coton cardé du Nord et de l'Ouest,* 22 March 1968, p. 6 (cotton spinning industry).
70. Ibid.
71. *Rapport de la Commission Technique des Ententes, Journal Officiel n° 2,* 7 February 1964, p. 13.
72. *Rapport de la Commission Technique des Ententes, Journal Officiel n° 2,* 7 February 1964, *entente entre armateurs et transitaires,* 21 April 1961, p. 29 (shipping).

Commission's investigations. Since the Commission, given its lack of means, can examine only a very limited number of cases each year, the probability that a cartel will go undetected for a number of years is quite high; therefore, if firms are willing and able to abandon their illegal practices quickly enough, the pay off from forming a restrictive agreement may be quite high. Conversely, the Commission will take a tough stand when the firms have not reacted to a previous warning.[73]

b. *Behaviour of customers.* The fact that customers such as public utilities have had knowledge of and have not reacted to obviously illegal collusive agreements has long been considered by the Commission as an indirect incentive to cartelization and as grounds for decreasing the responsability of firms guilty of violating the antitrust statutes.[74] In some cases, public utilities have even directed firms to share the market.[75] The nature of public utilities and local governments is such that they are often more concerned with ensuring continuing public service than with the price of their supplies.

The continuity of the public service depends, among other things, on the ability to have diversified sources of supply. For these reasons public utilities and local governments have often attempted to distribute their orders among potential suppliers in order to keep each of them in business rather than contracting exclusively with the most efficient firm.

In its 1973 report to the Minister of Finance and Economic Affairs,[76] though, the Commission held that such extenuating circumstances would no longer be taken into account to decide whether a case should be taken to court.

c. *Behaviour of Ministries.* In a few cases, although an illegal agreement could not be exempted from the statutes prohibition for legal reasons, it was clear that a technical ministry had more or less actively supported the restrictive practices of the firms or had made it possible for the firms to be successful in a joint attempt to monopolize trade. In the case of semi-finished copper products,[77] the Commission noted that the copper import quotas had obviously been too restricted to satisfy the domestic demand for copper products and that the

---

73. *Rapport de la Commission Technique des Ententes, Journal Officiel n° 66,* 19 July 1974, p. 2606.
74. *Rapport de la Commission Technique des Ententes, n° 1193-72, entente entre laboratoires de développement et de tirage de films,* 16 January 1970, p. 5 (photographic processing laboratories).
75. *Rapport de la Commission Technique des Ententes, Journal Officiel n° 2,* 11 January 1974, *entente entre entreprises de pose de canalisations électriques souterraines de la région de Lyon,* 17 March 1972, p. 30 (installers of underground electrical pipes).
76. *Rapport de la Commission Technique des Ententes, Journal Officiel n° 66,* 19 July 1974, p. 2606.
77. *Rapport de la Commission Technique des Ententes, n° 1193-1, entente entre fabricants de demi produits en métaux cuivreux,* 21 February 1958, p. 47 (semi finished copper products).

Ministry of Industry had entrusted the trade organization with the distribution of imported copper among copper product manufacturers. For these reasons, the Commission held that the incentive to cartelize the industry given by the Ministry was so obvious that the firms could not be considered fully responsible for the market sharing agreement into which they had entered.

Similarly in the case of road construction material,[78] the Commission held that the fact that the illegal agreement had been set up and could have functioned only with the full approval of the Ministry of Industry was sufficient to recommend that the firms should not be taken to court. These examples clearly show the inconsistency of French public policy and the inability of the Commission to fight against the pro-cartel forces in other branches of government.

d. *The Commission's economic recommendations.* If it decides against recommending that a case be taken to court, the Commission usually makes far-reaching economic recommendations to the parties to the agreement or to the Government.

1. Economic recommendations to the firms

Most of these recommendations are based on the Commission's economic view that has been spelled out above. It is thus not necessary to detail them here. It is sufficient to say that they fall into three general categories.

a. *Some of them have to do with abandoning practices that violate the statutes.*
b. *Some try to spell out the conditions under which the illegal agreements could be exempted from the prohibition.* They can be either very general such as in the case of the flat glass industry[79] where the Commission stated that 'the firms must reinforce their efforts to maintain and develop positive economic results' or more specific such as in the case of semi-finished copper products[80] where the Commission held that future exemption of the illegal agreement would depend on a change in the quota system (from rigid to flexible), the efforts of the firms to further normalize and specialize their productions and the establishment of a common research and development centre.

---

78. *Rapport de la Commission Technique des Ententes, Journal Officiel n° 2,* 7 February 1964, *entente Franco-Belge sur le marché des matériaux de viabilité,* 5 November 1960, p. 32 (road construction material).
79. *Rapport de la Commission Technique des Ententes, n° 1193-1, entente entre fabricants de verre plat,* 23 November 1957, p. 36 (flat glass industry).
80. See footnote n° 2, previous page.

c. *Some deal with the necessity to change the structure of the industry.* Thus in the cigarette paper and thin paper cases,[81] the Commission held that in the future the illegal agreement would be exempted if the firms concentrated and renovated their plants and equipment.

The Commission also often specifies the time period it allots the firms to reform themselves or to meet the requirements of the exemption and defines the type of control that it will use to make sure that its recommendations are in fact followed. On the first point, the length of the time period alloted to the firms to reform themselves seems to be a negative function of the seriousness of the violation and a positive function of the extent of the changes associated with the return to a competitive situation. Thus not only will the Commission be more lenient about refering extremely cartelized industries to court (as has been shown previously), it will also give them longer delays to reform themselves.

On the central question, several systems are used. In some instances the Commission decides that it will re-examine a case after a given delay. In others, the Government (usually a division of the Ministry of Finance and Economic Affairs) will investigate the firms and report its findings to the Commission which will then decide whether or not it wants to re-examine the case. Sometimes, the Commission asks the Ministry of Finance and Economic Affairs to provide periodic information on the industry or the firms. Finally in a few cases, no special provision is made for controlling the firms in the future.

In its 1968 Report to the Minister of Finance and Economic Affairs,[82] the Commission stated that the best control procedure would be that it re-examine the cases. The Commission sees such re-examination as being all the more necessary when restrictive agreements have been exempted for economic reasons since the conditions that led to the exemption may no longer exist after a number of years. Unfortunately given its limited means, the Commission can examine only a few cases each year (nine at the most). Thus in the future it will have to rely more and more on the information provided by the price division of the Ministry of Finance and Economic Affairs. This information is often inadequate because the price division tends to focus its studies mainly on the rate of increase of prices and may fail to see

---

81. *Rapport de la Commission Technique des Ententes, n° 1193-70, entente entre fabricants de papier à cigarette,* 17 May 1968, p. 9 (cigarette paper).
Rapport de la Commission Technique des Ententes, n° 1193-71, entente dans l'industrie des papiers minces et spéciaux autres que le papier à cigarettes, 19 December 1969, p. 15 (Thin paper industry).
82. *Rapport de la Commission Technique des Ententes, n° 1193-70,* p. 2.

the implications of complex agreements designed by firms to maintain their cartels. This increased reliance on the price division is likely to significantly weaken administrative control of restrictive practices. This is all the more preoccupying since when the Commission re-examines the industry directly, it often finds that the efforts of firms to contribute to economic progress have been only marginal or that the illegal practices have not disappeared.[83]

Given all these constraints, one may wonder whether the Commission's attempt to bring about a satisfactory level of competition on formerly cartelized markets through administrative control and persuasion of firms rather than by prosecution in court is not doomed to be a failure.

2. Economic recommendations to Government

The Commission also quite frequently recommends that technical ministries should alter their course of action so as to no longer incite firms to enter into illegal agreements. Thus in the mushroom canning case,[84] the Commission held that a decree of the Minister of Agriculture which organized the cartel was both illegal and economically unsound. Also the Commission chastized public utilities and local government for not fighting, or in a few cases blatantly supporting, their suppliers who shared market or fixed prices.[85,86] Indeed it appears that in many instances, public utilities and local or central government agencies prefer to stick to a given number of known suppliers with whom they are used to dealing (and who thus have an easy time sharing markets and fixing prices) rather than widely publicizing their tenders and choosing the lowest bidder from a wide range of competitors. These public firms and agencies also seem to follow an unwritten rule of nearly always choosing a French supplier over a foreign one, regardless of the difference in price, thereby lessening potential foreign competition.

Finally, in a number of cases, the Commission recommended that technical ministries organize workable competition on individual markets and help the firms to reduce their costs, specialize or normalize their

---

83. *Rapport de la Commission Technique des Ententes, n° 1193-72, entente dans l'industrie des aciers étirés*, 20 February 1970, p. 8 (Steel drawing industry).
84. *Rapport de la Commission Technique des Ententes, n° 1193-70, entente dans l'industrie de la conserverie des champignons de couche*, 18 October 1968, p. 10 (mushroom canning industry).
85. *Rapport de la Commission Technique des Ententes, Journal Officiel n° 2*, 11 January 1974, *entente entre entreprises de pose de canalisations électriques souterraines dans la region de Lyon*, 17 March 1972, p. 30 (installers of underground electrical pipes).
86. *Rapport de la Commission Technique des Ententes, n° 1193-72, entente entre laboratoires de développement et tirage de films*, 16 June 1970, p. 5 (photographic processing laboratories).

production, etc.[87] The idea which seems to guide the Commission is that the 'invisible hand' of competition may not be totally trusted to bring about economic progress and that Government supervision may prove more efficient to reaching this goal. Given the anticompetitive attitude of most technical ministries and the ineptitude of their actions in the general field of Industrial Structures, one may seriously question their ability to bring about economic progress.

4. Overall appraisal of the current system and policy implications

The analysis of the Commission's record between 1954 and 1973 does not provide much to refute Scherer's view that

'Up to the present, there has been little zeal in governmental circles for systematic promotion of competitive market processes. Enforcement, carried out in an atmosphere of secrecy by a commission whose membership includes businessmen and bankers, has been lackadaisical.'[88]

But it may be useful to summarize the main limits of the French antitrust enforcement system and to present a few tentative conclusions on the ways in which it could be improved.

The definition of a coherent antitrust policy

French public policy in the field of Industrial Organization has shown many inconsistencies. We have seen that some powerful ministries, unconvinced of the benefits of a satisfactory level of competition and eager to please various professional groups, have facilitated or encouraged cartelization of a number of industries while the Commission tried rather unsuccessfully to restore competition on these markets. At a more general level, there also seems to be some inconsistency between systematic promotion of mergers, based on the idea that large firms systematically perform more efficiently than smaller ones, and the desire to avoid the social costs associated with market power. It now seems that French public policy is about to modify its course slightly. First some public officials have expressed disappointment with the performances of larger firms

87. F. M. Scherer, *Industrial Market Structure and Economic Performance*, Rand McNally, Chicago, 1970, p. 438.
88. F. M. Scherer, *Industrial Market Structure and Economic Performance*, Rand McNally, Chicago, 1970, p. 438.

(notably on the export market) and seem to feel that further concentration of markets may not be the panacea it was once held to be. Second, the current administration, through the Minister of Finance and Economic Affairs has implied on several occasions that it intends to reinforce the antitrust statutes. If a higher level of competition on individual markets and a more coherent industrial policy are desired, a few suggestions can be made:

– Both mergers and interfirm agreements (whether initiated by private firms or by the Government) could be subjected to some kind of *a priori* control. More specifically, it could be useful to devise a system where mergers between firms would be notified to the Commission before they actually take place so that either the Commission or a specialized administrative body could evaluate the potential efficiency gains to be obtained from such mergers and weigh these gains against the potential social costs associated with increased market power, at least at the horizontal level. Such a procedure might deter those mergers whose only justification is the acquisition of a dominant position. Such a procedure would not exclude a statute prohibiting abuse of market power.
– It seems that given the limited size of French markets a *per se* prohibition of dominant positions or of monopolies would be economically unsound; but as we have seen, the system of control of firms having such a position leaves much to be desired. Therefore it would be useful if the Commission gave a clearer definition of what constitutes a dominant position. Firms having a market share larger than the level defined by the Commission could then expect close scrutinization of their market behaviour and this alone could have a deterrent effect on them. Furthermore, as we have seen, the definition of abuse of market power is still quite hazy. It would also be useful if the Commission would concentrate on this point and examine a sufficient number of cases to provide guidelines for firms in dominant positions.
– On the question of inter-firm restrictive agreements, we have argued that most of the justifications presented by the firms seeking exemptions from the statutes were either economically unsound or probably not the direct result of the agreement. It then seems that a *per se* prohibition of all restrictive agreements would be likely to significantly increase the level of competition without hampering economic progress. In addition it would leave the Commission more time to concentrate on the problem of dominant position.
– Finally it seems obvious from previous discussion that it would be quite difficult, if not impossible, in many instances to bring about a satisfactory level of competition on the domestic market unless artificial barriers to entry resulting from international restrictive agreements are detected and elim-

inated. Thus a policy of close cooperation with the EEC Commission seems to be one prerequisite to the success of French antitrust policy.

The means necessary to investigate and deal with anticompetitive practices

We have given numerous examples of what we thought was poor economic reasoning on the part of the Commission and it is our opinion that to enforce a more vigourous antitrust policy, the Commission's composition should be changed by significantly decreasing the number of representatives of the business community. But besides the question of the Commission's composition, there looms the more general question of the means available for the detection of restrictive agreements or abuse of market power and the enforcement of the antitrust statutes. Indeed in the past the Commission has quite often defined the scope of its analysis much too narrowly and has treated restrictive agreements that were obviously linked to each other as separate questions.

Thus in the pipe industry cases, the Commission successively examined cast iron pipes,[89] steel pipes,[90] reinforced concrete pipes,[91] and vinyl pipes.[92] Given that these products are to a large extent substitutes and given that some of the implicated firms manufacture more than one type of pipe, it would appear quite obvious that there is a general cartel in the pipe industry and that much was lost by treating the individual agreements separately. Similarly in the advertising case,[93] the trade association had set up a system through which it could bar entry, fix prices and share markets. Such a system could not have worked if newspapers had not refused ad space to advertising agencies that were not members of the trade association. Therefore there must have been some kind of bilateral cartel under which the advertising industries directed their customers towards newspaper advertising and the newspaper cartel, in return, protected the agencies from potential competition. But the Commission examined only the restrictive practices among advertising agencies and did not examine the possibility of a cartel in the newspaper industry. It seems that the Commission's extremely

89. *Rapport de la Commission Technique des Ententes, Journal Officiel n° 2,* 7 February 1964, *entente dans l'industrie des tuyaux de fonte,* 19 May 1961, p. 29 (cast iron pipes).
90. *Rapport de la Commission Technique des Ententes, Journal Officiel n° 2,* 7 February 1964, *entente dans l'industrie des tubes d'acier,* 1 April 1960, p. 16 (Steel pipes).
91. *Rapport de la Commission Technique des Ententes, n° 1193-69. entente dans le négoce des produits d'amiante ciment,* 16 June 1967, p. 6 (reinforced concrete).
92. *Rapport de la Commission Technique des Ententes, Journal Officiel n° 66,* 19 July 1974, *entente dans l'industrie des tuyaux en chlorure de polyvinyle,* 17 Octobre 1973, p. 2619 (Vinyl pipe).
93. *Rapport de la Commission Technique des Ententes, n° 1193-1, entente professionnelle dans le domaine de la publicité,* 4 January 1958, p. 38 (advertising).

limited means are partially responsible for such an incomplete approach. The Commission's means are limited both regarding investigative capacity and ability to rule on cases.

The Commission has been able to employ only six full-time investigators since 1970 and it is quite obvious that it has had to make a choice between having its investigators examine each case fully or bring to light only the most obvious facts about the agreements. But one may wonder whether the Commission can make a real contribution to the promotion of competition if it is not given the means to make more sophisticated and complete investigations of trade practices. What is more, as we have argued, the French antitrust enforcement system relies heavily on administrative controls and the Commission's workload will thus necessarily increase over time if this control is to be performed seriously. Even if the Commission were to refer all illegal agreements to court its investigative capacity is so limited that the number of cases treated each year would not be sufficient to deter firms tempted to violate the statutes.

Even if the investigative capacity is increased, there remains the problem of the Commission's ability to rule on more than a limited number of cases per year. The Commission's fourteen members all occupy important positions either in the Government or in the business community and because of these outside activities have never been able to deal with more than nine cases a year. The Commission has always defended its member's part-time activity both on the grounds that it is only fair that representatives of the business community should be present and that this system insured a higher level of coherence between the Government's general economic and industrial policy and the Commission's work. At least on the grounds of coherency, as we have mentioned above, the results do not seem to match the Commission's expectations. This is all the less surprising since the six government representatives have outside positions that have nothing to do whatsoever with industrial problems. What is more, given that industrial policy makers at the Planning Commission and in technical ministries do not concern themselves with the general problem of competition, one may wonder whether there is not a basic imbalance between the full-time industrial policy and the part-time competition policy which should be its necessary counterpart.

The role of the courts

Finally, because court judges usually have only limited understanding of economic problems, they tend to adopt the Commission's opinion on whether specific agreements or behaviour of firms violate the statutes. As we have seen previously the Commission may decide not to take an illegal agreement to court on the grounds that the violation was not sufficiently serious. For these two reasons, the Commission which is in principle an administrative body also exercises an implicit judicial power. Although this confusion of power may seem undesirable to private citizens, an economist as such is not entitled to make a judgement on this point. Nevertheless, the situation in France has important consequences as far as the efficiency of the enforcement system is concerned. Namely, the number of cases which can be tried in court is extremely limited because the Commission has to determine whether or not an agreement or the behaviour of a firm in a dominant position violates the statutes before any trial can take place. Thus as only a few cases reach court the deterrent effect of the system is limited. On this point one may wonder if a system in which *per se* prohibitions were more prevalent (particularly as far as restrictive agreements are concerned) and in which some courts specialized in economic problems and could apply the Commission's guidelines without having to ask its opinion first, would not significantly improve the enforcement system.

INDEX